CHINESE:
A COMPREHENSIVE GRAMMAR

Routledge Comprehensive Grammars

Comprehensive Grammars are available for the following languages:

Cantonese
Catalan
Chinese
Danish
Dutch
Greek
Indonesian
Japanese
Modern Welsh
Modern Written Arabic
Slovene
Swedish
Ukrainian

Titles of related interest

Basic Chinese: A Grammar and Workbook
by Yip Po-Ching and Don Rimmington

Intermediate Chinese: A Grammar and Workbook
by Yip Po-Ching and Don Rimmington

Colloquial Chinese
by Kan Qian

CHINESE: A COMPREHENSIVE GRAMMAR

Yip Po-Ching and
Don Rimmington

Routledge
Taylor & Francis Group

LONDON AND NEW YORK

First published 2004
by Routledge
2 Park Square, Milton Park, Abingdon, Oxon OX14 4RN

Simultaneously published in the USA and Canada
by Routledge
270 Madison Ave, New York, NY 10016

Reprinted 2006 (twice)

Routledge is an imprint of the Taylor & Francis Group, an informa business

© 2004 Yip Po-Ching and Don Rimmington

Typeset in Times by Graphicraft Limited, Hong Kong
Printed and bound in Great Britain by TJ International Ltd, Padstow, Cornwall

British Library Cataloguing in Publication Data
A catalogue record for this book is available from the British Library

Library of Congress Cataloging in Publication Data
Yip, Po-Ching, 1935–
    Chinese : a comprehensive grammar / Yip Po-Ching and Don Rimmington.
        p. cm. – (Routledge comprehensive grammars)
    1. Chinese language–Grammar.   I. Title.   II. Series.
    PL1107.Y56 2003
    495.1′82421–dc21   2003010198

ISBN10: 0–415–15031–0 (hbk)
ISBN10: 0–415–15032–9 (pbk)

ISBN13: 978–0–415–15031–6 (hbk)
ISBN13: 978–0–415–15032–3 (pbk)

CONTENTS

ACKNOWLEDGEMENTS

The authors wish to thank Ms Li Quzhen for all her help with the *pinyin* annotations of the illustrative examples. Without her assistance and support the project would never have been completed.

The authors also wish to thank members of the British Chinese Language Teaching Seminar (an affiliated body of the British Association of Chinese Studies, under the Oxford China Centre) for valuable suggestions on grammatical problems.

Any errors are, of course, entirely the responsibility of the authors.

Yip Po-Ching and Don Rimmington
May 2003

ABBREVIATIONS

adj.	adjective
cl.	clause
class.	classical
colloq.	colloquial
cv	coverb
dial.	dialect
dv	dummy verb
fml.	formal
infml.	informal
lit.	literally
mv	modal verb
mw	measure word
n.	noun
neut.	neutral
num.	numeral
obs.	obsolete
p.	predicate
pron.	pronoun
s.	subject
svo	subject-verb-object
vb.	verb
vs.	versus

INTRODUCTION

This book aims to provide a comprehensive grammar of Chinese. It is intended for readers who have some knowledge of the language and are at ease with its written form, whether in traditional characters or romanisation. We have endeavoured to minimise the use of technical expressions, but, where linguistic terms are introduced, we have provided explanations.

We believe that a comprehensive grammar has to be comprehensive in two senses. First, it must highlight the specific characteristics of the language being described and, where appropriate, indicate how they differ from those of other languages. In the case of Chinese, for example, syntactic rules are often seen to be operational in conjunction with semantic, prosodic and discoursal principles. Second, the grammar must be able to cover (and therefore generate) all possible (and acceptable) constructions in the language. We have consequently adopted an eclectic approach and have made reference to a range of grammatical theories in order to achieve what we hope is a multi-perspective approach: semantic, pragmatic, stylistic, prosodic, structural, functional, discoursal, transformational and generative. In our view syntactic generalisations become comprehensive only when they are underpinned by judgements on particular language characteristics that draw on theoretical approaches relevant to those characteristics.

THE LAYOUT OF THE GRAMMAR

For ease of reference, each chapter provides an independent exposition of a particular grammatical feature and can be consulted by readers wishing to investigate that feature. Footnotes offer cross-references to related issues in other chapters. Lists of language examples are given throughout to illustrate points under discussion, and each example is in Chinese script and romanisation, with an English translation and, where needed, a literal translation.

The book lays particular stress on functional types of sentence in Chinese, and this has influenced the sequencing of chapters. The non-morphological nature of the language with the resultant absence of noun and verb inflection, and of general markers for definite and indefinite reference, means that most grammatical features have to be seen in the context of the sentence, or more usefully the sentence type, as a whole. We have identified four basic sentence types and a fifth overriding type, and these are discussed in detail in Chapters 20 and 21. The four basic types are: **narrative** (action-verb based and associated with the completed action marker); **descriptive** (again generally featuring action verbs, but with continuous action markers); **expository** (covering a range of explanatory statements, relating to existence, possession, cognition, experience, etc., with no verbal markers apart from one indicating experience); and **evaluative** (also explanatory statements, but with a more judgemental tone, featuring modal verbs, etc., but with no verbal markers). Narrative and descriptive sentences have a subject–predicate structure, while expository and evaluative sentences are more likely to follow a topic–comment pattern. The endless variability and invention of language means that this typology will inevitably have loose ends and overlapping dimensions, and the presence or function of sentence elements will sometimes blur the boundaries between types, but nonetheless we hope that the structure we propose will offer some clarification of the complexities of Chinese grammar.

The fifth overriding type we have called *le*-**expository**, because the particle *le* 了 is present at the end of the sentence, and its presence introduces a notion of change or reversal which the speaker expresses with varying degrees of personal involvement. *Le* can in fact be added to any of the four sentence types identified above, and, as we shall see, it has a significant impact on the meaning of the sentence. *Le*-expository sentences are a highly distinctive feature of the Chinese language, and, because they express some degree of endorsement by a speaker, they are a particular feature of the spoken language.

The layout of the book reflects this typology. The first five chapters deal with noun-related issues; Chapters 6 to 14 discuss elements in narrative and descriptive sentences; Chapters 15 to 19 are more concerned with expository and evaluative sentences; Chapters 20 and 21, as we have said, analyse sentence functional types; the final six chapters cover conjunctions, non-declarative sentences (interrogative and imperative) and other elements at work in sentences (omissions, and prosodic and stylistic features).

THE CHINESE LANGUAGE

The Chinese language, or group of related languages, is spoken by the Hans, who constitute 94 per cent of China's population. One word for the language in Chinese is *Hanyu* 汉语, the Han language. Different, non-Han languages are spoken by the other 6 per cent of the population, the so-called minority peoples, such as the Mongols and the Tibetans.

The Chinese language is divided into a number of major dialects (with their many sub-dialects). Speakers of different dialects in some cases find each other unintelligible, but dialects are brought together by the fact that they share a common script. This book describes the main and official dialect, which is known by a number of names: Mandarin, modern standard Chinese, or *putonghua* ('common speech'). It is spoken in its various sub-dialect forms by almost three-quarters of the Hans across the northern, central and western regions of the country, but its standard pronunciation and grammar are associated with the Beijing area of north China, though not with Beijing city itself. The other dialects are Wu (spoken in Jiangsu and Zhejiang, including Shanghai), Xiang (in

Hunan), Cantonese (in Guangdong), Min (in Fujian), Hakka (in northeast Guangdong and other southern provinces) and Gan (in Jiangxi).

Cantonese, Min and Hakka are widely spoken among overseas Chinese communities. In Taiwan a form of Min dialect is used, though the official language is Mandarin, brought over by the Nationalists in 1949, and called there *guoyu* ('national language'). Mandarin in also widely used in Singapore, where it is known as *huayu* ('Chinese language'). Elsewhere, Chinese emigrants took their particular dialects with them, and in Britain, for instance, the Chinese people, who are largely from Hong Kong, almost all speak Cantonese.

The Chinese character script existed virtually unchanged for two thousand years until a range of simplified forms began to be introduced by the mainland Chinese government in the 1950s. These simplified characters, which we employ in this book, are used throughout China and increasingly in Chinese communities outside China, though not Taiwan. Chinese has been transcribed into Western alphabetic script through various systems for over one hundred years and this book makes use of the standard romanisation *pinyin*.

The formal written language of China until the early decades of the twentieth century was Classical Chinese, which, as the vehicle for all publicly acknowledged literature and for official documentation, was at the heart of the Chinese cultural tradition. However, it had grown remote from spoken Chinese in syntax and lexis, and had a position somewhat akin to medieval Latin in relation to the Romance languages it had spawned. It was left behind by modern written styles, based on spoken Chinese, which evolved over the last hundred years, but echoes of Classical Chinese remain in contemporary speech and writing, especially in literary and aphoristic registers. This continuing presence of the Classical today will be mentioned at various points in our analysis.

1 NOUNS AND NOMINALISATIONS

Nouns in Chinese are not specifically identified as being nouns except in the case of those with suffixes like 子 **zi**, 儿 **er**,[1] 头 **tou**, etc. They are mainly disyllabic, but there are also quite a number of monosyllabic nouns in everyday vocabulary. Trisyllabic nouns are rare and polysyllabic nouns are even rarer, the latter being often regarded as nominal phrases. Chinese nouns do not under any circumstances inflect for case, gender or number,[2] though an unmarked common noun is normally assumed as being plural, e.g. 书 **shū** 'books' rather than 'book'.

1.1 NOUNS AND CATEGORISATION

Nouns can be assigned to different categories with reference to their grammatical properties. Such categorisation, as we shall see, helps to highlight their usages, and identifies distinctive features relating to the use of measure words, definite and indefinite reference, plurality, etc.

1.1.1 COMMON NOUNS

Certain nouns are referrable to classes of tangible (and sometimes discrete) entities, categories, events and phenomena in the natural or human world. They are generally known as common nouns, and are linguistic labels we attach to ourselves and our surroundings. For example:

诗人	**shīrén**	poet
山	**shān**	hill; mountain
商店	**shāngdiàn**	shop
狗	**gǒu**	dog
牡丹	**mǔdān**	peony
鞋	**xié**	shoe(s)
盐	**yán**	salt

---

[1] 儿 **er** is essentially a nominal suffix, but occasionally is found with other word classes, e.g. the verb 玩儿 **wánr** 'to play, enjoy oneself', and with some reduplicated adjectives, e.g. 好好儿 **hǎohāor** 'well, good'.

[2] An unmarked common noun is normally assumed as being plural. Also see §1.3 for the specific use of the plural suffix 们 **men**.

语言	**yǔyán**	language
音乐	**yīnyuè**	music
广告	**guǎnggào**	advertisement
电影	**diànyǐng**	film; movie
比赛	**bǐsài**	contest
战争	**zhànzhēng**	war
地震	**dìzhèn**	earthquake

Tangibility is not to be understood only in a macroscopic sense. Some entities may not be visibly observable, but their existence can be verified by means of instruments or by accompanying phenomena.

电	**diàn**	electricity
细胞	**xìbāo**	[biology] cell
分子	**fēnzǐ**	molecule
原子	**yuánzǐ**	atom

The so-called discreteness, on the other hand, does not necessarily imply separateness. Sometimes such discreteness may be more pragmatic than real. For instance, 树枝 **shùzhī** 'branch, twig' is discrete but not separated from 树干 **shùgàn** 'tree trunk', and there is a similar pragmatic distinction between 腿 **tuǐ** 'leg' and 脚 **jiǎo** 'foot'.

However, a most distinctive feature of a Chinese common noun is that some kind of measure word is normally used in conjunction with a number or demonstrative. In some cases the measure is a classifier (**a**) and in others it is a universal or standard measure (**b**),[3] which is generally associated with material nouns:[4]

(**a**)	一座山	**yī zuò shān**	a hill; a mountain
	两朵花儿	**liǎng duǒ huār**	two flowers; two blossoms
	四家商店	**sì jiā shāngdiàn**	four shops
	五栋房子	**wǔ dòng fángzi**	five houses
	那个人	**nèi ge rén**	that person
	这本书	**zhèi běn shū**	this book
(**b**)	一滴水	**yī dī shuǐ**	a drop of water
	三片面包	**sān piàn miànbāo**	three slices of bread
	一杯茶	**yī bēi chá**	a cup of tea
	十度电	**shí dù diàn**	ten units of electricity (for billing a consumer)
	五公斤米	**wǔ gōngjīn mǐ**	five kilos of rice
	二十公升汽油	**èrshí gōngshēng qìyóu**	twenty litres of petrol

[3] See Chapter 2 for a full discussion of measure words in all their forms.
[4] See §1.1.2 below.

1.1.2 MATERIAL NOUNS

There are a number of common nouns that may be regarded as **material nouns**. One important feature of these nouns is that, unlike other common nouns, which have their own specific measure words, material nouns must first be grouped, packaged, partitioned or measured in terms of national or international standards before they can be counted. For example:

玻璃	**bōli**	glass
铁	**tiě**	iron
水	**shuǐ**	water
空气	**kōngqì**	air

They may only be used in connection with grouping, packaging, partitioning or standard measures:

一块玻璃	**yī kuài bōli**	a (thick) piece of glass	(partitioning)
一片铁	**yī piàn tiě**	a (thin) piece of iron	(partitioning)
三瓶牛奶	**sān píng niúnǎi**	three bottles of milk	(packaging)
四堆泥	**sì duī ní**	four heaps of earth	(grouping)
两吨铁	**liǎng dūn tiě**	two tons of iron	(standard measure)

Material nouns can also be distinguished from other common nouns in two further ways:

(**a**) While, as indicators of small or imprecise number or amount, 一些 **yīxiē** 'some' and 几 **jǐ** (plus measure) 'several; a few' can be used with any common nouns, 一点(儿) **yīdiǎn(r)** 'a little' occurs only with material nouns:

一些书	**yīxiē shū**	some books
几本书	**jǐ běn shū**	a few books
*一点(儿)书	***yīdiǎn(r) shū**	*a little books

一些水	**yīxiē shuǐ**	some water
几桶水	**jǐ tǒng shuǐ**	a few buckets/pails of water
一点(儿)水	**yīdiǎn(r) shuǐ**	a little water

(**b**) When suffixed by the particle 的 *de*, a material noun more often indicates composition rather than possession:

铜的	**tóng de**	(made of) brass
塑料的	**sùliào de**	(made of) plastic
玻璃的	**bōli de**	(made of) glass

Compare the following sentences:

这个盒子是塑料的。 **zhèi ge hézi shì sùliào de**
(lit. this mw box is plastic *de*)
This is a plastic box. (material composition)

这个盒子是爸爸的。 **zhèi ge hézi shì bàba de**
(lit. this mw box is father *de*)
This box belongs to father. (possession)

1.1.3 COLLECTIVE NOUNS

Another group of Chinese common nouns has an inbuilt notion of plurality.
They are known as **collective nouns**, and are usually formed by juxtaposing two
hyponyms (**a**) or by tagging a measure to a noun (**b**). For example:

(**a**) 父母 **fùmǔ**   parents (father and mother)
夫妇 **fūfù**   a married couple (husband and wife)
子女 **zǐnǚ**   children (sons and daughters)

(Others include: 师生 **shīshēng** 'teachers and students', 亲友 **qīnyǒu** 'friends and relatives', 男女
nánnǚ 'men and women; boys and girls', 人民 **rénmín** 'people (as opposed to government)', 城乡
chéngxiāng 'cities and villages', 院校 **yuànxiào** 'academic institutions', 书报 **shūbào** 'publications
(books and newspapers)', 文具 **wénjù** 'stationery', 树木 **shùmù** 'trees', 饭菜 **fàncài** 'food (cooked
rice and dishes for a meal)', 财产 **cáichǎn** 'possessions', etc.)

(**b**) 车辆 **chēliàng** vehicles   (一辆车 **yī liàng chē** a/one car)
花朵 **huāduǒ** flowers   (一朵花 **yī duǒ huā** a/one flower/blossom)
马匹 **mǎpǐ** horses   (一匹马 **yī pǐ mǎ** a/one horse)

(Others include: 人口 **rénkǒu** 'population', 枪支 **qiāngzhī** 'rifles', 船只 **chuánzhī** 'shipping', 书本
shūběn 'books', 纸张 **zhǐzhāng** 'paper', 砖块 **zhuānkuài** 'bricks', 事项 **shìxiàng** 'matters', 布匹
bùpǐ '(bolts of) cloth', 田亩 **tiánmǔ** 'cultivated land', etc.)

A common feature of these collective nouns is that they are not differentiable
into individual items by means of numerals and measures. For example:

*两个父母   *liǎng ge fùmǔ   *two parents
*三辆车辆   *sān liàng chēliàng   *three vehicles

The only measure words that may be used with them are those of grouping,
location or indeterminate amount. For example:

一对夫妻   **yī duì fūqī**   a couple
一批人马   **yī pī rénmǎ**   a cohort of people (assembled
                for a particular job)

一桌饭菜	**yī zhuō fàncài**	a table of food
一些亲朋	**yīxiē qīnpéng**	some relatives and friends

1.1.4 ABSTRACT NOUNS

A second major set of nouns is generally known as **abstract nouns**. Unlike common nouns, they are non-referrable to concrete objects or entities in the natural or human world. They are rather products of human epistemology, being convenient, summary labels used holistically to refer to complex or sophisticated situations, experiences, processes, qualities or phenomena in diverse areas of human endeavour. For example:

矛盾	**máodùn**	contradiction
名声	**míngshēng**	reputation
真理	**zhēnlǐ**	truth
范围	**fànwéi**	scope
前景	**qiánjǐng**	prospect
影响	**yǐngxiǎng**	influence
印象	**yìnxiàng**	impression

While common nouns are the basic stock of words sufficient for general purposes, abstract nouns are tools for conceptualisation and argument.

Abstract nouns may also be defined by a numeral/demonstrative and a measure word, but this measure is restricted to either the more general 个 **gè** or a measure word indicating type, e.g. 种 **zhǒng** 'type, kind, category' or the indeterminate number/amount measure 一些 **yīxiē** 'some' or 一点 **yīdiǎn** 'a little'. For example:

那个真理	**nèi ge zhēnlǐ**	that truth
一个印象	**yī ge yìnxiàng**	an impression
一种影响	**yī zhǒng yǐngxiǎng**	a certain influence
两种(不同的)情况	**liǎng zhǒng (bù tóng de) qíngkuàng**	two (different) situations
这些矛盾	**zhèixiē máodùn**	these contradictions
一点效果	**yīdiǎn xiàoguǒ**	a little effect

1.1.5 PROPER NOUNS

A third important set of nouns is **proper nouns**. They are unique labels used to identify particular individuals, items, places, etc. In other words, proper nouns have unique referents in the universe. For example:

孔子	**kǒngzǐ**	Confucius
中国	**zhōngguó**	China

| 火星 | **huǒxīng** | Mars |
| 佛教 | **fójiào** | Buddhism |

Proper nouns do not usually associate themselves with numerals and measure words except in a metaphorical sense. For example:

| *三个火星 | ***sān ge huǒxīng** | *three Mars |
| *两个孔子 | ***liǎng ge kǒngzǐ** | *two Confucius's |

but:

| 另一个孔子 | **lìng yī ge kǒngzǐ** | another Confucius |
| 两个中国 | **liǎng ge zhōngguó** | two Chinas |

1.1.6 TEMPORAL AND SPATIAL NOUNS

A group of time and location words can be defined as **temporal–spatial nouns**. These nouns cut right across common, abstract and proper nouns to focus on the notions of time and space. They are, in fact, habitual cognitive linchpins in a speaker's awareness of daily happenings and events, their precedences, consequences and developments, and their venues and associations, and they help to order and rationalise thought processes. Without these temporal and spatial labels, narration would become impossible and argument would be devoid of logic.

Temporal nouns:

昨天	**zuótiān**	yesterday
去年	**qùnián**	last year
下周	**xiàzhōu**	next week
每天	**měitiān**	every day
新石器时代	**xīnshíqì shídài**	the Neolithic Age

Spatial nouns:

中国	**zhōngguó**	China
北京	**běijīng**	Beijing
伦敦	**lúndūn**	London
飞机场	**fēijīchǎng**	airport
火车站	**huǒchēzhàn**	railway station

What differentiates this group of nouns from the rest is their normal usage as adverbials with or without the help of the preposition-like coverb 在 **zài** 'at, in, on, exist'. For example:

| 他昨天来看我。 | **tā zuótiān lái kàn wǒ** | He came to see me yesterday. |
| 他在中国访问。 | **tā zài zhōngguó fǎngwèn** | He is touring China at the moment. |

1.2 NOUNS AND REFERENCE

1.2.1 DEFINITE OR INDEFINITE/GENERIC REFERENCE

Proper nouns have unique referents and are therefore always of **definite reference** while abstract and material nouns usually have **indefinite** or **generic reference** when unqualified. Collective nouns, too, are by nature of indefinite reference. With common nouns, however, we are faced with a clear choice between definite and indefinite reference.

In a language without definite or indefinite articles like Chinese, the reference of unmarked nouns is influenced by a number of factors: context, sentence type, the position of the noun in relation to the verb in the sentence, and the nature of the verb itself.[5] When we use the noun 书 **shū** 'book', for instance, we have no way of determining whether it means 'the book(s)' or 'books' in general until we place it in a sentence.

In a sentence with an action verb, whether transitive or intransitive, all pre-verbal unmarked nouns (being given information) are of definite reference whereas all post-verbal unmarked nouns (new information) are generally of indefinite reference. For example:

书已经还了。 **shū yǐjīng huán le**
The book/books has/have already been returned.

我去借书。 **wǒ qù jiè shū**
I am going/went to borrow a book/some books.

孩子回来了。 **háizi huílái le**
The child/children has/have come back.

In some contexts, however, a post-verbal unmarked noun may be part of given information and therefore be of definite reference:

她去照顾孩子。 **tā qù zhàogù háizi**
She went to look after the children.

With an expository verb like 是 **shì** 'to be', the pre-verbal position may also feature new information. It is therefore not impossible for pre-verbal nouns in expository sentences to acquire indefinite or generic reference as well as definite reference, depending on the context. For example:

---

[5] See Chapter 23 for a full discussion of reference in relation to sentence types.

书是知识与文化的使者。
shū shì zhīshí yǔ wénhuà de shǐzhě (indefinite/generic reference)
<u>Books</u> are messengers of knowledge and culture.

书是我买的。 **shū shì wǒ mǎi de** (definite reference)
(lit. books are I buy *de*)
I bought <u>the</u> books.

Definite or indefinite reference may, of course, be formally marked by **demonstratives** or '**numerals + measure word' phrases**.

这本书	**zhèi běn shū**	this book	(definite reference)
那本书	**nèi běn shū**	that book	(definite reference)
一本书	**yī běn shū**	a book/one book	(indefinite reference)
几本书	**jǐ běn shū**	a few books	(indefinite reference)
一些书	**yīxiē shū**	some books	(indefinite reference)

With the help of demonstratives and measure words, a definite-referenced noun may also be used post-verbally:

我看过这本书。 **wǒ kàn guo zhèi běn shū**
I have read this book.

However, an indefinite-referenced noun, despite the fact that it has been specified by a 'numeral + measure word' phrase, cannot normally be featured in a pre-action-verb position:[6]

*一本书放在桌子上。 ***yī běn shū fàng zài zhuōzi shàng**
*A book was placed on the table.

As a general rule, the shift of an indefinite-referenced noun to a pre-action-verb position will entail the use of the verb 有 **yǒu** 'there is/are, to exist, to have':[7]

有(一)本书放在桌子上。 **yǒu (yī) běn shū fàng zài zhuōzi shàng**[8]
There was a book on the table.

这时候，有(一)辆车开来了。 **zhè shíhou yǒu (yī) liàng chē kāi lái le**
At this moment a car drove up.

---

[6] This, however, happens increasingly in modern translations: e.g. 这时候，一辆车开来了。 **zhè shíhou yī liàng chē kāi lái le** 'At this moment a car drove up', but it is still felt to be translationese by most Chinese readers.
[7] See Chapter 6: the verb 有 **yǒu**.
[8] The numeral 一 **yī** 'one' is often omitted for reasons of speech rhythm.

1.2.2 EXCLUSIVE REFERENCE

Apart from definite and indefinite/generic reference, **exclusive references** can also be expressed through the use of 一 **yī** 'one'[9] plus a measure word or the adjective 什么 **shénme** 'any'. Exclusive-referenced nouns are invariably positioned pre-verbally, and are always accompanied by the obligatory use of an adverb 也 **yě** 'also' or 都 **dōu** 'all' in the predicate or comment:

我一本书也没借。 **wǒ yī běn shū yě méi jiè**
I didn't borrow a single book.

他什么书都看。 **tā shénme shū dōu kàn**
He reads any books.

1.3 NOUNS AND PLURALITY

Collective nouns, as we have seen, possess inbuilt notion of plurality and are therefore not definable by precise numbers (see §1.2).

Proper nouns derive their singularity or plurality from their corresponding referents.

英国	**yīngguó**	Britain	(singular)
基督教徒	**jīdū jiàotú**	Christians	(singular/plural)

With **abstract nouns**, the notion of plurality does not normally arise. If it does, it is in a metaphorical and non-numerical sense. An abstract noun can usually only be made to associate with the numeral 一 **yī** 'one'. For example:

一线希望	**yīxiàn xīwàng**	a gleam of hope
一派胡言	**yī pài húyán**	a pack of nonsense

It is only with **common nouns** that there is an obvious choice as to whether they are plural or singular, and plurality is generally indicated by a 'numeral + measure word' phrase:

五个学生	**wǔ ge xuésheng**	five students
两只小猫	**liǎng zhī xiǎomāo**	two kittens
三把刀	**sān bǎ dāo**	three knives

---

[9] See also §6.2.

In addition 一些[10] **yīxiē** 'some', 几 **jǐ** plus a measure word 'a few', and other established adjectives like 许多 **xǔduō** 'many', 不少 **bùshǎo** 'quite a few', etc., can be used:

一些苹果	**yīxiē píngguǒ**	some apples
几个人	**jǐ ge rén**	a few people
许多商店	**xǔduō shāngdiàn**	many shops
不少书	**bùshǎo shū**	quite a few books

Similarly, in the case of **material nouns**, plurality is expressed in conjunction with their measures or through rough estimation. For example:

一块布	**yī kuài bù**	a piece of cloth	(singular: partitioning)
两匹布	**liǎng pǐ bù**	two bolts of cloth	(plural: packaging)
一批布	**yī pī bù**	a batch of cloth	(singular: group)
两尺布	**liǎng chǐ bù**	two Chinese feet of cloth	(plural: standard measures)
一些/一点儿布	**yīxiē/yīdiǎnr bù**	some cloth	(rough estimate)

With **human nouns** there is a standard plural suffix form 们 **men**. Some restrictions, however, apply to its use: it normally relates to people in groups, and therefore regularly occurs as a term of address in gatherings, e.g. 朋友们 **péngyoumen** 'friends', 先生们、女士们 **xiānshengmen nǚshìmen** 'ladies and gentlemen'; it is not used with numbers, e.g. 'three children' will therefore be 三个孩子 **sān ge háizi** rather than *三个孩子们 ***sān ge háizimen**; and when it is present in a sentence, the noun to which it is suffixed is invariably of definite reference:

客人们	**kèrenmen**	<u>the</u> guests
孩子们	**háizimen**	<u>the</u> children

It should also be noted that there are a small number of nouns in the language that, whatever their category, cannot be quantified at all (unless metaphorically). They provide some form of overall description: from natural phenomena to social conditions and human traits.[11] For example:

大自然	**dàzìrán**	nature
天空	**tiānkōng**	the sky

---

[10] The indeterminate plural measure 些 **xiē** occurs with the numeral 一 **yī** and no others. It is also used with the demonstratives 这 **zhè** and 那 **nà** to form the plural demonstrative adjectives 这些 **zhèixiē** 'these' and 那些 **nèixiē** 'those' (see §3.2). The 一 **yī** 'one' in 一些 **yīxiē** 'some' may sometimes be omitted.

[11] The list is not exhaustive.

海洋	**hǎiyáng**	the ocean
波涛	**bōtāo**	billows, great waves
潮汐	**cháoxī**	the morning and evening tides
地势	**dìshì**	topography, terrain
风水	**fēngshuǐ**	fengshui, geomancy
烈日	**lièrì**	the scorching sun

国防	**guófáng**	national defence
金融	**jīnróng**	finance
民意	**mínyì**	public opinion, the will of the people
行政	**xíngzhèng**	administration
全局	**quánjú**	the overall situation
人类	**rénlèi**	humankind
商业	**shāngyè**	commerce
政治	**zhèngzhì**	politics

身心	**shēnxīn**	body and mind
体魄	**tǐpò**	physical condition
外表	**wàibiǎo**	physical appearance
心灵	**xīnlíng**	heart, soul
仪表	**yíbiǎo**	demeanour
智能	**zhìnéng**	intelligence
眼界	**yǎnjiè**	outlook, field of vision
胸怀	**xiōnghuái**	frame of mind

1.4 NOUNS AND SYNTACTIC FUNCTIONS

Nouns, whatever their category, and noun phrases may contract the following syntactic relationships with other word classes in a syntactic construction – phrasal as well as sentential:

Phrasal:
(a) as an attributive with or without 的 *de* indicating attribution or possession:

| 电脑世界 | **diànnǎo shìjiè** | the computer world |
| 电脑的将来 | **diànnǎo de jiānglái** | the future of computers |

(b) as a headword modified by an adjectival attributive with or without 的 *de*:

新书	**xīn shū**	new books
年轻的诗人	**niánqīng de shīrén**	a young poet
美丽的风景	**měilì de fēngjǐng**	a beautiful view

(c)   as a headword modified by a 'numeral + meaure word' phrase:

一个诗人   **yī ge <u>shīrén</u>**   a poet
两架飞机   **liǎng jià <u>fēijī</u>**   two aircraft

(d)   as an object governed by a preposition or coverb:

靠墙   **kào <u>qiáng</u>**   against the wall
沿着大路   **yánzhe <u>dàlù</u>**   along the road

(e)   as a headword followed by a full or abbreviated postposition:

桌子上边   **<u>zhuōzi</u> shàngbian**   on the table
桌子上   **<u>zhuōzi</u> shàng**   on the table

(f)   as items juxtaposed to each other or joined together by conjunctions:

楼上楼下   **<u>lóushàng lóuxià</u>**   upstairs and downstairs
桌子和椅子   **<u>zhuózi</u> hé <u>yǐzi</u>**   tables and chairs

Sentential:
(g)   as the subject of a sentence:

飞机起飞了。   **<u>fēijī</u> qǐfēi le**   The plane took off.

(h)   as the topic of a sentence:

电脑十分有用。   **<u>diànnǎo</u> shífēn yǒuyòng**   Computers are extremely useful.

(i)   as a predicative after 是 **shì** 'to be':

这位是诗人。   **zhèi wèi shì <u>shīrén</u>**   This gentleman/lady is a poet.

(j)   as a nominal predicate:[12]

今天星期五。   **jīntiān <u>xīngqī wǔ</u>**   Today is Friday.
小孩今年四岁。   **xiǎohái jīnnián <u>sì suì</u>**   My child is 4.

---

[12] A nominal predicate can always be reworded to include the expository verb 是 **shì** 'to be': e.g. 今天是星期五。 **jīntiān shì xīngqī wǔ** 'Today is Friday'. Predicates like these are restricted to the predication of time, date, size, weight, length, height, price, age, nationality, birthplace, personal physical or psychological traits, etc. Physical and psychological traits are represented by phrases like 高个儿 **gāogèr** 'a tall person', 急性子 **jíxìngzi** 'a person of fiery temper', etc. For example, 这个人急性子。 **zhèi ge rén jíxìngzi.** 'This person is hot-tempered'.

(**k**) as the object of a transitive verb:

他很尊敬<u>老师</u>。 **tā hěn zūnjìng <u>lǎoshī</u>** He respects teachers
very much.

(**l**) as an adverbial:

他<u>昨天</u>回来。 **tā <u>zuótiān</u> huílai** He came back yesterday.
他<u>一个人</u>回来。 **tā <u>yī ge rén</u> huílai** He came back on his own.

Apart from temporal nouns, which are almost always used as adverbials, there are
a very restricted number of nouns that may be sometimes used (with or more often
without the adverbial marker 的 *de*) as adverbials. The most common ones are:

表面	**biǎomiàn**	surface > superficially
部分	**bùfèn**	part > partially
集体	**jítǐ**	collective > collectively
和平	**hépíng**	peace > peacefully
本能	**běnnéng**	instinct > instinctively
历史	**lìshǐ**	history > historically
逻辑	**luóji**	logic > logically

1.5 NOUNS AND SEMANTIC FIELDS

Nouns may be compartmentalised into definable categories in terms of meaning.
These definable categories are generally known as **semantic fields**. One salient
feature of these categories is their established or potential **hyponymic relationship** with one another. For example, a semantic field concerning meteorological
phenomena in Chinese may have a superordinate term 气象 **qìxiàng** 'meteorology'
dominating the following hyponyms:

雨	**yǔ**	rain
雪	**xuě**	snow
冰	**bīng**	ice
雹子	**báozi**	hailstone
风	**fēng**	wind
云	**yún**	cloud
霜	**shuāng**	frost
露水	**lùshuǐ**	dew
虹	**hóng**	rainbow
彩霞	**cǎixiá**	sunset clouds
雾	**wù**	fog
烟雾	**yānwù**	smog
雷	**léi**	thunder
闪电	**shǎndiàn**	lightning

These terms may seem different from one another, but in their written form they mostly share the common radical 雨 **yǔ** 'rain': 雪 **xuě**, 霜 **shuāng**, 雹 **báo**, 露 **lù**, 霞 **xiá**, 雾 **wù**, 雷 **léi**, and the original, unsimplified versions of 电 **diàn** (電) and 云 **yún** (雲). If we go further and try to retrieve co-hyponyms of, for example, 雨 **yǔ** 'rain' or 风 **fēng** 'wind' down the semantic ladder, we will find that most terms are organised with the superordinate terms themselves as headwords:

雨 **yǔ** 'rain':

大雨	**dà yǔ**	heavy rain
毛毛雨	**máomáo yǔ**	drizzle
阵雨	**zhèn yǔ**	shower
暴风雨	**bàofēng yǔ**	storm

风 **fēng** 'wind':

微风	**wēi fēng**	breeze
大风	**dà fēng**	gale
台风	**táifēng**	typhoon
飓风	**jùfēng**	hurricane
龙卷风	**lóngjuǎnfēng**	tornado

In the Chinese lexicon, in fact, hyponymic or co-hyponymic relationships like the above are often realised in terms of a **suffix-like form** shared by the hyponyms or co-hyponyms in the field. For example:

superordinate term:	专家	**zhuānjiā**	specialist; professional
co-hyponyms:	作家	**zuòjiā**	writer
	画家	**huàjiā**	painter
	音乐家	**yīnyuèjiā**	musician
	艺术家	**yìshùjiā**	artist
	探险家	**tànxiǎnjiā**	explorer
	慈善家	**císhànjiā**	philanthropist

superordinate term:	交通工具	**jiāotōng gōngjù**	means of transport
co-hyponyms:	火车	**huǒchē**	train
	电车	**diànchē**	tram; trolley
	汽车	**qìchē**	car
	缆车	**lǎnchē**	cable car
	摩托车	**mótuōchē**	motorcyle
	自行车	**zìxíngchē**	bicycle

co-hyponyms of 汽车 **qìchē** 'car':

长途汽车	**chángtú qìchē**	coach
公共汽车	**gōnggòng qìchē**	bus

出租汽车[13]	**chūzū qìchē**	taxi
小汽车	**xiǎoqìchē**	private car
货车	**huòchē**	lorry, truck

Another salient feature of these semantic fields are the sets of **metonymic relationships** which are often expressed in terms of a **prefix-like form** shared by the members of the same field. For example:

车头	**chētóu**	the front of a car
车身	**chēshēn**	the body of a car
车尾	**chēwěi**	the rear of a car
车轮	**chēlún**	wheel (of a car)
车胎	**chētāi**	tyre
车闸	**chēzhá**	brake
车牌	**chēpái**	number plate

山顶	**shāndǐng**	peak; summit
山腰	**shānyāo**	halfway up (a mountain)
山脚	**shānjiǎo**	foot (of a mountain)
山坡	**shānpō**	slope
山脊	**shānjǐ**	ridge
山谷	**shāngǔ**	ravine; valley
山坞	**shānwù**	glen; col

鞋底	**xiédǐ**	sole (of shoe)
鞋跟	**xiégēn**	heel
鞋帮	**xiébāng**	upper (of shoe)
鞋带	**xiédài**	shoelace

花瓣	**huābàn**	petal
花蕾	**huālěi**	bud
花蕊	**huāruǐ**	stamen or pistil
花粉	**huāfěn**	pollen

Such metonymic associations are not limited to **part-and-whole relationship**, but extend to **spatial affinity** in diverse senses. For example,

花盆	**huāpén**	flower pot
花瓶	**huāpíng**	flower vase
花篮	**huālán**	basket of flowers
花园	**huāyuán**	garden
花匠	**huājiàng**	gardener

---

[13] Nowadays there is an increasing use of 的士 **dìshì** for 'taxi' (in place of 出租汽车 **chūzū qìchē**) in everyday speech, 的士 **dìshì** borrows the Cantonese transliteration of 'taxi'.

1.6 NOMINALISATIONS

Nominalisation in Chinese does not usually seek morphological conversions. It is always **context-dependent**. In other words, all nominalisations are contextual nominalisations.

A verb or an adjective may be taken as a noun therefore only in a given context or grammatical framework: for example 广播 **guǎngbō** 'to broadcast' in origin is a verb, as in 广播新闻 **guǎngbō xīnwén** 'to broadcast news'. However, if the order of the two words is reversed, 新闻广播 **xīnwén guǎngbō** will mean 'news broadcast', in which the word 'broadcast' may be said to have been nominalised according to its headword status in the collocation.

Again, 美 **měi** 'beautiful' in 这个菜的味道真美 **zhèi ge cài de wèidào zhēn měi** 'This dish tastes really delicious' (literally: the taste is really beautiful) is undoubtedly an adjective. However, in a context such as the following, it functions as a noun: 外表的美不等于内心的美 **wàibiǎo de měi bù děngyú nèixīn de měi** 'Beauty in appearance is not the same as beauty at heart'.

Contextual nominalisation, as we can see, occurs essentially with verbs and adjectives when they are used as grammatical topics or objects. Other word classes are less likely to become nominalised. Here are a few more examples, in which the verbs 研究 **yánjiū** 'to study, to research into', 发现 **fāxiàn** 'to discover' and 判断 **pànduàn** 'to judge' have been made nouns:

他对这个问题进行了研究。 **tā duì zhèi ge wèntí jìnxíng le yánjiū**
He conducted some research into/made a study of the problem.

他然后根据自己的发现，对这个问题作出了判断。
tā ránhòu gēnjù zìjǐ de fāxiàn | duì zhèi ge wèntí zuòchū le pànduàn
He then, based on his discovery, made a judgement on the problem.

2 NUMERALS AND MEASURES

2.1 DIGITS, UNITS AND CARDINAL NUMBERS

There are eleven **digital notations** in Chinese:

零	**líng**[1]	zero
一	**yī**	one
二	**èr** (两 **liǎng**)[2]	two
三	**sān**	three
四	**sì**	four
五	**wǔ**	five
六	**liù**	six
七	**qī**	seven
八	**bā**	eight
九	**jiǔ**	nine
十	**shí**	ten

Cardinal integers or round figures from eleven to ninety-nine are formed by arranging in different sequences the ten digits from one to ten. For example:

twelve	十二	**shí'èr**
nineteen	十九	**shíjiǔ**
twenty	二十	**èrshí**
ninety	九十	**jiǔshí**
twenty-nine	二十九	**èrshí jiǔ**
ninety-two	九十二	**jiǔshí èr**

Numbers above 100 make use of a set of **unitary notations**, some of which are peculiar to Chinese. They are:

百	**bǎi**	hundred
千	**qiān**	thousand

---

[1] The digit 零 **líng** 'zero', apart from indicating itself, is only used in ordinals, decimals or numbers larger than 100.

[2] 两 **liǎng** 'two' is used with measures and nouns rather than 二 **èr**: 两个人 **liǎng ge rén** 'two people', 两点钟 **liǎng diǎn zhōng** 'two o'clock'. However, this does not apply to numbers over ten, e.g. 十二个人 **shí'èr ge rén** 'twelve people', 五十二岁 **wǔshí èr suì** '52 years old'. Also, when 两 **liǎng** itself is used as a measure word meaning 'tael' or '50 grams', 二 **èr** is preferred to avoid a euphonic clash.

万	**wàn**	ten thousand
亿	**yì**	hundred million
兆	**zhào**	million million/trillion

The differences between Chinese and English unitary notations are therefore as follows:

		十亿	百万				
English	trillion	billion	million	thousand	hundred	ten	one
	1, 0 0	0, 0	0 0, 0 0	0 0,	0	0	0.
Chinese	兆	亿	万	千	百	十	个[3]
		hundred million	ten thousand				

We can see that, compared with English where beyond a thousand a new unitary notation is introduced every three places, in the Chinese system, a new notation is used every four places beyond ten thousand (万 **wàn**).

Here are some examples demonstrating the conversion:

100	一百	**yī bǎi**
125	一百二十五	**yī bǎi èrshī wǔ**
3,236	三千二百三十六	**sān qiān èr bǎi sānshí liù**
54,321	五万四千三百二十一	**wǔ wàn sì qiān sān bǎi èrshí yī**
543,217	五十四万三千二百一十七	**wǔshí sì wàn sān qiān èr bǎi yīshí qī**
1,200,000	一百二十万	**yī bǎi èrshí wàn**
1,100,000,000	十一亿	**shíyī yì**

Note that in counting numbers larger than one hundred, 一 **yī** 'one' has to be incorporated before tens as well. Compare:

18	十八	**shíbā**
118	一百一十八	**yī bǎi yīshí bā**

零 **líng** 'zero' has to be introduced into a number where one or more consecutive unitary notations are missing. Compare:

1,981	一千九百八十一	**yī qiān jiǔ bǎi bāshí yī**
1,081	一千零八十一	**yī qiān líng bāshí yī**
1,001	一千零一	**yī qiān líng yī**
10,101	一万零一百零一	**yī wàn líng yī bǎi líng yī**

---

[3] 个 **gè**, the most commonly used measure word (see §2.8.2 below), is generally used to represent one digit numbers (个位数 **gè wèi shù**).

2.2 ORDINALS

Ordinals in Chinese are formed simply by adding the prefix 第 **dì** to cardinal numbers. For example:

一	**yī**	one	>	第一	**dì yī**	first
五	**wǔ**	five	>	第五	**dì wǔ**	fifth
一百零一	**yī bǎi líng yī**		>	第一百零一 **dì yī bǎi líng yī**		
	one hundred and one			one hundred and first		

Other examples are:

第十一图	**dì shíyī tú**	Diagram 11
第八表	**dì bā biǎo**	Chart 8
第二卷	**dì èr juǎn**	Volume 2 (of a set of books)
第十二页	**dì shí'èr yè**	Page 12

However, not all sequencing in ordinals in English is convertible into corresponding ordinals in Chinese. For example:

Year Two (i.e. the second year)		二年级	**èr niánjí**
	not:	*第二年级	*dì èr niánjí
second floor		三楼	**sān lóu**
	not:	*第三楼	*dì sān lóu

If there are any rules which can be followed, it seems that in classification or gradation 第 **dì** will normally be dropped:

一等舱	**yī děng cāng**	first class (on a ship or plane)
二级商品	**èr jí shāngpǐn**	second-class commodities
三流作品	**sān liú zuòpǐn**	third-class works (of art or literature)

And if the item is one from an established series,[4] it is customary, too, for 第 **dì** to be left out:

五路车	**wǔ lù chē**	Bus Route 5, the number 5 bus
六号房	**liù hào fáng**	Room 6

Also for the sake of succinctness, ordinals are often represented by cardinals following nouns:[5]

---

[4] Books and journals are exceptions, e.g. 第四册 **dì sì cè** 'Vol. 4', 第七期 **dì qī qī** 'Issue No. 7', because without the ordinal marker 第 **dì**, the phrases may respectively mean: '4 volumes (of books)' and '4 issues (of journals)'.

[5] This is more so in written Chinese. In spoken Chinese cardinals more commonly precede nouns.

图四	**tú sì**	Diagram 4
表五	**biǎo wǔ**	Chart 5
例六	**lì liù**	Example 6
练习七	**liànxí qī**	Exercise 7
附录三	**fùlù sān**	Appendix 3

2.3 ENUMERATION

Cardinal numbers indicate amounts and ordinal numbers position in a sequence. **Enumeration** is the expression of a number, particularly a large number, for its own sake, e.g. in a telephone directory or on a meter.

Enumeration requires that the numbers be used one after another in a linear succession:

2783697	二七八三六九七	**èr qī bā sān liù jiǔ qī**
(0113) 2333463	零一一三二三三三四六三	**líng yāo yāo sān èr sān sān sān sì liù sān**[6]

It is also used to refer to particular years:

2001	二零零一年	**èr líng líng yī nián** (lit. two zero zero one year)[7]

However, centuries and decades are expressed in terms of cardinal numbers:

二十一世纪	**èrshí yī shìjì**	the twenty-first century
八十年代	**bāshí niándài**	the nineteen eighties

2.4 FRACTIONS, PERCENTAGES AND DECIMALS

2.4.1 FRACTIONS

Fractions (分数 **fēnshù**) in Chinese are linguistically expressed in the standard way as a **numerator** (分子 **fēnzǐ**) which is a proportion of a **denominator** (分母 **fēnmǔ**). Both the numerator and the denominator are encoded in terms of cardinal numbers, formulaically, as:

denominator + 分之 **fēn zhī** + numerator

---

[6] Note that 一 **yī** 'one' can often be expressed orally, particularly over the telephone, as 一 **yāo** 'one' to rule out the possibility of its being confused with 七 **qī** 'seven'.

[7] Please also note the widespread use of arabic numerals rather than Chinese numerals in modern documentation.

For example:

$^1/_2$	二分之一	**èr fēn zhī yī**
$^2/_3$	三分之二	**sān fēn zhī èr**
$^5/_6$	六分之五	**liù fēn zhī wǔ**
$^1/_{10}$	十分之一	**shí fēn zhī yī**

Literally, 二分之一 **èr fēn zhī yī** means 'one out of two parts', 三分之二 **sān fēn zhī èr** 'two parts out of three', and so on and so forth.

Improper fractions (假分数 **jiǎ fēnshù**), where the numerator is bigger than the denominator, are expressed in the same way:

$^6/_5$	五分之六	**wǔ fēn zhī liù**

Complex fractions (繁分数 **fán fēnshù**), where the numerator or the denominator itself is a fraction, are expressed in a similar fashion:

$^2/_3/^1/_2$ 二分之一分之三分之二   **èr fēn zhī yī fēn zhī sān fēn zhī èr**
(two thirds
over a half)

Integers followed by fractions (带分数 **dài fēnshù**) adopt the following pattern:

cardinal number + 又 **yòu** 'plus' + denominator + 分之 **fēn zhī** + numerator

$1^1/_2$	一又二分之一	**yī yòu èr fēn zhī yī**
$5^3/_4$	五又四分之三	**wǔ yòu sì fēn zhī sān**

2.4.2 PERCENTAGES

Percentages (百分比 **bǎi fēn bǐ**) as fractions with one hundred as their denominator, are expressed in the same way as fractions in Chinese. The only thing to note is that the number 'hundred' in the denominator is encoded in the formula as 百 **bǎi** on its own rather than its full form 一百 **yī bǎi**:

64%	百分之六十四	**bǎi fēn zhī liùshí sì**
101%	百分之一百零一	**bǎi fēn zhī yī bǎi líng yī**

2.4.3 DECIMALS

Decimals (小数 **xiǎo shù**) have two forms: the number before the decimal point may be read as a cardinal number or as an enumeration with the number after it always an enumeration. For example:

275.63	either	二百七十五点六三	**èr bǎi qīshí wǔ diǎn liù sān**
	or	二七五点六三	**èr qī wǔ diǎn liù sān**

| 1038.94 | either | 一千零三十八点九四 | yī qiān líng sānshí bā diǎn jiǔ sì |
| | or | 一零三八点九四 | yī líng sān bā diǎn jiǔ sì |

Note that the **decimal point** is always expressed as 点 **diǎn** 'point'.

2.5 IMPRECISE NUMBERS, HALVES AND MULTIPLES

2.5.1 IMPRECISE NUMBERS (约数 yuēshù)

In this section we are including **juxtaposition** (one or two); **approximation** (about); **indeterminate excess** (over, more than).

2.5.1.1 Juxtaposition

This places two consecutive numbers under ten one after the other in the following kinds of formulation:

一两年	**yī liǎng nián**	one or two years; a year or two
一、二十天	**yī èrshí tiān**	ten to twenty days
一、二/两百人	**yī èr/liǎng bǎi rén**	one to two hundred people
三、四千人	**sān sì qiān rén**	three to four thousand people
七、八万头牛	**qī bā wàn tóu niú**	seventy to eighty thousand cattle
十二、三万只羊	**shí'èr sān wàn zhī yáng**	one hundred and twenty to thirty thousand sheep

but not:

| *六十、七十匹马 | *liùshí qīshí pǐ mǎ | *sixty to seventy horses |

2.5.1.2 Approximation

This is expressed in a number of ways:

(a) by placing 大约 **dàyuē** 'approximately' before the number:

大约五十三公斤	**dàyuē wǔshí sān gōngjīn**	around 53 kilos
大约四十来天	**dàyuē sìshí lái tiān**	about forty days
大约七十多岁	**dàyuē qīshí duō suì**	about 70 years of age
大约一百人	**dàyuē yī bǎi rén**	around one hundred people
大约三分之一强	**dàyuē sān fēn zhī yī qiáng**	slightly over one-third

Note that 来 **lái** and 多 **duō** are sometimes added after unitary notations such as 十 **shí** 'ten', 百 **bái** 'hundred', etc., to emphasize the approximation.

(b) by putting 左右 **zuǒyou** 'around, about, more or less' (lit. left-right) after a 'number + measure' phrase, where the associated noun is not usually identified but can be retrieved from the context:

两斤左右	**liǎng jīn zuǒyòu**	about two catties
三百名左右	**sān bǎi míng zuǒyòu**	around 300 people[8]

(c) by adding 来 **lái** to numbers rounded to ten after unitary notations such as 十 **shí** 'ten', 百 **bǎi** 'hundred', and 千 **qiān** 'thousand', etc.:

十来天	**shí lái tiān**	about ten days
二十来岁	**èrshí lái suì**	around 20 years old
三百来人	**sān bǎi lái rén**	around 300 people

(d) similarly, by adding 把 **bǎ** to the single unitary notations 个 **gè** 'one', 百 **bǎi** 'hundred', 千 **qiān** 'thousand' and 万 **wàn** 'ten thousand':

个把星期	**gè bǎ xīngqī**	around a week
百把人	**bǎi bǎ rén**	around one hundred people
千把块钱	**qiān bǎ kuài qián**	around 1,000 *yuan*[9]

2.5.1.3 Indeterminate excess

This is usually conveyed by adding 多 **duō** 'many' to numbers rounded to ten, and this applies to any such number from ten upwards:

十多[10]	**shí duō**	over ten; more than ten
二十多	**èrshí duō**	twenty and more
一百多年	**yī bǎi duō nián**	over one hundred years
两百多人	**liǎng bǎi duō rén**	more than two hundred people
三千多	**sān qiān duō**	over three thousand
四万多	**sì wàn duō**	more than forty thousand
五亿多	**wǔ yì duō**	over five hundred million
一百一十多	**yī bǎi yīshí duō**	over a hundred and ten[11]
两千三百六十多	**liǎng qiān sān bǎi liùshí duō**	more than 2,360

[8] 名 **míng** is a measure for people in lists, e.g. candidates, recruits, team members, etc.

[9] Some of these expressions derive from dialect speech.

[10] Note that one does not say *一十多 **yī shí duō**, though one has to say 一百多 **yī bǎi duō**, 一千多 **yī qiān duō**, etc.

[11] A sequence like this with 多 **duō** is not possible if any of the consecutive unitary notations is missing: *四千零八十多 *sì qiān líng bāshí duō * 'over four thousand and eighty'.

三万五千六百七十多   **sān wàn wǔ qiān**   over 35,670
                liù bǎi qīshí duō

多 **duō** may of course come between two unitary notations when the former qualifies the latter:

十多万	**shí duō wàn**[12]	over one hundred thousand
二十多万	**èrshí duō wàn**	more than 200,000
三百多万	**sān bǎi duō wàn**	over three million
四千五百六十多万	**sì qiān wǔ bǎi**	more than 45,600,000
	liùshí duō wàn	

For all the above numbers with 多 **duō**, when the number is associated with a noun or measure and noun, 多 **duō** comes after the number and before the measure or noun:

八十多个人[13]	**bāshí duō ge rén**	over 80 people
三百多张纸	**sān bǎi duō zhāng zhǐ**	over 300 sheets of paper

多 **duō** can also be used with single digit numbers up to ten when they occur with standard measures or with temporal nouns, which are de facto measures. In these cases, 多 **duō** comes after the standard measure and before the noun if there is one:

四公升多(汽油)	**sì gōngshēn duō (qìyóu)**	over 4 litres (of petrol)
六英里多(路)	**liù yīnglǐ duō (lù)**	over six miles
五年多(时间)	**wǔ nián duō (shíjiān)**	over five years
两点多(钟)	**liǎng diǎn duō (zhōng)**	shortly past 2 o'clock
三个多月[14]	**sān ge duō yuè**	over three months

几 **jǐ** 'a few' has a similar function to 多 **duō** with numbers rounded to ten, between ten and ninety, conveying the meaning 'slightly more than'. This holds for larger numbers too, provided the final digit is ten (or a multiple of ten):

十几人	**shí jǐ rén**	slightly more than ten people
五十几岁	**wǔshí jǐ suì**	a little over 50 years of age
九十几天	**jiǔshí jǐ tiān**	over ninety days
三百六十几本	**sān bǎi liùshí jǐ běn**	over 360 copies

---

[12] If the quantifying unitary notation is 十 **shí**, two possibilities exist. One may say either 十多万 **shí duō wàn** 'over ten thousand' or 十万多 **shǐ wàn duō** 'ten thousand and more'.

[13] In more formal styles, the measure word can be omitted with 人 **rén** e.g. 八十多人 **bāshí duō rén**.

[14] The measure word 个 **gè** may only be used in the case of time words such as 钟头 **zhōngtou** 'hour', 礼拜 **lǐbài** 'week'.

几 **jǐ** 'a few' is of course itself an indicator of an imprecise number below ten and is used in the same way as numerals and placed before measure words:

几本书[15]	**jǐ běn shū**	a few books
几个人	**jǐ ge rén**	several people

In addition 强 **qiáng** 'strong' and 弱 **ruò** 'weak' are added to fractions or percentages to mean respectively 'slightly more' or 'slightly less':

三分之一强	**sān fēn zhī yī qiáng**	slightly over one-third
百分之二十弱	**bǎi fēn zhī èrshí ruò**	slightly below 20 per cent

2.5.2 HALVES

Half is expressed by 半 **bàn** which, as a numeral is followed by a measure word:[16]

半个苹果	**bàn ge píngguǒ**	half an apple
半天	**bàn tiān**	half a day
半年	**bàn nián**	half a year
半个月	**bàn ge yuè**	half a month

However, when it means a half in addition to a number, it is placed after the measure and before the noun, if there is one:

一个半西瓜	**yī ge bàn xīguā**	one and half melons
两天半	**liǎng tiān bàn**	two and a half days
三个半月	**sān ge bàn yuè**	three and a half months

2.5.3 MULTIPLES

Multiples (倍数 **bèishù**) are expressed by 倍 **bèi** '(one) time as much' linked with the cardinal number that precedes it:

一倍半	**yī bèi bàn**	one and a half times as much
两倍	**liǎng bèi**	twice as much
三倍	**sān bèi**	three times as much
一百倍	**yī bǎi bèi**	a hundred times as much

Further examples are:

六是三的两倍。 **liù shì sān de liǎng bèi.** (lit. six is three's two times)
Six is twice as much as three.

---

[15] In the same capacity, 几 **jǐ** may also be used to mean 'how many' when asking about a number below ten: e.g. 几本书? **jǐ běn shū** 'How many books?' (with the speaker presuming a number below ten).
[16] See §2.8 below on measure words.

Note that the same multiple may be expressed in the form of a comparison:

六比三多一倍。 **liù bǐ sān duō yī bèi**.
(lit. six compared-with three more one time) Six is twice as much as three.

今年的粮食比去年增加了一倍。
jīn nián de liángshí bǐ qù nián zēngjiā le yī bèi.
(lit. this year's grain output compared-with last year increase *le* one time)
This year's grain output increased to twice as much as last year's.

2.6 MATHEMATICAL SYMBOLS AND SIMPLE ARITHMETIC EQUATIONS

The mathematical symbols for addition, subtraction, multiplication and division, etc., are expressed in Chinese in the following terms:

+	加	**jiā**	add, plus
−	减	**jiǎn**	subtract, minus
×	乘	**chéng**	multiply
÷	除以	**chú yǐ**	divided by
=	等于	**děngyú**	equal/be equal to

$1 + 1 = 2$	一加一等于二	**yī jiā yī děngyú èr**
$2 - 1 = 1$	二减一等于一	**èr jiǎn yī děngyú yī**
$3 \times 3 = 9$	三乘三等于九	**sān chéng sān děngyú jiǔ**
$12 \div 4 = 3$	十二除以四等于三	**shí'èr chú yǐ sì děngyú sān**

Other common symbols are expressed as:

>	大于	**dà yú**	bigger than
<	小于	**xiǎo yú**	smaller than
:	比	**bǐ**	as compared with/proportionate to
[ ]^4	四次方	**sì cì fāng**	to the power of 4, etc.

For example:

$2 : 5$	二比五	**èr bǐ wǔ**	two as against five
4^3	四的三次方	**sì de sān cì fāng**	the cube of four

2.7 THE MULTIPLICATION TABLE

Multiplication tables in Chinese have a rhythm similar to English. When the result is a single digit or a multiple of ten, the word 得 **dé** 'obtain' is added. Otherwise the pattern consists simply of enumerations followed by cardinal numbers.

二二 得四	**èr èr | dé sì**	Two twos are four.
二四 得八	**èr sì | dé bā**	Two fours are eight.
四五 得二十	**sì wǔ | dé èrshí**	Four fives are twenty.
三七 二十一	**sān qī | èrshí yī**	Three sevens are twenty-one.
六八 四十八	**liù bā | sìshí bā**	Six eights are forty-eight.
九九 八十一	**jiǔ jiǔ | bāshí yī**	Nine nines are eighty one.

2.8 MEASURE WORDS

Chinese, like other languages, has standard measure words relating to distance, weight, volume, etc., or to such universal notions as parts, groups or packages:

| 一磅蘑菇 | **yī bàng mógu** (mw: 磅 **bàng** pound in weight) | a pound of mushrooms |
| 一片面包 | **yī piàn miànbāo** (mw: 片 **piàn** piece; slice) | a slice of bread |

However, Chinese is unique in that all nouns, when occurring with a number or demonstrative,[17] generally incorporate a measure, whether or not there is any notion of 'measuring':

| 一本书 | **yī běn shū** (mw: 本 **běn** copy) | a book |
| 一张桌子 | **yī zhāng zhuōzi** (mw: 张 **zhāng** spread) | a table |

In what follows, we will therefore distinguish between **standard measure words** and **classifying measure words** (or **classifiers**).

2.8.1 STANDARD MEASURES

Standard measure words express universally accepted concepts of measurement on the one hand and packaging, grouping and partitioning on the other. For example:

2.8.1.1 National or international measures

一英里路	**yī yīnglǐ lù**	a mile
一品脱啤酒	**yī pǐntuō píjiǔ**	a pint of beer
二十公升汽油	**èrshí gōngshēng qìyóu**	20 litres of petrol
两公斤苹果	**liǎng gōngjīn píngguǒ**	2 kilos of apples
三平方米(地毯)	**sān píngfāng mǐ (dìtǎn)**	3 square metres (of carpet)

---

[17] Virtually all the examples we will cite in the following sections will use the numeral 一 **yī** 'one'. When unstressed 一 **yī** has the meaning 'a(n)' and our translations will reflect this.

Others include: *length*: 公里 **gōnglǐ** 'kilometre', 公尺/米 **gōngchǐ/mǐ** 'metre', i.e. 公分/厘米 **gōngfēn/ límǐ** 'centimetre', 码 **mǎ** 'yard', 英尺 **yīngchǐ** 'foot', 英寸 **yīngcùn** 'inch', 尺 **chǐ** 'Chinese foot', 寸 **cùn** 'Chinese inch'; *weight*: 吨 **dūn** 'ton', 斤 **jīn** 'catty', 两 **liǎng** 'tael', 盎司 **àngsī** 'ounce', 克 **kè** 'gram', 毫克 **háokè** 'milligram'; *volume*:加仑 **jiālún** 'gallon', 立方米 **lìfāng mǐ** 'cubic metre'; *area*: 公顷 **gōngqǐng** 'hectare', 英亩 **yīngmǔ** 'acre', 亩 **mǔ** 'Chinese acre'; 打 **dǎ** 'dozen'.

2.8.1.2 Packaging measures

Packaging measures usually identify the containers concerned:

一包香烟	**yī bāo xiāngyān**	a packet of cigarettes
一筒饼干	**yī tǒng bǐnggān**	a (tube-shaped) packet of biscuits
一盒巧克力	**yī hé qiǎokèlì**	a box of chocolate
一瓶酒	**yī píng jiǔ**	a bottle of wine
一杯茶	**yī bēi chá**	a cup of tea

Others include: 壶 **hú** '(tea) pot', 罐 **guàn** 'tin; can', 锅 **guō** 'pan; wok', 碗 **wǎn** 'bowl', 盆 **pén** 'basin', 盘 **pán** 'plate', 碟 **dié** 'dish; saucer', 袋 **dài** 'bag', 箱 **xiāng** 'box; suitcase', 桶 **tǒng** 'bucket; pail', 篮 **lán** 'basket', 勺 **sháo** 'spoonful', 车 **chē** 'car-load', 船 **chuán** 'shipload'.

2.8.1.3 Grouping measures

Small indeterminate numbers or amounts

Some group measures are more precise while others are less so. The two most common ones in Chinese are 一些 **yīxiē** 'some' and 一点儿 **yīdiǎnr** 'a little'. As we can see, they are used invariably with the numeral 一 **yī** 'one':

一些苹果	**yīxiē píngguǒ**	some apples
一些朋友	**yīxiē péngyou**	some friends
一点儿牛奶	**yīdiǎnr niúnǎi**	a little milk
一点儿希望	**yīdiǎnr xīwàng**	a bit of hope

As we saw in Chapter 1, while 一些 **yīxiē** 'some' occurs with both common and material nouns, 一点儿 **yīdiǎnr** 'a little' is used only with material nouns:

一些钱	**yīxiē qián**	some money
一点儿钱	**yīdiǎnr qián**	a little money
一些朋友	**yīxiē péngyou**	some friends
*一点儿朋友	**yīdiǎnr péngyou**	*a few friends

However, although 一点儿 **yīdiǎnr** 'a little' and 一些 **yīxiē** 'some' are generally interchangeable when used with material nouns, 一点儿 **yīdiǎnr** 'a little' tends to connote a smaller amount, and, as a result, 一些 **yīxiē** 'some' never features when scarcity is the focal point:

我一点儿钱也没有。	**wǒ yīdiǎnr qián yě méiyǒu**	I haven't got a penny.
*我一些钱也没有。	**wǒ yīxiē qián yě méiyǒu**	*I haven't got a penny.

Clusters

Other group measure words can in most cases be used with any numerals. They are applicable either to animate beings or to inanimate objects, but in a few instances they occur with both.

For animate beings:

一班年轻人	**yī bān niánqīng rén**	a bunch of young people
一队战士	**yī duì zhànshì**	a file of soldiers
一帮孩子	**yī bāng háizi**	a group of children
一股土匪	**yī gǔ tǔfěi**	a gang of bandits
一群羊[18]	**yī qún yáng**	a flock of sheep

Others include: 伙 **huǒ** 'group' (e.g. students), 批 **pī** 'batch', 起 **qǐ** 'batch', 拨 **bō** 'group'.

For inanimate objects:

一束鲜花	**yī shù xiānhuā**	a bunch of flowers
一串钥匙	**yī chuàn yàoshi**	a bunch of keys
一挂鞭炮	**yī guà biānpào**	a string of firecrackers
一沓纸	**yī dá zhǐ**	a pile of paper
一笔钱	**yī bǐ qián**	a sum of money
一份报纸	**yī fèn bàozhǐ**	a newspaper

Others include: 套 **tào** 'set' (e.g. stamps), 叠 **dié** 'pile' (e.g. books), 排 **pái** 'row' (e.g. houses), 嘟噜 **dūlu** 'cluster' (e.g. grapes), 丛 **cóng** 'clump' (e.g. grass), 簇 **cù** 'bunch' (e.g. flowers), 汪 **wāng** 'pool' (e.g. water), 剂 **jì** 'dose' (e.g. medicine), 绺 **liǔ** 'lock; skein' (e.g. hair; thread).

For both animate beings and inanimate objects:

一堆人	**yī duī rén**	a throng of people
一堆土	**yī duī tǔ**	a heap of earth

[18] 群 **qún** 'crowd; group' is a cluster measure for all animate beings:

一群牛	**yī qún niú**	a herd of cows
一群羊	**yī qún yáng**	a flock of sheep
一群狼	**yī qún láng**	a pack of wolves
一群鸟	**yī qún niǎo**	a flight of birds
一群鱼	**yī qún yú**	a shoal of fish
一群蜜蜂	**yī qún mìfēng**	a swarm of bees
一群人	**yī qún rén**	a crowd of people

| 一批人 | yī pī rén | a group of people |
| 一批货 | yī pī huò | a batch of goods |

Others include: 行 háng 'row', 列 liè 'file'.

Pairs and couples

对 duì and 双 shuāng, both meaning 'pair', are used with nouns, animate and inanimate, that exist in some form of duality:

一对夫妇	yī duì fūfù	a married couple
一对枕头	yī duì zhěntou	a pair of pillows
一对耳环	yī duì ěrhuán	a pair of ear-rings

一双手	yī shuāng shǒu	a pair of hands
一双眼睛	yī shuāng yǎnjing	a pair of eyes
两双鞋	liǎng shuāng xié	two pairs of shoes
三双袜子	sān shuāng wàzi	three pairs of socks

(Also for: 手套 shǒutào 'gloves', 筷子 kuàizi chopsticks.)

The difference between 对 duì and 双 shuāng seems to be that the former emphasises complementarity while the latter indicates functioning together.

Pairs of things which are physically inseparable, and in English are viewed as 'pairs', do not use 对 duì or 双 shuāng in Chinese. For example:

一条裤子	yī tiáo kùzi	a pair of trousers
一把剪刀	yī bǎ jiǎndāo	a pair of scissors
一副眼镜	yī fù yǎnjìng	a pair of spectacles

Parts or series

Part is expressed by 一部分(的) yī bùfen (de) and series by 一系列(的) yī xìliè (de). Both of these terms may only be preceded by the numeral 一 yī 'one' and the particle 的 de is optional.

一部分人	yī bùfen rén	a section of the people
一部分工作	yī bùfen gōngzuò	part of the work
一部分时间	yī bùfen shíjiān	part of the time
一系列问题	yī xìliè wèntí	a series of problems
一系列政策	yī xìliè zhèngcè	a whole set of policies

2.8.1.4 Partitioning measures

Partitioning measure words, which represent part of a whole, are common in many languages. For example:

一块蛋糕	**yī kuài dàngāo**	a piece of cake
两片面包	**liǎng piàn miànbāo**	two slices of bread
一瓣儿蒜	**yī bànr suàn**	a clove of garlic
一截儿木头	**yī jiér mùtou**	a chunk of wood
一滴水	**yī dī shuǐ**	a drop of water

Others include: 节 **jié** 'section' (e.g. railway coaches), 段 **duàn** 'length' (e.g. rope; string).

In the above, we see the partitioning of concrete objects. In fact, this process of partitioning may be applied to less concrete and more abstract things where the measure is an item or an instance:

一起案子	**yī qǐ ànzi**	a crime
一项政策	**yī xiàng zhèngcè**	a policy
一桩事儿	**yī zhuāng shìr**	a matter
一门课程	**yī mén kèchéng**	an academic discipline
一宗心事	**yī zōng xīnshì**	a worrying matter

In a number of cases, this part–whole relationship can be extended to part of a series, concrete or less concrete:

一幕戏	**yī mù xì**	a scene in a play, opera, etc.
一顿饭	**yī dùn fàn**	a meal
一届毕业生	**yī jiè bìyèshēng**	graduates of a particular year
一班飞机	**yī bān fēijī**	a scheduled flight
一茬麦子	**yī chá màizi**	a crop of wheat
一期杂志	**yī qī zázhì**	an issue of a magazine

Others include: 页 **yè** 'page', 味 **wèi** 'ingredient' (e.g. of (herbal) medicine).

These part-series measure words are in fact often used on their own in an ordinal form with the associated headword being understood from the context:

第一届	**dì yī jiè**	the first batch (of graduates)
下一班	**xià yī bān**	the next (flight, train, etc.)
第二册	**dì èr cè**	Volume 2
第二版	**dì èr bǎn**	the second edition
上一期	**shàng yī qī**	the previous issue
这一代	**zhèi yī dài**	this generation (of people)

第三幕	**dì sān mù**	the third act (of a play)
第四组	**dì sì zǔ**	Group 4
第五批	**dì wǔ pī**	the fifth batch (of people, goods, etc.)
第六项	**dì liù xiàng**	the sixth item
第七页	**dì qī yè**	Page 7

2.8.2 CLASSIFYING MEASURES

The so-called classifying measure words constitute the great majority of measure words in Chinese. They are not measures in the real sense of the word, but indicators of prominent features which can be attached to a particular set or class of nouns. That is why they are sometimes called classifiers by some grammarians. As with standard measures, these classifying measure words must be used when their associated nouns are qualified by numerals or demonstratives. For example, 把 **bǎ** which is derived from 把 **bǎ** 'handle' is used as a classifier for things with a handle:

一把刀	**yī bǎ dāo**	a knife
两把锉	**liǎng bǎ cuò**	two files/rasps
三把锹	**sān bǎ qiāo**	three spades
四把扇子	**sì bǎ shànzi**	four (folding) fans
五把伞	**wǔ bǎ sǎn**	five umbrellas
六把扫帚	**liù bǎ sàozhou**	six brooms
七把剑	**qī bǎ jiàn**	seven swords
八把锯	**bā bǎ jù**	eight saws
这把斧子	**zhèi bǎ fǔzi**	this axe
那把茶壶	**nèi bǎ cháhú**	that teapot

This usage is then extended to everything that can be 'held by the hand as if by a handle':

一把尺	**yī bǎ chǐ**	a ruler (for measuring)
两把梳子	**liǎng bǎ shūzi**	two combs
三把钥匙	**sān bǎ yàoshi**	three keys
四把锁	**sì bǎ suǒ**	four locks
五把椅子	**wǔ bǎ yǐzi**	five chairs

and then further extended to anything that can be 'held or scooped up by the handful':

一把米	**yī bǎ mǐ**	a handful of rice
一把土	**yī bǎ tǔ**	a handful of earth
一把花	**yī bǎ huā**	a bunch of flowers
一把眼泪	**yī bǎ yǎnlèi**	a flood of tears
一把胡子	**yī bǎ húzi**	a beard

Metaphorical extensions are also possible:

一把年纪	**yī bǎ niánjì**	getting on in years (年纪 **niánjì** age)
一把力气	**yī bǎ lìqi**	quite strong (力气 **lìqi** strength)
一把劲儿	**yī bǎ jìnr**	quite an effort

Other classifying measure words in the language are derived and used in a similar fashion. We will now discuss their particular usages in turn.

The most versatile multi-purpose measure word is 个 **gè** (usually unstressed as *ge* in its role as a measure word), which can be associated with most nouns, from human beings to inanimate objects and abstract concepts. For example:

一个人	**yī ge rén**	a person
一个朋友	**yī ge péngyou**	a friend
一个手表	**yī ge shǒubiǎo**	a watch
一个西瓜	**yī ge xīguā**	a watermelon
一个岛	**yī ge dǎo**	an island
一个城市	**yī ge chéngshì**	a city
一个电影	**yī ge diànyǐng**	a film
一个主意	**yī ge zhǔyì**	an idea

More often, however, particular sets of nouns which share common characteristics or belong to the same type are linked with more specific measure words. These associations are generally derived from shape, category or related activity. For example:

2.8.2.1 Shape-oriented

Long and narrow

| 一枝笔 | **yī zhī bǐ** | a pen |

(Also for: 蜡烛 **làzhú** 'candle', 枪 **qiāng** 'rifle', 箭 **jiàn** 'arrow'.)[19]

| 一支火箭 | **yī zhī huǒjiàn** | a rocket |

(Also for: 军队 **jūnduì** 'army or column of troops', 牙膏 **yágāo** 'tube of toothpaste', 香 **xiāng** 'joss-stick',[20] 乐曲 **yuèqǔ** 'musical composition or piece of music'.)

| 一根针 | **yī gēn zhēn** | a needle |

---

[19] Nouns associated with 枝 **zhī** may generally also use 支 **zhī**, but this does not apply the other way round in that, where 支 **zhī** is the normal measure for a noun, it cannot be replaced by 枝 **zhī**.

[20] Another measure word for 香 **xiāng** 'joss-stick' is 炷 **zhù**, particularly if the joss-stick is burning.

(Also for: 线 **xiàn** 'thread', 弦 **xián** 'string' (on a violin, etc.), 铁丝 **tiěsī** 'wire', 头发 **tóufa** 'hair' (on the head), 毛 **máo** 'hair' (on the body), 火柴 **huǒchái** 'match' (to light, set fire), 香肠 **xiāngcháng** 'sausage', 香蕉 **xiāngjiāo** 'banana', 骨头 **gǔtou** 'bone', 柱子 **zhùzi** 'pillar; column', 竹子 **zhúzi** 'bamboo'.)

| 一杆枪 | **yī gǎn qiāng** | a rifle |

(Also for: 称 **chèn** 'steelyard', 旗子 **qízi** 'flag'.)

| 一管毛笔 | **yī guǎn máobǐ** | a writing brush |

(Also for: 牙膏 **yágāo** 'tube of toothpaste', 箫 **xiāo** 'vertical flute', 笛子 **dízi** 'flute'.)

| 一条虫 | **yī tiáo chóng** | a worm |

(Also for: 蛇 **shé** 'snake', 绳子 **shéngzi** 'rope', 沟 **gōu** 'ditch', 河 **hé** 'river', 街 **jiē** 'street', 路 **lù** 'road', 鱼 **yú** 'fish', 狗 **gǒu** 'dog', 腿 **tuǐ** 'leg', 尾巴 **wěiba** 'tail', 黄瓜 **huángguā** 'cucumber', 裤子 **kùzi** 'a pair of trousers', 裙子 **qúnzi** 'skirt', 被单 **bèidān** 'blanket', 被子 **bèizi** 'quilt', 围巾 **wéijīn** 'scarf', 船 **chuán** 'boat'.)

| 一道光 | **yī dào guāng** | a ray of light |

(Also for: 闪电 **shǎndiàn** 'lightning', 虹 **hóng** 'rainbow', 篱笆 **líba** 'bamboo or twig fence', 河堤 **hédī** 'dyke', 眉毛 **méimáo** 'eyebrow', 伤疤 **shāngbā** 'scar'.)

| 一缕炊烟 | **yī lǚ chuīyān** | a wisp/curl of smoke (from a chimney) |
| 一股泉水 | **yī gǔ quánshuǐ** | a stream of spring water |

Round or oval

| 一颗珠子 | **yī kē zhūzi** | a pearl |

(Also for: 种子 **zhǒngzǐ** 'seed', 炸弹 **zhàdàn** 'bomb', 子弹 **zǐdàn** 'bullet', 手榴弹 **shǒuliúdàn** 'hand-grenade', 心 **xīn** 'heart', 牙齿 **yáchǐ** 'tooth', 星 **xīng** 'star', 糖 **táng** 'sweet, candy'.)

| 一粒米 | **yī lì mǐ** | a grain of rice |

(Also for: 豆子 **dòuzi** 'pea; bean', 花生 **huāshēng** 'peanut', 葡萄 **pútao** 'grape', 钻石 **zuànshí** 'diamond', 沙子 **shāzi** 'a grain of sand; grit'.)[21]

| 一团毛线 | **yī tuán máoxiàn** | a ball of wool |

(Also for: 面 **miàn** 'dough', 棉花 **miánhuā** 'cotton wool', 火 **huǒ** 'fire', 云 **yún** 'a dense patch of cloud'.)

---

[21] 粒 **lì** and 颗 **kē** are generally interchangeable unless the object is larger, when only 颗 **kē** may be used.

一轮明月   **yī lún míngyuè**   a bright moon

(Also for: 红日 **hóngrì** 'red sun'.)

Spread out and/or with a flat surface

一张纸   **yī zhāng zhǐ**   a piece of paper

(Also for: 表 **biǎo** 'chart', 布告 **bùgào** 'public notice', 票 **piào** 'ticket', 邮票 **yóupiào** 'stamp', 照片 **zhàopiàn** 'photograph', 明信片 **míngxìnpiàn** 'postcard', 唱片 **chàngpiàn** '(music) record', 床 **chuáng** 'bed', 桌子 **zhuōzi** 'table'.)

一幅画[22]   **yī fú huà**   a painting

(Also for: 地图 **dìtú** 'map'.)

一片叶子   **yī piàn yèzi**   a leaf

(Also for: 面包 **miànbāo** 'slice of bread', 雪 **xuě** 'snowflake'.)

一面镜子   **yī miàn jìngzi**   a mirror

(Also for: 锣 **luó** 'gong', 旗 **qí** 'flag'.)

一扇门   **yī shàn mén**   a door

(Also for: 窗 **chuāng** 'window')

一块玻璃   **yī kuài bōli**   a piece of glass

(Also for: 冰 **bīng** 'ice', 饼干 **bǐnggān** 'biscuit', 豆腐 **dòufu** 'beancurd', 肉 **ròu** 'meat', 肥皂 **féizào** 'soap', 地 **dì** 'land', 石头 **shítou** 'stone; rock', 砖 **zhuān** 'brick'.)

Resemblance

一口井	**yī kǒu jǐng**	a well (口 **kǒu** mouth; opening)
一头蒜	**yī tóu suàn**	a head or bulb of garlic (头 **tóu** head)
一尾鱼	**yī wěi yú**	a fish (尾 **wěi** tail)
两撇小胡子	**liǎng piě xiǎo húzi**	a moustache (lit. two strokes of moustache) (撇 **piě** left-falling stroke in writing)

---

[22] 幅 **fú** can be usually replaced by 张 **zhāng**.

2.8.2.2 Category-oriented

Human beings

个 **gè** (often unstressed) is the general measure word for human nouns:

一个人	**yī ge rén**	one person
一个老师	**yī ge lǎoshī**	a teacher
一个医生	**yī ge yīshēng**	a doctor
一个工程师	**yī ge gōngchéngshī**	an engineer

Alternatives to 个 **gè**, in appropriate contexts, are 位 **wèi**, 名 **míng**, 员 **yuán**, 条 **tiáo**, 口 **kǒu**, etc. For example:

一位客人	**yī wèi kèren**	a guest	(位 **wèi**: polite alternative)
五名学生	**wǔ míng xuésheng**	five students	(名 **míng**: for counting people)
四口人	**sì kǒu rén**	four in the family	(口 **kǒu**: for family members)
一员大将	**yī yuán dàjiàng**	a senior general	(员 **yuán**: for generals)
一条好汉	**yī tiáo hǎohàn**	a brave man	(条 **tiáo**: for strong men)

Animals and insects

All animals, birds, and insects use the measure word 只 **zhī**:

一只羊	**yī zhī yáng**	a sheep
一只狼	**yī zhī láng**	a wolf
一只老虎	**yī zhī lǎohǔ**	a tiger
一只老鼠	**yī zhī lǎoshǔ**	a mouse, rat

一只鸟	**yī zhī niǎo**	a bird
一只燕子	**yī zhī yànzi**	a swallow
一只麻雀	**yī zhī máquè**	a sparrow
一只鸡	**yī zhī jī**	a chicken
一只甲虫	**yī zhī jiǎchóng**	a beetle
一只蜻蜓	**yī zhī qīngtíng**	a dragonfly
一只蝴蝶	**yī zhī húdié**	a butterfly

一只青蛙	**yī zhī qīngwā**	a frog
一只蟹	**yī zhī xiè**	a crab

The only exceptions are fish, reptiles and worms which are associated with 条 **tiáo**, as we saw at §2.8.2.1, and also the following:

一匹马	**yī pǐ mǎ**	a horse

(Also for: 骡子 **luózi** 'mule', 骆驼 **luòtuo** 'camel'.)

一头牛	**yī tóu niú**	a bull/cow; an ox

(Also for: 驴 **lú** 'donkey', 象 **xiàng** 'elephant'.)

一条狗	**yī tiáo gǒu**	a dog

Plants

棵[23] **kē** is the measure word generally used with plants. For example:

一棵菜	**yī kē cài**	a cabbage
一棵草	**yī kē cǎo**	a tuft of grass[24]
一棵葱	**yī kē cōng**	a spring onion
一棵麦子	**yī kē màizi**	a stalk of wheat
一棵树	**yī kē shù**	a tree

However, for flowers there are four measure words, each used in different contexts:

一朵花	**yī duǒ huā**	a flower/blossom
一枝花	**yī zhī huā**	a flower or blossom on a stem or twig
一束花	**yī shù huā**	a bouquet (of flowers)
一簇花	**yī cù huā**	a cluster of flowers

Imposing natural or architectural structures

一座山	**yī zuò shān**	a mountain/hill
一座塔	**yī zuò tǎ**	a tower/pagoda
一座桥	**yī zuò qiáo**	a bridge

(Also for: 坟 **fén** 'tomb', 水库 **shuǐkù** 'reservoir', 宫殿 **gōngdiàn** 'palace', 楼房 **lóufáng** 'storeyed building', 大厦 **dàshà** 'mansion'.)

For buildings, the following are also commonly used:

所 **suǒ**: for those with institutional association
间 **jiān**: for smaller constructions, e.g. rooms, etc.

---

[23] 棵 **kē** and 株 **zhū** are generally used interchangeably in this context.
[24] A blade of grass is expressed by another measure word, 茎 **jīng** (一茎草 **yī jīng cǎo**).

家[25] **jiā**: for enterprises, etc.
栋 **dòng** and 幢 **zhuàng**, as well as 所 **suǒ**: for houses

For example:

| 一所学校 | **yī suǒ xuéxiào** | a school |

(Also for: 医院 **yīyuàn** 'hospital'.)

| 一家旅馆 | **yī jiā lǚguǎn** | a hotel |

(Also for: 饭店 **fàndiàn** 'restaurant', 商店 **shāngdiàn** 'shop', 剧院 **jùyuàn** 'opera house', 工厂 **gōngchǎng** 'factory', 银行 **yínháng** 'bank'.)

| 一间教室 | **yī jiān jiàoshì** | a classroom |

(Also for: 屋子 **wūzi** 'room'.)

Vehicles

辆 **liàng** or 部 **bù**: for 车 **chē** car
列 **liè**: for 火车 **huǒchē** train
艘 **sōu** or 条 **tiáo**: for 船 **chuán** ship or boat
架 **jià**: for 飞机 **fēijī** aircraft
顶 **dǐng**: for 轿子 **jiàozi** sedan chair

Machines

台[26] **tái**, which implies a raised platform or table:

| 一台机器 | **yī tái jīqì** | a machine |
| 一台马达 | **yī tái mǎdá** | a motor |

(Also for: 车床 **chēchuáng** 'lathe', 缝纫机 **féngrènjī** 'sewing-machine', 收音机 **shōuyīnjī** 'radio', 仪器 **yíqì** 'instrument; apparatus'.)

Natural or social events

The same written form 场 with two different pronunciations is used for natural or social events, 场 **cháng** (second tone) for a period or spell of a natural event or condition; and 场 **chǎng** (third tone) for social events or recreational or sporting activities. For example:

---

[25] 家 **jiā** and 间 **jiān** can in fact be used interchangeably, and they may replace all other measure words for buildings with specific functions.
[26] 台 **tái** may always be used interchangeably with 架 **jià** 'frame; shelf' in the context of machines. Sometimes 部 **bù** can also be used.

| 一场大雪 | **yī cháng dà xuě** | a heavy snowfall |
| 一场大病 | **yī cháng dà bìng** | a (period of) serious illness |

| 一场电影 | **yī chǎng diànyǐng** | a film show |
| 一场球赛 | **yī chǎng qiúsài** | a ball game |

Publications, writings, expressions, etc.

| 一本书 | **yī běn shū** | a book |

(Also for: 杂志 **zázhì** 'magazine', 期刊 **qīkān** 'journal', or any publication that is bound into a volume.)

| 一首诗 | **yī shǒu shī** | a poem |

(Also for: 歌 **gē** 'song'.)

一阕词	**yī què cí**	a *ci* poem
一篇文章	**yī piān wénzhāng**	a piece of writing, an essay
一出戏	**yī chū xì**	an opera/a play
一句话	**yī jù huà**	a few words/a sentence
一声谢谢	**yī shēng xièxie**	a word of thanks

Articles of clothing

For garments worn on the upper part of the body or on the whole body, 件 **jiàn** is the measure word:

一件衬衫	**yī jiàn chènshān**	a shirt
一件外套	**yī jiàn wàitào**	a jacket
一件毛衣	**yī jiàn máoyī**	a woollen sweater
一件大衣	**yī jiàn dàyī**	an overcoat

For garments worn on the lower part of the body, 条 **tiáo** is normally used:

| 一条裤子 | **yī tiáo kùzi** | a pair of trousers |
| 一条裙子 | **yī tiáo qúnzi** | a skirt |

Accessories have individual measure words:

一条围巾	**yī tiáo wéijīn**	a scarf
一条领带	**yī tiáo lǐngdài**	a tie
一顶帽子	**yī dǐng màozi**	a hat/cap
一副手套	**yī fù shǒutào**	a pair of gloves
一双鞋	**yī shuāng xié**	a pair of shoes

Abstract notions

In Chinese, abstract notions may either be seen as categories or types and the measures used are generally 种 **zhǒng** 'kind', 类 **lèi** 'category', 样 **yàng** 'type':

一种哲学	**yī zhǒng zhéxué**	a kind of philosophy
这类角色	**zhèi lèi juésè**	this kind of role
各样商品	**gè yàng shāngpǐn**	different kinds of commodities

2.8.2.3 Action-oriented

A number of nouns derive their measure words from the actions or activities associated with them. For example:

一服药	**yī fú yào**	a dose of medicine	(服 **fú** to take medicine)
一封信	**yī fēng xìn**	a letter	(封 **fēng** to seal)
一发子弹	**yī fā zǐdàn**	a bullet	(发 **fā** to fire; to discharge)
一卷软片	**yī juǎn ruǎnpiàn**	a roll of film	(卷 **juǎn** to roll)

(Also for: 手纸 **shǒuzhǐ** 'toilet paper', 铺盖 **pūgài** 'bedding'.)

一捆柴	**yī kǔn chái**	a bundle of firewood	(捆 **kǔn** to tie up)
一包糖	**yī bāo táng**	a packet of sweets	(包 **bāo** to wrap up)
一撮盐	**yī cuō yán**	a pinch of salt	(撮 **cuō** to pick up between the thumb and the first finger)
一把沙	**yī bǎ shā**	a handful of sand	(把 **bǎ** to hold; grasp)
一捧枣儿	**yī pěng zǎor**	a double handful of dates	(捧 **pěng** to carry in both hands)
一抱草	**yī bào cǎo**	an armful of hay	(抱 **bào** to hug; embrace)
一担水	**yī dàn shuǐ**	a shoulder pole of water – with a bucket hanging at the two ends	(担 **dān** to carry on a shoulder pole)
一贴膏药	**yī tiē gāoyào**	a piece of (medicated) plaster	(贴 **tiē** to stick; glue)
一堵墙	**yī dǔ qiáng**	a wall	(堵 **dǔ** to block up)
一任首相	**yī rèn shǒuxiàmg**	a period of office as prime minister	(任 **rèn** to assume a post)

2.8.2.4 Location-oriented

Location measure come in many forms, in that they identify the actual location involved:

一身泥	yī shēn ní	the whole body covered in mud (lit. a body of mud)
一脸汗	yī liǎn hàn	a face dripping with sweat
一顶帽子	yī dǐng màozi	a hat/cap (lit. a crown of hat)
一手墨水	yī shǒu mòshuǐ	the whole hand covered in ink (lit. a handful of ink)
一下巴胡子	yī xiàba húzi	a hairy chin (lit. a chin of beard)
一鼻子灰	yī bízi huī	a nose covered with dirt
一嘴油	yī zuǐ yóu	a mouth (lips) covered with grease
一口黄牙	yī kǒu huángyá	a mouthful of stained/yellow teeth
一肚子坏	yī dùzi huài	a bellyful of bad ideas
一地水	yī dì shuǐ	water all over the floor/ground (lit. a floor of water)
一桌子菜	yī zhuōzi cài	a table laden with food
一席酒	yī xí jiǔ	a banquet (lit. a tableful of wine)
一柜子衣服	yī guìzi yīfu	a cabinet full of clothes
一树花	yī shù huā	a tree covered in blossoms
一池荷花	yī chí héhuā	a pond of lotus flowers
一处名胜	yī chù míngshèng	a scenic spot (lit. a place of scenery)

2.8.2.5 Metaphor-oriented

A number of measure words are associated with more abstract and descriptive notions. These metaphorical measures occur only with the numeral 一 yī 'one'. For example:

一线希望	yīxiàn xīwàng	a ray/gleam of hope
一团漆黑	yī tuán qīhēi	complete darkness (lit. a ball/lump of darkness)
一派新气象	yī pài xīn qìxiàng	a new and dynamic atmosphere
一片欢腾	yī piàn huānténg	a scene of rejoicing
一泓流水	yī hóng liúshuǐ	a stream of flowing water
一把年纪	yī bǎ niánjì	a good age
一股劲儿	yī gǔ jìnr	a burst of energy
一丝笑意	yī sī xiàoyì	a hint of a smile

2.9 MEASURE WORDS AND OTHER ATTRIBUTIVES

To convert a cardinally numbered item into an ordinal one, 第 **dì** is added before the numeral and measure word.[27] For example:

一个人 **yī ge rén**　　　>　　第一个人 **dì yī ge rén**
a person; one person　　　　the first person

---

[27] See §2.2.

两个人 **liǎng ge rén**   >   第二个人[28] **dì èr ge rén**
two persons   the second person

When words like 这 **zhè** 'this', 那 **nà** 'that', 每 **měi** 'every', 某 **mǒu** 'certain', 哪 **nǎ** 'which', etc. are used with numbers, they are placed before the numeral and measure phrase. If the numeral is 一 **yī** 'one', it is usually dropped. For example:

this person	这个人	**zhèi ge rén**
that person	那个人	**nèi ge rén**
every person	每个人	**měi ge rén**
a certain person	某个人	**mǒu ge rén**
which person?	哪个人	**něi ge rén**

However, when numerals other than 一 **yī** 'one' are involved, they obviously cannot be omitted:

这四个苹果	**zhèi sì ge píngguǒ**	these four apples
那五个杯子	**nèi wǔ ge bēizi**	those five cups/mugs/glasses
每两个月	**měi liǎng ge yuè**	every other month
某两个人	**mǒu liǎng ge rén**	two certain persons
哪三个人?	**něi sān ge rén**	Which three people?

When descriptive adjectives form part of the attributive to a noun qualified by a 'numeral + measure word' phrase, they go between the 'numeral + measure word' phrase and the noun. For example:

这本书	**zhèi běn shū**	this book
这本新书	**zhèi běn xīn shū**	this new book
一个姑娘	**yī ge gūniang**	a girl
一个漂亮的姑娘	**yī ge piàoliang de gūniang**	a pretty girl
那个年轻人	**nèi ge niánqīng rén**	that young man/woman
那个勇敢的年轻人	**nèi ge yǒnggǎn de niánqīng rén**	that brave young man/woman

Verbal attributives, on the other hand, either go between the 'numeral + measure word' phrase and the noun or precede the whole phrase altogether. For example:

每个学生	**měi ge xuésheng**	every student
每个不会用电脑的学生	**měi ge bù huì yòng diànnǎo de xuésheng**	every student who can't use a computer
不会用电脑的每个学生	**bù huì yòng diànnǎo de měi ge xuésheng**	every student who can't use a computer

---

[28] 第 **dì** as an indicator of 'sequence' can only be used with 二 **èr** and not 两 **liǎng**.

两个老师	**liǎng ge lǎoshī**	two teachers
两个新来的老师	**liǎng ge xīn lái de lǎoshī**	two teachers who have newly arrived
新来的两个老师	**xīn lái de liǎng ge lǎoshī**	two teachers who have newly arrived
八家商店	**bā jiā shāngdiàn**	eight shops
八家卖衣服的商店	**bā jiā mài yīfu de shāngdiàn**	eight shops which sell clothes
卖衣服的八家商店	**mài yīfu de bā jiā shāngdiàn**	eight shops which sell clothes
一个家庭	**yī ge jiātíng**	a family
一个夫妻经常 吵架的家庭	**yī ge fūqī jīngcháng chǎojià de jiātíng**	a family in which the husband and wife often quarrel
夫妻经常吵架 的一个家庭	**fūqī jīngcháng chǎojià de yī ge jiātíng**	a family in which the husband and wife often quarrel

In fact, the longer the attributive, the more likely it is for the 'numeral + measure' phrase to go closer to its headword, rather than follow the normal 'numeral + measure word + attributive + headword sequence'.

2.10   REDUPLICATION OF MEASURE WORDS

Measure words may often be reduplicated to mean plurality, profusion, or exclusiveness. For example:

条条大路通罗马。	**tiáo tiáo dàlù tōng luómǎ**	All roads lead to Rome.
个个都有责任。	**gè gè dōu yǒu zérèn**	Everybody bears responsibility.

These reduplications may be preceded by the numeral 一 **yī** 'one' to mean 'every' and may be used attributively like a 'numeral + measure word' phrase:

一朵朵花	**yī duǒ duǒ huā**	every single flower
一门门课程	**yī mén mén kèchéng**	each and every course
一个个旅客	**yī gè gè lǚkè**	every passenger

The attributive indicator 的 **de** may also be included after the reduplication to mean 'many':

一座座的桥	**yī zuò zuò de qiáo**	many a bridge
一台台的电脑	**yī tái tái de diànnǎo**	many computers

Reduplication of measure words together with their attached numeral 一 **yī** 'one', however, means 'one after another':

一个一个地[29]	**yī gè yī gè de**	one after another
一步一步地	**yī bù yī bù de**	step by step
一口一口地	**yī kǒu yī kǒu de**	mouthful after mouthful

2.11 MISSING MEASURE WORDS

Measure words, as we have seen, must accompany any noun associated with a numeral. However, sometimes measure words may seem to be missing from certain structures. One possibility is that the noun itself may be a measure. For example:

| 一个人 | **yī ge rén** | one person (where 人 **rén** is a noun) |
| 一人 | **yī rén** | one person (where 人 **rén** is a measure) |

For example:

一人船	**yī rén chuán**	a one-man boat
一个星期	**yī ge xīngqī**	one week (where 星期 **xīngqī** is a noun)
一星期	**yī xīngqī**	one week (where 星期 **xīngqī** is a measure)

For example:

| 一星期假期 | **yī xīngqī jiàqī** | a one-week holiday |

There is some ambiguity with temporal nouns. Some of them are only nouns, some may be both nouns and measures and while others may only be used as measures:

一个小时	**yī ge xiǎoshí**	one hour (where 小时 **xiǎoshí** is a noun)
一小时	**yī xiǎoshí**	one hour (where 小时 **xiǎoshí** is a measure)
一个钟头	**yī ge zhōngtou**	(colloq.) one hour (钟头 **zhōngtou** can only be used as a noun)
*一钟头	***yī zhōngtou**	*one hour
*一个天[30]	***yī ge tiān**	*one day (天 **tiān** is normally used only as a measure)
一天	**yī tiān**	one day

---

[29] 地 **de** is a particle used to mark descriptive adverbials. See §18.2.

[30] 天 **tiān** may sometimes be used as a noun when qualified by an attributive, e.g. 一个大晴天 **yī ge dà qíngtiān** 'a bright sunny day'.

一个礼拜	**yī ge lǐbài**	(colloq.) one week (礼拜 **lǐbài** is only used as a noun)
*一礼拜	***yī lǐbài**	*one week
*一个周	***yī ge zhōu**	*one week (周 **zhōu** can only be used as a measure)
一周	**yī zhōu**	(formal) one week
一个月	**yī ge yuè**	one month (where 月 **yuè** is a noun)
一月	**yī yuè**	January (where 月 **yuè** is still a noun)
*一个年[31]	***yī ge nián**	*one year
一年	**yī nián**	one year (where 年 **nián** is a measure)

Another situation, where a measure word seems to be missing, is in quadrisyllabic expressions and established idioms. As the use of measure words is a relatively recent development in the history of the language, it is not unusual that in expressions derived from Classical Chinese one finds numerals directly associated with nouns. For example:

一事无成 **yī shì wú chéng**
(lit. one thing without success) to have accomplished nothing

一蟹不如一蟹 **yī xiè bùrú yī xiè**
(lit. one crab smaller than another crab) each one is worst than the last

一叶障目，不见泰山 **yī yè zhàng mù | bù jiàn tàishān**
(lit. one leaf screens one's eye, one does not see Mount Tai)
one's view of the important is obscured by the trivial

三言两语 **sānyán liǎngyǔ**
(lit. three words, two expressions) in a few words

五湖四海 **wǔhú sìhǎi** (lit. five lakes, four seas) all corners of the world

A speaker/writer of the language can create expressions modelled on this omission pattern:

(**a**) when using 一 **yī** 'one' with a quadrisyllabic rhythm:

| 这一问题 | **zhèi yī wèntí** | this problem |
| 某一特点 | **mǒu yī tèdiǎn** | a certain characteristic |

---

[31] 年 **nián** to indicate period of time may only be used as a measure. The exception is the expression 给你拜个年 **gěi nǐ bài ge nián** 'wish you a Happy New Year' where it is a noun.

| 另一要求[32] | **lìng yī yāoqiú** | another request/demand |
| 哪一方面? | **něi yī fāngmiàn** | Which aspect? |

(**b**) when using 那 **nèi** or 这 **zhèi** in colloquial speech without 一 **yī**:

| 这年纪 | **zhèi niánjì** | at this age |
| 那事儿 | **nèi shìr** | as far as that matter is concerned |

On the other hand, the numeral 一 **yī** 'one' is usually omitted before a measure word and a noun which is the object of a monosyllabic verb: e.g. 买本书 **mǎi běn shū** 'to buy a book' instead of 买一本书 **mǎi yī běn shū** or 喝杯酒 **hē bēi jiǔ** 'to drink a glass of wine' instead of 喝一杯酒 **hē yī bēi jiǔ**.[33]

2.12 DISYLLABIC MEASURE WORDS

The number of measure words in Chinese is approximately 450, half of which are in common use. By far the great majority of them, as we have seen, are monosyllabic, but a small number of established or ad hoc disyllabic measure words are used in colloquial speech. For example:

一嘟噜葡萄	**yī dūlu pútao**	(colloq.) a bunch of grapes
一疙瘩糕儿	**yī gēda gāor**	(colloq.) a small piece of cake
一掐子盐	**yī qiāzi yán**	(dial.) a pinch of salt

2.13 COMPOUND MEASURE WORDS

Measure words, particularly in technical texts, can appear as compounded measurements. Generally speaking, the compounding usually takes place between an average or universal measure and a duration or frequency measure. The average or standard measure is mentioned first followed immediately by the duration or frequency measure. For example:

人次	**réncì**	number of [for example] visits from people (within a designated period)
架次	**jiàcì**	number of flights (within a designated period)
千瓦小时	**qiānwǎ xiǎoshí**	kilowatts per hour

2.14 DURATION AND FREQUENCY MEASURES

Duration and frequency measures are used in a different way from nominal measures. They will be discussed in full in Chapter 8 which deals with duration and frequency complements.

---

[32] If the quadrisyllabic rhythm is not adhered to, the necessary measure word needs to be supplied, e.g. 另外一个要求 **lìngwài yī ge yāoqiú**.

[33] See Chapter 26 on Prosodic Features.

3 PRONOUNS, PRONOMINALS AND PRO-WORDS

3.1 PERSONAL PRONOUNS

The system of personal pronouns in Modern Standard Chinese is laid out in the following table:

person	singular			plural		
				speaker only	speaker and hearer	
first person	我 **wǒ** 'I; me'			我们 **wǒmen** 'we; us'	咱们 **zánmen** 'we; us'	
	normal		polite			
second person	你 **nǐ** 'you'		您 **nín** 'you'	你们 **nǐmen** 'you'		
	masculine	feminine	neuter	masculine	feminine	neuter
third person	他 **tā** 'he; him'	她 **tā** 'she; her'	它 **tā** 'it'	他们 **tāmen** 'they; them'	她们 **tāmen** 'they; them'	它们 **tāmen** 'they; them'

We can see that, first, no distinction is made between subject and object cases in the pronominal system in Chinese. For example, 我 **wǒ** stands for either 'I' or 'me'.

Second, the distinction between the two forms of first person plural 我们 **wǒmen** and 咱们 **zánmen** as indicated in the table is not always made by native speakers, particularly those from the south of the country.

Third, the polite form for the second person singular 您 **nín**, is in practice most commonly used in addressing superiors or new acquaintances. There is no corresponding form in the plural, and, therefore, other supplementary phrases have to be used to convey the kind of politeness intended, e.g. 你们两位 **nǐmen liǎng wèi** 'you two (honourable sirs)', etc.

Fourth, in the third person singular, the differentiation between genders only appears in the written script and no attempt is made in the spoken form to register such differences.

The possessive forms corresponding to these pronouns are expressed by adding the particle 的 **de** after the pronouns; and there is no distinction between possessive adjectives and possessive pronouns. For example:

my; mine	我的	**wǒde**
our; ours (inclusive)	咱们的	**zánmende**
your; yours	你的	**nǐde**
your; yours (polite)	您的	**nǐnde**
her; hers	她的	**tāde**
their; theirs (masculine)	他们的	**tāmende**

这是您的茶。 **zhè shì nínde chá**
This is your tea. (possessive adjective)

这封信是您的。 **zhèi fēng xìn shì nínde**
This letter is yours. (possessive pronoun)

3.2 DEMONSTRATIVE PRONOUNS

In Modern Standard Chinese, there are only two sets of demonstrative pronouns in common use:

close to the speaker	away from the speaker
这 **zhè** 'this'	那 **nà** 'that'
这儿 **zhèr** or 这里 **zhèli** 'here'	那儿 **nàr** or 那里 **nàli** 'there'

For example:

这是我的。	**zhè shì wǒde**	This is mine.
那是你的。	**nà shì nǐde**	That is yours.

These two demonstrative pronouns on their own can only be used in the topic[1] position. When they function as **demonstrative adjectives**, they combine with measure words or 'numeral + measure' phrases, and like other pronouns can then occur in any position in a sentence:

---

[1] The forms of topic–comment sentences as opposed to subject–predicate sentences are discussed in Chapter 21.

这(一)个	**zhèi (yī) gè**	this one
这两个	**zhèi liǎng gè**	these two
这(一)些	**zhèi (yī) xiē**	these

那(一)本	**nèi (yī) běn**	that copy
那几本	**nèi jǐ běn**	those few copies
那(一)些	**nèi (yī) xiē**	those

我买那两个。	**wǒ mǎi nèi liǎng gè**	I'd like to buy those two.
我不要这几本。	**wǒ bùyào zhèi jǐ běn**	I don't want these few copies.
我对那些不感兴趣。	**wǒ duì nèixiē bù gǎn xìngqù**	I'm not interested in those.

Note that 这 'this' and 那 'that' are always pronounced respectively as **zhè** and **nà** when used as demonstrative pronouns on their own. However, as demonstrative adjectives, when they are followed by a measure, they are also pronounced **zhèi** and **nèi** by many speakers. This is almost certainly a phonetic fusion of **zhe** + **yi** 'one' and **na** + **yi** 'one'. Even when **yi** 'one' is present in its own right in an utterance, the pronunciation **zhèi** and **nèi** can still be used. For example:

| 这(一)件大衣 | **zhèi (yī) jiàn dàyī** | this overcoat |
| 那(一)天 | **nèi (yī) tiān** | that day |

It also naturally follows that 这些 'these' and 那些 'those' are pronounced **zhèixiē** and **nèixiē**, since the plural measure 些 **xiē** 'some' is it itself used only with the measure 一 **yī** 'one'.[2]

The location words here and there are also based on the two demonstratives:

| here | 这儿 **zhèr** | or | 这里 **zhèli** |
| there | 那儿 **nàr** | or | 那里 **nàli** |

| 这儿/这里有牛奶。 | **zhèr/zhèli yǒu niúnǎi** | Here is some milk. |
| 你的书包在那儿/那里。 | **nǐde shūbāo zài nàr/nàli** | Your schoolbag is over there. |

Finally there are a number of demonstratives (used both as pronouns and adjectives), that occur as established words, expressions, idioms, or sayings.[3] These expressions are more literary than colloquial.

---

[2] See §1.3.

[3] These demonstratives, being classical in origin, do not occur with measure words and are followed immediately by nouns.

this	此 cǐ	此外	**cǐwài**	apart from this
		此地/此处	**cǐdì/cǐchù**	this place; here
		此刻	**cǐkè**	this moment; now
		从此	**cóngcǐ**	since then; from now on
		由此	**yóucǐ**	from here
	斯 sī	斯人	**sī rén**	(fml.) this person
	者 zhě	者番	**zhě fān**	(obs.) on this occasion
that	彼 bǐ	彼时	**bǐ shí**	(fml.) at that time
	其 qí	其时	**qí shí**	(fml.) just at that time
this or that	是 shì	如是	**rúshì**	(fml.) like this
		是日	**shìrì**	(fml.) that day
	该 gāi	该校	**gāi xiào**	(fml.) this or that school

In writings which adopt a more formal tone, 此 **cǐ** 'this; here' and 该 **gāi** 'that; the said; the above-mentioned' are still commonly used:

formal in tone	colloquial equivalent	English
此地/此处 **cǐdì/cǐchù**	这儿/这里 **zhèr/zhèli**	in this place
此事 **cǐshì**	这件事儿 **zhèi jiàn shìr**	this matter
该项工作 **gāi xiàng gōngzuò**	那项工作 **nèi xiàng gōngzuò**	that job
该地区 **gāi dìqū**	那个地区 **nèi ge dìqū**	that area

3.3 INTERROGATIVE PRONOUNS

	English	Chinese
human beings	who/whom	谁 **shuí** or (colloq.) **shéi**
inanimate objects	what	什么 **shénme**
human beings or inanimate objects	which	哪 **nǎ/něi** + measure word
one of an ordered closed set	which	几 **jǐ** (+ measure word)
place	where[4]	哪儿/哪里 **nǎr/nǎli**

---

[4] Though 'where' is an interrogative adverb in English, 哪儿 **nǎr** in Chinese is a pronoun, e.g. 你上哪儿去? **nǐ shàng nǎr qù** (lit. you to where go) 'Where are you off to?'.

From the table we can see that there are only two interrogative pronouns 谁 **shuí** (or **shéi**) and 什么 **shénme**, and that there is no case differentiation with 谁 **shuí**.

谁不去?	**shuí /shéi bù qù**	Who is not going?
你找谁?	**nǐ zhǎo shuí/shéi**	Whom are you looking for?
这是什么?	**zhè shì shénme**	What is this?
你要什么?	**nǐ yào shénme**	What do you want?

谁 **shuí/shéi** may of course be turned into a possessive pronoun or adjective by the addition of 的 **de**:

| 这本书是谁的? | **zhèi běn shū shì shuíde/shéide** | Whose is this book? |
| 这是谁的书? | **zhè shì shuíde/shéide shū** | Whose book is this? |

什么 **shénme** may also be used as an interrogative adjective:[5]

| 你喜欢听什么音乐? | **nǐ xǐhuan tīng shénme yīnyuè** | What music do you like listening to? |
| 你什么时候走? | **nǐ shénme shíhou zǒu** | What time are you leaving? |

On the other hand, 哪 **nǎ/něi** is an interrogative adjective which is always used in conjunction with an appropriate measure word or 'measure + noun' phrase (preceded or not preceded by a numeral) to form an interrogative pronominal expression meaning 'which one/two/ etc'. Here are some examples:

哪(一)天?	**nǎ/něi (yī) tiān**[6]	Which day?
哪(一)年?	**nǎ/něi (yī) nián**	Which year?
哪(一)件?	**nǎ/něi (yī) jiàn**	Which jacket/shirt/coat/, etc.?
哪本书?	**nǎ/něi běn shū**	Which book?
哪两支笔?	**nǎ/něi liǎng zhī bǐ**	Which two pens?
哪些椅子?	**nǎ/něi xiē yǐzi**	Which chairs?
哪条裤子?	**nǎ/něi tiáo kùzi**	Which pair of trousers?
哪班飞机?	**nǎ/něi bān fēijī**	Which flight?
哪个大夫?	**nǎ/něi ge dàifu**	Which doctor?

As we can see, 哪 **nǎ/něi** is used to single out a particular one or number from an unlimited group of people or things. If the selection is made from an ordered and closed set of items, 几 **jǐ** is often used instead. For example:

---

[5] When 什么 **shénme** is used as an interrogative adjective, it can be linked with human nouns to connote contempt: e.g. 你是什么人? **nǐ shì shénme rén** 'Who/What are you?', 什么积极分子? **shénme jījí fènzǐ** 'What an activist!', etc.

[6] As with **zhè/zhèi** 'this' and **nà/nèi** 'that' above 哪 **nǎ** followed by 一 **yī** may also be pronounced as **něi**.

哪(一)天 **nǎ/něi (yī) tiān**	= 几号 **jǐ hào**[7]	Which day of the month?
哪个月 **nǎ/něi ge yuè**	= 几月 **jǐ yuè**	Which month?
哪(一)年 **nǎ/něi (yī) nián**		Which year?[8]
	几时 **jǐ shí**	What time (i.e. which hour, day, etc.)[9]
	几点(钟) **jǐ diǎn (zhōng)**	What time (i.e. which hour)?
	几年级 **jǐ niánjí**	Which year (in a school, etc.)?
	几号房 **jǐ hào fáng**	Which room?/What number room?
	第几 **dì jǐ**	What place (in a race, exam, etc.)?

哪儿 **nǎr** has an alternative form in 哪里 **nǎli**, which is commonly used by southern speakers:

你去哪儿/哪里?	**nǐ qù nǎr/nǎli**	Where are you going?
他在哪儿/哪里?	**tā zài nǎr/nǎli**	Where is he?
哪儿/哪里有厕所?	**nǎr/nǎli yǒu cèsuǒ**	Where is there a toilet?

3.4 INDEFINITE PRONOUNS

By indefinite pronouns we mean words like 'everybody', 'anybody', 'nobody', 'everything', 'anything', 'nothing', and so on. In Chinese, these pronouns are created by using the appropriate interrogative word[10] in conjunction with a **reference adverb**, either 都 **dōu** 'all' or 也 **yě** 'also':

谁都/也	**shuí/shéi dōu/yě**	everyone, anyone
什么都/也	**shénme dōu/yě**	everything, anything
哪个都/也	**nǎ/něi ge dōu/yě**	all, any
哪儿/哪里都/也	**nǎr/nǎli dōu/yě**	everywhere, anywhere

They generally occur in the topic position, that is at the beginning of an expository or evaluative sentence,[11] and they can be followed by either a positive or negative comment:

---

[7] Please note however that the answer to 哪(一)天 **nǎ/něi (yī) tiān** may for instance be: (a) today; or (b) Tuesday; or (c) 21st; while to 几号 **jǐ hào**, can only be 21st; likewise the answer to 哪个月 **nǎ/něi ge yuè** is either (a) this month; or (b) May; but to 几月 **jǐ yuè**, can only be May.

[8] As 年 **nián** 'year' is an open set, it is therefore not usually used with 几 **jǐ**.

[9] 时 **shí** 'time' is not normally used on its own but often occurs with 几 **jǐ** to ask meaning 'which hour, day, month', etc. in general terms.

[10] In these constructions, the interrogative pronoun becomes indefinite: 谁 **shuí/shéi** 'who(m)ever', 什么 **shénme** 'whatever', 哪个 **nǎ ge/něi ge** 'whichever', and 哪儿/哪里 **nǎr/nǎli** 'wherever'.

[11] See Chapter 20.

谁都认识他。	shuí/shéi dōu rènshi tā	Everybody knows him.
谁都不喜欢他。	shuí/shéi dōu bù xǐhuan tā	Nobody likes him.
什么都行。	shénme dōu xíng	Anything will do.
(我)什么都吃。	(wǒ) shénme dōu chī	I eat everything.
(我)什么也不要。	(wǒ) shénme yě bùyào	I do not want anything.
(我)哪件也不买。	(wǒ) nǎ/něi jiàn yě bù mǎi	I am not going to buy any (of these clothes).
(我)哪儿/哪里都不去。	(wǒ) nǎr/nǎli dōu bù qù	I am not going anywhere.

As happens with its interrogative usage, the addition of 的 **de** to the indefinite pronoun 谁 **shuí/shéi** 'whoever' converts it to an indefinite possessive 谁的 **shuíde/shéide** 'whose'. For example:

谁的都没有关系。 **shuí/shéide dōu méiyǒu guānxi**
It does not matter whose it is.

However, if these Chinese indefinite pronouns are used in any other than the topic position in a sentence, the sentence generally takes the form of a dependent clause followed by, or embedded in, another larger and independent construction:

见到谁，请替我问候一声。 **jiàndào shuí | qǐng tì wǒ wènhòu yī shēng**
Please remember me to anyone you come across.

我肚子一饿，就想吃点儿什么。 **wǒ dùzi yī è | jiù xiǎng chī diǎnr shénme**
I like to have something to eat as soon as I feel hungry.

去哪儿都行。 **qù nǎr dōu xíng**
(I'll) go wherever it is/(I) don't mind where (we) go.

Very often the same indefinite pronoun is used in a similar position in two clauses within a sentence, the second echoing the first:

有什么，吃什么。 **yǒu shénme | chī shénme**
(lit. have what, eat what) I'll eat whatever you've got.

你去哪儿，我就去哪儿。 **nǐ qù nǎr | wǒ jiù qù nǎr**
(lit. you go where, I then go where) I'll go wherever you go.

谁弄错，谁负责。 **shuí nòng cuò | shuí fùzé**
(lit. who gets wrong, who is responsible)
Whoever makes a mistake will be responsible.

他跟谁好，我也跟谁好。 **tā gēn shuí hǎo | wǒ yě gēn shuí hǎo**
(lit. he with whom good, I also with whom good)
I'll be nice to anyone he is nice to.

你帮谁，我就帮谁。 **nǐ bāng shuí | wǒ jiù bāng shuí**
(lit. you help whom, I then help whom) I'll help anyone you help.

One important thing to note about these interrogatives-turned-indefinite pronouns is that, while their interrogative originals are always stressed in a sentence, as indefinites they never are.

3.5 ENUMERATIVE PRONOUNS

By enumerative pronouns we mean fixed pronominal expressions used in Chinese which are similar to 'etc.' or 'and so on (and so forth)' in English:

他在超市买了一些水果，如梨、苹果、橘子，<u>等等</u>。
tā zài chāoshì mǎi le yīxiē shuǐguǒ | rú lí | píngguǒ | júzi | <u>děngdeng</u>
He bought some fruit, such as pears, apples, oranges, etc. at the supermarket.

where 等等 **děngdeng** 'etc, and the like' is an enumerative pronoun indicating a thing or things of a similar kind in a list that remains open.

Indefinite pronouns also sometimes occur as enumerative pronouns when they are reduplicated and integrated into an object clause. For example,

他说老王、老张，还有<u>谁谁</u>(谁)也没有去。 **tā shuō lǎowáng | lǎozhāng |
háiyǒu <u>shuí shuí</u> (<u>shuí</u>)/<u>shéi shéi</u> (<u>shéi</u>) yě méiyǒu qù**
He said Old Wang, Old Zhang and <u>various other people</u> had not gone either.

她认为他不但懂天文、地理、数学，还懂别的<u>什么什么</u>的。 **tā rènwéi tā
bùdàn dǒng tiānwén | dìlǐ | shùxué | hái dǒng biéde <u>shénme shénme</u> de**
She thought he understood not only astronomy, geography and mathematics but also all other <u>kinds of things</u>.

3.6 PRONOMINALS

Pronominals are words or phrases which function like pronouns. The most common type is either a 'numeral + measure' phrase on its own or an attributive followed by 的 **de**. Take the following noun phrase:

两件红色的外套 **liǎng jiàn hóngsè de wàitào**   two red jackets

Enquiries deriving from it about the number and/or colour of the jackets might invite the following pronominal responses:

我买了两件。	**wǒ mǎi le <u>liǎng jiàn</u>**	I bought two.
我买了红色的。	**wǒ mǎi le <u>hóngsè de</u>**	I bought the red ones.
我买了两件红色的。	**wǒ mǎi le <u>liǎng jiàn hóngsè de</u>**	I bought two red ones.

两件 **liǎng jiàn**, as a 'numeral + measure' phrase and 红色的 **hóngsède**, as an attributive with 的 **de**, both represent their associated noun 外套 **wàitào** 'jacket' in this context, and are both pronominals. We will look at some other examples in different contexts:

At a fruit stall selling mandarin oranges:

你买<u>几斤</u>? **nǐ mǎi <u>jǐ jīn</u>**
(lit. you buy how many catties) How many catties do you want?
我买<u>三斤</u>。 **wǒ mǎi <u>sān jīn</u>**
(lit. I buy three catties) I'd like to have three catties, (please).
你要<u>大的</u>还是<u>小的</u>? **nǐ yào <u>dà de</u> háishi <u>xiǎo de</u>**
(lit. you want big *de* or small *de*) Do you want big ones or small ones?
我要<u>中等</u>的。 **wǒ yào <u>zhōngděng de</u>**
(lit. I want medium *de*) I'd like the medium-sized ones.

A scene on the beach:

海滩上有很多人。<u>有的</u>在晒太阳；<u>有的</u>要么跑着，跳着，要么在玩泥沙。
hǎitān shàng yǒu hěnduō rén ‖ <u>yǒude</u> zài shài tàiyáng | <u>yǒude</u> yàome pǎo zhe | tiào zhe | yàome zài wán níshā ‖
There are a lot of people on the beach, some sun-bathing, others running, jumping or playing with the sand.

<u>晒太阳的</u>大半是大人。<u>跑着</u>、<u>跳着</u>或者<u>在玩泥沙的</u>大多是小孩。
<u>shài tàiyáng de</u> dàbàn shì dàrén | <u>pǎo zhe</u> | <u>tiào zhe</u> huòzhě <u>zài wán níshā de</u> dàduō shì xiǎohái ‖
Those sun-bathing are mostly adults while those running, jumping or playing with the sand are mostly children.

卖冰激凌的车一来，那些<u>跑着</u>、<u>跳着</u>，<u>在玩泥沙的</u>马上停下来，蜂拥而上，团团围住卖<u>冰激凌的</u>，使他忙得喘不过气来。
mài bīngjīlíng de chē yī lái | <u>nèixiē</u> <u>pǎo zhe</u> | <u>tiào zhe</u> | <u>zài wán níshā de</u> mǎshàng tíng xiàlai | fēngyōng ér shàng | tuántuán wéizhù <u>mài bīngjīlíng de</u>, shǐ tā máng de chuǎn bu guò qì lái ‖
As soon as the ice-cream van arrives, those running, jumping or playing with the sand immediately stop what they are doing and swarm around the ice-cream man in a tight circle, making him so busy he can't get his breath.

It must, however, be remembered that 的 **de** pronominals always imply a contrast, whether the original forms are adjectival or verbal. In the case of adjectival pronominals, one may, say, for example:

| 大的 | **dà de** | a big one |
| 最大的 | **zuì dà de** | the biggest one |

but never:

| *很大的 | **hěn dà de** | *very big one |
| *大大的 | **dàdà de** | *biggish one |

3.7 PRO-WORDS

Apart from the rule-governed *ad hoc* pronominals, there are a number of established **pro-words** in the lexicon. They are items that are often used to replace other words or expressions. One common set takes the place of personal pronouns:

person	singular or plural		plural	
	formal	**colloquial**	**formal**	**colloquial**
first person	自己[12] **zìjǐ** 'oneself'	自个儿 **zìgěr** 'oneself'		
second person			诸位 **zhūwèi** 'every one here' 各位 **gèwèi** 'every one here'	大家 **dàjiā** 'everybody' 大伙儿 **dàhuǒr** 'everyone'
third person	别人 **biérén** 'others' 前者 **qiánzhě**[13] 'the former' 后者 **hòuzhě** 'the latter'	人家 **rénjiā**[14] 'others'		

[12] 自己 **zìjǐ** and 自个儿 **zìgěr** may also be used as emphatic pronouns, e.g. 我自己 **wǒ zìjǐ** 'I myself', 他们自个儿 **tāmen zìgěr** 'they themselves', etc.

[13] 前者 **qiánzhě** and 后者 **hòuzhě** are somewhat formal, and are generally used to refer to inanimate objects rather than animate beings.

[14] 人家 **rénjiā** normally indicates a third party, e.g. 把书送给人家 **bǎ shū sòng gěi rénjiā** 'Take the book to him (her, them)'; however, it may sometimes be used to refer to the speaker him or herself, that is, referring to oneself as if one is a third party when discussing or arguing with somebody, e.g. 他让人家生气了 **tā ràng rénjiā shēngqì le** 'He made me angry'.

The possessive forms of these pro-words are formulated in the same way as personal pronouns by adding the particle 的 **de**:

自己的	**zìjǐ de**	one's own
大家的	**dàjiā de**	everybody's

Here are some sentence examples:

自己不愿意做，就别叫别人做。 **zìjǐ bù yuànyi zuò | jiù bié jiào biérén zuò**
Don't ask others to do what you are unwilling to do yourself.

请大家安静点儿。 **qǐng dàjiā ānjìng diǎnr**
Please (would everyone) be a bit quiet.

人家的事儿你别管。 **rénjiā de shìr nǐ bié guǎn**
Don't poke your nose into other people's affairs. (i.e. Mind your own business.)

The **pro-word** 怎么样 **zénmeyàng** is an interrogative, and often constitutes the whole of a predicate. For example:

你今天怎么样?	**nǐ jīntiān zénmeyàng**	How are you today?
你明天怎么样?	**nǐ míngtiān zénmeyàng**	What are you doing tomorrow?
今天的电影怎么样?	**jīntiān de diànyǐng zénmeyàng**	How was today's film?
你怎么样?	**nǐ zénmeyàng**	How about you?
你怎么样了?	**nǐ zénmeyàng le**	What's wrong with you?
我没怎么样。	**wǒ méi zénmeyàng**	There's nothing wrong with me.[15]

---

[15] A speaker, in responding to a question, will often borrow or repeat a phrase in this way from the question.

4 ADJECTIVES AS ATTRIBUTIVES AND PREDICATIVES

4.1 ADJECTIVES IN CHINESE

Syntactically, adjectives in Chinese may function as **attributives** when placed in front of noun headwords (with or without 的 *de*) (= formulaically: Attr. + Noun); or as **predicatives** when placed behind nominal headwords (with or without 的 *de*) (= formulaically: Noun + Pred.);[1] or even as **adverbials** if placed before verbs (with or without 地 *de*). We will defer the discussion of adjectives functioning as adverbials until Chapter 9. Here, we will concentrate on attributive and predicative uses.

An adjective (e.g. 漂亮 **piàoliang** 'pretty') used attributively with a noun headword produces an extended nominal expression:

一条漂亮的裙子　　**yī tiáo piàoliang de qúnzi**　a pretty skirt

When an adjective is used predicatively with a nominal headword, the result is a clause or sentence:

这条裙子真漂亮。　**zhèi tiáo qúnzi zhēn**　　　This skirt is really pretty.
　　　　　　　　　piàoliang

Apart from differences in syntactic function and in syllabicity, which directly affects collocability,[2] adjectives also differ in many other respects: qualifiers vs quantifiers, gradable vs non-gradable, conditional vs unconditional, derivable vs non-derivable, reduplicable vs non-reduplicable, phonaesthetic vs non-phonaesthetic, derogatory vs commendatory, and so on. These differences, which invariably affect their syntactic capability, are discussed in turn in §4.2 and 4.6 below.

---

[1] See §4.4 for discussion of the descriptive indicator 的 *de*.
[2] Generally speaking, monosyllabic adjectives tend to form words or set expressions and are therefore more restrictive in their collocability, whereas disyllabic adjectives can be used freely as qualifiers (or quantifiers).

4.2 QUALIFIERS OR QUANTIFIERS

Adjectives in Chinese are used, like adjectives in other languages, to **qualify** or **quantify**[3] noun headwords. For example:

好学生	**hǎo xuésheng**	a good student/good students
许多学生	**xǔduō xuésheng**	many students

where 好 **hǎo** 'good' qualifies and 许多 **xǔduō** 'many' quantifies. As we can see, both precede their respective headwords. When they come together to qualify and quantify one and the same headword, the quantifier always comes before the qualifier:[4]

许多好学生	**xǔduō hǎo xuésheng**	many good students

and not:

*好许多学生	***hǎo xǔduō xuésheng**	*good many students

Qualifiers are used freely as either attributives or predicatives, but **quantifiers** for the most part function only as attributives. For example:

所有问题	**suǒyǒu wèntí**	all the problems
*问题所有	***wèntí suǒyǒu**	

多数人	**duōshù rén**	the majority of the people
*人多数	***rén duōshù**	

The exceptions are 多 **duō** 'many, much' and 少 **shǎo** 'few, little', which, when duly modified by a degree adverb, may be used predicatively. For example:

很多东西	**hěn duō dōngxi**	a lot of things
东西很多	**dōngxi hěn duō**	there are a lot of things (lit. things are (very) many)
不少人	**bùshǎo rén**	quite a few people
人不少	**rén bùshǎo**	there are quite a few people (lit. people are quite a few)

---

[3] The kind of quantification indicated by adjectives is generally rough and imprecise compared with the more precise or specific 'numeral and measure word' phrases.

[4] This is similar to noun phrases with a 'numeral + measure' and a qualifier where the former always precedes the latter: e.g. 一个好学生 **yī ge hǎo xuésheng** 'a good student', and not *好一个学生 ***hǎo yī ge xuésheng**.

Note, however, that this exception does not apply to 许多 **xǔduō** 'many, a lot of':

| 许多朋友 | **xǔduō péngyou** | quite a few friends |
| *朋友许多 | ***péngyou xǔduō** | *there are quite a few friends |

Other common quantifiers include: 大量 **dàliàng** 'a great deal', 好些 **hǎoxiē** 'quite a number'; 个别 **gèbié** 'individual', 点滴 **diǎndī** 'a little'; 一切 **yīqiè** 'all', 全部 **quánbù** 'whole'; 有些 **yǒuxiē** 'some', 有的 **yǒude** 'some'; 多数 **duōshù** 'majority of', 少数 **shǎoshù** 'minority of'; etc.

4.3 DEGREE ADVERBS AND COMPLEMENTS

Degree adverbs and **complements** occur respectively before and after adjectives to indicate the degree or extent to which the meaning encoded by an adjective is to be ascertained:

这本字典<u>很</u>好。 **zhèi běn zìdiǎn <u>hěn</u> hǎo**
This dictionary is <u>very</u> good. [degree adverb]

这本字典好<u>得很</u>。 **zhèi běn zìdiàn hǎo <u>de hěn</u>**
This dictionary is <u>really</u> good. [degree complement]

The presence of these degree adverbs and complements removes any implication of contrast that is latent in an unmarked predicative adjective.

If somebody says:

这本字典好。 **zhèi běn zìdiǎn hǎo**.　　This dictionary is good.

the speaker must be understood to be implying that some other dictionary is not as good as this one. In fact the degree adverb 很 **hěn** 'very', unless it is emphasised, does not really mean 'very', and its integration into an adjectival predicative is more often than not to counteract an implication of contrast.

Quantifying adjectives, with the exception of 多 **duō** 'many' and 少 **shǎo** 'few', do not normally occur with degree adverbs or degree complements. For example:

| *很许多人 | **hěn xǔduō rén*** | quite a number of people |
| *好些得很 | **hǎoxiē de hěn*** | quite a few |

Qualifying adjectives, on the other hand, as we have just seen, usually do require the modification of degree adverbs.

| 不重 | **bù zhòng** | not heavy |
| 很美 | **hěn měi** | very pretty |

较差	**jiào chà**	slightly worse
最好	**zuì hǎo**	best of all (lit. most good)
蛮有趣[5]	**mán yǒuqù**	fairly interesting
非常容易	**fēicháng róngyì**	extremely easy
有点儿可怜[6]	**yǒu diǎnr kělián**	somewhat pitiable
那么/这么漂亮	**nàme/zhème piàoliang**	so pretty
多么美丽	**duōme měilì**	how beautiful

不 **bù** 'not' is both negator and degree adverb. When it is used in conjunction with 很 **hěn** 'very', two different meanings are possible depending on word order:

| 不很好 | **bù hěn hǎo** | not very good |
| 很不好 | **hěn bù hǎo** | very bad |

较 **jiào** and 比较 **bǐjiào** 'comparatively' indicate a comparative degree and 最 **zuì** 'most' a superlative degree. For example:

这个较好。	**zhèi ge jiào hǎo**	This one is better.
这个比较好。	**zhèi ge bǐjiào hǎo**	This one is better.
这个最好。	**zhèi ge zuì hǎo**	This one is the best.

那么 **nàme** 'so' is usually used in negative sentences and 多么 **duōme** 'how' in exclamatory ones. For example:

我从没见过那么漂亮的孩子。
wǒ cóng méi jiàn guo nàme piàoliang de háizi
I have never seen such a pretty child before.

这儿的风景多么美丽呀! **zhèr de fēngjǐng duōme měilì ya**
How beautiful the view is from here!

Other degree adverbs are:

太	**tài**	too	真	**zhēn**	really
更/更加	**gèng/gèngjiā**	even more	十分	**shífēn**	very, extremely
万分	**wànfēn**	extremely	相当	**xiāngdāng**	quite, fairly
特别	**tèbié**	especially	极其	**jíqí**	most, exceeding
无比	**wúbǐ**	incomparably	绝顶	**juédǐng**	extremely
过分	**guòfèn**	excessively			

[5] 蛮 **mán** 'fairly', which occurs mainly in southern dialects of Chinese, is generally used with commendatory terms, e.g. 蛮好 **mán hǎo** 'fairly good', but not: *蛮坏 **mán huài** 'rather bad'.

[6] There is a tendency for 有点儿 **yǒu diǎnr** 'somewhat' to be used only with derogatory terms, e.g. 有点儿难 **yǒu diǎnr nán** 'somewhat difficult', but not *有点儿容易 **yǒu diǎnr róngyì** 'somewhat easy'.

Degree complements[7] follow the adjectives they modify:

好些	**hǎoxiē**	slightly better
好点儿	**hǎo diǎnr**	a little better
好得很	**hǎo de hěn**	really, really good
好得多	**hǎo de duō**	much/far better
美极了	**měi jí le**	exceptionally beautiful
糟透了[8]	**zāo tòu le**	thoroughly bad, totally rotten

Other degree complements are:

坏得不得了 **huài de bùdeliǎo** rotten to the core

饿死了 **è sǐ le** famished (lit. hungry to death)

贵得要命 **guì de yàomìng** impossibly expensive

高兴得了不得 **gāoxìng de liǎobùdé** exceedingly happy

快乐之极 **kuàilè zhī jí** extremely happy

热得要死 **rè de yàosǐ** unbearably hot

It must, however, be noted that only qualifying adjectives that are gradable[9] can take degree adverbs or complements. Non-gradable adjectives usually cannot. For example:

| *很男 | **hěn nán** | *very male |
| *女得很 | **nǚ de hěn** | *extremely female |

4.4   THE DESCRIPTIVE INDICATOR 的 *de*

The presence of the descriptive indicator 的 *de* in an adjectival phrase depends on factors, which are different for quantifying and qualifying adjectives.

Quantifying adjectives are not generally used with the descriptive indicator 的 *de* when they have no more than a quantifying capacity. For example:

许多人	**xǔduō rén**	many people
广大读者	**guǎngdà dúzhě**	a large number of general readers
大量信息	**dàliàng xìnxī**	a large quantity of information
个别地区	**gèbié dìqū**	individual areas
些许礼物	**xiēxǔ lǐwù**	a few presents
全部开支	**quánbù kāizhī**	total expenditure

However, when a quantifying adjective has a more descriptive than quantifying function, it does incorporate 的 *de*:

---

[7] For more precise degree complements like 高一公分 **gāo yī gōngfēn** 'one centimetre taller', 大两岁 **dà liǎng suì** 'two years older', etc., see §4.9.

[8] 透了 **tòu le** 'thoroughly, to the core' tends to occur only with a derogatory meaning, e.g. 坏透了 **huài tòu le** 'rotten to the core', but not *好透了 **hǎo tòu le*** 'good to the extreme'.

[9] For gradable and non-gradable adjectives, see §4.6 below.

| 无数的事实 | wúshù de shìshí | innumerable facts |
| 许许多多[10]的人 | xǔxǔduōduō de rén | a very many people |

With qualifying adjectives, on the other hand, the presence of 的 *de* depends on whether the adjective is monosyllabic or polysyllabic. Generally speaking, monosyllabic adjectives have greater collocational restrictions and hence greater structural bonds with the headwords they qualify. They are therefore often placed directly in front of their headwords without 的 *de*:[11]

红砖	hóng zhuān	red bricks
短裤	duǎn kù	shorts (lit. short trousers)
近路	jìn lù	a short-cut (rather than a detour)
热水	rè shuǐ	hot water
新书	xīn shū	a new book/new books
高个子	gāo gèzi	a tall person (lit. tall build/stature)
怪脾气	guài píqi	an odd/eccentric temperament
新房子	xīn fángzi	a new house/new houses
好天气	hǎo tiānqì	good weather

On the other hand, di- or polysyllabic adjectives usually require 的 *de*:

肥沃的土地	féiwò de tǔdì	fertile land
幽静的环境	yōujìng de huánjìng	quiet surroundings
幸福的生活	xìngfú de shēnghuó	a happy life
美丽的焰火	měilì de yànhuǒ	beautiful fireworks
凉爽的风	liángshuǎng de fēng	a cool breeze
蔚蓝的天空	wèilán de tiānkōng	a blue sky
茂密的树林	màomì de shùlín	a dense forest
平易近人的老师	píngyì jìnrén de lǎoshī	an approachable teacher
无穷无尽的力量	wúqióng wújìn de lìliàng	boundless energy/ strength
一个聪明伶俐的孩子	yī ge cōngming línglì de háizi	an intelligent, quick- witted child

All phonaesthetic or reduplicated forms, because of their inbuilt descriptive nature, are also usually followed by 的 *de*:

清清的河水	qīngqīng de héshuǐ	a clear stream
蓝蓝的天	lánlán de tiān	a blue sky
圆滚滚的卵石	yuángǔngǔn de luǎnshí	smooth, round pebbles

---

[10] All reduplicated forms in Chinese are in fact of a descriptive nature.

[11] Where the collocation is loose and/or the noun is long, it is possible for a monosyllabic adjective to occur with 的 *de*, e.g. 新的自来水笔 xīn de zìláishuǐbǐ a new fountain pen.

白蒙蒙的雾气	**báiméngméng de wùqì**	white haze
绿茸茸的草地	**lüróngróng de cǎodì**	a lush green lawn/meadow
弯弯曲曲的小道	**wānwānqūqū de xiǎodào**	a zigzag path
火热火热的太阳	**huǒrè huǒrè de tàiyáng**	a burning hot sun
一个老老实实的人	**yī ge lǎolǎoshíshí de rén**	an extremely honest person

Monosyllabic adjectives, when modified by degree adverbs, become more descriptive than restrictive, and therefore have to include the indicator:

很大的房子	**hěn dà de fángzi**	a very big house/very big houses
很脏的衣服	**hěn zāng de yīfu**	very dirty clothes
很高的评价	**hěn gāo de píngjià**	a very good appraisal

However, when disyllabic adjectives qualify disyllabic headwords, if the consequential quadrisyllabic rhythm forms a tightly knit expression, then the indicator may often be dropped.[12] For example:

公共场所	**gōnggòng chǎngsuǒ**	public places
首要任务	**shǒuyào rènwu**	the primary task
根本问题	**gēnběn wèntí**	the fundamental problem
关键时刻	**guānjiàn shíkè**	the critical juncture
保守势力	**bǎoshǒu shìlì**	conservative forces
耐心指导	**nàixīn zhǐdǎo**	patient guidance

In adjectival predicatives, which, as we have seen, normally incorporate a degree adverb or complement, 的 *de* is not usually present:

这个孩子很高。	**zhèi ge hǎizi hěn gāo**	This child is tall.
这个学生非常聪明。	**zhèi ge xuésheng fēicháng cōngming**	This student is very clever.
那儿的生活写意得很。	**nàr de shēnghuó xièyì de hěn**	Life there is extremely enjoyable.

However, this is not always the case. In the three examples above, the adjective is evaluative, conveying a comment or judgement, but it is also possible for the adjective to be descriptive rather than evaluative. When this is so, 的 *de* is likely to be present:

那个人老老实实的。 **nèi ge rén lǎolǎoshíshí de**
That man is an extremely honest person.

---

[12] This does not imply that the indicator 的 *de* must be omitted. It is still grammatical to say 首要的任务 **shǒuyào de rènwu** 'the primary task', etc.

太阳火热火热的。 **tàiyáng huǒrè huǒrè de** The sun is scorching.

河水清清的。 **héshuǐ qīngqīng de** The water in the river is crystal clear.

英国的草地一年到头绿茸茸的。 **yīngguó de cǎodì yī nián dào tóu lǜrōngrōng de** Lawns in Britain are pleasantly green all the year round.

他整天忙忙碌碌的。 **tā zhěngtiān mángmanglùlù de** He is busy doing this or that all day long.

Quadrisyllabic adjectival idioms, whether evaluative or descriptive, in a predicative position uniquely take neither 很 **hěn** nor 的 *de*:

那个孩子聪明伶俐。 **nèi ge háizi cōngming línglì** That child is intelligent and quick-witted.

河水清澈见底。 **héshuǐ qīngchè jiàn dǐ** The water in the river is crystal clear.

4.5 ATTRIBUTIVES AND PREDICATIVES

Adjectives, as we said earlier, may precede or follow their noun headwords respectively as **attributives** or **predicatives**.

4.5.1 ADJECTIVES AND THEIR FUNCTIONAL CAPACITY

While most adjectives will conform to the formulae for attributive or predicative uses described in the previous sections, not every adjective in all its senses may be used attributively or predicatively. In other words, they vary in their **functional capacity**. Take the monosyllabic adjective 大 **dà** 'big' for example.

When 大 **dà** is used to indicate that something is physically 'big' or to mean 'on a large scale', it may be used either:

(a) attributively:

大象	**dà xiàng**	a big elephant
大蚂蚁	**dà mǎyǐ**	a big ant
大箱子	**dà xiāngzi**	a big box
大规模	**dà guīmó**	on a big scale
大问题	**dà wèntí**	a big problem
大错误	**dà cuòwù**	a big mistake

or

(**b**) predicatively:

那头象很大。	**nèi tóu xiàng hěn dà**	That elephant is very large.
那只蚂蚁很大。	**nèi zhī mǎyǐ hěn dà**	That ant is very big.
这个箱子很大。	**zhèi ge xiāngzi hěn dà**	This box is very big.
规模很大	**guīmó hěn dà**	It is on a big scale (lit. the scale is very big)
问题很大	**wèntí hěn dà**	There is a big problem (lit. the problem is very big)
错误很大	**cuòwù hěn dà**	It is a big mistake (lit. the mistake is very big)

However, when 大 **dà** is used to mean 'big' in a metaphorical sense, i.e. when it is removed from its primary sense of physical size, it has to be modified by 很 **hěn** 'very' not only when it is used predicatively but also as an attributive:

*大影响	**dà yǐngxiǎng**	
很大的影响	**hěn dà de yǐngxiǎng**	a big influence
影响很大	**yǐngxiǎng hěn dà**	The influence is considerable.
*大区别	**dà qūbié**	
很大的区别	**hěn dà de qūbié**	a big difference
区别很大	**qūbié hén dà**	There is a major difference.
*大作用	**dà zuòyòng**	
很大的作用	**hěn dà de zuòyòng**	an important function
作用很大	**zuòyòng hěn dà**	The function is important.
*大权力	**dà quánlì**	
很大的权力	**hěn dà de quánlì**	enormous power
权力很大	**quánlì hěn dà**	The power is enormous.

There are other collocational restrictions. When 大 **dà** 'big' is used in the sense of 'important' with, say, 人物 **rénwù** 'personage', it can only occur attributively:

大人物	**dà rénwù**	a bigwig/an important personage
很大的人物	**hěn dà de rénwù**	a real bigwig

but not:

*这个人物很大。	***zhèi ge rénwù hěn dà**	*This personage is important.

Nor can 大 **dà** 'big' function predicatively in the sense of 'serious' in relation to 病 **bìng** 'illness':

| 大病 | **dà bìng** | a serious illness |
| 很大的病 | **hěn dà de bìng** | an extremely serious illness |

nor:

| *他的病很大。 | ***tāde bìng hěn dà** | *His illness is serious. |

On the other hand, when 大 **dà** 'big' means 'fiery' of 脾气 **píqì** 'temper', it is generally used predicatively:

| 她的脾气很大。 | **tāde píqì hěn dà** | She has (got) a fiery temper. |

If it is to be used attributively, 很 **hěn** 'very' or some other modifier will have to be incorporated and the resultant phrase is restricted in meaning to somebody flying into a rage on a particular occasion:

| 发很大的脾气 | **fā hěn dà de píqì** | to fly into a temper |
| *大脾气 | **dà píqì** | *a bad temper |

This goes to show that, while most adjectives can be used either attributively or predicatively, some are restricted to one function in particular collocations.

4.5.2 ATTRIBUTIVE-ONLY ADJECTIVES

These are generally non-gradable.[13] They differentiate rather than describe, and most of them therefore have extremely restricted collocations. Monosyllabic adjectives in this category are relatively infrequent:

正数	**zhèngshù**	a positive number
负数	**fùshù**	a negative number
公鸡	**gōngjī**	rooster (lit. male fowl)
母牛	**mǔniú**	cow (lit. mother ox)

Monosyllabic attributive-only adjectives include: 单 **dān**/复 **fù** '(of number) singular/plural', 单 **dān**/双 **shuāng** 'single/double/, 雌 **cí**/雄 **xióng** '(of animals) female/male', 公 **gōng**/母 **mǔ** '(of animals) male/female', 正 **zhèng**/副 **fù** '(of presidents, for example) the president/the vice president', 正 **zhèng**/反 **fǎn** 'one side/the reverse side', 总 **zǒng**/分 **fēn** 'headquarters/branches', 横 **héng**/竖 **shù** 'horizontal/vertical'.

Disyllabic attributive-only adjectives usually convey a formal tone, and they are more likely to have an internal lexical structure.[14] The following attributive-only adjectives, for example, all have a modificational structure:

---

[13] See §4.6.

[14] By internal lexical structure we mean the internal syntactic relationship between the two composing morphemes of a disyllabic adjective.

慢性病	**mànxìng bìng**	a chronic disease (慢性 lit. slow nature)
头等舱	**tóuděng cāng**	first class cabin (头等 lit. first grade)
现代音乐	**xiàndài yīnyuè**	modern music (现代 lit. present generation)
大型水库	**dàxíng shuǐkù**	a big reservoir (大型 lit. big type)

Attributive-only adjectives of a modificational structure include: 初步 **chūbù** 'initial', 短期 **duǎnqī** 'short-term', 长途 **chángtú** 'long distance', 人工 **réngōng** 'artificial', 不断 **bùduàn** 'continuous', 正式 **zhèngshì** 'formal', 良性 **liángxìng** 'benign', 妃色 **fēisè** 'pink', 高级 **gāojí** 'high quality', 中号 **zhōnghào** 'medium-sized', 野生 **yěshēng** 'wild', 万能 **wànnéng** 'almighty', 真正 **zhēnzhèng** 'true', 弱智 **ruòzhì** 'mentally handicapped'.

Attributive-only adjectives may also have a governmental or predicational structure:

忘我	**wàngwǒ**	selfless (lit. forgetting oneself)
无私	**wúsī**	unselfish (lit. not having selfishness)
有益	**yǒuyì**	beneficial (lit. having benefit)

人造	**rénzào**	artificial (lit. 'man made')
国营	**guóyíng**	state-owned (lit. 'state-managed')
自动	**zìdòng**	automatic (lit. 'self-propelled')

4.5.3 PREDICATIVE-ONLY ADJECTIVES

These, on the other hand, are generally more colloquial in tone, and are mostly monosyllabic:

我很累。	**wǒ hěn lèi**	I am very tired.
你的话很对。	**nǐde huà hěn duì**	What you said is correct.
他写的字真棒。	**tā xiě de zì zhēn bàng**	His handwriting is remarkably beautiful.
他的成绩很差。	**tāde chéngjī hěn chà**	His examination results are poor.

The most commonly used predicative-only adjectives include: 背 **bèi** 'hard of hearing', 吵 **chǎo** 'noisy', 沉 **chén** 'heavy', 烦 **fán** 'annoyed', 够 **gòu** 'enough', 滑 **huá** 'sly', 活 **huó** 'lively', 困 **kùn** 'sleepy', 懒 **lǎn** 'lazy', 牢 **láo** 'firm', 紧 **jǐn** 'tight', 闷 **mēn** 'stifling'; **mèn** 'bored', 腻 **nì** 'greasy', 松 **sōng** 'loose', 稳 **wěn** 'stable', 响 **xiǎng** 'loud', 香 **xiāng** 'fragrant', 行 **xíng** 'feasible', 痒 **yǎng** 'itchy', 匀 **yún** 'even; well-mixed', 准 **zhǔn** 'accurate'.

However, there is no absolute divide between the two types of adjective which cannot be crossed. Though the result may sometimes sound a little forced, a predicative-only adjective can be made to function attributively by placing it in a 'degree adverb + 的 *de*' frame (e.g. 很差的学校 **hěn chà de xuéxiào** 'a badly governed school'). Likewise, an attributive-only adjective can be made to function predicatively by setting it in a '是 **shì** + 的 **de**' format (e.g. 这项工程是大型的。 **zhèi xiàng gōngchéng shì dàxíng de** 'This is an enormous project'.).

4.6 VARIOUS INHERENT FEATURES OF ADJECTIVES

The syntactic function of adjectives in Chinese varies with their inherent features. In the following sections we will see these variances through a number of dichotomies.

4.6.1 GRADABLE VS NON-GRADABLE

Gradable adjectives form the greater part of the adjectival lexicon. They are of a descriptive nature and can be used freely both as attributives and as predicatives. Their most salient feature is that they can be modified by degree adverbs or complements:

高	**gāo**	tall	很高	**hěn gāo**	very tall
苦	**kǔ**	bitter	有点儿苦	**yǒu diǎnr kǔ**	somewhat bitter
穷	**qióng**	poor	穷得很	**qióng de hěn**	really poor
嫩	**nèn**	tender	嫩极了	**nèn jí le**	extremely tender

那儿起了一座<u>很高</u>的楼房。 **nàr qǐ le yī zuò <u>hěn gāo</u> de lóufáng**
A very tall building was erected there.

我不喜欢喝<u>太浓</u>的茶。 **wǒ bù xǐhuan hē <u>tài nóng</u> de chá**
I don't like my tea too strong. (lit. I don't like drinking very strong tea)

这个问题<u>难极</u>了。 **zhèi ge wèntí <u>nán jí</u> le**
This question is (simply) too difficult.

Non-gradable adjectives cannot be modified in this way:

男	**nán**	male	*很男	***hěn nán**	*very male
单	**dān**	single	*相当单	***xiāngdāng dān**	*quite single
现代	**xiàndài**	modern	*现代得很	***xiàndài de hěn**	*modern to the extreme
合法	**héfǎ**	legal	*合法极了	***héfǎ jí le**	*extremely legal

For non-gradable adjectives the general predicative schema is 是 **shì** . . . 的 *de* and not 很 **hěn** . . . :

*这很非法。 ***zhè hěn fēifǎ** *This is illegal.
这是非法的。 **zhè shì fēifǎ de** This is illegal.

*那个人很女。 ***nèi ge rén hěn nǚ** *That person is very female.
那个人是女的。 **nèi ge rén shì nǚ de** That person is a woman/girl.

Further examples:

| 那张桌子是方的。 | **nèi zhāng zhuōzi shì fāng de** | That table is square. |
| 这个人是残废的。 | **zhèi ge rén shì cánfèi de** | This person is handicapped. |

Non-gradable adjectives include: 假 **jiǎ** 'false', 错 **cuò** 'wrong'.

There are, of course, a small number of adjectives that straddle the two categories:

他的话是对的。	**tā de huà shì duì de**	His words are correct.
他的话很对。	**tā de huà hěn duì**	His words are very correct.
那张桌子是圆的。	**nèi zhāng zhuōzi shì yuán de**	That table is round.
那张桌子很圆。	**nèi zhāng zhuōzi hěn yuán**	That table is truly round.

4.6.2   CONDITIONAL VS UNCONDITIONAL

Apart from the wide range of standard adjectives such as 大 **dà** 'big', 美丽 **měilì** 'beautiful', etc., which can be said to be used unconditionally as adjectives, there are adjectives which are derived from other word classes. These adjectives may be viewed as being conditional adjectives, which can be made to function as adjectives only in certain collocations and structures. They are therefore either collocation-specific or structure-specific. For example, the adjectival use of the noun 贼 **zéi** 'thief' to mean 'sly' is conditional on it occurring in a predicative position: 这个人真贼 **zhèi ge rén zhēn zéi** 'This person is really cunning'. It can function attributively, but this is limited only to a few established idioms like 贼眉贼眼 **zéi méi zéi yǎn** 'shifty' (lit. thievish eyebrows and thievish eyes), 贼头贼脑 **zéi tóu zéi nǎo** 'stealthy' (lit. thievish head and thievish brain). The adjectival use of the verb 闹 **nào** 'make a noise' to mean 'noisy', too, is conditional on it being used in a predicative position: 这儿太闹了 **zhèr tài nào le** 'It is too noisy here'. In fact, most of these conditional adjectives are predicative-only.

4.6.3   DERIVABLE VS NON-DERIVABLE

A large part of the Chinese adjectival lexicon consists of disyllabic adjectives that are formed on the basis of monosyllabic adjectives, which we may call stems. These disyllabic adjectives are therefore derivations or derivatives. For example, from 光 **guāng** 'polished', are derived such commonly used adjectives as 光滑 **guānghuá** 'smooth', 光亮 **guāngliàng** 'luminous', 光明 **guāngmíng** 'bright', 光洁 **guāngjié** 'bright and clean', 光溜 **guāngliu** 'slippery', 光润 **guāngrùn** 'smooth (of skin)', etc. From 冷 **lěng** 'cold', come 冷淡 **lěngdàn** 'indifferent', 冷寂 **lěngjì** 'still', 冷静 **lěngjìng** 'sober, calm', 冷酷 **lěngkù** 'callous', 冷落 **lěngluò** 'desolate', 冷漠 **lěngmò** 'unconcerned', 冷僻 **lěngpì** 'deserted', 冷涩 **lěngsè** 'dull' as well as 寒冷 **hánlěng** 'frigid', 冰冷 **bīnglěng** 'ice-cold'.

There are however a small number of monosyllabic adjectives that do not normally act as stems for other adjectives, e.g. 嗲 **diǎ** 'coquettish', 帅 **shuài** 'smart', etc.

4.6.4   REDUPLICABLE VS NON-REDUPLICABLE

Monosyllabic adjectives indicating physical traits and appealing to the senses are usually reduplicable for descriptive purposes often with an affectionate tone, e.g. 白白的 **báibái de** 'white as white can be', 高高的 **gāogāo de** 'towering', 甜甜的 **tiántián de** 'very sweet', 香香的 **xiāngxiāng de** 'sweet-smelling', 软软的 **ruǎnruǎn de** 'soft to the touch', 静静的 **jìngjìng de** 'very quiet', etc. Once reduplicated, they describe rather than differentiate as is the case normally with monosyllabic adjectives.

On the other hand, monosyllabic adjectives indicating absolute values, derogatory qualities or psychological traits cannot normally be reduplicated. For example:

*假假的	**jiǎjiǎ de**	*false
*丑丑的	**chǒuchǒu de**	*ugly
*恶恶的	**è'è de**	*fierce

They can nevertheless adopt the phonaesthetic type of extension, e.g. 恶狠狠 **èhěnhěn** 'ferocious', 懒洋洋 **lǎnyāngyāng** 'languid', 乐滋滋 **lèzīzī** 'contented', 傻乎乎 **shǎhūhū** 'simple-minded', 羞答答 **xiūdādā** 'bashful', 假惺惺 **jiǎxīngxīng** 'hypocritical', 臭烘烘 **chòuhōnghōng** 'stinking', etc. These phonaesthetic forms are more often used as adverbials than attributives.[15]

A number of monosyllabic adjectives that indicate sensory responses may also incorporate phonaesthetic suffixes to enhance their descriptive effect, e.g. 白皑皑 **bái'ái'ái** 'pure/snow white', 甜丝丝 **tiánsīsī** 'pleasantly sweet', 香喷喷 **xiāngpēnpēn** 'sweet-smelling', 软绵绵 **ruǎnmiánmián** 'extremely soft', 矮墩墩 **ǎidūndūn** 'pudgy', 静悄悄 **jìngqiāoqiāo** 'very quiet', etc.

Disyllabic adjectives AB can be reduplicable but only in an AABB sequence and if they are originally descriptive adjectives regarding a person's physical appearance, specific mannerisms, or inbuilt personality. For example,

---

[15] See Chapter 17 on adverbials.

| 白淨 **báijìng** | 白白淨淨 **báibáijìngjìng** | fair (of skin) |
| 高大 **gāodà** | 高高大大 **gāogāodàdà** | tall and big |

| 匆忙 **cōngmáng** | 匆匆忙忙 **cōngcōngmángmáng** | hastily |
| 随便 **suíbiàn** | 随随便便 **suísuíbiànbiàn** | casually |

| 散漫 **sǎnmàn** | 散散漫漫 **sǎnsǎnmànmàn** | sloppily |
| 仔细 **zǐxì** | 仔仔细细 **zǐzǐxìxì** | meticulously |

Reduplications like the above, as can be seen from the translations, are generally used as adverbials, apart from a few describing physical appearance.

Statistical analysis shows that less than 20 per cent of the adjectives in the language's lexicon are in fact reduplicable. These adjectives mostly have a juxtapositional type of lexical structure if they are disyllabic and the majority of them (over 90 per cent) belong to the colloquial rather than formal section of the vocabulary.

4.6.5 DEROGATORY VS COMMENDATORY

Adjectives may be divided semantically for the most part into two major categories: derogatory and commendatory. Those that do not fall into either category may be said to be neutral. There are a number of collocational restrictions that apply to the two non-neutral categories.

Derogatory adjectives cannot be modified by the degree adverb 蛮 **mán** 'fairly' or complemented by the degree complement 得了不得 **de liǎobude** 'to an enormous extent':

| *蛮臭 | **mán chòu** | *fairly smelly |
| *悲观得了不得 | **bēiguān de liǎobude** | *pessimistic to the extreme |

Derogatory adjectives include: 坏 **huài** 'bad', 笨 **bèn** 'stupid', 丑 **chǒu** 'ugly', 懒 **lǎn** 'lazy', 粗心 **cūxīn** 'careless', 固执 **gùzhí** 'stubborn', 糊涂 **hútu** 'muddle-headed', 危险 **wēixiǎn** 'dangerous', 小气 **xiǎoqì** 'stingy', 自私 **zìsī** 'selfish'.

Commendatory adjectives, on the other hand, cannot be modified by the degree adverb 有点儿 **yǒu diǎnr** 'somewhat' or complemented by a degree complement like 得要命 **de yàomìng** 'to death':

| *有点儿香 | **yǒu diǎnr xiāng** | *somewhat sweet-smelling |
| *暖和得要命[16] | **nuǎnhuo de yàomìng** | *warm in the extreme |

---

[16] Sometimes such degree complements are used with commendatory adjectives for rhetorical purposes, e.g. as hyperbole. 高兴得要死 **gāoxìng de yàosǐ** 'happy in the extreme', etc.

Commendatory adjectives include: 好 **hǎo** 'good', 乖 **guāi** 'well-behaved', 灵 **líng** 'clever; effective', 准 **zhǔn** 'accurate', 安全 **ānquán** 'safe', 聪明 **cōngming** 'intelligent', 方便 **fāngbiàn** 'convenient', 合适 **héshì** 'suitable', 漂亮 **piàoliang** 'pretty', 干净 **gānjìng** 'clean', 高兴 **gāoxìng** 'high-spirited', 健康 **jiànkāng** 'healthy', 容易 **róngyì** 'easy'.

Neutral adjectives, however, have no such restrictions. For example:

蛮大	**mán dà**	fairly big
大得不得了	**dà de bù de liǎo**	extremely big
有点儿大	**yǒu diǎnr dà**	somewhat big
大得要命	**dà de yàomìng**	exceedingly big

4.7 ADJECTIVES AND VALENCY

There are a number of adjectives in the language which, when used in a predicative position, will need to be associated with coverbal phrases or plural number subjects to convey their inherent dual- or multi-valency meanings. For example, one cannot very well say:

| *他很生疏。 | **tā hěn shēngshū** | *He is unfamiliar with. |
| *她很不和。 | **tā hěn bùhé** | *She does not get along very well with. |

Sentences along the following lines are, on the other hand, perfectly natural:

他对这儿的情况很生疏。 **tā duì zhèr de qíngkuàng hěn shēngshū**
He is not familiar with the situation here.

她们很不和。 **tāmen hěn bùhé**
They do not get along very well with each other.

or

她跟他很不和。 **tā gēn tā hěn bùhé**
She does not get along very well with him.

Dual- or multi-valency adjectives include: 熟悉 **shúxī** 'familiar with', 陌生 **mòshēng** 'unfamiliar with', 不满 **bùmǎn** 'not happy with', 要好 **yàohǎo** 'on good terms with', 一样 **yīyàng** 'the same as'.

4.8 ADJECTIVES AND COLLOCATION

Adjectives also vary in their **collocational capacity**. Some like 大 **dà** 'big' and 新 **xīn** 'new', as we have seen, are of such a general nature that they can be used with many noun headwords without too many restrictions.

Most adjectives, however, are **collocationally specific**. In other words, particular adjectives tend to be linked with specific noun headwords. For example:

(a) attributively:

严格	**yángé**	stringent
严格的规定	**yángé de guīdìng**	stringent rules
严厉	**yánlì**	severe
严厉的批评	**yánlì de pīpíng**	severe criticism
严肃	**yánsù**	solemn
严肃的气氛	**yánsù de qìfēn**	a solemn atmosphere
严重	**yánzhòng**	serious
严重的后果	**yánzhòng de hòuguǒ**	serious consequences

(b) predicatively:

严格	**yángé**	strict
要求很严格	**yāoqiú hěn yángé**	the demands are strict
严厉	**yánlì**	stern
声音很严厉	**shēngyīn hěn yánlì**	the voice is stern
严肃	**yánsù**	serious
态度很严肃	**tàidù hěn yánsù**	the attitude is serious
严重	**yánzhòng**	grave
事态很严重	**shìtài hěn yánzhòng**	the situation is grave

There is some degree of flexibility in these collocational rules (e.g., 严厉 **yánlì** 'stern' and 严肃 **yánsù** 'serious' can both be used with 态度 **tàidù** 'attitude'), but in practice they are closely adhered to by native speakers.

4.9   ADJECTIVES AND COMPARISON[17]

Comparison between two entities A and B is generally expressed in the formula: A + 比[18] **bǐ** 'compare with' + B + adjective. For example,

你比我高。 **nǐ bǐ wǒ gāo**
You are taller than me. (lit. you cv: compare with me tall)

我比你大。 **wǒ bǐ nǐ dà**
I am older than you. (lit. I cv: compare with you big)

In the formula, A can be a phrase or a clause with B being often pruned to the minimum, keeping only the key point for comparison and dropping other repetitive elements. For example:

这件衬衫比那件[衬衫]贵。 **zhèi jiàn chènshān bǐ nèi jiàn [chènshān] guì**
This shirt is more expensive than that one.

---

[17] For comparisons with the verb 有 **yǒu**, see §17.5.
[18] 比 **bǐ** is in fact a coverb. For a fuller discussion of coverbs, see Chapter 11.

这个菜比那个[菜]好吃。 **zhèi ge cài bǐ nèi ge [cài] hǎochī**
This dish is tastier than that one.

他跑得比我[跑得]快。 **tā pǎo de bǐ wǒ [pǎo de] kuài**
He runs faster than me. (lit. . . . than I run)

我吃得比他[吃得]多。 **wǒ chī de bǐ tā [chī de] duō**
I eat more than him. (lit. . . . than he eats)

It is possible to retain the repeated elements (given in the square brackets) but the sentence then sounds a little unnatural.

In fact, the last two examples can be reworded so that the two subjects/topics in the comparison share the same verb:

他比我跑得快。 **tā bǐ wǒ pǎo de kuài** He runs faster than me.
我比他吃得多。 **wǒ bǐ tā chī de duō** I eat more than him.

This indicates that the comparison is made not between the two actions, but between the two people concerned.

The adjective in the formula cannot be premodified,[19] but it may be complemented by a quantifier, indeterminate or precise:

*我比你很大。 **wǒ bǐ nǐ hěn dà** *I am much older than you.

我比你大(一)些。 **wǒ bǐ nǐ dà (yī)xiē** I am a little older than you.
我比你大两岁。 **wǒ bǐ nǐ dà liǎng suì** I am two years older than you.
他比我高(一)点儿。 **tā bǐ wǒ gāo (yī)diǎnr** He is slightly taller than me.
他比我高一厘米。 **tā bǐ wǒ gāo yī límǐ** He is one centimetre taller than me.
我比他吃得多得多。 **wǒ bǐ tā chī de duō de duō** I eat much more than he does.
我比他吃得多一倍。 **wǒ bǐ tā chī de duō yī bèi** I eat twice as much as he does.
这个比那个贵一点。 **zhèi ge bǐ nèi ge guì yīdiǎn** This is a little dearer than that.
这个比那个贵三镑。 **zhèi ge bǐ nèi ge guì sān bàng** This is three pounds dearer than that.

---

[19] Premodification would take away the contrast necessary for the comparison. The only exception is the adverb 更 **gèng** 'even more' which is used as a premodifier, e.g. 我比你更大。 **wǒ bǐ nǐ gèng dà** 'I am even older than you'.

5 ATTRIBUTIVES OTHER THAN ADJECTIVES

Attributives come in all forms and types and their function is to qualify or quantify nouns, to describe and delimit them. They may be (**a**) adjectives, (**b**) nouns, (**c**) verbs, (**d**) clauses, (**e**) prepositional or postpositional phrases, (**f**) numeral or demonstrative and measure word phrases, (**g**) pronouns, (**h**) idioms, etc.

For instance:

(**a**) 黄狗 **huánggǒu**	brown dog	adjective + noun
(**b**) 笔名 **bǐ míng**	pen name	noun + noun
(**c**) 滚水 **gǔnshuǐ**	boiling water	verb + noun
(**d**) 我买的东西 **wǒ mǎi de dōngxi**	the things I bought	clause + noun
(**e**) 沿路的商店 **yán lù de shāngdiàn**	the shops along the road	prepositional phrase + noun
家里的人 **jiā li de rén**	the people at home	postpositional phrase + noun
(**f**) 两个女人 **liǎng ge nǚrén**	two women	numeral + mw + noun
那个男人 **nèi ge nánrén**	that man	demonstrative + mw + noun
(**g**) 我的书 **wǒde shū**	my book(s)	pronoun + noun
(**h**) 一望无际的草原 **yī wàng wújì de cǎoyuán**	a boundless stretch of grassland	idiom + noun

From the above list, two features of the attributive in Chinese can be observed. First, it almost invariably precedes the noun it modifies;[1] and, second, the marker 的 **de** is regularly placed between the attributive and the noun. The presence of 的 **de** depends on the type of attributive being used, and details are given in the list of attributives below.

A further feature to be noted is that the presence of an attributive makes any item it qualifies or quantifies become automatically nominalised, whatever grammatical category it originally belonged to. Verbs and adjectives are often found to be nominalised in such a way. For example:

---

[1] Where attributives are very long, they can occur after the noun for stylistic reasons. See §5.3.2 below.

谢谢您无微不至的<u>关怀</u>。 **xièxie nín wú wēi bù zhì de guānhuái**
(lit. thank you (polite) meticulous *de* care)
Thank you for your meticulous care. (关怀 **guānhuái** v. to care for)

请宽恕我刚才的<u>鲁莽</u>。 **qǐng kuānshù wǒ gāngcái de lǔmǎng**
(lit. please forgive me just now *de* being rude)
Please excuse my rudeness just now. (鲁莽 **lǔmǎng** adj. rude)

我在此向您表示热烈的<u>欢迎</u>。 **wǒ zài cǐ xiàng nín biǎoshì rèliè de huānyíng**
(lit. I hereby cv: to you (polite) express warm *de* welcome)
I hereby express a warm welcome to you. (欢迎 **huānyíng** v. to welcome)

5.1 THE DIFFERENT FORMS OF ATTRIBUTIVE

Adjectives are attributives par excellence, and they have been fully discussed in the previous chapter. In this chapter we shall concentrate on other forms of attributives, which are either of different word classes (e.g. nouns, verbs, etc.) or of different levels of structure (e.g. phrases, clauses, etc.).

5.1.1 NOUNS

5.1.1.1 Nouns with zero marker

Nominal items as attributives have the tendency to form established words or expressions. They are usually placed directly in front of the headword they qualify:

冷水澡	**lěngshuǐ zǎo**	a cold bath (lit. cold water bath)
繁体字	**fántǐ zì**	unsimplified Chinese characters
双方意见	**shuāngfāng yìjian**	ideas put forward by both parties
世界记录	**shìjiè jìlù**	world record

5.1.1.2 Nouns with an obligatory or optional 的 *de*

If a nominal item does not form an established quadrisyllabic expression, it will need 的 *de*:

现在的情况	**xiànzài de qíngkuàng**	present situation
童年(的)生活	**tóngnián (de) shēnghuó**	childhood days
个人(的)体会	**gèrén (de) tǐhuì**	personal experience
色彩的浓淡	**sècǎi de nóngdàn**	lighter or darker shades of colours

5.1.1.3 Nouns with phonaesthemes and 的 *de*

泪汪汪的眼睛	**lèiwāngwāng de yǎnjing**	tearful eyes
水淋淋的头发	**shuǐlínlín de tóufa**	hair dripping with water

5.1.2 VERBS

5.1.2.1 Verbs with zero marker

If a verbal item with the noun constitutes an established expression, it does not take 的 *de*:

敲门声	**qiāomén shēng**	the sound of knocking at the door
修订版	**xiūdìng bǎn**	revised edition
印刷体	**yìnshuā tǐ**	printed forms
退休生活	**tuìxiū shēnghuó**	life of retirement

5.1.2.2 Verbs with 的 *de*

Otherwise in most cases, verbal attributives do require 的 *de*:

开会的日期	**kāihuì de rìqī**	date for the meeting
要办的事情	**yào bàn de shìqing**	matters to attend to
渐渐远去的火车	**jiànjiàn yuǎn qù de huǒchē**	a train disappearing into the distance
今天来参观的人	**jīntiān lái cānguān de rén**	people who came to visit today

5.1.3 CLAUSES

Clausal attributives will always need 的 *de*:

他讲的话	**tā jiǎng de huà**	what he said
你要的书	**nǐ yào de shū**	the book you want
笔画多的字	**bǐhuà duō de zì**	Chinese characters with many strokes
我们没有见过的东西	**wǒmen méiyǒu jiànguo de dōngxi**	things we have not seen before

5.1.4 PREPOSITIONAL OR POSTPOSITIONAL PHRASES WITH 的 *de*

5.1.4.1 Prepositional/coverbal phrases with 的 *de*

Prepositional or coverbal phrases as attributives are always followed by 的 *de*:

对北京的访问	**duì běijīng de fǎngwèn**	visit to Beijing
在英国的日子	**zài yīngguó de rìzi**	days in Britain
有关水利的著作	**yǒuguān shuǐlì de zhùzuò**	writings on water conservation
沿路的商店	**yánlù de shāngdiàn**	shops along the road

5.1.4.2   Postpositional phrases with 的 *de*

Postpositional phrases are essentially nominal in nature, and they will also generally need the presence of 的 *de* to function as attributives:

路上的行人	**lù shàng de xíngrén**	pedestrians on the road
壶里的水	**hú li de shuǐ**	water in the pot
室内的空气	**shìnèi de kōngqì**	air inside the room
公路两旁的水渠	**gōnglù liǎngpáng de shuǐqú**	ditches on either side of the highway

5.1.5   NUMERALS OR DEMONSTRATIVES AND MEASURE WORDS

5.1.5.1   Numerals and measure words

Numeral and measure word expressions, strictly speaking, are not standard
attributives, but are quantifiers that indicate number as well as indefinite reference.[2] They do not require 的 *de*:

一群青年	**yī qún qīngnián**	a group of young people
几个孩子	**jǐ ge háizi**	several children
五天期限	**wǔ tiān qīxiàn**	five days' limit
两种说法	**liǎng zhǒng shuōfǎ**	two ways of putting it

5.1.5.2   Demonstratives and measure words

As with numerals and measure words, demonstrative and measure word expressions do not need 的 *de* when they are associated with noun headwords:

这些问题	**zhèixiē wèntí**	these problems
那首诗	**nèi shǒu shī**	that poem
这场比赛	**zhèi chǎng bǐsài**	this match
那一件大衣	**nèi yī jiàn dàyī**	that overcoat

5.1.5.3   Demonstratives without measure words

On the other hand, in more formal writing, demonstratives may be used as
attributives on their own without measure words, placed directly in front of noun
headwords:

| 这人 | **zhèi rén** | this person |
| 这城市 | **zhèi chéngshì** | this city |

---

[2] There are adjectives in the language other than numeral and measure word expressions that indicate indeterminate numbers, and they are likewise used without 的, e.g. 许多人 **xǔduō rén** 'a lot of
people', 不少钱 **bùshǎo qián** 'a large sum of money'.

| 这孩子 | **zhèi háizi** | this child |
| 那时候 | **nèi shíhou** | at that time |

5.1.5.4 Reduplicated measure words with or without 的 *de*

Reduplicated measure word expressions indicating numerousness or exclusiveness may or may not be preceded by 一 **yī** 'one'. Where 一 **yī** is present, the marker 的 *de* is usually required; otherwise 的 *de* is not generally used:

阵阵芳香	**zhènzhèn fāngxiāng**	puffs of fragrance
条条大路	**tiáotiáo dàlù**	every road
一片片的白云	**yī piànpiàn de báiyún**	white clouds one after another
一封封的来信	**yī fēngfēng de láixìn**	every letter that arrived

5.1.6 PRONOUNS

5.1.6.1 Personal pronouns with or without 的 *de*

Personal pronouns used in their possessive forms may delimit their noun headwords with or without 的 *de*. The presence of 的 *de* usually depends on the intimacy of the association or on the rhythm of the utterance. If the association is close, 的 *de* is more likely to be omitted:

你妈妈	**nǐ māma**	your mother
他的脾气	**tāde píqì**	his temperament
她的名字	**tāde míngzi**	her name
我的请求	**wǒde qǐngqiú**	my request

5.1.6.2 Interrogative pronouns with or without measure words

Interrogative pronouns, if disyllabic or when incorporating a measure word, do not generally need 的 *de* to function as attributives. Monosyllabic interrogative pronouns on the other hand definitely do require 的 *de*:

多少钱?	**duōshǎo qián**	how much?
什么时候?	**shénme shíhou**	what time, when?
怎么回事?	**zénme huí shì**	what is the matter?
哪些问题?	**něixiē wèntí**	what problems?
谁的东西?	**shuí/shéi de dōngxi**	whose things?

5.1.7 IDIOMS

5.1.7.1 Quadrisyllabic or trisyllabic idioms with 的 *de*

Quadrisyllabic or trisyllabic idioms must always be followed by 的 *de* to function as attributives:

一举两得的事	**yījǔ liǎngdé de shì**	a stone that kills two birds
似是而非的论点	**sì shì ér fēi de lùndiǎn**	a specious argument
久别重逢的亲人	**jiǔbié chóngféng de qīnrén**	relatives reunited after a long parting
谦虚谨慎的作风	**qiānxū jǐnshèn de zuòfēng**	a modest and prudent style
绕弯子的话	**rào wānzi de huà**	beating about the bush (lit. words that go round bends)

5.1.7.2 Disyllabic expressions with 之 **zhī** qualifying a monosyllabic noun headword

One of the functions of 之 **zhī** in Classical Chinese was to be an attributive marker, and this function persists in the modern language in a number of set expressions. These expressions are always quadrisyllabic:

敬慕之心	**jìngmù zhī xīn**	feelings of admiration and respect
无稽之谈	**wújī zhī tán**	sheer nonsense (lit. a talk without evidence)
一孔之见	**yī kǒng zhī jiàn**	a narrow view (lit. a view through one hole)
十天之内	**shí tiān zhī nèi**	within ten days

5.1.7.3 Onomatopoeic terms with/without 的 **de** qualifying headword 一声 **yī shēng**

These expressions, like the previous ones, are formulaic and likewise must always be quadrisyllabic including the headword 一声 **yī shēng** 'the sound as indicated'. 的 **de** is used if the onomatopoeic term is monosyllabic; but not if it is disyllabic:

| 砰的一声 | **pēng de yī shēng** | with a bang |
| 哐啷一声 | **kuānglāng yī shēng** | with a crushing sound |

So we see that attributives in Chinese are generally placed before their headwords. They have the capacity to qualify or quantify. For some, 的 **de** must be present, for some it must not. In other cases 的 **de** is optional and its presence or absence is usually dictated by the needs of rhythm and balance.

5.2 THE SEQUENCING OF ATTRIBUTIVES

When different types of attributives come together, they follow a definite pattern of sequencing. If we take the 'numeral + measure word' phrase as the dividing point, we see that some types of attributives generally go before the 'num + mw' phrase while others usually follow it. Under certain conditions, post- 'num + mw' attributives may cross the boundary and become pre- 'num + mw' attributives. However, this is not usually the case the other way round.

Pre- 'num + mw' attributives tend to display the following semantic features:

(a) possession

> 她的一个朋友 **tāde yī ge péngyou** (lit. her one mw friend)
> A friend of hers.

> 我大儿子的那(一)辆汽车 **wǒ dà érzi de nèi (yī) liàng qìchē**
> (lit. my eldest son's that (one) mw car) That car of my eldest son.

> 邻居的那(一)栋房子 **línjū de nèi (yī) dòng fángzi**
> (lit. neighbour's that (one) mw house) That house of my neighbour.

(b) location

> 门上的那(一)层油漆 **mén shàng de nèi (yī) céng yóuqī**
> (lit. door-on de that (one) mw: layer paint)
> The coat of paint on the door.

> 厨房里的两个柜子 **chúfáng li de liǎng ge guìzi**
> (lit. kitchen-inside de two mw cupboards)
> The two cupboards in the kitchen.

> 花瓶里的那(一)些鲜花 **huāpíng li de nèi (yī) xiē xiānhuā**
> (lit. flower vase-inside de those (one) mw: some fresh flowers)
> Those fresh flowers in the vase.

(c) time

> 明天的三节课 **míngtiān de sān jié kè**
> (lit. tomorrow de three mw classes) The three lessons tomorrow.

> 两年来的一些积蓄 **liǎng nián lai de yīxiē jīxù**
> (lit. last two years de one mw: some savings)
> Some savings from the last two years.

> 上个月的一次聚会 **shàng ge yuè de yī cì jùhuì**
> (lit. last month de one mw: time gathering) One gathering last month.

(d) scope

> 这几种颜色 **zhèi jǐ zhǒng yánsè** (lit. these a few mw: kinds colours)
> These few colours.

> 别的一些事情 **biéde yīxiē shìqing** (lit. other one mw: some matters)
> Some other matters.

Post- 'num + mw' attributives tend to be in the following semantic groups:

(e) state or activity

一些剩下的时间 **yīxiē shèngxia de shíjiān**
(lit. one mw: some remaining *de* time) Some remaining time.

一个到海滨去度假的计划 **yī ge dào hǎibīn qù dùjià de jìhuà**
(lit. one mw cv: to seaside go pass holiday *de* plan)
A plan to go for a seaside holiday.

那些她做的菜 **nèixiē tā zuò de cài**
(lit. those mw: some she make de food/dishes)
The food/dishes she made/cooked.

(f) characteristics

一个很直爽的人 **yī ge hěn zhíshuǎng de rén**
(lit. one mw very forthright *de* person) A very forthright man/person.

一片朦胧的晨雾 **yī piàn ménglóng de chénwù**
(lit. one mw: stretch hazy *de* morning mist)
A stretch of hazy morning mist.

两只水汪汪的大眼睛 **liǎng zhī shuǐwāngwāng de dà yǎnjing**
(lit. two mw limpid *de* big eyes) Two big bright eyes.

(g) shape

一个圆圆的脑袋 **yī ge yuányuán de nǎodài**
(lit. one mw round *de* head) A round head.

一顶伞形的帽子 **yī dǐng sǎnxíng de màozi**
(lit. one mw umbrella shape *de* hat) An umbrella-shaped hat.

(h) colour

几朵白云 **jǐ duǒ báiyún** (lit. a few mw white clouds) A few white clouds.

四个金字 **sì ge jīn zì** (lit. four mw gold characters)
Four golden characters.

一条天蓝色的裙子 **yī tiáo tiānlánsè de qúnzi**
(lit. one mw sky blue colour de skirt) A sky-blue skirt.

(i) material

一件棉布衬衫 **yī jiàn miánbù chènshān**
(lit. one mw cotton cloth shirt) A cotton shirt.

一面铜镜 **yī miàn tóngjìng** (lit. one mw bronze mirror)
A bronze mirror.

三个搪瓷脸盆 **sān ge tángcí liǎnpén**
(lit. three mw enamel wash basin) Three enamel wash basins.

两三团毛线 **liǎng sān tuán máoxiàn**
(lit. two three mw: ball wool thread) Two or three balls of wool

(**j**) function

一个茶杯 **yī ge chábēi** (lit. one mw tea cup) A tea cup.

一双跑鞋 **yī shuāng pǎoxié** (lit. one mw: pair run shoes)
A pair of running shoes.

In theory, it is possible for all forms of attributive to come together to qualify and quantify the same headword. When this happens, the sequence of attributives will normally be:

(**a**) possession (noun or pronoun)
(**b**) location (postpositional or prepositional/coverbal phrase)
(**c**) time (noun)
(**d**) scope (demonstrative adjective, etc.)
    numeral + measure word expression
(**e**) state or activity (verbal phrase or clause)
(**f**) characteristics (adjective)
(**g**) shape (adjective)
(**h**) colour (adjective)
(**i**) material (noun)
(**j**) function (noun or verb)

For example:

attributive || headword

她 | 鞋架上 | 去年 | 那 | (一)双 | 穿了又穿(的) | 破破烂烂的 | 尖头的 | 黑色 |
棉布 || 拖鞋 **tā xiéjià shàng qùnián nèi (yī) shuāng chuān le yòu chuān (de) pòpòlànlàn de jiāntóu de hèsè miánbù tuōxié**
(lit. her | shoe-rack-top | last year | that | (one) mw: pair | wear *le* again wear (de) | tattered de | pointed toe de | black colour | cotton cloth || drag shoes (i.e. slippers))

That pair of tattered, black cotton slippers on the shoe rack with pointed toes that she wore over and over again last year.

If we arrange the sentence vertically, we shall see the order of the attributives more clearly:

她	**tā**	possession	her
鞋架上	**xiéjià shàng**	location	shoe rack top
去年	**qùnián**	time	last year
那	**nèi**	scope	that
(一)双	**(yī) shuāng**	numeral + measure word	(one) pair
穿了又穿(的)	**chuānle yòu chuān de**	activity	wore and wore again
破破烂烂的	**pòpòlànlàn de**	characteristics	tattered
尖头的	**jiāntóu de**	shape	pointed
黑色	**hēisè**	colour	black
棉布	**miánbù**	material	cotton
拖	**tuō**	function	drag
鞋	**xié**	headword	shoes (i.e. slippers)

For the sake of rhythm or clarity of message, the 'state and activity' attributive can often be placed in a position immediately before the 'scope' attributive, if there is one, and the 'numeral + measure word'. The middle section of the sentence above would therefore become:

... 穿了又穿的那一双 ... **chuān le yòu chuān de nèi yī shuāng**

instead of

... 那一双穿了又穿的 ... **nèi yī shuāng chuān le yòu chuān de**

5.3 COMBINATION, EMBEDDING AND DELAYING

5.3.1 COMMAS OR CONJUNCTIONS

When attributives of the same type occur with a headword, they are joined by commas[3] or conjunctions:

远远地驶来了一艘轻捷、美观、整洁的游艇。
yuǎnyuǎn de shǐlai le yī sōu qīngjié | měiguān | zhěngjié de yóutǐng
(lit. distant de sail-come le one mw light-quick, attractive, neat yacht)
In the distance an attractive, neat, light yacht approached.

他是一个思想活跃而又谦虚谨慎的人。
tā shì yī ge sīxiǎng huóyuè ér yòu qiānxū jǐnshèn de rén
(lit. he is one mw thinking lively but also modest prudent *de* person)
He is someone who has a lively mind, but is also modest and cautious.

---

[3] Note that, when listing items, the Chinese convention is to use a reversed (dun) comma, / 、 /.

缺页<u>或</u>装订上有误差的书，都可以退换。
quē yè <u>huò</u> zhuāngdīng shàng yǒu wùchā de shū | dōu kěyǐ tuìhuàn
(lit. lack pages or binding-on have faults de books, all may return exchange)
Any book with missing pages or faulty binding can be exchanged.

整个城市沉浸在热烈<u>和</u>欢快的气氛中。
zhěng ge chéngshì chénjìn zài rèliè <u>hé</u> huānkuài de qìfēn zhōng
(lit. whole mw city immersed cv: in enthusiastic and happy *de* atmosphere-in)
The whole city was immersed in an enthusiastic and happy atmosphere.

谁都喜欢这个真诚<u>而</u>热情的姑娘。
shuí dōu xǐhuan zhèi ge zhēnchéng <u>ér</u> rèqíng de gūniang
(lit. everyone all like this mw sincere but warm girl)
Everyone likes this sincere and enthusiastic young woman.

5.3.2 LONGER ATTRIBUTIVES

Longer attributives may sometimes have other 'attributive + headword' constructions embedded in them. For example:

草地上出现了一条来来往往的行人踏出来的小道
cǎodì shàng chūxiànle yī tiáo [(láiláiwǎngwǎng de xíngrén) tà chūlai de] xiǎodào
(lit. grassland-on appear *le* one mw [coming going *de* pedestrians] tread out come *de* small path)
On the grass, appeared a small path made by the steps of constant passers-by.

她买了一套跟浅绿色的地毯配起来特别和谐、悦目的家具。
tā mǎile yī tào [gēn(qiǎn lǜ sè de dìtǎn)pèi qǐlai tèbié héxié yuèmù de] jiājù
(lit. she buy *le* one mw: suite [cv: with (light green colour *de* carpet) match especially harmonious, attractive de] furniture)
She bought a suite of furniture that match particularly harmoniously and attractively with the light-green carpet.

However, Chinese is not a language that is comfortable with long attributives, and the examples above would quite likely be divided into two sections:

草地上出现了一条小道，是来来往往的行人踏出来的。
cǎodì shàng chūxiànle yī tiáo xiǎodào | shì láiláiwǎngwǎng de xíngrén tà chūlai de
(lit. grassland-on appear *le* one mw small path, is coming going *de* pedestrian tread out come *de*)
On the grass, appeared a small path made by the steps of constant passers-by.

她买了一套家具，跟浅绿色的地毯配起来，特别和谐、悦目。
tā mǎile yī tào jiājù | gēn qiǎn lǜ sè de dìtǎn pèi qǐlai | tèbié héxié yuèmù
(lit. she buy *le* one mw:suite furniture, cv:with light green colour *de* carpet
match, especially harmonious, attractive)
She bought a suite of furniture matching particularly harmoniously and
attractively with the light-green carpet.

This unease with long attributives leads to a stylistic preference to have two or
more short attributives placed in sequence after a noun headword and separated
from each other by commas. For example:

草地上出现了一条<u>小道</u>，〈是来来往往的行人踏出来的，〈弯弯曲曲，〈一直
伸向山颠，〈远远看去，忽隐忽现，〈好象一条条巨大的<u>蚯蚓</u>，《一伸一缩，
《奋力向上游着。

**cǎodì shàng chūxiànle yī tiáo xiǎodào |<shì láiláiwǎngwǎng de xíngrén
tà chūlai de |<wānwānqūqū |<yīzhí shēn xiàng shāndiān | <yuǎnyuǎn
kàn qù | hū yǐn hū xiàn |<hǎoxiàng yī tiáotiáo jùdà de qiūyǐn |<<yī shēn
yī suō |<<fènlì xiàngshàng yóuzhe**
(lit. grassland on appear *le* one mw small path, <is coming going de
pedestrians tread out come *de*, <winding, <straight stretch cv: towards
mountain peak, <distantly look, suddenly disappear suddenly appear,
<resemble one mw mw huge *de* earthworm <<one stretch one contract,
<<strive cv: towards travel *zhe*)
On the grass appeared a small path, made by the steps of constant passers-
by, which wound right up to the mountain peak appearing and disappearing
in the distance like a series of giant earthworms that, stretching and
recoiling, were striving to move upwards.

All the sections marked with < are clearly attributable to their fronted headword
小道 **xiǎodào** 'small path', but when we come to the nominal 蚯蚓 **qiūyǐn**
'earthworm', it then becomes a second headword and the two sections marked
<< are attributable to it. Theoretically, an articulated attributive chain like this
could stretch even further but it would naturally be curtailed by stylistic and
other constraints.

6 ACTION VERBS

Action verb is a portmanteau term used here to cover all the verbs in the language apart from non-action verbs such as 是 **shì** 'to be' and 有 **yǒu** 'to have' and verbs of emotion or cognition. Their major distinctive feature is that they generally indicate **transient performance**. Therefore they are more narrative or descriptive, recounting past events or depicting ongoing actions; whereas non-action verbs tend to register more or less **permanent states** or **characteristics** and are therefore more expository. In other words, actions verbs play a more prominent role in narration or description while non-action verbs focus more on explanation. This, of course, does not imply that action verbs cannot be used for purposes other than narration or description, but there is a clear distinction between the subject of an action verb predicate and the topic of a comment expressed by 是 **shì** 'to be', 有 **yǒu** 'to have' or an emotional or cognitive verb. In the former case, the subject either initiates or tolerates the action encoded in the predicate, while in the latter, the topic is linked to further explanations expressed in the comment. Compare the following.

subject–predicate structures:

我吃了一碗面。 **wǒ chī le yī wǎn miàn**　　　　(narrative)
I ate a bowl of noodles.

他收到了两封信。 **tā shōudào le liǎng fēng xìn**　(narrative)
He received two letters.

妹妹在弹钢琴。 **mèimei zài tán gāngqín**　　　(descriptive)
My younger sister is playing the piano.

topic–comment structures:

我是大学教师。 **wǒ shì dàxué jiàoshī**　　　　(expository)
I am a university teacher.

他有两个弟弟。 **tā yǒu liǎng ge dìdi**　　　　　(expository)
He has two younger brothers.

哥哥喜欢喝啤酒。 **gēge xǐhuan hē píjiǔ**　　　(expository)
My elder brother likes drinking beer.

We will pick up these differences again in later chapters, and, in particular, in Chapter 21, but here, we will focus on the intrinsic features of action verbs: their diverse structural categories and their formal and semantic relations with the subject and the object. In the next two chapters, we will discuss relationship of action verbs with time and location expressions.

6.1 TRANSITIVE AND INTRANSITIVE

Action verbs can be transitive or intransitive. The difference is that the former takes an object while the latter does not. For example:

(a) transitive verbs:

| 他在学中文。 | **tā zài xué zhōngwén** | He is studying Chinese. |
| 她去了伦敦。 | **tā qù le lúndūn** | She went to London. |

(b) intransitive verbs:

| 春天到了。[1] | **chūntiān dào le** | Spring has come. |
| 太阳出来了。 | **tàiyáng chū lái le** | The sun has come out. |

Quite often, a verb can be used both transitively and intransitively:

(a)	请原谅。	**qǐng yuánliàng**	Please excuse me.[2]
	我原谅了他。	**wǒ yuánliàng le tā**	I forgave him.
(b)	她笑了。	**tā xiào le**	She laughed/smiled.
	别笑我。	**bié xiào wǒ**	Don't laugh at me.
(c)	菜来了。	**cài lái le**	The food has arrived.
	请来两个菜。	**qǐng lái liǎng ge cài**	Please bring two dishes.
(d)	他已经离开了。	**tā yǐjīng líkāi le**	He has already left.
	他已经离开这儿了。	**tā yǐjīng líkāi zhèr le**	He has already left here.

The term 'object' broadly refers to any nominal or pronominal item (or nominalised verbal or clausal expression) coming immediately after the verb, whether it indicates animate beings or inanimate objects, time, location, result, instrument or activity. The possible semantic diversity of objects bespeaks the

---

[1] The inclusion of end-of-sentence particle 了 **le** actually turns an action verb predicate into an explanation, thus making the whole sentence expository. This will be fully discussed in Chapter 20.

[2] The English translation requires a transitive verb and object.

general flexibility of syntactic rules in languages. Very often a transitive verb may take objects of different semantic orientations. For example:

母鸡在孵小鸡。	**mǔjī zài fū xiǎojī**	The hen is hatching (its) chicks.
母鸡在孵蛋。	**mǔjī zài fū dàn**	The hen is hatching eggs.
母亲在喂小孩。	**mǔqīn zài wèi xiǎohái**	The mother is feeding her child.
母亲在喂奶。	**mǔqīn zài wèi nǎi**	(lit. the mother is feeding milk [to her baby]) The mother is breast-feeding.

There are far more transitive than intransitive verbs in Chinese. Apart from those indicating posture (e.g. 站 **zhàn** 'to stand', 坐 **zuò** 'to sit'), body movement (e.g. 跳 **tiào** 'to jump', 爬 **pá** 'climb; crawl'), emotion (e.g. 笑 **xiào** 'to smile; laugh', 哭 **kū** 'to cry; weep') and physical or chemical changes (e.g. 变 **biàn** 'to change', 溶化 **rónghuà** 'to dissolve'), which are essentially intransitive, the great majority of action verbs are transitive in nature. Many intransitive verbs or intransitive uses of transitive verbs in English, for example, will find their Chinese counterparts encoded in a disyllabic 'verb + object' structure. For example:

sing	唱歌 **chànggē**	(lit. sing songs)
dance	跳舞 **tiàowǔ**	(lit. leap dances)
swim	游泳 **yóuyǒng**	(lit. swim swims)
read	看书 **kànshū**	(lit. see books)
talk	谈话 **tánhuà**	(lit. talk words)
walk	走路 **zǒulù**	(lit. walk paths)
run	跑步 **pǎobù**	(lit. run steps)
sleep	睡觉 **shuìjiào**	(lit. sleep a sleep)
drive	开车 **kāichē**	(lit. drive a car)
cook	煮饭 **zhǔfàn**	(lit. boil rice)
rain	下雨 **xiàyǔ**	(lit. pour down rain)

These apparently intransitive verbs nonetheless remain strictly 'verb + object' constructions and as such they cannot be followed by additional grammatical items in a sentence. For example, 'to walk for ten miles' or 'to sleep for three hours' is expressed by interposing a time modification before the object:

走路	**zǒulù**	to walk
走了十英里(的)路	**zǒu le shí yīnglǐ (de) lù**	(he) walked for
*走路了十英里	***zǒulù le shí yīnglǐ**	ten miles

睡觉	**shuìjiào**	to sleep
睡了三个钟头(的)觉	**shuì le sān ge zhōngtóu (de) jiào**	(he) slept for three hours
*睡觉了三个钟头	***shuìjiào le sān ge zhōngtóu**	

下雨	**xiàyǔ**	to rain
下了两天雨	**xià le liǎng tiān yǔ**	(it) rained for two days
*下雨了两天	***xiàyǔ le liǎng tiān**	

In other cases a coverb[3] will be introduced:

见面	**jiànmiàn**	to meet (lit. to see face)
他跟她见了面。	**tā gēn tā jiàn le miàn**	He met her.
*他见面了她。	***tā jiànmiàn le tā**	

接吻	**jiēwěn**	to kiss (lit. to link lips)
他在跟她接吻。	**tā zài gēn tā jiēwěn**	He is kissing her.
*他在接吻她。	***tā zài jiēwěn tā**	

6.2 DYNAMIC AND STATIC DIFFERENCES

A noticeable semantic dimension that affects the use of action verbs in Chinese is the difference between dynamic and static verbs. A dynamic action verb implies that the action travels across a certain space whereas a static action verb does not. This can be clearly illustrated by the difference between 'walk' and 'stand': when one walks, one moves from one location to another; whereas when one stands, one either stays in one place or changes from a sitting position to a standing position and no change of location is involved.

The dynamic or static nature of an action verb will decide whether a location phrase associated with it precedes or follows it. A dynamic action verb will have location phrases preceding it whereas a static action verb may have a location phrase either preceding it or following it. For example:

他在公园里散步。	**tā zài gōngyuán li sànbù**	He is having a walk in
*他散步在公园里。	***tā sànbù zài gōngyuán li**	the park.

他在草地上坐着。[4]	**tā zài cǎodì shàng zuò zhe**	He is sitting on
他坐在草地上。	**tā zuò zài cǎodì shàng**	the grass.

6.3 DATIVE VERBS

With some transitive verbs (dative verbs), two objects rather than one are present, in the sequence of an indirect object followed by a direct object. In other words, while the valency of ordinary transitive verbs is two (i.e. subject and object) that of dative verbs is three (subject, indirect object and direct object). For example:

---

[3] See Chapter 11 on coverbs.

[4] The addition of the particle 着 **zhe** to the verb changes it from narrative mode to descriptive mode. This will be discussed in Chapter 20.

姐姐给了我一个苹果。 **jiějie gěi le wǒ yī ge píngguǒ**
(My) elder sister gave me an apple.

爸爸送了我一个很漂亮的生日礼物。
bàba sòng le wǒ yī ge hěn piàoliang de shēngrì lǐwù
Father gave me a very beautiful birthday present.

王老师在教我们英文。[5] **wáng lǎoshī zài jiāo wǒmen yīngwén**
Teacher Wang is teaching us English.

我还了他两镑钱。 **wǒ huán le tā liǎng bàng qián**
I gave him back two pounds.

我收了他两镑钱。 **wǒ shōu le tā liǎng bàng qián**
I received two pounds from him.

他们赔了我十块钱。 **tāmen péi le wǒ shí kuài qián**
They paid me ten yuan/dollars compensation.

Dative verbs, as we can see, are primarily verbs that indicate giving, receiving, paying, returning, and so on where two parties (usually the subject and the indirect object) are transmitting something (usually the direct object) between them.

Other similar verbs are:

退 **tuì** 'to return (unwanted goods)', 找 **zhǎo** 'to give change', 付 **fù** 'to pay', 奖 **jiǎng** 'to award', 赏 **shǎng** 'to reward', 赠 **zèng** 'to present with', 分 **fēn** 'to apportion'.

给 **gěi** 'to give' is used not only as a dative verb on its own but also in tandem with other verbs to form disyllabic dative verbs. The subject of these verbs must be the giver and the indirect object the beneficiary:

我还给他两镑钱。 **wǒ huán gěi tā liǎng bàng qián**
I returned/gave back two pounds to him.

我交给他一封信。 **wǒ jiāo gěi tā yī fēng xìn**
I handed over a letter to him.

她递给我一杯啤酒。 **tā dì gěi wǒ yī bēi píjiǔ**
She handed me a glass of beer.

师傅传给我不少技艺。 **shīfu chuán gěi wǒ bùshǎo jìyì**
The master (worker) passed on to me many skills.

---

[5] Teacher (老师 **lǎoshī**) is a commonly used title in Chinese.

The following verbs often incorporate 给 **gěi** 'to give' as the second syllable:

捐 **juān** 'to donate', 卖 **mài** 'to sell', 输 **shū** 'to lose (in a game)', 补 **bǔ** 'to supplement', 扔 **rēng** 'to throw to', 发 **fā** 'to distribute', 寄 **jì** 'to send by post', 派 **pài** 'to despatch (people) to', 介绍 **jièshào** 'to introduce', 推荐 **tuījiàn** 'to recommend', 分配 **fēnpèi** 'to assign or allocate to', 贡献 **gōngxiàn** 'to contribute'.

In the case of 借 **jiè** which means both 'to borrow' and 'to lend' and 租 **zū** which means both 'to hire' and 'to rent', 给 **gěi** 'to give' must be incorporated to express the difference between the two meanings:

他借了我两镑钱。 **tā jiè le wǒ liǎng bàng qián**
He borrowed two pounds from me.

他借给我两镑钱。 **tā jiè gěi wǒ liǎng bàng qián**
He lent me two pounds.

我租了他们一间屋子。 **wǒ zū le tāmen yī jiān wūzi**
I rented a room from them.

我租给他们一间屋子。 **wǒ zū gěi tāmen yī jiān wūzi**
I rented a room to them.

As well as being incorporated into disyllabic verbs 给 **gěi** 'to give' may also be placed before the verb or towards the end of the sentence to create a coverbal construction. Used in this way, it can occur with a wider range of verbs:

她给我倒了杯茶。 **tā gěi wǒ dào le bēi chá**
她倒了杯茶给我。 **tā dào le bēi chá gěi wǒ**
She poured me a cup of tea.

他给我做了碗面。 **tā gěi wǒ zuò le wǎn miàn**
他做了碗面给我。 **tā zuò le wǎn miàn gěi wǒ**
He made me a bowl of noodles.

我给他打了个电话。 **wǒ gěi tā dǎ le ge diànhuà**
我打了个电话给他。 **wǒ dǎ le ge diànhuà gěi tā**
I telephoned him.

给 **gěi** 'to give' itself incorporates 予 **yǔ** 'to give' to form the disyllabic 给予 **gěiyǔ** 'to give'. Its direct object is abstract rather than concrete, and is generally modified by a degree adjective and preceded by an optional 以 **yǐ**:

他们给予我极大的支持。 **tāmen gěiyǔ wǒ jídà de zhīchí**
They gave me very great support.

这番话给予他们(以)极大的鼓舞。 **zhèi fān huà gěiyǔ tāmen (yǐ) jídà de gǔwǔ**
These words gave them great encouragement.

Other abstract nouns commonly used with 给予 **gěiyǔ** 'to give' include:

影响 **yǐngxiǎng** 'influence', 印象 **yìnxiàng** 'impression', 力量 **lìliàng** 'strength', 帮助 **bāngzhù** 'help', 支持 **zhīchí** 'support', 安慰 **ānwèi** 'consolation', 勇气 **yǒngqì** 'courage', 教育 **jiàoyù** 'education', 鼓励 **gǔlì** 'encouragement'.

With certain dative verbs the subject is the beneficiary or recipient:

我拿了你一瓶酱油。 **wǒ ná le nǐ yī píng jiàngyóu**
I took a bottle of soy sauce from you.

他们罚了你多少钱？ **tāmen fá le nǐ duōshao qián**
How much did they fine you?

Other similar verbs include:

欠 **qiàn** 'owe', 赢 **yíng** 'to win (in a game)', 扣 **kòu** 'to deduct', 偷 **tōu** 'to steal', 抢 **qiǎng** 'to rob', 骗 **piàn** 'to cheat out of', 赚 **zhuàn** 'to earn'.

If what is given is information of one form or another, verbs like the following are used:

大家都叫我小李。 **dàjiā dōu jiào wǒ xiǎolǐ**
Everyone calls me Xiao (Little) Li.

我托你一件事。 **wǒ tuō nǐ yī jiàn shì**
(lit. I entrust a matter to you) Can you do me a favour?

他瞒了我一件事儿。 **tā mán le wǒ yī jiàn shìr**
He hid a matter from me./He did not tell me about something.

他们限我两天。 **tāmen xiàn wǒ liǎng tiān**
They limited me to two days.

他告诉我明天开会。 **tā gàosu wǒ míngtiān kāihuì**
He told me the meeting was/is tomorrow.

人人都说他糊涂。 **rénrén dōu shuō tā hútu**
Everyone says he is stupid.

她看中他聪明。 **tā kànzhòng tā cōngming**
She was attracted by his intelligence.

他责备我没把这件事儿办好。 **tā zébèi wǒ méi bǎ zhèi jiàn shìr bàn hǎo**
He blamed me for not doing this well/getting this done.

As we can see from the last few examples, the direct object is a verbal message, and, as such, it can be an adjectival or verbal expression, or even a clause.

Other such verbs include:

> 劝 **quàn** 'to persuade', 求 **qiú** 'to plead with', 称呼 **chēnghū** 'to call (by a certain name)', 骂 **mà** 'to criticise', 问 **wèn** 'to ask', 请教 **qǐngjiào** 'to consult', 通知 **tōngzhī** 'to inform', 嘱咐 **zhǔfu** 'to warn or advise', 答应 **dāying** 'to promise', 回答 **huídá** 'to reply to', 抱怨 **bàoyuàn** 'to complain', 表扬 **biǎoyáng** 'to praise'.

Finally, some dative verbs express physical or psychological infliction:

> 他打了我一拳。 **tā dǎ le wǒ yī quán**
> (lit. He hit *le* me one fist) He gave me a punch.

> 她看了我一眼。 **tā kàn le wǒ yī yǎn**
> (lit. She look *le* me one eye) She gave me a look.

> 我踢了他一脚。 **wǒ tī le tā yī jiǎo**
> (lit. I kick *le* him one foot) I gave him a kick.

> 这件事儿吓了我一身汗。 **zhèi jiàn shìr xiā le wǒ yī shēn hàn**
> (lit. This mw business startle *le* me one body of swcat)
> This business brought me out in a sweat.

In these cases, the indirect object is always a noun preceded by the numeral 一 **yī** 'one' with a measure.

Other such verbs include:

> 吐 **tǔ** 'to spit', 溅 **jiàn** 'to splash', 累 **lèi** 'to tire', 急 **jí** 'to worry', 告 **gào** . . . 状 **zhuàng** 'to accuse . . . of', 出 **chū** . . . 丑 **chǒu** 'to put . . . to shame'.

6.4   CAUSATIVE VERBS

Some transitive action verbs, on the other hand, not only transmit an action on to an object, but also cause the object to produce a further action or actions itself. They therefore produce a knock-on effect, with one action leading to another. Theoretically, this knock-on effect can continue to repeat itself as long as the meaning remains clear.

> 妈妈叫我叫哥哥教妹妹写字。 **māma jiào wǒ jiào gēge jiāo mèimei xiězì**
> Mother told me to tell [my] elder brother to teach [my] younger sister to write.

> 他求我帮他做一件事。 **tā qiú wǒ bāng tā zuò yī jiàn shì**
> He asked me to help him do something.

Generally, however, one follow-up action is more common:

我朋友请我吃饭。 **wǒ péngyou qǐng wǒ chīfàn**
My friend invited me to eat/for a meal.

什么使东西落到地上? **shénme shǐ dōngxi luò dào dì shàng**
What causes things to fall to the ground?

医生让她好好休息。 **yīshēng ràng tā hǎohāo xiūxi**
The doctor told her to have a good rest.

我劝他戒烟，他劝我戒酒。 **wǒ quàn tā jièyān | tā quàn wǒ jièjiǔ**
I urged him to give up smoking, and he urged me to give up drinking.

奶奶要我替她写信。 **nǎinai yào wò tì tā xiěxìn**
Grandma wanted me to write a letter for her.

It is worth noting that despite the fact that causative verbs help to narrate events, they do not usually incorporate the particle 了 **le**. The second verb in the chain may, of course, take 了 **le** to emphasise that the desired action has already been carried out.

我朋友请我吃了一顿饭。 **wǒ péngyou qǐng wǒ chī le yī dùn fàn**
My friend invited me to a meal.

医生让她好好地休息了几天。 **yīshēng ràng tā hǎohāo de xiūxi le jǐ tiān**
The doctor told her to make sure she rested for a few days.

奶奶要我替她写了一封信。 **nǎinai yào wǒ tì tā xiě le yī fēng xìn**
Grandma had me write a letter for her.

Causative verbs with the underlying notion of making somebody do something range from request to requirement and from order to coercion:

我挽留他多坐一会儿。 **wǒ wǎnliú tā duō zuò yīhuìr**
I pressed him to stay a bit longer.

妈妈催弟弟快睡。 **māma cuī dìdi kuài shuì**
Mother urged younger brother to hurry up and go to bed.

别惹你爸爸生气。 **bié rě nǐ bàba shēngqì**
Don't make your father angry.

这个孩子真逗人喜欢。 **zhèi ge háizi zhēn dòu rén xǐhuan**
This child really makes people like him.

大家选我当经理。 **dàjiā xuǎn wǒ dāng jīnglǐ**
Everyone elected/chose me to be the manager.

法官传证人出庭作证。 **fǎguān chuán zhèngren chūtíng zuòzhèng**
The judge summoned the witness to appear in the court and give evidence.

Other such verbs include:

> 烦 **fán** 'to bother', 烦劳 **fánláo** 'to trouble', 指望 **zhǐwàng** 'to expect', 托 **tuō** 'to entrust', 要求 **yāoqiú** 'to require', 嘱咐 **zhǔfu** 'to enjoin', 安排 **ānpái** 'to arrange', 组织 **zǔzhí** 'to organise', 命令 **mìnglìng** 'to order', 指定 **zhǐdìng** 'to designate', 指示 **zhǐshì** 'to instruct', 打发 **dǎfā** 'to send sb away', 派 **pài** 'to despatch sb', 召集 **zhàojí** 'to muster', 逼 **bī** 'to force', 强迫 **qiángpò** 'to coerce'.

Sometimes the subject of the sentence does not make somebody do something but rather allows, encourages, or prevents an action:

他支持我提出抗议。 **tā zhīchí wǒ tíchū kànyì**
He supported me in my protest.

她怂恿弟弟去干坏事。 **tā sǒngyǒng dìdi qù gàn huàishì**
She incited [her] younger brother to do something wrong.

管理员禁止游客乱扔果皮纸屑。
guǎnlǐyuán jìnzhǐ yóukè luàn rēng guǒpí zhǐxiè
The person on duty told the tourists not to drop litter.

爸爸不准我去打猎。 **bàba bù zhǔn wǒ qù dǎ liè**
Father won't let me go hunting.

Other such verbs include:

> 允许 **yǔnxǔ** 'to allow', 鼓励 **gǔlì** 'to encourage', 勉励 **miǎnlì** 'to spur on', 影响 **yǐngxiǎng** 'to affect', 制止 **zhìzhǐ** 'to prevent', 劝阻 **quànzǔ** 'to dissuade'.

The subject may be involved or become involved in the subsequent action:

我约他到城里去逛逛。 **wǒ yuē tā dào chéng lǐ qù guàngguang**
I arranged with/made an appointment with him to go for a stroll in town.

我来帮你收拾行李吧。 **wǒ lái bāng nǐ shōushi xíngli ba**
I'll/Why don't I come and help you pack your luggage.

我陪客人吃了一顿饭。 **wǒ péi kèren chī le yī dùn fàn**
I accompanied the guests for a meal.

老师带领学生参观展览会。 **lǎoshī dàilǐng xuésheng cānguān zhǎnlǎnhuì**
The teacher took the students to visit the exhibition.

他扶我上楼。 **tā fú wǒ shàng lóu**
He helped me upstairs.

我送他到火车站。 **wǒ sòng tā dào huǒchēzhàn**
I saw him off to the station.

If the subject is inanimate, 使 **shǐ** and its more colloquial or formal counterparts are generally used:

这件事使我十分失望。 **zhèi jiàn shì shǐ wǒ shífēn shīwàng**
This business makes me extremely disappointed.

这种精神使人十分钦佩。 **zhèi zhǒng jīngshén shǐ rén shífēn qīnpèi**
This kind of vitality/spirit fills people with admiration.

那样的话教人作呕。 **nàyàng de huà jiāo rén zuò'ǒu**
Talk like that makes one sick.

这个消息令人高兴。 **zhèi ge xiāoxi lìng rén gāoxìng**
This news makes people/one happy.

这儿的风景引人入胜。 **zhèr de fēngjǐng yǐn rén rù shèng**
The scenery here enchants one/is enchanting.

A causative construction may sometimes work in conjunction with a dative construction. The causative verb in these cases usually links with 给 **gěi** 'to give':

老奶奶倒给我一杯茶喝。 **lǎo nǎinai dào gěi wǒ yī bēi chá hē**
Grandma poured out a cup of tea for me (to drink).

老公公递给我一条毛巾擦汗。
lǎo gōnggong dì gěi wǒ yī tiáo máojīn cā hàn
Grandpa handed me a towel to wipe (my) sweat.

我朋友送给我一张照片留念。
wǒ péngyou sòng gěi wǒ yī zhāng zhàopiàn liúniàn
My friend gave me a photograph as/to be a keepsake.

6.5 COVERBS[6]

Some transitive verbs, particularly those that indicate location, destination or instrument, are used to accompany other verbs expressing more specific actions.

---

[6] For a detailed discussion of coverbs, see See Chapter 11.

These transitive verbs are generally known as coverbs, that is, verbs that commonly occur with other verbs. They in fact express concepts very similar to those expressed by prepositions in English, which can be seen from the English translations of the following examples. However, unlike English prepositional phrases, Chinese coverbal expressions are generally placed before the main predicate verbs:

他在图书馆借书。 **tā zài túshūguǎn jiè shū**
He borrowed a book <u>from</u> the library.

他到车站去坐车。 **tā dào chēzhàn qù zuò chē**
He went <u>to</u> the station to catch a train/bus.

她给爸爸、妈妈写信。 **tā gěi bàba | māma xiěxìn**
She wrote <u>to</u> her mother and father.

她跟朋友一起去看电影。 **tā gēn péngyou yīqǐ qù kàn diànyǐng**
She went <u>with</u> a friend/friends to see a film.

我用电脑画了一幅画儿。 **wǒ yòng diànnǎo huà le yī fú huàr**
I drew a picture <u>on</u> my computer.

6.6 AGREEMENT BETWEEN THE SUBJECT AND ITS ACTION VERB PREDICATE

The agreement between the subject and its action verb predicate is threefold.

First is the principle of **reference agreement**. The subject of an action verb predicate in Chinese must be of definite reference. In other words, only an entity known to the participants of a communication can be featured as the initiator (or tolerator) of an action. Being a language devoid of definite or indefinite articles, Chinese uses the relative positions of items in a narrative or descriptive sentence to establish different points of reference. That is to say, all pre-verbal positions tend to be reserved for definite reference and post-verbal ones for indefinite reference.[7] The following examples and their English translations will make things clear:

女主人唱了一首歌。 **nǚ zhǔrén chàng le yī shǒu gē**
The hostess sang **a song**.

老师在黑板上写字。 **lǎoshī zài hēibǎn shàng xiě zì**
The teacher was writing **characters** on the blackboard.

---

[7] For a full discussion of reference, see Chapter 20.

Second is the principle of **number agreement**. Generally speaking, most action verbs are compatible with a subject of any number, i.e., singular or plural. However, there are some action verbs which may only relate to a plural subject. For example:

他们共事了三年。 **tāmen gòngshì le sān nián**
They worked together for three years.

大家在门口集中。 **dàjiā zài ménkǒu jízhōng**
Everyone assembled at the entrance.

If the subject is singular, a coverbal phrase has to be introduced to indicate the involvement of another party:

他在跟她聊天。 **tā zài gēn tā liáotiān**
He is chatting with her.

弟弟在跟妹妹吵架。 **dìdi zài gēn mèimei chǎojià**
Younger brother is quarrelling with younger sister.

Otherwise, the rule of agreement is violated and the sentence becomes wrong:

*他通信。 **tā tōngxìn** *He corresponded.
*她争论。 **tā zhēnglùn** *She argued.

The most common verbs of this type in the lexicon include:

接吻 **jiēwěn** 'kiss', 见面 **jiànmiàn** 'meet', 再见 **zàijiàn** 'say goodbye to', 分手 **fēnshǒu** 'part company', 谈判 **tánpàn** 'negotiate'.

In most cases, such verbs have a first morpheme implying 'mutuality', 'collaboration' or 'coming together'. For example:

相处 **xiāngchǔ** 'deal with', 互助 **hùzhù** 'help each other', 合作 **hézuò** 'collaborate', 会面 **huìmiàn** 'meet', 联合 **liánhé** 'unite with', 团圆 **tuányuán** 'reunite (of a family)', 聚餐 **jùcān** 'come together for a meal', 交流 **jiāoliú** 'exchange views with', 对立 **duìlì** 'oppose', 商量 **shāngliang** 'consult', 并列 **bìngliè** 'list together'.

Third is the principle of **semantic** or **stylistic agreement**. Some action verbs are more subject-specific than others in terms of meaning or style. The verb 啼 **tí** 'to crow', for example, is only relatable in meaning to roosters and some other birds; and the verb 光临 **guānglín** 'to honour somebody with one's presence' is stylistically applicable exclusively to the second person. If these semantic or stylistic principles are violated, the sentence is unacceptable:

*他在啼。	**tā zài tí**	*He is crowing.
*我光临了。	**wǒ guānglín le**	*I am honouring (you) with my presence.

6.7 AGREEMENT BETWEEN AN ACTION VERB AND ITS OBJECT

The first agreement between an action verb and its object is **collocation**. Every action verb has a collocation range, large or small. An action verb like 遵守 **zūnshǒu** 'to abide by', for instance, takes only objects like 法律 **fǎlǜ** 'laws', 规章制度 **guīzhāng zhìdù** 'rules and regulations' or 诺言 **nuòyán** 'promises'. Its collocation range is therefore comparatively small. An action verb like 吃 **chī** 'to eat', on the other hand, has a large collocation range in that many things are edible. But with an action verb like 打 **dǎ** 'to hit', the collocation range is even larger, not only because many things can be hit, but also because the verb's collocation embraces a range of set expressions such as 打字 **dǎzì** 'to type (words)', 打气 **dǎqì** 'to pump air into', 打鱼 **dǎyú** 'to catch fish', 打电话 **dǎ diànhuà** 'to make a telephone call'.

This so-called collocation agreement, which is partly of a semantic and partly of a lexical nature, occurs in all languages. There is, however, an agreement between an action verb and its object in terms of **rhythm**,[8] which is peculiar to Chinese. A 'verb + object' expression can be invalidated, even when it conforms with grammar, meaning and collocation, if it violates a rhythmic principle. The general rule with this principle is that while a monosyllabic action verb may be followed by objects of any length, a disyllabic verb may only be followed by objects which are disyllabic or longer. For example:

to read:	看书 **kànshū**	看书报 **kàn shūbào**
	阅读书报 **yuèdú shūbào**	*阅读书 **yuèdú shū**
to return books:	还书 **huán shū**	还图书 **huán túshū**
	归还图书 **guīhuán túshū**	*归还书 **guīhuán shū**
to drive:	开车 **kāichē**	开汽车 **kāi qìchē**
	驾驶汽车 **jiàshǐ qìchē**	*驾驶车 **jiàshǐ chē**

The difference between these rhythmic patterns is one of registral formality:

monosyllabic verb + monosyllabic object:		neutral
e.g. 看书 **kànshū**	to read	
开会 **kāihuì**	to go to or attend a meeting	

monosyllabic verb + disyllabic object:		colloquial or metaphorical
e.g. 看电影 **kàn diànyǐng**	to go to the cinema	
开夜车 **kāi yèchē**	to burn the midnight oil	

[8] See Chapter 26 for a wider discussion of prosodic features like these.

disyllabic verb + disyllabic object: formal or written

e.g. 浏览书籍 **liúlǎn shūjí**   to read extensively

召开会议 **zhàokāi huìyì** to hold or convene a meeting

6.8 ACTION VERBS: COMPLETION AND CONTINUATION

Action verbs, as we have seen, are designed primarily for narrative or descriptive purposes, and every piece of narration or description must be lodged in a time frame. English and other languages specify the time and aspect of an action verb through the so-called tense framework, which can be summarised as follows:

time	aspect
past	
	perfect
present	continuous
	perfect continuous
future	

The manipulation of time and aspect creates tenses like present perfect, past continuous or present perfect continuous, and so on.

In Chinese, the tense and aspect framework looks rather different. Tense is encoded solely by time expressions and not reflected in the form of the verbs while aspect is indicated as follows:

the completion aspect by 了 **le** following the verb
the continuation aspect by 在 **zài** preceding the verb

他写了一首诗。 **tā xiě le yī shǒu shī** He wrote a poem. (narration)
他在写一首诗。 **tā zài xiě yī shǒu shī** He is writing a poem.
                                             (description)

These two aspect markers have a far wider function to fulfil than merely indicating such notions as completion or continuation. In this chapter, however, we shall only focus on their aspectual significations.

6.8.1 THE COMPLETION ASPECT

The completion aspect indicator 了 **le**, as a desemanticised particle derived from the verb 了 **liǎo** 'to bring to completion', is a marker in the narrative indicating that something has already taken place. The subject of the verb in a narrative, as we have seen, must be of definite reference. The object, on the other hand, can be of either reference. In general, following a verb marked by a perfect aspect 了 *le*, a noun object on its own, unqualified by a 'numeral + measure' phrase, will be of definite reference. Where both the subject and the object are of definite reference and are part of known information, the sentence remains incomplete unless something further is added. For example, these two sentences are incomplete:

他写完了诗 . . . **tā xiě wán le shī** . . .
He finished the poem . . . (and then what?)

我吃了饭 . . . **wǒ chī le fàn**
I ate/had my meal . . . (and then what?)

but are readily completed by an additional clause:

他写完了诗就去睡觉了。[9] **tā xiě wán le shī jiù qù shuìjiào le**
(lit. He write-finish *le* then go sleep *le*)
He went to bed as soon as he finished writing the poem.

我吃完了饭就去上班了。 **wǒ chī wán le fàn jiù qù shàngbān le**
(lit. I eat-finish *le* then go attend-duty *le*)
I went to work as soon as I had eaten.

A sentence is of course acceptable, if the object is qualified by a numeral phrase to indicate indefinite or generic reference. For example:

他收到了三封信。 **tā shōudào le sān fēng xìn**
He received three letters.

他碰见了不少老朋友。 **tā pèngjiàn le bùshǎo péngyou**
He bumped into quite a few friends.

The notion of completion indicated by 了 *le* is naturally associated with past time:

他昨天收到了三封信。 **tā zuótiān shōudào le sān fēng xìn**
He received three letters yesterday.

那一年他碰见了不少老朋友。
nèi yī nián tā pèngjiàn le bùshǎo lǎo péngyou
That year he bumped into quite a few friends.

---

[9] Note that the end-of-sentence 了 *le* functions entirely differently from the verbal suffix 了 *le*, and makes the initial narrative sentence expository. See Chapter 21.

了 *le* can only be used with future time in incomplete clauses (which are resolved by further information):

明天你下了课来找我。 **míngtiān nǐ xià le kè lái zhǎo wǒ**
Come and see me when you have finished class tomorrow.

我写完了三封信就去睡觉。 **wǒ xiě wán le sān fēng xìn jiù qù shuìjiào**
I will go to bed when I have written three letters.

One cannot say, for example:

*明天我上了三节课。 **míngtiān wǒ shàng le sān jié kè**
*Tomorrow I will have attended three classes.

*下个礼拜你吃了三次中餐。 **xià ge lǐbài nǐ chī le sān cì zhōngcān**
*Next week you will have eaten three Chinese meals.

Negative counterparts of 了 *le* sentences are expressed by using 没有 **méiyǒu** or 没 **méi** without a quantified object:[10]

昨天我没(有)上课。 **zuótiān wǒ méi (yǒu) shàngkè**
I did not go to class yesterday.

他那天没(有)碰见老朋友。 **tā nèi tiān méi (yǒu) pèngjiàn lǎo péngyou**
That day he did not bump into his old friend.

The quantification of an object in negative sentences occurs only for contrast:

昨天我没(有)写三封信，只写了两封。
zuótiān wǒ méi (yǒu) xiě sān fēng xìn | zhǐ xiě le liǎng fēng
Yesterday I did not write three letters but only two. (lit. only wrote two)

那天我并没碰见两个老朋友，只碰见了一个。
nèi tiān wǒ bìng méi pèngjiàn liǎng ge lǎo péngyou | zhǐ pèngjiàn le yī ge
I did not bump into two old friends that day but only one.
(lit. only bumped into one)

Finally, it must be pointed out that causative verbs and disyllabic dative verbs with 给 **gěi** cannot be encoded in the completion aspect:

*他逼了我撒谎。 ***tā bī le wǒ sāhuǎng**
*He forced me to lie.

---

[10] See §16.9.

*市长发给了他一张奖状。 **shìzhǎng fāgěi le tā yī zhāng jiǎngzhuàng**
*The mayor awarded him a certificate of merit.

6.8.2   THE CONTINUATION ASPECT

The continuation aspect marker 在 **zài** is placed before the verb and the action indicated can be ongoing, continual, or repetitive. In all cases, the continuation aspect makes the sentence descriptive.

他们在唱歌。 **tāmen zài chànggē**
They are singing.

这几天他们都在研究这个问题。
zhèi jǐ tiān tāmen dōu zài yánjiū zhèi ge wèntí
They have all been studying this question for the last few days.

他们在调查情况。 **tāmen zài diàochá qíngkuàng**
They are investigating the situation.

演员们在排演。 **yǎnyuánmen zài páiyǎn**
The performers are rehearsing.

The notion of continuation can be further emphasised by the addition of 正 **zhèng** before 在 **zài**:

上星期天下午我正在看球赛。
shàng xīngqī tiān xiàwǔ wǒ zhèngzài kàn qiúsài
Last Sunday afternoon I was just watching a match.

她正在接电话。 **tā zhèngzài jiē diànhuà**
She is just taking a call.

明年这个时候，我们正在度假。
míngnián zhèi ge shíhou | wǒmen zhèngzài dùjià
This time next year we will (just) be on holiday.

河水正在上涨。 **héshuǐ zhèngzài shàngzhǎng**
The river water is (just) rising.

Adding 呢 *ne* at the end of a sentence also indicates the continuation aspect (with or without the marker 在 **zài** or 正 **zhèng**), but adds a rhetorical tone to the utterance:

外面在下雨呢。 **wàimian zài xiàyǔ ne**
(Don't you know) it's raining [outside].

孩子们正睡觉呢。 **háizimen zhèng shuìjiào ne**
(Can't you see) the children are sleeping.

别吵他。他准备明天的考试呢。
bié chǎo tā | tā zhǔnbèi míngtiān de kǎoshì ne
Don't disturb him. (Can't you see) he is preparing for tomorrow's exam.

In contrast with completion aspect, a noun object following a verb with the continuation aspect will be generally of indefinite reference, whether or not it is qualified by a 'numeral + measure' phrase, and there is no question of a sentence with an unqualified object sounding incomplete. For example:

他在写诗。 **tā zài xiěshī** He is writing poems.

他在写一首诗。 **tā zài xiě yī shǒu shī** He is writing a poem.

学生在做作业。 **xuésheng zài zuò zuòyè**
The students are doing their coursework.

姐姐在编织一件毛衣。 **jiějie zài biānzhī yī jiàn máoyī**
(My) elder sister is knitting a woollen sweater.

This aspectual function of 在 **zài** is thought to derive from its use as a coverb in locational phrases like 在这儿 **zài zhèr** 'at this place; here', 在那儿 **zài nàr** 'at that place; there', 在家 **zài jiā** 'at home', 在学校 **zài xuéxiào** 'at school'. This may explain why the presence of a coverbal 在 **zài** phrase with a specified location also expresses continuous action:

有许多人在沙滩上晒太阳。 **yǒu xǔduō rén zài shātān shàng shài tàiyáng**
Lots of people are sunbathing on the beach.

小猫在火炉前打瞌睡。 **xiǎo māo zài huǒlú qián dǎ kēshuì**
The kitten is dozing in front of the fire.

Continuation aspect, unlike completion aspect, is naturally associated with any time: past, present and future:

他现在正在洗澡。 **tā xiànzài zhèngzài xǐzǎo**
He is taking a bath at the moment.

那时候她在读博士学位。 **nà shíhou tā zài dú bóshì xuéwèi**
At that time she was reading for her Ph.D. degree.

昨天晚上他们在打扑克(牌)。 **zuótiān wǎnshàng tāmen zài dǎ pūkè (pái)**
They were playing cards last night.

明年这个时候，我们在度假。 **míngnián zhèi ge shíhou | wǒmen zài dùjià**
This time next year we will be on holiday.

The negation of the continuation aspect is usually effected by the use of 不 **bù** with 在 **zài** (but not 正在 **zhèngzài**):

上星期天下午我不在看球赛。
shàng xīngqī tiān xiàwǔ wǒ bù zài kàn qiúsài
I wasn't watching a match last Sunday afternoon.

她不在接电话。 **tā bù zài jiē diànhuà**
She isn't taking a call.

明年这个时候，我们不在度假。
míngnián zhèi ge shíhou | wǒmen bù zài dùjià
We won't be on holiday this time next year.

河水不在上涨。 **héshuǐ bù zài shàngzhǎng**
The river water isn't rising.

6.9 ACTION VERBS: MANNER DESCRIBED AND EXPERIENCE EXPLAINED

There are two other verbal indicators which are often used with action verbs. They are 着 *zhe* and 过 *guo*. It is a common misunderstanding that they, like 了 *le* and 在 **zài**, are also aspectual markers. In fact they have entirely different functions to serve. 着 *zhe* is suffixed to an action verb so that the resultant verbal phrase is used as a descriptive element in sentences to indicate 'manner of existence', 'manner of movement' or 'accompanying manner', whereas 过 *guo* is attached to an action verb in order to explain that what has happened is part of the speaker's past experience. The explanatory function of 过 *guo* gives the sentence, in which it occurs, an expository tone.

6.9.1 MANNER OF EXISTENCE WITH 着 *zhe*

Action verbs suffixed with the manner indicator 着 *zhe* constitute descriptive sentences indicating particular manner of existence:

Location expression + verb + 着 *zhe* + numeral and measure phrase + noun

天空中飘着几朵白云。 **tiānkōng zhōng piāo zhe jǐ duǒ bái yún**
(lit. sky in float-in-the-air *zhe* several mw white clouds)
A few patches of white clouds were floating in the sky.

炉子里烤着一只鸭子。 **lúzi li kǎo zhe yī zhī yāzi**
(lit. oven in roast **zhe** one mw duck)
A duck is being roasted in the oven.

屋子里亮着灯火。 **wūzi li liàng zhe dēnghuǒ**
(lit. room in bright **zhe** lamp-fire)
A light is/was shining in the room.

这个将军胸前挂着不少勋章。
zhèi ge jiāngjūn xiōng qián guà zhe bùshǎo xūnzhāng
(lit. this mw general chest front hang **zhe** not-a-few medals)
On the front of this general's coat were hanging quite a few medals.

6.9.2 PERSISTENT POSTURE OR CONTINUOUS MOVEMENT WITH 着 *zhe*

Action verbs with 着 **zhe** may be used after the aspect marker 在 **zài** or a 在 **zài** phrase to indicate persistent posture/state or continuous movement:

Noun + 在 zài (phrase) + verb + 着 zhe

游客们在海滩上躺着。 **yóukèmen zài hǎitān shàng tǎng zhe**
(lit. tourists *zai* beach on lie *zhe*)
The tourists were lying on the beach.

他们在树林里走着。 **tāmen zài shùlín li zǒu zhe**
(lit. they *zai* woods *in* walk *zhe*)
They were walking in the woods.

篝火在熊熊地燃烧着。 **gōuhuǒ zài xióngxióng de ránshāo zhe**
(lit. bonfire *zai* brightly *de* burn *zhe*)
The bonfire was burning brightly.

风在不停地刮着。 **fēng zài bù tíng de guā zhe**
(lit. wind *zai* non-stop *de* blow *zhe*)
The wind was blowing incessantly.

6.9.3 ACCOMPANYING MANNER WITH 着 *zhe*

A verb phrase marked by 着 *zhe* describing accompanying manner may occur within any type of sentence. With its specifying function it always comes before the main verb. Here are some examples:

他<u>笑着</u>朝我走了过来。 **tā <u>xiào zhe</u> cháo wǒ zǒu le guòlai**
(lit. he smile *zhe* cv:towards me walk *le* over-come)
He walked towards me smiling.

孩子流着眼泪向妈妈认错。 **hǎizi liú zhe yǎnlèi xiàng māma rèncuò**
(lit. child flow *zhe* tears towards mother admit wrong)
The child with tears in his eyes admitted to his mother that he was wrong.

护士蹑着脚走近了病床。 **hùshi niè zhe jiǎo zǒu jìn le bìngchuáng**
(lit. nurse tiptoe *zhe* foot walk near *le* illness-bed)
The nurse tiptoed towards the patient's bed.

小狗摇着尾巴跑了过来。 **xiǎo gǒu yáo zhe wěiba pǎo le guòlai**
(lit. small dog shake *zhe* tail run *le* across-come)
The puppy came over wagging its tail.

他低着头坐在那儿。 **tā dī zhe tóu zuò zài nàr**
(lit. he lower *zhe* head sit cv:at there)
He was sitting there with his head lowered.

Two consecutive 着 *zhe* expressions of this type indicate that the action is continued or repeated:

她说着说着哭了起来。 **tā shuō zhe shuō zhe kū le qǐlai**
(lit. she speak *zhe* speak *zhe* weep *le* begin)
As she spoke, she started to weep.

她哭着哭着昏了过去。 **tā kū zhe kū zhe hūn le guòqu**
(lit. she weep *zhe* weep *zhe* faint *le* over)
She wept and wept and finally fainted.

6.9.4   EXPERIENCE AND 过 *guo*

The presence of 过 *guo* following an action verb conveys the meaning that the action of the verb is something that has been experienced in the past, and the tone of the sentence is therefore expository:

我看过那本小说。 **wǒ kàn guo nèi běn xiǎoshuō**
I have read that novel.

他们已经去过中国三次。 **tāmen yǐjīng qù guo zhōngguó sān cì**
They have already been to China three times.

我以前来过这儿。 **wǒ yǐqián lái guo zhèr**
I've been here before.

The past experience may relate to a specified time:

我年轻的时候写过不少诗。 **wǒ niánqīng de shíhou xiě guo bùshǎo shī**
I wrote a lot of poems when I was young.

她的女儿两年前当过导游。 **tāde nǚ'ér liǎng nián qián dāng guo dǎoyóu**
Her daughter worked as a tourist guide two years ago.

The negator for verbs with 过 *guo* is 没(有) **méi(yǒu)**:

我没(有)吃过中国菜。 **wǒ méi(yǒu) chī guo zhōngguó cài**
(lit. I not (have) eat *guo* Chinese dishes) I have never eaten Chinese food.

你喝过绍兴酒没有? **nǐ hē guo shàoxìng jiǔ méiyǒu?**
Have you ever had Shaoxing (rice) wine?

The difference in function between 过 *guo* and the aspect marker 了 *le* is that, while the former explains an experience, the latter narrates an event. Compare the following sentences:

他去了中国没有? **tā qù le zhōngguó méiyǒu**
Did he go/Has he gone to China?

他去过中国没有? **tā qù guo zhōngguó méiyǒu**
Has he (ever) been to China?

你见了他没有? **nǐ jiàn le tā méiyǒu**
Did you see/Have you seen him?

你见过他没有? **nǐ jiàn guo tā méiyǒu**
Have you (ever) met him before?

他那年参加了马拉松。 **tā nèi nián cānjiā le mǎlāsōng**
He ran the marathon that year.

他以前参加过马拉松。 **tā yǐqián cānjiā guo mǎlāsōng**
He has run the marathon before.

If the object is a common noun, it is always definite reference in a verb + 了 *le* sentence and indefinite in a verb + 过 *guo* sentence:

你查了字典没有? **nǐ chá le zìdiǎn méiyǒu**
Have you consulted **the** dictionary?

你查过字典没有？　**nǐ chá guo zìdiǎn méiyǒu**
Have you ever consulted **a** dictionary?

Finally, 过 *guo* is less commonly attached to verbs that are not action verbs. This normally occurs when the reference is to a previous situation that subsequently changed:

我曾经有过钱。　**wǒ céngjīng yǒu guo qián**
(lit. I at one time have *guo* money) I was very rich at one time.

前年他身体好过一阵子。　**qián nián tā shēntǐ hǎo guo yīzhènzi**
The year before last his health did improve for a while.

7   ACTION VERBS AND TIME

As Chinese action verbs do not change morphologically for tense, the time concept associated with them is therefore encoded in terms of time expressions. The positioning of these time expressions, whether pre-verbal or post-verbal, depends on whether they refer to definite or indefinite time. **Point-of-time** expressions are by nature of definite reference and are therefore always featured in a pre-verbal position. **Duration** or **frequency** expressions, on the other hand, in that their purpose is to measure *how long* or *how often* an action has been carried out, are likely to be of indefinite reference, and therefore follow the verb. They are moved to a pre-verbal position only when a period of time or number of times serves as the time backdrop against which a particular action encoded in a verb is supposed to be taking place.

7.1   POINT OF TIME

Point-of-time expressions refer to the particular time in or at which an action takes place, and they are by their very nature of definite reference. For Chinese speakers, the time reference has to be established before the action of the verb is stated and point-of-time expressions are therefore positioned either at the beginning of the sentence or immediately after the subject.

昨天我去商场买东西。 **<u>zuótiān</u> wǒ qù shāngchǎng mǎi dōngxi**
<u>Yesterday</u> I went to the shop to buy some things.

他今天没(有)来。 **tā <u>jīntiān</u> méi (yǒu) lái**
He has not come <u>today</u>.

去年冬天这儿下了一场大雪。 **<u>qùnián dōngtiān</u> zhèr xià le yī chǎng dà xuě**
There was a heavy snowfall here <u>last winter</u>.

我下午三点半在大学门口等你。
wǒ <u>xiàwǔ sān diǎn bàn</u> zài dàxué ménkǒu děng nǐ
I will wait for you <u>at half past three this afternoon</u> at the entrance to the University.

In contrast with English, point-of-time expressions in Chinese follow the order of year, month, day, week, part of the day, hour, minute and second; that is, the larger unit always precedes the smaller one:

一九八七年六月五日星期五上午九时四十三分二十一秒
**yī jiǔ bā qī nián liù yuè wǔ rì xīngqī wǔ shàngwǔ jiǔ shí sìshí sān fēn
èrshí yī miǎo**
21 seconds after 9:43 on the morning of Friday, 5 June 1987

我明天下午两点二十分来。 **wǒ míngtiān xiàwǔ liǎng diǎn èrshí fēn lái**
I'll come at twenty past two tomorrow afternoon.

Duration or frequency expressions, usually come after the verb,[1] but they are
placed in a pre-verbal position, when they are posed, often in a contrastive
sense, for particular comment or action. As such, they take on definite reference
and in effect become point-of-time expressions:

那两天他没上过街。 **nèi liǎng tiān tā méi shàng guo jiē**
He did not go out for those two days.

明年头两个月我要到北京去学习。
míngnián tóu liǎng ge yuè wǒ yào dào běijīng qù xuéxí
I am going to study in Beijing for the first two months next year.

头三次我们都输了。 **tóu sān cì wǒmen dōu shū le**
The first three times we lost.

As we can see from these examples, a duration or frequency expression used in
this way is usually preceded by a demonstrative or specifying adjective. A
duration expression may also be followed by the word 来 **lái** 'till now', which
confirms that it indicates point of time:

| 这一年来 | **zhèi yī nián lái** | in this last year |
| 两个月来 | **liǎng ge yuè lái** | in the last two months |

7.2 DURATION

Duration expressions refer to the length of time a particular action lasts. Logically speaking, the duration will not become known until the action concerned
has taken place and it will naturally be of indefinite reference. A duration expression therefore is normally positioned post-verbally as a complement.

我们在巴黎待了一个星期。 **wǒmen zài bālí dāi le yī ge xīngqī**
We stayed in Paris for a week.

---

[1] See §§7.2 and 7.4 below.

会议继续了一个多小时。 **huìyì jìxù le yī ge duō xiǎoshí**
The meeting continued for over an hour.

我们要等多少时间? **wǒmen yào děng duōshǎo shíjiān**
How long will we have to wait?

If the verb is a transitive verb with an inanimate object or an intransitive verb with an internal 'verb + object' structure, the duration expression is positioned between the verb and the object. Grammatically, the duration expression is now no longer a complement of the verb in question but an attributive to the noun object. Under such circumstances, the attributive indicator 的 **de** may be optionally incorporated:

我学了两年(的)中文。 **wǒ xué le liǎng nián (de) zhōngwén**
I studied Chinese for two years.

我们跳了三个小时(的)舞。 **wǒmen tiào le sān ge xiǎoshí (de) wǔ**
We danced for three hours.

我们聊了一个晚上(的)天。 **wǒmen liáo le yī ge wǎnshàng (de) tiān**
We chatted for a whole evening.

If the object is a human or other animate being or is a pronoun, the duration complement comes after the noun object:

警察盘问了那个小偷三天三夜。
jǐngchá pánwèn le nèi ge xiǎotōu sān tiān sān yè
The police interrogated that petty thief for three days and nights.

校长训了那个调皮的小学生半个钟头。
xiàozhǎng xùn le nèi ge tiáopí de xiǎoxuésheng bàn ge zhōngtóu
The headteacher gave a telling-off to that mischievous pupil for half an hour.

爸爸在经济上支持了我两年。
bàba zài jīngjì shàng zhīchí le wǒ liǎng nián
Father supported me financially for two years.

However, if the focus is divided between the object and the duration, that is, if the construction is bifocal, the verb is repeated after the verb–object and the duration complement comes after the repeated verb:

我们跳舞就(跳)了三个小时。 **wǒmen tiàowǔ (jiù) tiào le sān ge xiǎoshí**
We (actually) danced for three hours.

我们(光是)聊天(就)聊了一个晚上。
wǒmen (guāng shì) liáotiān (jiù) liáo le yī ge wǎnshang
We simply chatted the whole evening.

校长训那个调皮的学生训了半个钟头。
xiàozhǎng xùn nèi ge tiǎopí de xuésheng xùn le bàn ge zhōngtóu
The headteacher gave a telling-off to that mischievous pupil for (all of) half an hour.

爸爸在经济上支持我支持了两年。
bàba zài jīngjì shàng zhīchí wǒ zhīchí le liǎng nián
Father gave me financial support for (a period of) two years.

A range of duration expressions is given below. It is important to note that some of them take the measure word 个 *gè* when associated with numerals while others do not. This stems from the fact that in some cases the duration expressions are derived from original nouns while in others they are measures themselves.

duration expression	with or without measure word 个 gè	example	English translation
年 **nián** 'year'	–	一年 **yī nián**	one year
月 **yuè** 'month'	+	两个月 **liáng ge yuè**	two months
日 **rì** 'day' (class.) 天 **tiān** 'day' (colloq.)	– –	三日 **sān rì** 三天 **sān tián**	three days three days
星期 **xīngqī** 'week' (neu.) 礼拜 **lǐbài** 'week' (infrml.)	± +	四(个)星期 **sì (ge) xīngqī** 四个礼拜 **sì ge lǐbài**	four weeks four weeks
小时 **xiǎoshí** 'hour' (neut.) 钟头 **zhōngtóu** 'hour' (infrml.)	± +	半(个)小时 **bàn (ge) xiǎoshí** 半个钟头 **bàn ge zhōngtóu**	half an hour half an hour
刻钟 **kè (zhōng)** 'quarter of an hour'	–	一刻钟 **yī kè (zhōng)**	a quarter of an hour
分钟 **fēn zhōng** 'minute'	–	五分钟 **wǔ fēn zhōng**	five minutes
秒(钟) **miǎo (zhōng)** 'second'	–	六秒(钟) **liù miǎo (zhōng)**	six seconds
上午 **shàngwǔ** 'morning'	+	整个上午 **zhěng ge shàngwǔ**	the whole morning
中午 **zhōngwǔ** 'noon'	+	两个中午 **liǎng ge zhōngwǔ**	two noons
下午 **xiàwǔ** 'afternoon'	+	半个下午 **bàn ge xiàwǔ**	half the afternoon
晚上 **wǎnshang** 'evening'	+	整个晚上 **zhěng ge wǎnshang**	the whole evening
夜 **yè** 'night'	–	整夜 **zhěng yè**	the whole night

7.3 BRIEF DURATION

Brief duration expressions take a few specific forms in Chinese. They indicate short periods of time and are generally placed after the verb like other duration expressions. They are associated with the numeral 一 **yī** 'one', and the two most common are: 一会儿 **yīhuìr** 'a little while' and 一下 **yīxià** 'briefly, a bit'. The difference between the two expressions is that the former focuses on the duration while the latter focuses on the action itself. For example:

我在他家坐了一会儿。 **wǒ zài tā jiā zuò le yīhuìr**
I sat for a while in his place.

他随随便便地看了一下。 **tā suísuíbiànbiàn de kàn le yīxià**
He casually gave it a look./He gave it a cursory glance.

If there is a nominal object in the sentence, the brief duration expression, like other duration expressions, is placed between the verb and the object:

我们聊了一会儿天。 **wǒmen liáo le yīhuìr tiān**
We chatted for a while.

她梳了一下头。 **tā shū le yīxià tóu**
She gave her hair a comb.

他们研究了一下那个问题。 **tāmen yánjiū le yīxià nèi ge wèntí**
They gave some thought to that question.

If the object is pronominal, the brief duration expression usually comes after the object:

他在胳膊上轻轻地碰了我一下。
tā zài gēbo shàng qīngqīng de pèng le wǒ yīxià
He touched me lightly on the arm.

If the object is animate, the brief duration expression may come either before or after the object:

妈妈吻了她的孩子一下。 **māma wěn le tāde háizi yīxià**

or

妈妈吻了一下她的孩子。 **māma wěn le yīxià tāde háizi**
Mother gave her child a kiss.

An alternative way to indicate brief duration is to repeat the verb. In a narrative sentence relating a past completed action, 了 *le* is inserted after the first verb. This, however, is only possible with a monosyllabic verb.[2] The verb may take an object, but, if so, only the verb is repeated:

她笑了笑。 **tā xiào le xiào**
She gave a smile.

她梳了梳头。 **tā shū le shū tóu**
She gave her hair a comb.

他在胳膊上轻轻地碰了碰我。
tā zài gēbo shàng qīngqīng de pèng le pèng wǒ
He touched me lightly on the arm.

*我们研究了研究那个问题。 **wǒmen yánjiū le yánjiū nèi ge wèntí**
*We gave some thought to that question.

In an expository sentence, where the brief activity is habitual or regular, 了 *le* is not needed:

星期天我们常到公园里去走走。
xīngqītiān wǒmen cháng dào gōngyuán li qù zǒuzou
We often go for a walk in the park on Sunday.

她每天都拿出他的照片来看一看。
tā měitiān dōu ná chū tāde zhàopiàn lái kàn yī kàn
Every day she took out his photograph to look at.

However, in questions or imperatives requiring further action, both monosyllabic and disyllabic verbs may be repeated to indicate brief duration. With disyllabic verbs, there is a simple repetition; but with monosyllabic verbs, the repetition may incorporate the numeral 一 **yī**.

咱们先休息休息。 **zánmen xiān xiūxi xiūxi**
We'll have a rest first.

咱们能好好地研究研究这个问题吗?
zánmen néng hǎohāo de yánjiū yánjiū zhèi ge wèntí ma
Can we give some proper thought to this question?

---

[2] In a narrative sentence with 了 *le*, a disyllabic verb cannot be repeated to mean brief duration: it may only use the brief duration expression 一下 **yīxià**.

请你等(一)等！ **qǐng nǐ děng (yī) děng**
Please wait a moment.

让我看(一)看！ **ràng wǒ kàn (yī) kàn**
Let me have a look.

你来尝(一)尝！ **nǐ lái cháng (yī) cháng**
Come and have a taste.

你也想试(一)试吗？ **nǐ yě xiǎng shì (yī) shì ma**
Would you like to have a try too?

The repetition brief duration construction also implies a degree of eagerness on the part of the speaker:

你猜猜谁来了！ **nǐ cāicai | shéi lái le**
Have a guess who's come!

你们见过面没有？我来介绍介绍。
nǐmen jiàn guo miàn méiyǒu | wǒ lái jièshao jièshao
Have you two met before? I'll introduce you to each other.

你有空就弹弹钢琴吧。 **nǐ yǒukòng jiù tántan gāngqín ba**
Have a go on the piano when you've got time.

Involuntary action verbs or verbs that indicate actions or situations beyond one's control, however, cannot be reduplicated. For example, one cannot say:

*你害怕害怕！　　 **nǐ hàipà hàipà**　　 *Be afraid!

Nor can brief duration reduplication occur with a negative:

*不要哭哭！ 　　 **bù yào kūku**　　 *Don't cry!
*别动动！ 　　 **bié dòngdong**　　 *Don't move!

7.4 FREQUENCY

Frequency expressions in Chinese are generally monosyllabic. They refer to the number of times an action takes place, and like duration expressions, become known only when the action has taken place. They therefore naturally come after the verb, and the most common are: 次 **cì**, 回 **huí**, 遍 **biàn** and 趟 **tàng**. They all mean 'time(s)', but 遍 **biàn** implies 'from beginning to end' and 趟 **tàng** refers to 'trips or journeys'.

这个问题我们讨论了两次。 **zhèi ge wèntí wǒmen tǎolùn le liǎng cì**
We discussed this question twice.

那篇课文我复习了三遍。 **nèi piān kèwén wǒ fùxí le sān biàn**
I revised that lesson three times.

那个人我见过几回。[3] **nèi ge rén wǒ jiàn guo jǐ huí**
I have met that man a few times.

北京我去过两趟。 **běijīng wǒ qù guo liǎng tàng**
I have been to Beijing twice.

If the verb, whether transitive or intransitive, has a nominal object, the frequency expression, like a duration expression, will generally have to go between the verb and the object:

我们见过两次面。 **wǒmen jiàn guo liǎng cì miàn**
We have met twice.

我复习了三遍课文。 **wǒ fùxí le sān biàn kèwén**
I revised the lesson three times.

If the object is a location, the frequency expression may go before or after it:

我去过两趟北京。 **wǒ qù guo liǎng tàng běijīng**
我去过北京两趟。 **wǒ qù guo běijīng liǎng tàng**
I've been to Beijing twice.

If the object is a pronoun or a human noun, the frequency expression must follow it:

我见过他两次。 **wǒ jiàn guo tā liǎng cì**
I have met him twice.

他们拜访了他们的老师三趟。 **tāmen bàifǎng le tāmen de lǎoshī sān tàng**
They visited their teacher three times.

*我见过两次他。 **wǒ jiàn guo liǎng cì tā**
*I have met him twice.

*他们拜访了三趟他们的老师。 **tāmen bàifǎng le sān tàng tāmende lǎoshī**
*They have visited their teacher three times.

---

[3] 过 **guo** 'have had the experience of' is an expository indicator. See §6.9.4.

7.5 每 **měi** 'every'

The adjective 每 **měi** 'every', like a numeral, indicates exclusive time reference, and it precedes a time noun with or without a measure word.[4] 每 **měi** is positioned pre-verbally, either at the beginning of the sentence or immediately after the subject, and it is often echoed by the monosyllabic adverb 都 **dōu** 'in every instance', which comes immediately before the verb:

我每天都去上课。 **wǒ měitiān dōu qù shàngkè**
I go to class every day.

李家每年都去瑞士旅游。 **lǐ jiā měi nián dōu qù ruìshì lǚyóu**
The Li family goes touring in Switzerland every year.

她每个星期都买彩卷。 **tā měi ge xīngqī dōu mǎi cǎiquàn**
She buys lottery tickets every week.

7.6 OTHER TIME EXPRESSIONS

In previous sections, we have looked at point of time, specified duration, brief duration, frequency and exclusive repetition. There are however other non-specific time expressions that are adverbial rather than nominal and indicate concepts like 'immediately', 'gradually', 'punctually', 'all along', 'constantly', 'always', 'regularly', 'already', 'finally', 'suddenly', and so on. These adverbs are invariably placed before the verb:[5]

他马上赶去学校。 **tā mǎshàng gǎn qù xuéxiào**   (narrative)
He immediately hurried off to school.

孩子渐渐长大了。 **háizi jiànjiàn zhǎngdà le**   (le-expository)
The child gradually grew up.

他们如期到达目的地。 **tāmen rúqī dàodá mùdìdì**   (narrative)
They reached their destination on time.

她是素食者，从(来)不吃肉。[6]
tā shì sùshízhě | cóng (lái) bù chī ròu   (expository)
She is a vegetarian and has never (all along not) eaten meat.

---

[4] See the table of time nouns in §7.2 on duration.
[5] Most of these adverbs can be used in all types of sentence, but some, specifying point of time, are by definition found most commnoly in narrative sentences, and others, implying change or passage of time, will tend to occur more often in expository sentences. See Chapter 20 on sentence types.
[6] Time adverbs like 从来 **cónglái** and 向来 **xiànglái** 'all along, always' are invariably followed by negators like 不 **bù** 'not', etc.

我们<u>无时无刻</u>不在想念他。 (descriptive)
wǒmen <u>wúshí wúkè</u> bù zài xiǎngniàn tā
We think about him <u>all the time/constantly</u>.

我<u>永远</u>记住您的话。 **wǒ <u>yǒngyuǎn</u> jìzhù nínde huà** (expository)
I'll <u>always</u> remember your words/what you said.

我女儿<u>经常</u>来探望我们。 (expository)
wǒ nǚ'ér <u>jīngcháng</u> lái tànwàng wǒmen
My daughter <u>regularly</u> comes to visit us.

他<u>已经</u>离开上海了。 **tā <u>yǐjīng</u> líkāi shànghǎi le** (*le*-expository)
He has <u>already</u> left Shanghai.

他们<u>终于</u>成功了。 **tāmen <u>zhōngyú</u> chénggōng le** (*le*-expository)
They were successful <u>in the end</u>.

奶奶<u>突然</u>晕倒了。 **nǎinai <u>tùrán</u> yūndǎo le** (*le*-expository)
Grandma <u>suddenly</u> fainted.

Similar adverbs include:

已经 **yǐjīng** 'already', 常常 **chángcháng** 'often', 立刻 **lìkè** 'immediately', 立即 **lìjí** 'at once', 及时 **jíshí** 'in time', 赶快 **gǎnkuài** 'in a hurry', 逐渐 **zhújiàn** 'gradually', 慢慢 **mànmàn** 'slowly', 临时 **línshí** 'temporarily', 预先 **yùxiān** 'in advance', 首先 **shǒuxiān** 'first of all', 准时 **zhǔnshí** 'on time', 按时 **ànshí** 'on schedule', 一再 **yīzài** 'again and again', 一向 **yīxiàng** 'all along', 不断 **bùduàn** 'constantly', 一直 **yīzhí** 'always, all along', 随时 **suíshí** 'at any time', 曾经 **céngjīng** 'at one time', 刚刚 **gānggāng** 'just now', 接着 **jiēzhe** 'after that', 就要 **jiùyào** 'soon'.

7.7   NEGATION AND TIME REFERENCE

In Chinese, the particular negator used to negate an action verb is often determined with reference to time and intention.

There are two negators of action verbs in Chinese: 不 **bù** and 没(有) **méi(yǒu)**. 不 **bù** mainly negates habitual and intended action, while 没(有) **méi(yǒu)** indicates that an action has not taken place or been completed. In general this means that 不 **bù** is largely associated with expository sentences and 没(有) **méi(yǒu)** with narrative sentences.

7.7.1   NEGATIVE EXPOSITORY SENTENCES

不 **bù** negating habitual actions (past, present or future):

他常常不上班。 **tā chángcháng bù shàngbān**
He often doesn't go to work.

他以前常常不上班。 **tā yǐqián chángcháng bù shàngbān**
In the past he often didn't go to work.

我怕他将来也常常不上班。
wǒ pà tā jiānglái yě chángcháng bù shàngbān
I'm afraid in the future he won't often go to work.

不 **bù** as a negator of intention and future action:

我明天不去开会。 **wǒ míngtiān bù qù kāihuì**
I will not go to the meeting tomorrow.

我不买那么贵的书。 **wǒ bù mǎi nàme guì de shū**
I won't buy a book as expensive as that.

Note that with unintentional actions 不 **bù** cannot be used:

*明天不下雨。[7] **míngtiān bù xià yǔ**
*It will not rain tomorrow.

7.7.2 NEGATIVE NARRATIVE SENTENCES

没(有) **méi(yǒu)** negating action that has not taken place:

他昨天没(有)来。 **tā zuótiān méi(yǒu) lái**
He did not come yesterday.

我们没(有)在那儿住两个月。 **wǒmen méi (yǒu) zài nàr zhù liǎng ge yuè**
We did not stay there for two months.

那天她没(有)吃三次药。 **nèi tiān tā méi (yǒu) chī sān cì yào**
That day she did not take her three doses of medicine.

If a past action did not take place as a result of deliberate non-action on the part of the subject, the negator 不 **bù** is used. A sentence like this is in fact expository:

他昨天(故意)不来。 **tā zuótiān (gùyì) bù lái**
He (deliberately) would not come yesterday.

---

[7] In a conditional clause, however, 不 **bù** may be used to indicate possibility rather than intention, and hence it is correct to say: 如果明天不下雨，球赛照常进行。 **rúguǒ míngtiān bù xiàyǔ | qiúsài zhàocháng jìnxíng** 'The match will go ahead tomorrow as scheduled if it doesn't rain'.

那年我们不(打算)在那儿住两个月。
nèi nián wǒmen bù (dǎsuan) zài nàr zhù liǎng ge yuè
That year we would not (i.e. we had no intention to) stay there for two
months.

那天她(决定)不吃三次药。 **nèi tiān tā (juédìng) bù chī sān cì yào**
That day she would not (i.e. she was determined not to) take her three
doses of medicine.

没(有) **méi(yǒu)** also occurs in expository sentences in particular circumstances:

(**a**) with the experiential verb suffix 过 **guo**:

我没(有)看过那本小说。 **wǒ méi(yǒu) kàn guo nèi běn xiǎoshuō**
I haven't read that novel.

他们没(有)去过美国。 **tāmen méi(yǒu) qù guo měiguó**
They have not been to America.

(**b**) in conjunction with the adverb 还 **hái** 'still, yet':

我还没(有)写完我的论文。 **wǒ hái méi(yǒu) xiě wán wǒ de lùnwén**
I haven't finished my thesis yet.

他们还没(有)作出决定。 **tāmen hái méi(yǒu) zuò chū juédìng**
They still have not come to a decision.

7.7.3 NEGATIVE DESCRIPTIVE SENTENCES

In descriptive sentences which are characterised by the presence of the continuation aspect marker 在 **zài**, 不 **bù** is normally used but 没(有) **méi(yǒu)** also
occurs, particularly when the reference is to a past unrealised action. The difference between them is that 没(有) **méi(yǒu)** is simply factual and objective while
不 **bù** implies a degree of intention:

昨天上午我没(有)在打球。 **zuótiān shàngwǔ wǒ méi(yǒu) zài dǎqiú**

or

昨天上午我不在打球。 **zuótiān shàngwǔ wǒ bù zài dǎqiú**
I wasn't playing any ball games yesterday morning.

In fact the distinction between these two sentences is that the first is descriptive
and the second expository.

8 ACTION VERBS AND LOCATIONS

Actions may be associated not only with time but also with location. In this chapter, we will look at the ways in which expressions of location, direction and destination in Chinese are linked with action verbs.

8.1 LOCATION EXPRESSIONS AND POSITION INDICATORS

In Chinese, location expressions are usually formed by placing one of the **position indicators** listed below after a noun. These position indicators have monosyllabic and disyllabic alternatives and the monosyllabic ones are known as postpositions (as opposed to prepositions). The disyllabic (and polysyllabic – see the second table below) forms can be location expressions in their own right.

meaning	postpositions colloq.	+ 面 mian neut.	+ 边 bian colloq.	+ 头 tou more colloq.	+ 方 fāng frml.
above; on	上 **shàng**	上面 **shàngmian**	上边 **shàngbian**	上头 **shàngtou**	上方 **shàngfāng**
below; under	下 **xià**	下面 **xiàmian**	下边 **xiàbian**	下头 **xiàtou**	下方 **xiàfāng**
inside; in	里[1] **lǐ**	里面 **lǐmian**	里边 **lǐbian**	里头 **lǐtou**	
outside	外 **wài**	外面 **wàimian**	外边 **wàibian**	外头 **wàitou**	
before; in front	前 **qián**	前面 **qiánmian**	前边 **qiánbian**	前头 **qiántou**	
behind	后 **hòu**	后面 **hòumian**	后边 **hòubian**	后头 **hòutou**	
left-hand side		左面 **zuǒmian**	左边 **zuǒbian**		左方 **zuǒfāng**
right-hand side		右面 **yòumian**	右边 **yòubian**		右方 **yòufāng**

In addition there are: 旁 **páng**/旁边 **pángbian** 'by the side of', 边 **bian** 'at the edge of', 底下 **dǐxia** 'directly under', 中 **zhōng**/中间 **zhōngjiān** 'in the middle of', 对面 **duìmiàn** 'opposite', 附近 **fùjìn** 'nearby', 隔壁 **gébì** 'next door to', 四周 **sìzhōu**/周围 **zhōuwéi** 'all round', 之间 **zhī jiān** 'among, between'.

For larger areas like a country, a city, etc., there are the following additional possibilities:

---

[1] There is a classical equivalent of 里 **li**, 内 **nèi**, which is generally used with more abstract notions, e.g. 范围内 **fànwéi nèi** 'within the scope'.

meaning	+ 部 bù neut.	+ 面 mian neut.	+ 边 bian colloq.	+ 方 fāng frml.
east of	东部 dōngbù	东面 dōngmian	东边 dōngbian	东方 dōngfāng
south of	南部 nánbù	南面 nánmian	南边 nánbian	南方 nánfāng
west of	西部 xībù	西面 xīmian	西边 xībian	西方 xīfāng
north of	北部 běibù	北面 běimian	北边 běibian	北方 běifāng
southeast of	东南部 dōngnánbù	东南面 dōngnánmian	东南边 dōngnánbian	东南方 dōngnánfāng
northeast of	东北部 dōngběibù	东北面 dōngběimian	东北边 dōngběibian	东北方 dōngběifāng
southwest of	西南部 xīnánbù	西南面 xīnánmian	西南边 xīnánbian	西南方 xīnánfāng
northwest of	西北部 xīběibù	西北面 xīběimian	西北边 xīběibian	西北方 xīběifāng

The position indication with 部 **bù** mean 'in the east of', 'in the south of', etc., while those with 面 **mian**, 边 **bian** and 方 **fāng** mean 'to the east of', 'to the south of', etc.

Here are some examples of location expressions:

桌子上	**zhuōzi shàng**	on the table
桌子上面	**zhuōzi shàngmian**	
桌子上边	**zhuōzi shàngbian**	
桌子上头	**zhuōzi shàngtou**	
桌子上方	**zhuōzi shàngfāng**	

树下	**shù xià**	under the tree
树下面	**shù xiàmian**	
树下边	**shù xiàbian**	
树下头	**shù xiàtou**	
树底下	**shù dǐxia**	

屋子里	**wūzi li**	in the room
屋子里面	**wūzi lǐmian**	
屋子里边	**wūzi lǐbian**	
屋子里头	**wūzi lǐtou**	

湖旁	**hú páng**	by the side of the lake
湖旁边	**hú pángbian**	
湖边	**hú bian**	

中国东部	**zhōngguó dōngbù**	in the east of China

中国东方	**zhōngguó dōngfāng**	to the east of China
中国东面	**zhōngguó dōngmian**	
中国东边	**zhōngguó dōngbian**	

大学对面	**dàxué duìmiàn**	opposite the university
商店附近	**shāngdiàn fùjìn**	near the shop
两棵树之间	**liǎng kē shù zhījiān**	between the two trees
公园四周	**gōngyuán sìzhōu**	all round the park

8.2 在 **zài** WITH LOCATION EXPRESSIONS

To indicate location, the preposition or coverb[2] 在 **zài** '(exist) in or at' usually combines with a location expression.

The 在 **zài** coverbal phrase can be positioned earlier or later in a sentence depending on the meaning it contracts with the verb. It comes before the verb if the initiator of the action (usually the subject) has to be at a particular location before the action can be carried out and it is placed post-verbally if the location indicates the position a particular being or object reaches following the action expressed in the verb. In other words, a pre-verbal location expression is usually concerned with the whereabouts of the subject (the initiator of the action) and a post-verbal location expression is more often than not concerned with the whereabouts of the object (which is usually topicalised).[3] We will discuss the complemental (post-verbal) use of location expressions in §8.4 below, but here we are concerned with the adverbial use of location expressions with 在 **zài**, which come between the subject and the verb:

学生们都在图书馆(里)看书。 **xuéshengmen dōu zài túshūguǎn (li) kànshū**
The students are all reading in the library.

运动员们在操场上跑步。 **yùndòngyuánmen zài cāochǎng shàng pǎobù**
The athletes are running on the sportsground.

有不少人在海里游泳。 **yǒu bùshǎo rén zài hǎi lǐ yóuyǒng**
There are quite a few people swimming in the sea.

雪花在空中飞舞。 **xuěhuā zài kōng zhōng fēiwǔ**
The snowflakes are dancing in the air.

我在旧书店外边碰见了一个老朋友。
wǒ zài jiù shūdiàn wàibian pèngjiàn le yī ge lǎo péngyou
I bumped into an old friend outside the second-hand bookshop.

有许多外国商人在中国东南部建立了企业。
yǒu xǔduō wàiguó shāngrén zài zhōngguó dōngnánbù jiànlì le qǐyè
Many foreign traders set up businesses in southeast China.

---

[2] Coverbs have already been mentioned in §6.5 and they will be discussed in detail in Chapter 11.
[3] The object is regularly brought forward before the verb or topicalised through use of the 把 **bǎ** or notional passive construction, see Chapters 12 and 13.

If the main verb is monosyllabic or does not have an object, the descriptive marker 着 *zhe* will have to be added to obtain a disyllabic rhythm:[4]

鸟儿在树上吱吱喳喳地叫着。
niǎor zài shù shàng zhīzhīzhāzhā de jiào zhe
The birds are chattering in the trees.

小猫在火炉旁睡着。 **xiǎo māo zài huǒlú páng shuì zhe**
The kitten is dozing beside the stove.

洗好的衣服都在晾衣绳上晾着。
xǐ hǎo de yīfu dōu zài liàngyīshéng shàng liàng zhe
The clothes are drying on the line.

金鱼在鱼缸里不停地游着。 **jīnyú zài yúgāng li bùtíng de yóu zhe**
The goldfish swims unceasingly round its tank/bowl.

有两个卫兵在门口(旁)[5]站着。
yǒu liǎng ge wèibīng zài ménkǒu (páng) zhàn zhe
There are two guards standing at the entrance.

Though the addition of 着 *zhe* 'exist continuously in a particular manner' is motivated by rhythm, the sentence with its presence becomes even more descriptive. This point will be picked up again in Chapter 21.

8.3 LOCATION EXPRESSIONS AS SENTENCE TERMINATORS

If a location expression indicates the result of an action, it naturally comes after the verb. In other words, if a location expression emphasises the position the subject (the initiator of the action) or the topic (generally the notional object of the action) eventually reaches following the execution of the action implied in the verb, it is only natural for the location expression to come after the verb. Under such circumstances, the expression is always preceded by 在 *zài* 'at; in; on', etc. Location expressions as sentence terminators are particularly common with 把 *bǎ* constructions or with **notional passives**.[6] For example,

他把大衣挂在衣架上。 **tā bǎ dàyī guà zài yījià shàng**
He hung [his] overcoat on the coat hanger/stand.

---

[4] Monosyllabic rhythm may be possible in imperatives, e.g. 你在这儿等 **nǐ zài zhèr děng**, 'Would you wait here', 请在前面坐 **qǐng zài qiánmiàn zuò** 'Please sit at the front'.

[5] Disyllabic or trisyllabic nouns may combine with 在 *zài* to form location expressions without postpositions, e.g. 在图书馆 **zài túshūguǎn** 'in the library', 在门口 **zài ménkǒu** 'at the entrance' if there is no ambiguity as to the actual whereabouts.

[6] See Chapter 12 for 把 *bǎ* constructions and Chapter 13 for notional passives.

妈妈把妹妹抱在怀里。 **māma bǎ mèimei bào zài huái li**
Mother took/held younger sister in her arms.

爸爸把汽车停在路边。 **bàba bǎ qìchē tíng zài lùbian**
Father parked the car at the roadside.

钱都存在银行里。 **qián dōu cún zài yínháng li**
The money is all deposited in the bank.

信息都存在软盘上。 **xìnxī dōu cún zài ruǎnpán shàng**
The information is all stored on the floppy (disk).

游客们都躺在树荫下。 **yóukèmen dōu tǎng zài shùyīn xià**
The visitors all lay down in the shade of the tree(s).

客人们都站在房子前面。 **kèrenmen dōu zhàn zài fángzi qiánmian**
The guests all stood in front of the house.

If the emphasis is the verb itself, the location expression becomes a coverbal phrase. For example, the last three examples may be reworded as:

信息都在软盘上存着。 **xìnxī dōu zài ruǎnpán shàng cún zhe**
The information is being stored on the floppy (disk).

游客们都在树荫下躺着。 **yóukèmen dōu zài shùyīn xià tǎng zhe**
The visitors are all lying in the shade of the tree(s).

客人们都在房子前面站着。 **kèrenmen dōu zài fángzi qiánmian zhàn zhe**
The guests are all standing in front of the house.

We can see that the post-verbal complemental use of the location expression focuses on the location while the pre-verbal adverbial use of the location expression focuses on the action itself. The only case where the alternative structures do not make any difference in meaning is the use of verbs like 住 **zhù** 'to live'. However, there will be a difference in their function: the former is a descriptive (with a 在 **zài** location phrase) while the latter an expository (with an unmarked verb):

他们住在伦敦。 **tāmen zhù zài lúndūn**
他们在伦敦住。[7] **tāmen zài lúndūn zhù**
They live in London.

---

[7] Note that in this case 住 **zhù** 'to live; to stay' is used monosyllabically without the addition of 着 *zhe*, or it would be a descriptive sentence again.

8.4 LOCATION EXPRESSIONS AS SENTENCE BEGINNERS

Location expressions in a sentence naturally indicate places which the speaker/writer is sure about, and, like point of time expressions, they are of definite reference. As we have seen, expressions of definite reference come before the verb, and location expressions are naturally found as coverbal phrases placed pre-verbally (e.g. the 在 **zài** phrases seen above) or as sentence beginners.[8] An expository sentence which states that 'there is something somewhere' is therefore often couched in Chinese as 'somewhere has that something'. For example, 'there is a book on the table' will have to become literally 'the top of the table has a book', 桌子上面有一本书 **zhuōzi shàngmian yǒu yī běn shū**. Similarly:

箱子里有不少新衬衫。 **xiāngzi li yǒu bùshǎo xīn chènshān**
There are quite a few new shirts in the case/box.

冰箱里还有橘子水。 **bīngxiāng li háiyǒu júzishuǐ**
There is also orange juice in the fridge.

书架上只有一本书。 **shūjià shàng zhǐyǒu yī běn shū**
There is only one book on the bookcase.

行李架上没有行李。 **xínglijià shàng méiyǒu xíngli**
There is no luggage on the luggage rack.

房子后面有一个小菜园。 **fángzi hòumian yǒu yī ge xiǎo càiyuán**
There is a small vegetable garden behind the house.

The verb 有 **yǒu** 'to have' may be replaced by an action verb marked by 着 *zhe* or 了 *le* so that what is indicated is not just that somewhere something exists but also in what fashion or manner something came to exist:

墙上挂着/了一幅画儿。 **qiáng shàng guà zhe/le yī fú huàr**
There is/was a picture hanging on the wall.

餐桌上放着/了十分精致的餐具。
cānzhuō shàng fàng zhe/le shífēn jīngzhì de cānjù
On the table is/was laid out an extemely fine dinner service.

花瓶里插着/了鲜花。 **huāpíng li chā zhe/le xiānhuā**
There are/were flowers (arranged/placed) in the vase.

---

[8] 在 **zài** does not usually occur with sentence beginners. For example, 他在图书馆看书。 **tā zài túshūguǎn kàn shū** 'He is reading in the library' vs 图书馆有很多中文书。 **túshūguǎn yǒu hěn duō zhōngwén shū** 'There are a lot of Chinese books in the library'. If 在 **zài** is present with a sentence beginner, it conveys an emphatic tone: e.g. 在车站外边有一个大铜像。 **zài chēzhàn wàibian yǒu yī ge dà tóngxiàng** 'Outside the station is a large bronze statue'.

The difference between 着 *zhe* and 了 *le* is that the former is more descriptive and the latter more narrative.

To indicate that something is the sole or dominant occupant of a particular place, 是 **shì** 'to be' is often used instead of 有 **yǒu** 'to have':

花园里到处都是野草。 **huāyuán li dàochù dōu shì yěcǎo**
Everywhere in the garden are weeds.

屋子里都是烟。 **wūzi li dōu shì yān**
The room is full of smoke.

大学入口处旁边是一个大钟楼。
dàxué rùkǒuchù pángbian shì yī ge dà zhōnglóu
Beside the entrance to the university is a large clock tower.

Similarly, an action verb can be used in this sense provided it is followed immediately by the monosyllabic complement 满 **mǎn** 'full of' and is marked by 了 **le**:

花园里到处长满了野草。 **huāyuán li dàochù zhǎng mǎn le yěcǎo**
Everywhere in the garden has grown full of weeds.

屋子里充满了烟雾。 **wūzi li chōngmǎn le yānwù**
The room is full of smoke.

汽车里挤满了人。 **qìchē li jǐ mǎn le rén**
The bus/car was crammed with people.

抽屉里塞满了旧报纸。 **chōuti li sāi mǎn le jiù bàozhǐ**
The drawer is/was stuffed (full) with old newspapers.

桌子上堆满了书。 **zhuōzi shàng duī mǎn le shū**
The table is/was piled high with books.

If the action verb indicates movement, the notion of existence gives way to that of **emergence** or **disappearance**. When this happens, complements indicating direction or result[9] have to be incorporated before the marker 了 *le* is added.

海面上飞来了一群海鸥。 **hǎimian shàng fēi lái le yī qún hǎi'ōu**
A flock of gulls came flying over the sea.

地平线上升起了一道黑烟。 **dìpíngxiàn shàng shēng qǐ le yī dào hēiyān**
A thread of black smoke rose on the horizon.

---

[9] See §§8.5.1 and 8.5.2 for direction complements; see Chapter 10 for result complements.

后面传来了一阵阵的警笛声。

hòumian chuán lái le yī zhènzhèn de jǐngdí shēng

From behind came the sound of police whistles one after another.

监狱里跑掉了两个犯人。 **jiānyù li pǎo diào le liǎng ge fànrén**

Two prisoners/convicts escaped from the prison.

8.5 DIRECTION INDICATORS

Direction indicator is a term used broadly to refer to a small set of verbs, which can be used as movement verbs on their own, or can be attached to other action verbs to indicate direction of movement or the beginning of a process involving the action. The set can be divided into two subsets, forming two tiers of possible attachment to an action verb.

8.5.1 SIMPLE DIRECTION INDICATORS
来 **lái** 'to come' and 去 **qù** 'to go'

来 **lái** 'to come' and 去 **qù** 'to go' are the two simple direction indicators on which other disyllabic direction indicators are built. 来 **lái** 'to come' indicates direction towards the speaker and 去 **qù** 'to go' away from the speaker:[10]

爷爷回来了[11]。 **yéye huí lái le**

(lit. Grandpa return come *le*) Grandpa has come/came back.

爷爷回去了 **yéye huí qù le**

(lit. Grandpa return go *le*) Grandpa has gone/went back.

If there is a location object, it is placed between the verb and its direction indicator:

爷爷回家来了。 **yéye huí jiā lái le**

(lit. Grandpa return home come *le*) Grandpa has come home.

爷爷出国去了。 **yéye chūguó qù le**

(lit. Grandpa exit country go *le*) Grandpa has gone abroad.

If there is a physical object, it comes after the verb, either before or after the direction indicator:

---

[10] 来 **lái/lai** 'to come' and 去 **qù/qu** 'to go' on their own and in other particular combinations may also respectively indicate related notions such as 'coming into, or disappearing from, view', 'regaining or losing consciousness'. These uses will be discussed below.

[11] Full discussion of the end-of-sentence particle 了 *le* can be found in Chapter 21.

爷爷带了一瓶酒来。 **yéye dài le yī píng jiǔ lái**
Grandpa brought a bottle of wine.

爷爷带来了一瓶酒。 **yéye dài lái le yī píng jiǔ**
Grandpa brought a bottle of wine.

8.5.2 DISYLLABIC DIRECTION INDICATORS

来 **lái** 'to come' and 去 **qù** 'to go' are combined with a set of movement verbs[12] to form disyllabic direction indicators, which are attached to a verb to indicate more precise directions:

		来 lai towards	去 qu away from
上 **shàng**	up	上来 **shànglai**	上去 **shàngqu**
下 **xià**	down	下来 **xiàlai**	下去 **xiàqu**
进 **jìn**	in(to)	进来 **jìnlai**	进去 **jìnqu**
出 **chū**	out (of)	出来 **chūlai**	出去 **chūqu**
过 **guò**	across/over	过来 **guòlai**	过去 **guòqu**
回 **huí**	back	回来 **huílai**	回去 **huíqu**
开 **kāi**	away	开来 **kāilai**	开去 **kāiqu**
起 **qǐ**	upward	起来 **qǐlai**	*起去 *qǐqu[13]

For example:

登山运动员爬上来了。 **dēngshān yùndòngyuán pá shànglai le**
The mountaineers have climbed up. (towards the speaker–observer above)

登山运动员爬上去了。 **dēngshān yùndòngyuán pá shàngqu le**
The mountaineers have climbed up. (away from the speaker–observer below)

If the sentence is narrative rather than expository (see Chapter 20), the completed action aspect marker 了 *le* comes after the verb and before the direction indicator:

---

[12] These direction indicators also constitute motion verbs themselves, e.g. 回来 **huílái** 'come back', 下去 **xiàqù** 'go down', 进来 **jìnlái** 'come in', 过去 **guòqù** 'go over', etc. (see examples under §8.5.1).
[13] The combination of 起去 **qǐqu** is no longer used.

登山运动员爬了上来。 **dēngshān yùndòngyuán pá le shànglai**
The mountaineers climbed up. (towards the speaker–observer)

登山运动员爬了上去。 **dēngshān yùndòngyuán pá le shàngqu**
The mountaineers climbed up. (away from the speaker–observer)

If a location object is present, it is placed between the two syllables of the disyllabic direction indicator:

登山运动员爬上山来了。 **dēngshān yùndòngyuán pá shàng shān lai le**
The mountaineers have climbed up the mountain. (towards the speaker–observer)

登山运动员爬上山去了。 **dēngshān yùndòngyuán pá shàng shān qu le**
The mountaineers have climbed up the mountain. (away from the speaker–observer)

Completed action in such location–object sentences is expressed either by the verb and direction indicator themselves or by placing 了 *le* after the first element in the indicator and omitting the second element, i.e. 来 **lai** or 去 **qu**:

松鼠爬上树去。 **sōngshǔ pá shàng shù qu**
松鼠爬上了树。 **sōngshǔ pá shàng le shù**
The squirrel climbed up the tree.

哥哥跑下楼来。 **gēge pǎo xià lóu lai**
哥哥跑下了楼。 **gēge pǎo xià le lóu**
Elder brother ran downstairs.

火车开过桥去。 **huǒchē kāi guò qiáo qu**
火车开过了桥。 **huǒchē kāi guò le qiáo**
The train went over a bridge.

Here are some more location–object examples where 来 **lái** or 去 **qù** has to be omitted due to the presence of 了 *le*:

大家都走进了屋子。 **dàjiā dōu zǒu jìn le wūzi**
Everyone came into the room.

他游到了对岸。 **tā yóu dào le duì'àn**
He swam to the opposite bank.

演员登上了舞台。 **yǎnyuán dēng shàng le wǔtái**
The actor went on stage.

If an object other than location (i.e. physical or abstract) is present, it can be placed either (**a**) between the verb and the direction indicator, or (**b**) after the verb and the direction indicator or (**c**) between the two parts of the direction indicator with 了 *le* omitted:

(**a**) 服务员提了一只箱子进来。 **fúwùyuán tí le yī zhī xiāngzi jìnlai**
(**b**) 服务员提进来了一只箱子。 **fúwùyuán tí jìnlai le yī zhī xiāngzi**
(**c**) 服务员提进一只箱子来。 **fúwùyuán tí jìn yī zhī xiāngzi lai**
The attendant brought a trunk in.

(**a**) 妈妈买了一只大火鸡回来。 **māma mǎi le yī zhī dà huǒjī huílai**
(**b**) 妈妈买回来了一只大火鸡。 **māma mǎi huílai le yī zhī dà huǒjī**
(**c**) 妈妈买回一只大火鸡来。 **māma mǎi huí yī zhī dà huǒjī lai**
Mum bought (and brought home) a big turkey.

(**a**) 工程师想了一个好办法出来[14]。
gōngchéngshī xiǎng le yī ge hǎo bànfǎ chūlai
(**b**) 工程师想出来了一个好办法。
gōngchéngshī xiǎng chūlai le yī ge hǎo bànfǎ
(**c**) 工程师想出一个好办法来。
gōngchéngshī xiǎng chū yī ge hǎo bànfǎ lai
The engineer came up with a good idea.

In relation to sentence (**c**), it would be less acceptable to keep 了 *le* in:

*服务员提进了一只箱子来。 **fúwùyuán tí jìn le yī zhī xiāngzi lai**
*The attendent brought a trunk in.

*妈妈买回了一只大火鸡来。 **māma mǎi huí le yī zhī dà huǒjī lai**
*Mum bought (and took home) a big turkey.

8.5.3 DIRECTION INDICATORS INDICATING MEANING OTHER THAN DIRECTION

Disyllabic direction indicators can also be used figuratively to convey meanings beyond those of directional motion, though a link with the basic idea of movement is retained. In sentences with these figurative meanings, the object has always to be placed between the two syllables of the disyllabic direction indicator, and the completion aspect marker 了 *le* may not be incorporated under any circumstances. However, if the verb is intransitive and there is no object present, 了 *le* can be used after the verb and before the disyllabic direction indicator.

---

[14] With an abstract noun object, this construction is probably less commonly used.

(a) 出来 **chūlai** can imply 'coming into view or having its presence felt' and 下去 **xiàqu**, 'disappearing from view':

他从口袋里拿出两镑钱来。
tā cōng kǒudài li ná chū liǎng bàng qián lai
He took two pounds (cash) out of his pocket.

没人提出任何问题来。 **méi rén tíchū rènhé wèntí lai**
No one raised any questions.

病人吞下一粒药丸去。 **bìngrén tūn xià yī lì yàowán qu**
The patient swallowed a pill.

(b) 过来 **guòlai** and 起来 **qǐlai** can respectively convey 'regaining consciousness' and 'regaining memory' and 过去 **guòqu**, 'losing consciousness':

醉汉最后醒了过来。 **zuìhàn zuìhòu xǐng le guòlai**
The drunkard finally came to.

他突然想起这件事来。 **tā tūrán xiǎng qǐ zhèi jiàn shì lai**
He suddenly remembered this.

那个坏消息使她昏了过去。 **nèi ge huài xiāoxi shǐ tā hūn le guòqu**
That bad news made her faint.

(c) 起来 **qǐlai** and 下去 **xiàqu** can respectively imply 'starting' and 'continuing' an action or process:

人人都唱起歌来。 **rénrén dōu chàng qǐ gē lai**
Everyone began to sing.

天下起雨来。 **tiān xià qǐ yǔ lai**
It began to rain.

老头儿正想说下去。 **lǎotóur zhèng xiǎng shuō xiàqu**
The old man was about to continue to speak.

我们只能等下去。 **wǒmen zhǐ néng děng xiàqu**
All we could do was carry on waiting.

我们不能再待下去了。 **wǒmen bù néng zài dāi xiàqu le**
We cannot stay here any longer.

Ambiguity as to whether the direction indicators refer to direction or process does not generally arise because of the semantic nature of the action verbs in the collocation. However, in some cases, such ambiguities do exist. The verb 跳 **tiào** 'to jump', for instance, is naturally compatible with upward motion and when combined with 起来 **qǐlai**, it may mean either 'to jump up' or 'to start jumping' or in particular contexts 'to start dancing'. The ambiguity is only resolved by the given context or co-text:

他吓得跳了起来。 **tā xiā de tiào le qǐlai**
He was so startled he jumped to his feet.

随着悠扬的舞曲，大家都跳了起来。
suízhe yōuyáng de wǔqǔ | dàjiā dōu tiào le qǐlai
Everyone began to dance with the rise and fall of the dance music.

(**d**) 下来 **xiàlai** indicates 'settling down or coming to a halt':

屋子里渐渐地静了下来。 **wūzi lǐ jiànjiàn de jìng le xiàlai**
The room slowly went quiet.

汽车慢慢地停了下来。 **qìchē mànmān de tíng le xiàlai**
The car slowly came to a halt.

8.6 THE DESTINATION INDICATOR 到 **dào** 'to arrive'

As an indicator of destination, 到 **dào** 'to arrive' is hybrid in nature, and may specify either location or direction. We will first look at 到 **dào** as a location indicator:

他一口气跑到火车站。 **tā yīkǒuqì pǎo dào huǒchēzhàn**
He ran to the railway station without stopping. (lit. in one breath)

她慢慢地走到河边。 **tā mànmān de zǒu dào hébian**
She slowly walked to the river bank.

Here the 到 **dào** phrases, as sentence terminators (similar to the location expressions with 在 **zài** in §8.4), clearly indicate the terminal point or destination of the movement verbs.

More often, however, 到 **dào** combines with 来 **lai** or 去 **qu** to indicate direction, and such combinations usually take the form of:

到 **dào** + location object + 来 **lai** or 去 **qu**

These structures are coverbal phrases, which are discussed in detail in Chapter 11, and may feature pre-verbally as adverbials or post-verbally as complements. As adverbials they identify where the subject is before the action in the verb is carried out and as complements they indicate where the subject or object is after the action.

(a) as adverbials:

他到车站去接朋友。[15] **tā dào chēzhàn qù jiē péngyou**
He went to the station to meet a friend.

妈妈到市场去买菜。 **māma dào shìchǎng qù mǎi cài**
Mother went to the market to buy vegetables/food.

叔叔到我家来探望我爸爸和妈妈。
shūshu dào wǒ jiā lái tànwàng bàba hé māma
Uncle came to my/our house to visit mother and father.

The subjects in these cases must get to their destination before they can carry out the various actions of meeting friends, buying food or visiting parents.

(b) as complements:

他急急忙忙地跑到我家来。 **tā jíjímángmáng de pǎo dào wǒ jiā lai**
He came running to my house in a great rush.

鸟儿飞到树上去。 **niǎor fēi dào shù shàng qu**
The bird flew on to the tree.

潜水员潜到海底去。 **qiánshuǐyuán qián dào hǎidǐ qu**
The divers dived to the bottom of the sea.

他们把楼上的家具搬到楼下去。
tāmen bǎ lóushàng de jiājù bān dào lóuxià qu
They moved the (upstairs) furniture downstairs.

她把省下来的钱存到银行里去。
tā bǎ shěng xiàlai de qián cún dào yínháng li qu
She put/deposited her savings in the bank.

The subjects here must carry out the actions before they or what they are moving reach their various destinations.

---

[15] In sentences like these 来 **lai** or 去 **qu** may colloquially be placed at the end of the sentence: e.g.
他到车站接朋友去。 **tā dào chēzhàn jiē péngyou qu** 'He went to the station to meet a friend'.

9 ADVERBIALS

Adverbials are words or expressions which modify verbs in the same way that attributives qualify nouns, and they are therefore placed immediately before the verb they modify. They may be divided into two categories: restrictive and descriptive.

Restrictive adverbials function to restrict the time frame, location, tone, structural orientation or referential scope of verbs. They consist of (**a**) time expressions; (**b**) a closed set of monosyllabic adverbs that refer forwards and backwards to particular words or expressions in a sentence or context to highlight or emphasise them; (**c**) set expressions used as mood or tone-setters of an utterance (e.g. 老实说 **lǎoshí shuō** 'to be honest'); (**d**) negators; and (**e**) coverbal expressions of all kinds.[1] Descriptive adverbials, on the other hand, describe the manner in which the action encoded in the verb is being carried out. They are usually, but not always, followed by the marker 地 **de** 'in the manner of'.

Restrictive adverbials, apart from coverbal expressions, generally come before descriptive ones. If there is a coverbal expression in the sentence, a descriptive adverbial can be placed either before or after it depending on meaning and emphasis. In contrast with this, a coverbal expression always occurs after restrictive adverbials.[2]

9.1 RESTRICTIVE ADVERBIALS

9.1.1 TIME EXPRESSIONS

As we saw in Chapter 7, point-of-time expressions always come before the verb, so that in the time-sequenced logic of a Chinese sentence the time reference can be made clear before the action of the verb is specified:

我每天早晨七点钟上学。 **wǒ měitiān zǎochen qī diǎn zhōng** shàngxué
I go to school <u>every morning at 7 o'clock</u>.

你们几时走? **nǐmen jǐ shí zǒu**
<u>When</u> are you leaving?

---

[1] See Chapter 11 on coverbs.
[2] Details of the relative position of adverbials are given in §9.5.

他两家过去常常来往。 **tā liǎng jiā guòqù chángcháng láiwǎng**
Their two families <u>in the past often</u> visited each other.

我一时想不起他是谁。 **wǒ yīshí xiǎngbuqǐ tā shì shuí**
I can't remember <u>for the moment/off hand</u> who he is.

他的理想终于实现了。 **tāde lǐxiǎng zhōngyú shíxiàn le**
His ideal <u>in the end</u> was realised.

咱们改天再谈吧。 **zánmen gǎitiān zài tán ba**
Let's talk again <u>another day</u>.

我这就来[3]。 **wǒ zhè jiù lái**
I'll come <u>straight away</u>.

他在一年之内两次打破(了)世界纪录。[4]
tā zài yī nián zhīnèi liǎng cì dǎpò (le) shìjiè jìlù
He broke the world record <u>twice</u> <u>in a year</u>.

我们好久没有通信了。 **wǒmen hǎojiǔ méiyǒu tōngxìn le**
We have not corresponded <u>for a long time</u>.

他向来不吸烟。 **tā xiànglái bù xīyān**
He has never (lit. <u>hitherto</u> not) smoked.

她不时向窗外探望。 **tā bùshí xiàng chuāngwài tànwàng**
She <u>from time to time</u> looked out of the window.

我昨天就把这篇文章写完了。
wǒ zuótiān jiù bǎ zhèi piān wénzhāng xiě wán le
I finished writing this essay <u>yesterday</u>.

那个日本妇女忽地[5]向他鞠了一躬。
nèi ge rìběn fùnǚ hūdì xiàng tā jūle yī gōng
That Japanese woman <u>suddenly</u> bowed to him.

---

[3] 这 **zhè** here means 马上 **mǎshàng** 'immediately'.

[4] This sentence and a few of the following ones are examples of duration and frequency expressions coming before the verb. For an explanation of this, see §7.1.

[5] A number of adverbs like 忽地 **hūdì**, e.g. 突地 **tūdì** 'abruptly', 陡地 **dǒudì** 'unexpectedly', 蓦地 **mòdì** 'suddenly', although they appear to be descriptive adverbials with 地 **dì** (see §9.2), in fact function as restrictive adverbials.

From these examples we can see that time adverbials generally come immediately after the subject and before the verb (or the co-verbal phrase if there is one). Sentences like the following are not acceptable:

*她向窗外不时探望。 *tā xiàng chuāngwài bùshí tànwàng
*我把这篇文章昨天就写完了。
*wǒ bǎ zhèi piān wénzhāng zuótiān jiù xiě wán le

Time expressions, however, may be placed at the beginning of the sentence before the subject if they are to be emphasised and if their scope of modification covers the whole sentence rather than the verb alone. For example:

每天早晨七点钟，弟弟还睡得很香的时候，我就背着书包上学去了。
**měitiān zǎochen qī diǎn zhōng | dìdi hái shuìde hěn xiāng de shíhou |
wǒ jiù bēizhe shūbāo shàngxué qu le**
<u>Every morning at 7 o'clock</u>, while younger brother is still fast asleep,
I go off to school with my satchel on my back.

几时你才能变得不那么调皮呢?
jǐshí nǐ cái néng biàn de bù nàme tiáopí ne
<u>When</u> are you ever going to stop being so mischievous?

Sometimes time expressions may take the form of short verbal expressions, which have the inbuilt meaning of 'while', 'after', 'before', etc. It is as if time words like 的时候 de shíhou, 时 shí 'while' or 之前 zhīqián, 以前 yǐqián 'before' or 之后 zhīhòu, 以后 yǐhòu 'after', which would normally be found after the verbal expression, have been omitted.[6]

她<u>干活儿</u>十分马虎。 **tā <u>gàn huór</u> shífēn mǎhu**
(lit. she do work extremely careless) She is extremely careless <u>with her
work</u>.

这种电池<u>充了电</u>可以再用。 **zhèi zhǒng diànchí <u>chōng le diàn</u> kěyǐ zài yòng**
(lit. this mw:kind battery fill/charge *le* electricity may again use)
This battery when it's charged can be used again.

这位老师<u>说起话来</u>喜欢比划手势。
zhèi wèi lǎoshī <u>shuō qǐ huà lái</u> xǐhuan bǐhuà shǒushì
(lit. this mw teacher begin to speak always like gesticulate gestures)
This teacher likes to gesticulate <u>when he speaks</u>.

你<u>临走</u>告诉我一声。 **nǐ <u>línzǒu</u> gàosu wǒ yī shēng**
(lit. you near-go tell me one mw:sound) Tell me <u>when you are leaving</u>.

[6] See Chapter 11 on time clauses.

9.1.2 MONOSYLLABIC REFERENTIAL ADVERBS

Referential adverbs are a set of monosyllabic adverbs which are placed immediately before verbs to refer backwards or forwards to a time, person or entity mentioned earlier or later in the sentence. They indicate immediacy, tardiness, inclusion, contrast, repetition, unexpectedness, etc. on the part of the referent in relation to the action which is about to take place or has just taken place.

The main referential adverbs[7] are:

就	**jiù**	immediately afterwards
才	**cái**	not until
都	**dōu**	all; both
也	**yě**	also
却	**què**	on the other hand; nevertheless
还	**hái**	in addition; still
倒	**dào**	on the contrary; but, however
再	**zài**	again (in future)
又	**yòu**	(once) again
只	**zhǐ**	only
竟	**jìng**	unexpectedly

Here are some examples:

一到冬天，天很快就黑了。 **yī dào dōngtiān | tiān hěn kuài jiù hēi le**
(lit. once arrive winter, sky very quickly <u>then</u> black *le*)
As soon as winter comes, it quickly gets dark.

我家就[8]在大学附近，几分钟就走到了。
wǒ jiā jiù zài dàxué fùjìn | jǐ fēnzhōng jiù zǒu dào le
(lit. my home <u>just</u> cv:at university vicinity, few minutes <u>then</u> walk-arrive *le*)
My home is nearby the university, and I can walk there in a few minutes.

他们大学毕业之后才结婚。 **tāmen dàxué bìyè zhīhòu cái jiéhūn**
(lit. they university graduate after <u>only then</u> marry)
They did not get married until they graduated from university.

与会的人都赞成他的提议。 **yǔhuì de rén dōu zànchéng tā de tíyì**
(lit. attend conference de people <u>all</u> approve his proposal)
The people at the conference/meeting all appproved/endorsed his proposal.

---

[7] See Chapter 22 for these adverbials discussed as conjunctives.
[8] The referential adverb 就 **jiù** 'just' here refers forward to indicate 'my home is near the university' rather than backwards.

这条路早晚都塞车。 **zhèi tiáo lù zǎowǎn <u>dōu</u> sāi chē**
(lit. this mw road morning-evening <u>both</u> block cars)
Morning and evening there is always a traffic jam on this road.

离合器坏了，刹车也坏了。 **líhéqì huài le | shāchē <u>yě</u> huài le**
(lit. clutch wrong *le*, brake <u>also</u> wrong *le*)
The clutch broke down, and so did the brake.

这条数学题老师也无法解答。 **zhèi tiáo shùxuétí lǎoshī <u>yě</u> wúfǎ jiědá**
(lit. this mw maths problem teacher <u>also</u> no way explain)
Even the teacher has no way to answer this maths problem.

那瞬间我却说不出话来。 **nèi shùnjiān wǒ <u>què</u> shuōbuchū huà lai**
(lit. that instant I <u>but</u> speak not out words come)
At that instant I could not say a word (however much I wanted to).

我妈妈还买了不少头巾。 **wǒ māma <u>hái</u> mǎile bùshǎo tóujīn**
(lit. my mother <u>in addition</u> buy *le* not a few scarves)
My mother in addition/also bought several scarves.

你还不明白我的意思吗？ **nǐ <u>hái</u> bù míngbai wǒde yìsi ma**
(lit. you <u>still</u> not understand my meaning *ma*)
Do you still not understand my meaning?

最后，他倒没有受到处罚。 **zuìhòu | tā <u>dào</u> méiyǒu shòudào chǔfá**
(lit. in the end, he <u>but</u> not have receive punishment)
In the end he did not receive any punishment (as he should).

这件事以后再说吧。 **zhèi jiàn shì yǐhòu <u>zài</u> shuō ba**
(lit. this mw matter <u>afterwards</u> again speak *ba*)
Let's talk about this again later.

一不小心，他又把球踢出了界外。 **yī bù xiǎoxīn | tā <u>yòu</u> bǎ qiú tīchū le jièwài**
(lit. once not careful, he <u>again</u> cv:grasping ball kick out *le* boundary-outside)
In a moment of carelessness, he kicked the ball out again.

这儿只有你一个人吗？ **zhèr <u>zhǐ</u> yǒu nǐ yī ge rén ma**
(lit. here <u>only</u> have/there is you one mw person *ma*)
Are you the only person here?

想不到事情竟发展到不可收拾的地步。
xiǎngbudào shìqing <u>jìng</u> fāzhǎn dào bùkě shōushi de dìbù
(lit. did not expect matter <u>unexpectedly</u> develop cv:to not able repair *de*
stage) Unexpectedly, the matter developed to an irretrievable stage/point.

9.2 DESCRIPTIVE ADVERBIALS

Descriptive adverbials are formed from adjectives or various kinds of adjectival constructions which must be at least two syllables long. They not only describe the way in which the action in the verb is being carried out but they also demonstrate an attitude or conscious effort on the part of the subject, that is, the initiator of the action (unless of course the subject is inanimate and cannot wilfully exert any influence). Descriptive adverbials invite appreciation by the senses (sight, hearing, touch, etc.) or understanding of human motives, qualities, etc. They are generally marked by the adverbial marker 地 **de** 'in the manner of', and are placed immediately before a verb or before or after a coverbal phrase:

他热情地接待了来宾。 **tā rèqíng de jiēdài le láibīn**
(lit. he warm de receive *le* guests) He received the guests warmly.

她敏捷地跑上前来。 **tā mǐnjié de pǎo shàng qiánlai**
(lit. she nimble de run up front come) She came running forward quickly.

老板很痛快地答应了我们的要求。
lǎobǎn hěn tòngkuài de dáyìng le wǒmende yāoqiú
(lit. the boss very quick de agree *le* our request(s)) The proprietor/boss agreed to our request promptly.

姐姐高高兴兴地跑回家来。 **jiějie gāogāoxìngxìng de pǎo huí jiā lai**
(lit. elder sister high-high-spirit-spirit de run back home come)
Elder sister came running home happily.

爸爸笼笼统统地解释了一下。 **bàba lǒnglǒngtǒngtǒng de jiěshì le yīxià**
(lit. father sweeping-sweeping de explain *le* one mw:time)
Father gave a sweeping explanation.

More rarely, verbs or noun phrases with or without 地 *de*[9] can also function as descriptive adverbials:

他合不拢嘴儿地笑着。 **tā hé bu lǒng zuǐr de xiào zhe**
(lit. he close-not-be-able mouth de grin *zhe*) He was grinning from ear to ear.

观众象潮水一样(地)涌进剧场。
guānzhòng xiàng cháoshuǐ yīyàng (de) yǒngjìn jùchǎng
(lit. audience like tide-water same de flood cv:into theatre)
The audience flooded into the theatre (like a tide).

她一个劲儿地诉说着。 **tā yī ge jìngr de sùshuō zhe**
(lit. she persistent de complain *zhe*) She went on complaining without stop.

---

[9] For descriptive adverbials without 地 **de**, see §9.4 below.

他自己<u>一个人</u>把房间收拾干净。 **tā zìjǐ <u>yī ge rén</u> bǎ fángjiān shōushi gānjìng**
(lit. he self <u>one mw person</u> cv:grasping room tidy up clean)
He cleaned up the room on his own.

Monosyllables (including onomatopoeic terms) have to be reduplicated to become adverbials. For example:

慢慢地	**mànmān de**	slowly
好好地	**hǎohāo de**	well
匆匆地	**cōngcōng de**	hurriedly
悄悄地	**qiāoqiāo de**	quietly
轻轻地	**qīngqīng de**	gently
呼呼地	**hūhū de**	whistling (of wind); noise (of snoring)

Trisyllabic (particularly phonaesthetic) adjectives, quadrisyllabic (often idiomatic) expressions and reduplicated disyllabic onomatopoeic terms are also used as adverbials:

静悄悄地	**jìngqiāoqiāo de**	very quietly
亮晶晶地	**liàngjīngjīng de**	glitteringly
一个个地	**yīgègè de**	one by one
齐心协力地	**qíxīn xiélì de**	with concerted effort
力不从心地	**lì bù cóng xīn de**	helplessly
翻来复去地	**fānláifùqù de**	repeatedly
咕嘟咕嘟地	**gūdūgūdū de**	gurgling, bubbling
劈劈啪啪地	**pīpīpāpā de**	with a cracking/clapping sound

The quadrisyllabic phrases can also be reduplications or intercalated expressions:

清清楚楚地	**qīngqīngchǔchu de**	clearly
认认真真地	**rènrènzhēnzhēn de**	earnestly
得意洋洋地	**déyì yángyáng de**	triumphantly, pleased with oneself
一起一伏地	**yī qǐ yī fú de**	rising and falling, up and down
又渴又累地	**yòu kě yòu lèi de**	both thirsty and tired
不高不低地	**bù gāo bù dī de**	neither high nor low

Adverbials longer than this are not common, but they are possible particularly if they incorporate words like 似的 **shì de** 'as if':

好象一点也不在乎似地 **hǎoxiàng yīdiǎn yě bù zàihu shì de**
as if not caring a bit/jot

被人骂了一顿似地 **bèi rén mà le yī dùn shì de**
as if rebuked (by someone)

9.3 INITIATOR-ORIENTED OR ACTION-ORIENTED DESCRIPTIVE ADVERBIALS

We have mentioned that a descriptive adverbial may come before or after a coverbal expression. This choice is not random, but is in most cases dictated by the underlying meaning. If the adverbial is **initiator-oriented** and relates more to the attitude or appearance of the subject of the sentence, it is usually placed before the coverbal expression[10] nearer to the initiator subject; if it relates more to the manner of the action it may be said to be more **action-oriented**, and is therefore generally placed after the coverbal expression and immediately before the verb.[11] Compare the following pair of sentences:

(a) 他漫不经心地把要带的东西塞进背包里。　　　　　(initiator-oriented)
tā màn bù jīngxīn de bǎ yào dài de dōngxi sāijìn bèibāo li
(lit. he casually cv:grasping want take *de* things stuff cv:into rucksack-inside)
All casual, he stuffed the things he wanted to take into the rucksack.

and:

他把要带的东西漫不经心地塞进背包里。　　　　　(action-oriented)
tā bǎ yào dài de dōngxi màn bù jīngxīn de sāijìn bèibāo li
(lit. he cv:grasping want take *de* things casually stuff cv:into rucksack)
He stuffed the things he wanted to take casually into the rucksack.

(b) 他满脸笑容地把要带的东西塞进背包里。　　　　　(initiator-oriented)
tā mǎnliǎn xiàoróng de bǎ yào dài de dōngxi sāijìn bèibāo li
(lit. he grinning all over cv:grasping want take *de* things stuff cv:into rucksack-inside)
Grinning all over, he stuffed the things he wanted to take into the rucksack.

but less acceptable as:

*他把要带的东西满脸笑容地塞进背包里。　　　　　(non-action-oriented)
***tā bǎ yào dài de dōngxi mǎnliǎn xiàoróng de sāijìn bèibāo li**
*(lit. he cv:grasping want take *de* things grinning all over stuff cv:into rucksack-inside)

(c) 他把要带的东西乱七八糟地塞进背包里。　　　　　(action-oriented)
tā bǎ yào dài de dōngxi luànqībāzāo de sāijìn bèibāo li
(lit. he cv:grasping want take *de* things messily stuff cv:into rucksack-inside)
He stuffed the things he wanted to take messily into his rucksack.

---

[10] Descriptive adverbials indicating intention or attitude may, however, often be used to indicate manner at the same time.

[11] The flexible word order of English sometimes makes these distinctions less marked.

but less acceptable as:

*他乱七八糟地把要带的东西塞进背包里。   (non-initiator-oriented)
*tā luànqībāzāo de bǎ yào dài de dōngxi sāijìn bèibāo li
*(lit. he messily cv:grasping want take *de* things stuff cv:into
rucksack-inside)

The first of the above pairs illustrates that these adverbials may be used before
or after the coverbal expression depending on whether they are describing
attitude/appearance or manner. However, descriptive adverbials that indicate
only attitude or appearance are less likely to be placed after the coverbal phrase
(second pair) and those of manner likewise are less likely to come before the
coverbal phrase (third pair).

Here are some more examples of either initiator-oriented or action-oriented
adverbials:

他<u>勇敢地</u>把球顶出界外。   (initiator-oriented)
tā yǒnggǎn de bǎ qiú dǐngchu jiè wài
(lit. he bravely cv:grasping ball head out boundary-outside)
He bravely headed the ball out of play.

but less acceptable as:

*他把球勇敢地顶出界外。
*tā bǎ qiú yǒnggǎn de dǐngchū jiè wài
*(lit. he cv:grasping ball bravely head out boundary-outside)

他迅速地把车刹住。   (initiator-oriented)
tā xùnsù de bǎ chē shāzhù
(lit. he rapidly cv:grasping car brake-stop)
Rapidly he put on the brake (and brought the car to a halt).

他把<u>车</u>迅速地刹住。   (action-oriented)
tā bǎ chē xùnsù de shāzhù
(lit. he cv:grasping car rapidly brake-stop)
He braked rapidly (and brought the car to a halt).

他诚诚恳恳地向她道歉。   (initiator-oriented)
tā chéngchéngkěnkěn de xiàng tā dàoqiàn
(lit. he sincerely cv:to her apologise) He apologised to her sincerely.

but less likely as:

*他向她诚诚恳恳地道歉。
*tā xiàng tā chéngchéngkěnkěn de dàoqiàn
(lit. he cv:to her sincerely apologise)

9.4 OMISSION OF THE DESCRIPTIVE MARKER 地 **de**

We have seen that the marker 地 **de** 'in the manner of' is usually present with descriptive adverbials. However, it is not used when the adverbial includes the numeral 一 **yī** in expressions indicating 'togetherness', 'swiftness', 'abruptness':[12]

他们一起去做义务工作。 **tāmen yīqǐ qù zuò yìwù gōngzuò**
(lit. they <u>together</u> go do voluntary work)
They are going <u>together</u> to do voluntary work.

孩子们一齐拥了上来。 **háizimen yīqí rōng le shànglai**
(lit. the children <u>in unison</u> swarm le up come)
The children swarmed over <u>all together</u>.

他一拳打在那个人的脸上。 **tā yī quán dǎ zài nèi ge rén de liǎn shàng**
(lit. he <u>one fist</u> hit cv:on that mw person's face-on)
He punched that man in the face.

他一头扎进水里。 **tā yī tóu zhājìn shuǐ li**
(lit. he <u>one head</u> plunge cv:into water-inside)
He plunged <u>headlong</u> into the water.

他一骨碌从床上爬起来。 **tā yī gūlu cóng chuáng shàng pá qǐlai**
(lit. he <u>rolling</u> cv:from bed-top crawl up come) He leapt out of bed.

他一个纵步跳过了小河。 **tā yī ge zōngbù tiàoguò le xiǎo hé**
(lit. he <u>one mw bound</u> jump over *le* little river)
<u>With one bound</u>, he leapt across the stream.

汽车嘎的一声刹住了。 **qìchē gā de yī shēng shāzhù le**
(lit. the car <u>with a screech</u> brake-stop *le*) The car screeched to a halt.

Monosyllabic adjectives can be used as adverbials in imperatives, brief responses, etc. and these adverbials are not followed by 地 **de**:

快来！ **kuàilái**
(lit. fast come) Come quickly!

慢走！ **mànzǒu**
(lit. slow leave) Take care, take it easy.

好说好说。 **hǎoshuō hǎoshuō**
(lit. well said well said) It's very kind of you to say so.

---

[12] Note, however, that if 一 **yī** in the expression indicates 'repetition or continuation', 地 **de** is retained: e.g. 一次又一次地 **yī cì yòu yī cí de** 'again and again', 一个劲儿地 **yī ge jìnr de** 'non-stop'.

A number of adverbs in the lexicon, though descriptive in nature, are not normally found with 地 **de**. This is simply a matter of usage and no generalisations can be made about them. For example:

大家连忙迎了上去。 **dàjiā liánmáng yíng le shàngqu**
(lit. everyone promptly welcome *le* up go)
Everyone hastened forward (to meet him/her/them).

两国会谈圆满结束。 **liǎng guó huìtán yuánmǎn jiéshù**
(lit. two country talks satisfactorily conclude)
The talks between the two countries were satisfactorily concluded.

他从不轻易发表意见。 **tā cóng bù qīngyì fābiǎo yìjian**
(lit. he hitherto not rashly express opinion) He never made rash comments.

列车徐徐开动。 **lièchē xúxú kāidòng**
(lit. the train slowly start-move) The train slowly started to move.

一缕炊烟袅袅上升。 **yī lǚ chuīyān niǎoniǎo shàngshēng**
(lit. one mw:thread kitchen smoke curling up rise)
A wisp of smoke curled up from the kitchen chimney.

我拉拉杂杂谈了这些，请大家指教。
wǒ lālāzázá tán le zhèixiē | qǐng dàjiā zhǐjiào
(lit. I in disorganised way talk le these, please everyone make comments)
I have chatted in no particular order about these things and so would everyone please make comments.

9.5 RELATIVE POSITION OF ADVERBIALS

When there is more than one adverbial in a sentence the normal order is for restrictive adverbials to come before descriptive ones. Within the descriptive category, initiator-oriented adverbials precede action-oriented adverbials. The overall sequence is something like:

(a) time expressions: from more general to more specific: 星期天早上十点钟 **xīngqī tiān zǎoshang shí diǎn zhōng**
(b) adverbials indicating mood or tone: 很不幸 **hěn bùxìng** 'unfortunately' (interchangeable in position with time expressions)
(c) monosyllabic referential adverbs: 也 **yě** 'also', 都 **dōu** 'all'
(d) negators: 不 **bù** 'not', 没有 **méiyǒu** 'did/has not'
(e) actor-oriented descriptive adverbials: 高高兴兴地 **gāogaoxìngxìng de** 'happily'
(f) 着 *zhe* phrases indicating accompanying manner

(g) action-oriented descriptive adverbials: 一步一步地 **yī bù yī bù de** 'step by step'

(h) 把 **bǎ** or 被 **bèi**

(i) coverbal expressions other than 把 **bǎ** or 被 **bèi** or location expressions: 跟他 **gēn tā** 'with him' (interchangeable in position with 把 **bǎ** or 被 **bèi** or location expressions)

(j) location expressions: 在花园 **zài huāyuán** 'in the garden'

(k) onomatopoeic terms: 哗哗哗地 **huāhuāhuā de** (interchangeable in position with location expressions)

An extended sentence illustrating all the above (presented here vertically) could be constructed along the following lines:

老实说 (tone),	**lǎoshi shuō**	frankly
这个孩子 (**subject**)	**zhèi ge háizi**	this mw child
每天 (time)	**měitiān**	every day
都 (referential)	**dōu**	all
不 (negator)	**bù**	not
肯 (**modal verb**)	**kěn**	willing
认认真真地 (actor-oriented)	**rènrènzhēnzhēn de**	seriously
看着课文 (着 *zhe* phrase)	**kàn zhe kèwén**	reading text
干脆利索地 (action-oriented)	**gāncuì lìsuo de**	briskly/ unhesitatingly
把生词 (把 **bǎ** phrase)	**bǎ shēngcí**	cv:grasping vocabulary
用铅笔 (coverbal phrase)	**yòng qiānbǐ**	use pencil
在练习本上 (location)	**zài liànxíběn shàng**	cv:on exercise book-on
唰唰唰地 (onomatopoeic term)	**shuāshuāshuā de**	with a scratching noise
抄 (**main verb**)	**chāo**	copy
几遍。(complement: frequency)	**jǐ biàn**	a few mw:times

English translation:

Frankly, this child is never willing any day to scratch out without fuss and with a careful eye on the text (of the lesson) a number of copies of the new vocabulary into his/her exercise book.

10   COMPLEMENTS

One of the most distinctive features of Chinese syntax is that a verb in a narrative sentence is rarely used without an object or a complement following it; that is to say, an unmarked verb would not normally be found at the end of a narrative sentence. Even so-called intransitive verbs in Chinese, as we saw in Chapter 6, are in most cases self-contained verb–object structures.

Complements are expressions that indicate in some way the result of the action of the verb or describe the way the action is or has been carried out. In the Chinese mind, they articulate a consequence that is observable in terms of outcome or manner and as such must logically follow the verb. We have already seen examples of complements in duration and frequency phrases (Chapter 7) and direction expressions (Chapter 8). Here we will deal with resultative and potential complements and those indicating manner and consequential state.

10.1   RESULTATIVE COMPLEMENTS

A **resultative complement** consists of either a result verb[1] or an adjective and it is placed immediately after the main verb. If there is a following noun, it comes after the verb + complement. The result indicated by the complement can be either intended or unintended, or it can be the natural outcome of the action of the verb. Resultative complements can occur in narrative, expository and evaluative sentences, but not in descriptive sentences.

10.1.1   ADJECTIVAL RESULTATIVE COMPLEMENTS

Virtually any adjective can function as a resultative complement, but some are used much more often than others for this purpose. Generally speaking, commendatory adjectives indicate intended result and derogatory adjectives unintended results. In cases where the subject is inanimate or the adjective neutral, the result produced may be a description of a natural phenomenon.

> 他修好了我的汽车。 **tā xiū hǎo le wǒde qìchē**
> (lit. he repair-<u>good</u> *le* my car) He repaired my car.

---

[1] There is a specific set of verbs in the vocabulary which indicates the end-result of an action rather than the action itself, e.g. 破 **pò** 'break', 倒 **dǎo** 'topple' (see §10.1.2 below).

他撞坏了我的汽车。 **tā zhuàng <u>huài</u> le wǒde qìchē**
(lit. he collide-<u>bad</u> *le* my car)
He damaged my car (in a collision).

他们还没弄²<u>清楚</u>这个问题。 **tāmen hái méi nòng <u>qīngchu</u> zhèi ge wèntí**
(lit. they still not handle-<u>clear</u> this mw problem)
They still haven't clarified this problem.

妹妹算错了那道题。 **mèimei suàn <u>cuò</u> le nèi dào tí**
(lit. younger sister calculate-<u>wrong</u> *le* that mw question)
Younger sister got that question <u>wrong</u>.

太阳照亮了大地。 **tàiyáng zhào <u>liàng</u> le dàdì**
(lit. sun shine-<u>bright</u> *le* earth) The sun lit up the world.

晚霞染红了西边的天空。 **wǎnxiá rǎn <u>hóng</u> le xībian de tiānkōng**
(lit. sunset clouds dye-<u>red</u> *le* western *de* sky)
The evening sun coloured the western sky red.

妈妈整理好(了)床铺。 **māma zhěnglǐ <u>hǎo</u> (le) chuángpū**
(lit. mother put-in-order-<u>well</u> bedclothes)
Mother straightened the bed-clothes.

姐姐抹干净(了)桌子。 **jiějie mā <u>gānjìng</u> (le) zhuōzi**
(lit. elder sister wipe-<u>clean</u> table) Elder sister wiped the table clean.

Note that in the last two examples the completed action aspect marker 了 *le* is likely to become optional for reasons of rhythm, when either the verb or the complement is disyllabic.

Common resultative adjectives are mostly monosyllables from the language's adjectival lexicon, including the following: 饱 **bǎo** 'full from eating', 醉 **zuì** 'drunk', 对 **duì** 'correct'.

10.1.2 VERBAL RESULTATIVE COMPLEMENTS

A limited set of so-called result verbs function as resultative complements. They tend to indicate the end result of an action rather than an action itself.

弟弟做完了他的作业。 **dìdi zuò <u>wán</u> le tāde zuòyè**
(lit. younger brother do-<u>finish</u> *le* his homework)
Younger brother finished his homework.

---

² 弄 **nòng** 'to handle' is used widely in colloquial speech, rather like 'get' in English.

爷爷寄走了那封给奶奶的信。 **yéye jì zǒu le nèi fēng gěi nǎinai de xìn**
(lit. grandpa send-go that mw give grandma *de* letter)
Grandpa sent the letter to grandma.

大风吹倒了那棵大树 。 **dà fēng chuī dǎo le nèi kē dà shù**
(lit. typhoon blow-topple *le* that large tree)
The typhoon blew down that large tree.

那个小男孩打破了一只盘子。 **nèi ge xiǎo nánhái dǎ pò le yī zhī pánzi**
(lit. that mw little boy hit-break *le* one mw plate)
That little boy broke a plate.

Other common verbal resultatives are: 掉 **diào** 'drop', 着 **zháo** 'reach, find', 到 **dào** 'attain, achieve', 开 **kāi** 'separate'.

10.1.3 RESULTATIVE COMPLEMENTS IN 把 **bǎ**, 被 **bèi** AND NOTIONAL PASSIVE CONSTRUCTIONS

Resultative complements feature commonly in 把 **bǎ**, 被 **bèi** and notional passive constructions, where the sentence ends with the outcome encoded by the complement:[3]

电工把电线剪断了。 **diàngōng bǎ diànxiàn jiǎn duàn le**
(lit. electrician *ba* wire cut-break *le*) The electrician cut the wire.

洪水把稻田淹没了。 **hóngshuǐ bǎ dàotián yān mò le**
(lit. flood *ba* paddy field inundate-submerge *le*)
The flood inundated the paddy fields.

剩菜被妈妈倒掉了。 **shèngcài bèi māma dào diào le**
(lit. left-overs *bei* mother tip-drop *le*)
The left-overs were thrown away by mother.

树被大风吹倒了。 **shù bèi dà fēng chuī dǎo le**
(lit. tree cv:by big wind blow-topple *le*)
The tree was blown down in the gale.

信已经寄走了。 **xìn yǐjīng jì zǒu le**
(lit. letter already send-go *le*) The letter has already been sent.

衣服都晾干了。 **yīfu dōu liàng gān le**
(lit. clothes all dry-in-air-dry *le*) The clothes are all dried.

---

[3] Note that sentences like these tend to be *le*-expository sentences.

电话马上接通了。 **diànhuà mǎshàng jiē <u>tōng</u> le**
(lit. telephone immediately connect-<u>through</u> *le*)
The telephone call immediately got <u>through</u>.

10.1.4 RESULTATIVE COMPLEMENTS AND INTENDED/ EXPECTED OUTCOMES IN IMPERATIVE SENTENCES

In addition to indicating results that have already been achieved in a narrative context, resultative complements, when they occur in imperative sentences, can point to outcomes that are intended or expected:

请叠好这些衣服！ **qǐng dié <u>hǎo</u> zhèixiē yīfu**
(lit. please fold-<u>well</u> these clothes) Please fold up these clothes.

别弄坏我的照相机！ **bié nòng <u>huài</u> wǒde zhàoxiàngjī**
(lit. don't handle-<u>bad</u> my camera) Don't break my camera.

拿走你的东西！ **ná <u>zǒu</u> nǐde dōngxi**
(lit. take-<u>go</u> your things) Take away your things.

请把垃圾倒掉。 **qǐng bǎ lājī dào <u>diào</u>**
(lit. please cv:grasp garbage tip-<u>fall</u>) Please tip out the garbage.

别把杯子摔破。 **bié bǎ bēizi shuāi <u>pò</u>**
(lit. don't cv:grasp glass drop-<u>break</u>) Please don't drop the glass.

10.2 POTENTIAL COMPLEMENTS

If resultative complements indicate results that are intended or unintended or are natural outcomes, potential complements point to results that are projected by the speaker to be possible or impossible. They are constructed by placing 得 *de* for positive potential or 不 *bu* for negative potential between the verb and the adjectival or verbal complements we have seen in §10.1 above. Sentences with potential complements tend to take an objective stance and the ability or inability to carry out the action expressed in the verb may arise at least in part from circumstances beyond the control of the speaker. Potential complements are therefore essentially expository.

10.2.1 ADJECTIVAL POTENTIAL COMPLEMENTS

这张照片放得大放不大? **zhèi zhāng zhàopiàn fàngdedà fàngbudà**
(lit. this mw photo expand *de* large expand not large)
Can this photograph be enlarged or not?

不戴眼镜，我看不清楚黑板上的字。
bù dài yǎnjìng | wǒ kànbuqīngchu hēibǎn shàng de zì
(lit. not wear glasses, I see-not-clear blackboard-on *de* Chinese characters)
I can't see the words on the blackboard clearly without my glasses on.

你弄得明白这个问题吗？ **nǐ nòngdemíngbái zhèi ge wèntí ma?**
(lit. you handle *de* clear this mw question *ma*)
Can you work out what the problem is?

10.2.2   VERBAL POTENTIAL COMPLEMENTS

昨晚我睡不着。 **zuó wǎn wǒ shuìbuzháo**
(lit. yesterday night I sleep not go-to-sleep)
I could not go to sleep last night.

婴儿还断不了奶。 **yīng'ér hái duànbuliǎo nǎi**
(lit. baby still stop not end milk)
The baby cannot be weaned from breast-feeding yet.

这场球打得赢吗？ **zhèi chǎng qiú dǎdeyíng ma**
(lit. this game ball hit *de* win ma)
Can [we] win this game (of football/basketball, etc.)?

10.2.3   POTENTIAL DIRECTIONAL COMPLEMENTS

这么多，我吃不下了。 **zhème duō | wǒ chībuxià le**
(lit. such a lot, I eat not down *le*) This is too much. I can't eat any more.

他的名字你想得起来吗？ **tāde míngzi nǐ xiǎngdeqǐlai ma**
(lit. his name you think *de* up *ma*) Can you remember his name?

你猜得出他的年龄吗？ **nǐ cāidechū tāde niánlíng ma**
(lit. you guess *de* out his age *ma*) Can you guess how old he is?

那么高的地方我们老人爬不上去。
nàme gāo de dìfang wǒmen lǎorén pábushàngqu
(lit. such high *de* place we old people climb not ascend-go)
Old people like us cannot climb to such a high place.

对不起，我现在走不开。 **duìbuqǐ | wǒ xiànzài zǒubukāi**
(lit. sorry, I now leave-not-separate) Sorry, I can't get away now.

10.2.4 FIGURATIVE USES AND OTHER FEATURES OF RESULTATIVE COMPLEMENTS

Verbal, particularly directional complements regularly have meanings beyond physical movement:

他这样说我受不了。 **tā zhèyàng shuō wǒ shòubuliǎo**
(lit. he this kind say I bear not end) I cannot put up with what he says.

他们看不起我。 **tāmen kànbuqǐ wǒ**
(lit. they look not up me) They look down on me.

这辆车坐得下五个人。 **zhèi liàng chē zuòdexià wǔ ge rén**
(lit. this mw car sit *de* down five mw people)
This car can seat/take five people.

我买不起那幅画儿。 **wǒ mǎibuqǐ nèi fú huàr**
(lit. I buy not rise that mw picture) I cannot afford (to buy) that picture.

你要想得开。 **nǐ yào xiǎngdekāi**
(lit. you should think *de* separate) You should take [it] philosophically.

10.3 COMPLEMENTS OF MANNER AND CONSEQUENTIAL STATE

Complements of manner are formed by placing 得 *de* after a verbal predicate followed by an adjectival phrase, which specifies the way in which the action of the verb is carried out or seen to be carried out. They delineate the observable manner or result of the action and by definition they are likely to be found in expository sentences. They can therefore be distinguished from pre-verbal adverbial modifiers of manner with 地 **de**,[4] which are more concerned with the attitude or approach of the initiator of the action, and which tend to feature more in narrative or descriptive sentences. If there is an object in a sentence with a complement of manner, it must be shifted to the beginning of the sentence as a topic or be placed pre-verbally after the coverb 把 **bǎ**. The words or expressions found in the complement are usually: (**a**) an adjective, normally modified by a degree adverb like 很 **hěn** 'very' or by a degree complement of its own; (**b**) a phonaesthetised adjective; or (**c**) a reduplicated adjective.

(**a**) degree adverb + adjective or adjective + degree complement:

那个姑娘打扮得很漂亮。 **nèi ge gūniang dǎban de hěn piàoliang**
(lit. that mw girl dress *de* very beautiful) That girl is beautifully dressed.

---

[4] See Chapter 9.

事情解决得十分完满。 **shìqing jiějué de shífēn wánmǎn**
(lit. matter resolve *de* entirely perfect)
The matter has been resolved perfectly.

她钢琴弹得好极了。 **tā gāngqín tán de hǎo jí le**
(lit. she piano play *de* good extremely *le*)
She plays the piano extremely well.

这个翻译中文说得流畅得很。
zhèi ge fānyì zhōngwén shuō de liúchàng de hěn
(lit. this mw interpreter Chinese speak *de* fluently *de* very)
This interpreter speaks Chinese extremely fluently.

(**b**) adjective + disyllabic phonaesthemes + 的 **de**:

他把杯子擦得亮铮铮的。 **tā bǎ bēizi cā de liàngzhēngzhēng de**
(lit. he cv:grasp glass rub *de* shining *de*)
He polished the glass so that it shone.

孩子长得胖乎乎的。 **háizi zhǎng de pànghūhū de**
(lit. child grow *de* chubby *de*) The child is/has grown chubby.

那个老头子喝得醉醺醺的。 **nèi ge lǎotóuzi hē de zuìxūnxūn de**
(lit. that mw old man drink *de* drunk *de*) That old man got drunk.

(**c**) reduplicated monosyllabic or disyllabic adjectives + (的 **de**):

大门关得紧紧的 。 **dàmén guān de jǐnjǐn de**
(lit. big gate shut *de* tight *de*) The main gate was tightly shut.

屋子整理得干干淨淨(的)。 **wūzi zhěnglǐ de gāngānjìngjìng (de)**
(lit. room tidy *de* clean *de*) The room was tidied nice and clean.

他把事件的经过说得清清楚楚的。
tā bǎ shìjiàn de jīngguò shuō de qīngqīngchǔchu de
(lit. he cv:grasp event *de* course tell *de* clear *de*)
He explained clearly the course of events.

In **complements of consequential state** the adjectival phrase is replaced by:
(**a**) a verbal phrase; (**b**) a clause; or (**c**) a quadrisyllabic idiom. They differ from
complements of manner in that they may follow either an adjectival or a verbal
predicate, but in other ways they are similar in function: an object, if present,
must come before the predicate; and they are likewise expository in tone, since
they elaborate on what is observed to result, intentionally or otherwise, from the

action of the predicate verb or from the situation described by the adjectival predicative.

(a) verbal phrase:

> 树被大风吹得左右摇摆。 **shù bèi dà fēng chuī de zuǒyòu yáobǎi**
> (lit. tree cv:by big wind blow *de* left-right-sway)
> The tree was swaying from left to right in the force of the gale.

> 他笑得直不起腰来。 **tā xiào de zhíbuqǐ yāo lai**
> (lit. he laugh *de* straight-not-rise-waist come)
> He laughed so much he couldn't straighten up.

> 妈妈伤心得睡不着觉。 **māma shāngxīn de shuìbuzháo jiào**
> (lit. mother sad *de* sleep not tight sleep)
> Mother was so sad that she could not go to sleep.

> 这个人胖得扣不上外衣的纽扣。
> **zhèi ge rén pàng de kòubushàng wàiyī de niǔkòu**
> (lit. this *ge* person fat *de* fasten-not up coat *de* buttons)
> This person was so fat he could not button up his coat.

(b) clause:

> 她哭得眼睛都红了。 **tā kū de yǎnjing dōu hóng le**
> (lit. she weep *de* eyes all red *le*) Her eyes were red with weeping.

> 老太太气得全身发抖。 **lǎo tàitai qì de quánshēn fādǒu**
> (lit. old lady angry *de* whole body tremble)
> The old lady trembled with anger.

> 她高兴得嘴巴都合不拢了。 **tā gāoxìng de zuǐba dōu hébulǒng le**
> (lit. she happy *de* mouth also close not together *le*)
> She was so happy that she was beaming all the time.

> 他们冷得牙齿直打战。 **tāmen lěng de yáchǐ zhí dǎzhàn**
> (lit. they cold *de* teeth continuously chatter)
> They were so cold their teeth were chattering.

(c) quadrisyllabic idioms:

> 桌子上的东西堆得乱七八糟。
> **zhuōzi shàng de dōngxi duī de luànqībāzāo**
> (lit. table-top *de* things pile *de* untidy)
> The things on the table were piled up untidily.

他回答得干脆利落。 **tā huídá de gāncuì lìluo**
(lit. he reply *de* clear-cut) He gave a clear-cut response.

地毯旧得一钱不值。 **dìtǎn jiù de yīqiánbùzhí**
(lit. carpet old *de* one-cash-not-worth)
The carpet was so old it was not worth a penny.

这种药苦得难以下咽。 **zhèi zhǒng yào kǔ de nányǐ xià yàn**
(lit. this kind medicine bitter *de* difficult to swallow)
This medicine is too bitter to swallow.

11 COVERBS

Coverbs are a specific set of verbs in the Chinese language which are similar to English prepositions. They are called coverbs because they almost invariably have to be used in conjunction with other verbs in a sentence.[1] For example:

小李对我笑了笑。 **xiǎolǐ duì wǒ xiào le xiào** (coverb: 对 **duì** 'towards; facing')
(lit. little Li cv:towards me smile *le* smile) Little Li smiled at me.

我们向前走去。 **wǒmen xiàng qián zǒu qu**
(coverb: 向 **xiàng** 'heading towards')
(lit. we cv:towards ahead go) We went forward/ahead.

他来自北方。 **tā lái zì běifāng** (coverb: 自 **zì** 'from')
(lit. he come cv:from north) He comes from the north.

她一口气走到学校。 **tā yīkǒuqì zǒu dào xuéxiào** (coverb: 到 **dào** 'arriving at')
(lit. she in one breath walk cv:arriving at school)
She walked straight through to school.

One cannot say:

*小李对我。	***xiǎolǐ duì wǒ**	*Xiao Li towards me.
*我们向前。	***wǒmen xiàng qián**	*We ahead.
*他自北方。	***tā zì běifāng**	*He from north.
*她到[2]学校。	***tā dào xuéxiào**	*She arriving at school.

Coverbs introduce expressions covering a wide range of factors including location, direction, timing, association, means, instrument, etc. and they are also essential elements in a number of grammatical constructions. These are all detailed below in §11.2. In most cases, coverbs are placed before the main verb in the sentence, the general formula being:

subject + coverbal expression + main verb

---

[1] Most coverbs must be followed by a verb in the sentence. Some, however, can function as independent verbs, e.g. 在 **zài**. In 他在家休息 **tā zài jiā xiūxi** 'He's resting at home', 在 **zài** is a coverb; but in 他不在家 **tā bù zài jiā** 'He's not at home', it is a verb.

[2] 到 **dào** like 在 **zài** can also be used as a full verb, but as such it needs to be aspect-marked, e.g. 她下午两点到了学校 **tā xiàwǔ liǎng diǎn dào le xuéxiào** 'She arrived at the school at two o'clock in the afternoon'.

In some cases, as can be seen from the third and fourth examples above, the coverb may come after the main verb. This positioning is determined by meaning, and is most common when the reference is to location or direction.[3]

The most important coverbs used in the language in terms of semantic categories are listed at §11.2. For example, 向 **xiàng** 'in the direction of', 朝 **cháo** 'towards', 往 **wǎng** or **wàng** 'going to', and 奔 **bèn** 'heading for' belong to the same semantic category. Coverbs like these within one category can generally be used interchangeably, but there are often particular features associated with their use as well as differences between them, which we will call **peer characteristics**.

We will first examine the nature of these peer characteristics before listing the semantic categories of coverbs.

11.1 PEER CHARACTERISTICS

11.1.1 REGISTRAL

Though coverbs in a semantic category broadly function in the same way, they do have differences in register usually associated with stylistic and regional distinctions.

For example, to say 'I'll go with him', the following options might be open:[4]

我和他一起去。	**wǒ hé tā yīqǐ qù**	(neut.)
我跟他一起去。	**wǒ gēn tā yīqǐ qù**	(northern dialect: colloq.)
我同他一起去。	**wǒ tóng tā yīqǐ qù**	(southern dialect: colloq.)
我与他同行。	**wǒ yǔ tā tóngxíng**	(fml. and class.)

The choice would be made purely in terms of formality of style.

11.1.2 COLLOCATIONAL

Collocational features are more lexical than grammatical in nature and they are part of language idiom. They dictate that some, if not all, the coverbs in a category may occur with a particular noun. Various possibilities are listed below within the category 'at the most opportune moment'. For example: 乘 **chéng**, 趁 **chèn**, and 随 **suí** may all collocate with 机 **jī** 'opportunity', but not 就 **jiù** and 顺 **shùn**:

乘机	**chéng jī**	making use of the opportunity
趁机	**chèn jī**	taking the opportunity
随机	**suí jī**	acting accordingly
*就机	**jiù jī**	
*顺机	**shùn jī**	

---

[3] See §11.1 below.
[4] See §11.2 below.

All five of them match with 便 **biàn** 'convenience':

顺便	**shùn biàn**	while one is at or about something
就便	**jiù biàn**	as is convenient
随便	**suí biàn**	as one pleases
趁便	**chèn biàn**	at one's convenience
乘便	**chéng biàn**	when convenient

顺 **shùn**, 就 **jiù**, 趁 **chèn** and 乘 **chéng** link with 势 **shì** 'momentum', but not 随 **suí**:

顺势	**shùn shì**	taking advange of someone's error
就势	**jiù shì**	making use of the momentum
趁势	**chèn shì**	taking advantage of a favourable situation
乘势	**chéng shì**	taking advantage of the situation
*随势	**suí shì**	

就 **jiù** and 随 **suí** both collocate with 地 **dì** 'place' while the others do not:

就地	**jiù dì**	on the spot
随地	**suí dì**	at any place where one is – anywhere

11.1.3 GOVERNMENTAL

Coverbs, like other transitive verbs, invariably take objects. Governmental characteristics refer to the fact that the object governed by a particular coverb may take diverse forms. Generally, the object is a noun or nominal expression, but in some cases it may be an adjective, a verb or verb phrase, or even a clause. For example, in the case of the coverb 趁 **chèn** 'taking the opportunity of' from the category cited above, the object may take the form of a noun, an adjective, a verb phrase, or a clause:

趁机 **chèn jī** taking the opportunity
(机 **jī** 'opportunity: an abbreviated noun)
趁热 **chèn rè** [eating or drinking something] while it is hot
(热 **rè** 'hot': an adjective)
趁下雨 **chèn xiàyǔ** [doing something] while it is raining
(下雨 **xiàyǔ** 'to rain': a verb)
趁天晴 **chèn tiān qíng** [doing something] while the weather is fine
(天晴 **tiān qíng** 'it is fine': a clause)

The governing capacity of individual coverbs varies greatly.

11.1.4 PROSODIC

Most coverbs are monosyllabic. However, there are quite a few which have disyllabic alternatives. While monosyllabic coverbs may occur with monosyllabic, disyllabic or multi-syllabic objects, disyllabic coverbs function only with disyllabic or multi-syllabic objects. For example, 按 **àn** 'according to' can be used freely as follows:

按理	**àn lǐ**	according to reason, normally
按道理	**àn dàolǐ**	according to reason
按实际情况	**àn shíjì qíngkuàng**	according to/in the light of actual circumstances

But its disyllabic alternative 按照 **ànzhào** 'in accordance with' is more restricted, with the following two phrases being acceptable:

| 按照道理 | **ànzhào dàolǐ** | according to reason |
| 按照实际情况 | **ànzhào shíjì qíngkuàng** | in the light of actual circumstances |

but not:

| *按照理 | ***ànzhào lǐ** | *according to reason |

11.1.5 SEQUENTIAL

As a general rule, coverbs occur before the main verb in the sentence. However, where a coverb indicates location or direction, it may come after the verb. For example, within the category with the meaning 'in the direction of' (see §11.2.1.1), 向 **xiàng** 'towards' and 往 **wàng/wǎng** 'heading for' may be used before or after the main verb in the sentence, while most of the others occur only pre-verbally.[5] It must however be noted that all post-verbal uses are restricted in one way or another. For example 向 **xiàng** in the pre-verbal position can govern any noun (or pronoun):

他向我走来。 **tā xiàng wǒ zǒu lai**
(lit. he cv:towards me walk come) He walked towards me.

whereas post-verbally its noun object is likely to be limited to an abstract idea:

我们从胜利走向胜利。 **wǒmen cóng shènglì zǒu xiàng shènglì**
(lit. we cv:from victory go cv:towards victory) We went from victory to victory.

---

[5] 于 **yú**, with its origins in Classical Chinese, is the only coverb in this category that is used post-verbally.

这不是走向光明；这是走向死亡。
zhè bù shì zǒu xiàng guāngmíng | zhè shì zǒu xiàng sǐwáng
(lit. this not is go cv:towards brightness; this is go cv:towards death)
This is not heading for glory; this is heading for death.

In the case of 往 **wàng/wǎng** the post-verbal restriction relates to the verb which is limited to examples like 开 **kāi** (of a car) 'to head for':

她往海边走去。 **tā wǎng hǎibiān zǒu qu**
(lit. she cv:heading for shore walk go) She walked towards the shore (sea).

这班车开往上海。 **zhèi bān chē kāiwǎng shànghǎi**
(lit. this mw vehicle travel cv:heading for Shanghai)
This bus/train is going to Shanghai.

In addition to the above, 到 **dào** 'arriving at, to' is used freely in pre- and post-verbal positions. For examples, see §11.2.1.3, and §11.2.2.3 below.

11.1.6 USAGE

Usage differences highlight the specific ways some coverbs are used. For example, in the category of 'along', 沿 **yán** 'alongside' does not occur with verbs of motion while its disyllabic counterpart 沿着 **yánzhe** does:

沿路都是商店。 **yán lù dōu shì shāngdiàn**
(lit. cv:alongside road all is shops) There are shops all along the road.

他们沿着大路走去。 **tāmen yán zhe dà lù zǒu qu**
(lit. they cv:along main road walk go) They walked along the road.

The first example above also illustrates the fact that 沿 **yán** is one of a limited number of coverbs that can be used as sentence beginners. Other examples are:

靠墙摆着一张床。 **kào qiáng bǎi zhe yī zhāng chuáng**
(lit. cv:against wall place *zhe* one mw bed) Against the wall was a bed.

临窗放着一张桌子。 **lín chuāng fàng zhe yī zhāng zhuōzi**
(lit. cv:beside window place *zhe* one mw table) Next to the window was a table.

11.2 SEMANTIC CATEGORIES

We list here the semantic categories of coverbs. For each category a table is given summarising peer characteristics: usage (indicating, where appropriate, dynamic and/or static nature, sentence beginners, etc.); register (informal, formal, colloquial, etc.); collocational (detailing specific association with specific nouns, where this occurs); governmental (identifying the possible grammatical form of the item governed by the coverb, e.g. noun, pronoun, etc.); prosodic (providing examples of alternative disyllabic coverbs, where they exist); and sequential (indicating whether the coverbs occur only before the main verb, or either before or after it).

11.2.1 DIRECTION AND POSITION

11.2.1.1 Towards or in the direction of

朝 **cháo**: towards, facing:

他朝我走过来。 **tā cháo wǒ zǒu guòlai**
(lit. he cv:towards me walk cross come) He walked over to me.

他朝我笑了笑。 **tā cháo wǒ xiào le xiào**
(lit. he cv:facing me smile *le* smile) He smiled at me.

我们朝前看去。 **wǒmen cháo qián kàn qu**
(lit. we cv:towards front look-go) We looked ahead.

向 **xiàng**: towards:

飞机向东边飞去。 **fēijī xiàng dōngbian fēi qu**
(lit. plane cv:towards east-side fly-go) The plane flew east.

走到路口，然后向左转。 **zǒu dào lù kǒu | ránhòu xiàng zuǒ zhuǎn**
(lit. walk cv:arriving crossroads, afterwards cv:towards left turn)
Go to the crossroads and then turn left.

我向窗外望去。 **wǒ xiàng chuāng wài wàng qu**
(lit. I cv.towards window-outside gaze-go) I looked out of the window.

我有点事儿向你请教。 **wǒ yǒudiǎn shìr xiàng nǐ qǐngjiào**
(lit. I have mw little matter cv:towards you seek advice)
I would like your advice on a small matter.

她向我点了点头。 **tā xiàng wǒ diǎn le diǎn tóu**
(lit. she cv:towards me nod *le* nod head) She nodded to me.

望 **wàng**: towards, to:

汽车望南开去。 **qìchē wàng nán kāi qu**
(lit. car cv:towards south drive-go) The car drove south.

往 **wǎng/wàng**: in the direction of:

妈妈往(**wàng**)厨房走去。 **māma wàng chúfáng zǒu qu**
(lit. mother cv:towards kitchen walk-go) Mother walked to the kitchen.

山脉往(**wàng**)东延伸。 **shānmài wàng dōng yánshēn**
(lit. mountain range cv:towards east stretch)
The mountain range stretched to the east.

这班车开往(**wǎng**)上海。 **zhèi bān chē kāiwǎng shànghǎi**
(lit. this mw train travel cv: towards Shanghai)
This train is going to Shanghai.

奔 **bèn**: heading for:

汽艇奔码头开去。 **qìtǐng bèn mǎtóu kāi qu**
(lit. motorboat cv:heading for dock travel-go) The motorboat headed for
the dock.

于 **yú**: to:

这是问道于盲。 **zhè shì wèn dào yú máng**
(lit. this is ask way cv:to blind) This is asking a blind person the way.

我得求救于人。 **wǒ děi qiújiù yú rén**
(lit. I had to cry for help cv: to person)
I had to call someone to come to the rescue.

为 **wèi**: to:

此事不足为外人道。 **cǐ shì bù zú wèi wàirén dào**
(lit. this matter not worth cv:to outsider speak)
This matter is not for outsiders to hear.

coverb	usage	register	collocational	governmental	prosodic	sequential
朝 **cháo**	dynamic/static	infml.		n, pron	朝着 **cháozhe**	pre-vb
向 **xiàng**	dynamic/static	fml.		n, pron	向着 **xiàngzhe**	pre-/post-vb
望 **wàng**	dynamic	colloq.		n		pre-vb
往 **wàng/wǎng**	dynamic	neut.		n		pre-/post-vb
奔 **bèn**	dynamic	slang		n		pre-vb
于 **yú**	static	class.		n		post-vb
为 **wèi**	static	obs.	. . . 道 **dào** 'to inform'	n		pre-vb

11.2.1.2   From (a starting-point)

从 **cóng**: from:

我刚从北京回来。 **wǒ gāng cóng běijīng huílai**
(lit. I just cv:from Beijing return-come) I have just come back from Beijing.

我从他那儿得到你的消息。 **wǒ cóng tā nàr dédào nǐde xiāoxi**
(lit. I cv:from his there obtain your news) I got your news from his place.

由 **yóu** from:

游行队伍由天安门出发。 **yóuxíng duìwu yóu Tiān'ānmén chūfā**
(lit. march ranks cv:from Tiananmen start out)
The procession started from Tiananmen.

风向突然变了，由北向南刮起来。
fēngxiàng tūrán biàn le | yóu běi xiàng nán guā qǐlai
(lit. wind direction suddenly change *le*, cv:from north cv:towards south
blow-begin)
The direction of the wind suddenly changed and it began to blow from
north to south.

打 **dǎ**: from:

咱们打这儿走吧。 **zánmen dǎ zhèr zǒu ba**
(lit. we cv:from here go *ba*) Let's go from here.

她打窗户里往外看。 **tā dǎ chuānghuli wǎng wài kàn**
(lit. she cv:from window-inside cv:towards outside look)
She looked out of the window.

起 **qǐ**: from:

您起哪儿来? **nín qǐ nǎr lái**
(lit. you (polite) cv:from where come) Where do you [polite] come from?

于 **yú**: from, at:

他毕业于英国利兹大学。 **tā bìyè yú yīngguó lìzī dàxué**
(lit. he graduate cv:from England Leeds university)
He graduated from Leeds University in England.

黄河发源于青海。 **huánghé fāyuán yú qīnghǎi**
(lit. Yellow River has source cv:from Qinghai) The Yellow River rises in Qinghai.

coverb	usage	register	collocational	governmental	prosodic	sequential
从 **cóng**	dynamic	neut.		n, pron		pre-vb
由 **yóu**	dynamic	fml.		n		pre-vb
打 **dǎ**	dynamic	colloq.		n		pre-vb
起 **qǐ**	dynamic	dial.		n, pron		pre-vb
于 **yú**	dynamic	class.		n, pron		post-vb

11.2.1.3 Going to or arriving at (a destination)

到 **dào**: to, arriving at:

你到哪儿去？ **nǐ dào nǎr qù**
(lit. you cv:to where go) Where are you going to?

我一口气跑到车站。 **wǒ yīkǒuqì pǎo dào chēzhàn**
(lit. I in one breath run cv:to station)
I ran straight to the bus/coach/railway station.

他下午到医院看病去。 **tā xiàwǔ dào yīyuàn kàn bìng qu**
(lit. he afternoon cv:to hospital see-to illness go)
He is going/went in the afternoon to the hospital for treatment.

coverb	usage	register	collocational	governmental	prosodic	sequential
到 **dào**	dynamic	neut.		n		pre-/post-vb

11.2.1.4 Along

沿 **yán**: along, alongside:

沿河开满了鲜花。 **yán hé kāi mǎn le xiānhuā**
(lit. cv:along river open-full *le* fresh flower)
There are flowers blooming all along the river.

沿着 **yán zhe**: along:

我们沿着大街一直走去。 **wǒmen yán zhe dàjiē yīzhí zǒu qu**
(lit. we cv:along main road straight walk-go)
We walked straight down the main road.

缘 **yuán**: along:

缘木求鱼。 **yuán mù qiú yú**
(lit. cv:along tree seek fish) Seek fish up a tree. [i.e. bark up the wrong tree]

挨 **āi**: in sequence:

他挨家挨户去询问。 **tā āijiā āihù qù xúnwèn**
(lit. he cv:in sequence house cv:in sequence door go enquire)
He made enquiries from door to door.

顺 **shùn**: along:

我顺手把门关上。 **wǒ shùnshǒu bǎ mén guān shàng**
(lit. I cv:along hand cv:grasp door close up)
I closed the door behind me/as I came in.

coverb	usage	register	collocational	governmental	prosodic	sequential
沿 **yán**	static	neut.		n	see 沿着 **yánzhe**	pre-vb
沿着 **yán zhe**	dynamic	neut.		n	see 沿 **yán**	pre-vb
缘 **yuán**	dynamic	class.	木 **mù** 'tree'	n		pre-vb
挨 **āi**	dynamic	colloq.	家 **jiā** 'house'	n		pre-vb
顺 **shùn**	dynamic	infml.	路 **lù** 'way' 藤 **téng** 'vine'	n		pre-vb

11.2.1.5 Facing

对 **duì**: to, facing:

你对他说了些什么？ **nǐ duì tā shuō le xiē shénme**
(lit. you cv:to him say *le* mw:some what) What did you say to him?

duìzhe: facing:

他对着镜子梳了梳头发。 **tā duì zhe jìngzi shū le shū tóufa**
(lit. he cv:facing mirror comb *le* comb hair)
He combed his hair in front of the mirror.

迎 **yíng**: facing, against:

彩旗迎风招展。 **cǎiqí yíng fēng zhāozhǎn**
(lit. coloured flag cv:facing wind flutter) The bunting fluttered in the wind.

当 **dāng**: facing, before:

阴谋当众败露。 **yīnmóu dāng zhòng bàilù**
(lit. plot cv:before crowd fail-expose)
The plot was exposed before everyone/in public.

当着 **dāng zhe**: facing, before:

请你当着大家的面把问题说清楚吧。
qǐng nǐ dāng zhe dàjiā de miàn bǎ wèntí shuō qīngchu ba
(lit. please you cv:before everyone's face cv:grasp problem speak-clear **ba**)
Please make clear the problem in front of everyone.

劈 **pī**: closely facing, right against:

我劈头碰见小王。 **wǒ pī tóu pèngjiàn xiǎowáng**
(lit. I cv:right against head bump-see little Wang)
I bumped straight into Xiao Wang.

冲 **chòng**: facing, towards:

他冲我眨了眨眼。 **tā chòng wǒ zhā le zhā yǎn**
(lit. he cv:towards me wink **le** wink eye) He winked at me.

冲着 **chòng zhe**: facing, towards:

风很大，别冲着窗口坐。
fēng hěn dà | bié chòng zhe chuāngkǒu zuò
(lit. wind very strong, don't cv:facing window sit)
The wind is very strong, don't sit facing the window.

coverb	usage	register	collocational	governmental	prosodic	sequential
对 **duì**	static	neut.		n, pron	对着 **duìzhe**	pre-vb
迎 **yíng**	dynamic	fml.	面 **miàn** 'face' 风 **fēng** 'wind'	n		pre-vb
当 **dāng**	static	colloq.	面 **miàn** 'face' 场 **chǎng** 'place'	n	当着 **dāngzhe**	pre-vb
劈 **pī**	dynamic	colloq.	脸 **liǎn** 'face' 头 **tóu** 'head'	n		pre-vb
冲 **chòng**	static	slang		n, pron	冲着 **chòngzhe**	pre-vb

11.2.1.6 Against

靠 **kào**: against, leaning on:

> 行人靠右边走。 **xíngrén kào yòubian zǒu**
> (lit. pedestrians cv:against right-side walk) Pedestrians keep to the right.

临 **lín**: next to:

> 他临床替病人诊治。 **tā línchuáng tì bìngrén zhěnzhì**
> (lit. she cv: next to bed cv:for patients diagnose treat)
> She diagnoses and treats patients at the bedside.

凭 **píng**: leaning against:

> 他凭栏远眺。 **tā pínglán yuǎntiào**
> (lit. he cv:leaning against balustrade distant-gaze)
> Leaning on the balustrade he gazes into the distance.

负 **fù**: relying on:

> 敌人负隅顽抗。 **dírén fùyú wánkàng**
> (lit. enemy cv:relying on corner stubbornly resist)
> The enemy with their backs to the wall resisted stubbornly.

coverb	usage	register	collocational	governmental	prosodic	sequential
靠 **kào**	static	neut.		n		pre-vb
临 **lín**	static	neut.		n		pre-vb
凭 **píng**	static	class.	栏 **lán** 'balustrate'	n		pre-vb
负 **fù**	static	class.	隅 **yú** 'corner'	n		pre-vb

11.2.1.7 At, in, on, etc.

在 **zài**: in, at, on:[6]

> 飞机在天空中盘旋。 **fēijī zài tiānkōng zhōng pánxuán**
> (lit. plane cv:in air-middle circle) The plane circled in the air.

---

[6] See also §8.2.

展览会在博物馆举行。 **zhǎnlǎnhuì zài bówùguǎn jǔxíng**
(lit. exhibition cv:in museum hold) The exhibition was held in the museum.

他在人群中挤来挤去。 **tā zài rénqún zhōng jǐlái jǐqù**
(lit. he cv.in crowd push-come push-go)
He pushed back and forth through the crowd.

在湖面上升起了一片水汽。 **zài húmiàn shàng shēngqǐ le yīpiàn shuǐqì**
(lit. cv:on lake surface-top rise-up *le* one mw:stretch vapour)
A bank of mist rose from the surface of the lake.

在 **zài** is the most versatile of coverbs, in the way it governs its locational objects. Most commonly the object requires a postposition which indicates its position precisely:

在花园<u>里</u> **zài huāyuán <u>li</u>**
(lit. cv:in garden-<u>inside</u>) in the garden

在大树<u>下</u> **zài dà shù <u>xià</u>**
(lit. cv:at large tree <u>below</u>) <u>beneath</u> the large tree

在桌子<u>上</u> **zài zhuōzi <u>shàng</u>**
(cv:on table-<u>top</u>) <u>on</u> the table

在房子<u>外面</u> **zài fángzi <u>wàimian</u>**
(cv:at house-<u>outside</u>) <u>outside</u> the house

However, if the location noun is trisyllabic, the postposition 里 **li** 'inside' is usually omitted for prosodic reasons. For example:

哥哥在图书馆复习功课。 **gēge zài túshūguǎn fùxí gōngkè**
(lit. elder brother cv:in library revise lesson)
Elder brother is revising his lessons in the library.

弟弟在游乐场玩儿。 **dìdi zài yóulèchǎng wánr**
(lit. younger brother cv:in funfair play)
Younger brother was having a good time at the funfair.

爸爸在办公室办公。 **bàba zài bàngōngshì bàngōng**
(lit. father cv:in office work) Father is working in [his] office.

Postpositions other than 里 **li**, can, of course, be used:

在游乐场外面 **zài yóulèchǎng wàimian**
outside the amusement park.

If the location is a place of work or study, a postposition is not needed:

姐姐在银行工作。 **jiějie zài yínháng gōngzuò**
(lit. elder sister cv:in bank work) Elder sister works in a bank.

弟弟在大学上学。 **dìdi zài dàxué shàngxué**
(lit. younger brother cv:in university attend)
Younger brother is at university.

Likewise the postpostion 里 **li** is not used with a location as large as a country or city:

他在中国旅游。 **tā zài zhōngguó lǚyóu**
(lit. he cv:in China tour) He is touring in China.

他们在北京居住。 **tāmen zài běijīng jūzhù**
(lit. they cv:in Beijing live) They live in Beijing.

于 **yú**: in, at:

熊猫产于中国西南山区。 **xióngmāo chǎn yú zhōngguó xīnán shānqū**
(lit. panda produce cv:in China south-west mountain region)
Pandas are found in the mountain regions of southwest China.

coverb	usage	register	collocational	governmental	prosodic	sequential
在 **zài**	static; as sentence beginner	neut.	里 **li** may be included/excluded depending on noun involved	n		pre-/post-vb
于 **yú**		class.	postposition not often used	n		post-vb

11.2.1.8 Through

透过 **tòuguò**: through:

阳光透过玻璃窗照射进来。 **yángguāng tòuguò bōlichuāng zhàoshè jìnlai**
(lit. sunlight cv:through glass window shine-in-come)
The sunlight shone through the (glass) window.

coverb	usage	register	collocational	governmental	prosodic	sequential
透过 **tòuguò**	neut.			n		pre-vb

11.2.1.9   Distance from

离 **lí**: from:

我家离大学不远。[7] **wǒ jiā lí dàxué bù yuǎn**
(lit. my home cv:from university not far)
My home is not far from the University.

这儿离车站有两英里的路。 **zhèr lí chēzhàn yǒu liǎng yīnglǐ de lù**
(lit. here cv:from station there-are two mile *de* road/distance)
Here is two miles from the station.

coverb	usage	register	collocational	governmental	prosodic	sequential
离 **lí**	static	neut.		n, pron		pre-vb

11.2.1.10   On the spot

就 **jiù**: at (where one is):

请大家就地坐下。 **qǐng dàjiā jiùdì zuòxia**
(lit. please everyone cv:where-one-is place sit down)
Would everyone please sit down where you are.

随 **suí**: at (any place one happens to be in):

请游客不要随地丢弃垃圾。 **qǐng yóukè bùyào suídì diūqì lājī**
(lit. please tourists do not cv:where-one-happens-to-be place discard
rubbish/litter)
Would tourists please not drop litter everywhere.

coverb	usage	register	collocational	governmental	prosodic	sequential
就 **jiù**		neut./fml.	地 **dì** 'place'	n		pre-vb
随 **suí**		neut.	地 **dì** 'place'	n		pre-vb

---

[7] The predicate in a 离 **lí** sentence is often represented by an adjective or the verb 有 **yǒu**.

11.2.2 TIME

11.2.2.1 At (a certain time)

在 **zài**: at:

教师在考试前帮助大家复习功课。
jiàoshī zài kǎoshì qián bāngzhù dàjiā fùxí gōngkè
(lit. teacher cv:at examination before help everyone revise lesson)
The teacher helped everyone with revision before the examination.

火车在中午十二点到达。 **huǒchē zài zhōngwǔ shí'èr diǎn dàodá**
(lit. train cv:at midday twelve o'clock arrive)
The train arrived at 12 o'clock midday.

开会日期定在下个月七号。 **kāihuì rìqī dìng zài xià ge yuè qī hào**
(lit. meeting time fix cv:at next mw month seventh day)
The time of the meeting is fixed for the 7th of next month.

于 **yú**: at:

大学于九月下旬开学。 **dàxué yú jiǔyuè xiàxún kāixué**
(lit. University cv:at nine month last ten-day period start-study)
The University will open in the last week of September.

他于去年去世。 **tā yú qùnián qùshì**
(lit. he cv:at last year leave-the-world)
He died last year.

我生于一九五六年三月二十八日。
wǒ shēng yú yī jiǔ wǔ liù nián sānyuè èrshí bā rì
(lit. I born cv:at 1956 year 3rd month 28th day)
I was born on 28th March 1956.

coverb	usage	register	collocational	governmental	prosodic	sequential
在 **zài**		neut.		n, pron		pre-/post-vb
于 **yú**		fml.		n, pron		pre-/post-vb

11.2.2.2 From or since (a certain time)

从 **cóng**: from, since:

他从小就喜爱音乐。 **tā cóng xiǎo jiù xǐ'ài yīnyuè**
(lit. he cv:from young then love music)
He has loved music since childhood.

她从来不失信用。 **tā cónglái bù shī xìnyòng**
(lit. she cv:from-past-till-now not break faith) She has never broken faith.

我从明天起开始吃斋。 **wǒ cóng míngtiān qǐ kāishǐ chī zhāi**
(lit. I cv:from tomorrow begin start eat vegetarian diet)
From tomorrow I will start being a vegetarian/go on a vegetarian diet.

自 **zì**: from, since:

本条例自即日起施行。 **běn tiáolì zì jírì qǐ shīxíng**
(lit. this mw regulation cv:from this day begin operate)
This regulation will come into operation from today.

由 **yóu**: from:

课程由明年起改为学分制。 **kèchéng yóu míngnián qǐ gǎi wéi xuéfēn zhì**
(lit. course cv:from next year begin change to credit system)
The courses will be changed to a credit-system from next year.

打 **dǎ**: from, since:

你打什么时候起学会这套本领？
nǐ dǎ shénme shíhou qǐ xuéhuì zhèi tào běnlǐng
(lit. you cv:from what time begin learn-acquire this mw skill)
Since when have you mastered this skill?

coverb	usage	register	collocational	governmental	prosodic	sequential
从 **cóng**		neut.	time word, phrase + 起 **qǐ** adj e.g. 从小 **xiǎo** 'since childhood' v. e.g. 从来 **lái** 'from past till now'	n, adj, v		pre-vb
自 **zì**		fml.	time word, phrase + 起 **qǐ**	n	自从 **zìcóng**	pre-/post-vb
由 **yóu**		class.	time word, phrase + 起 **qǐ**	n		pre-vb
打 **dǎ**		colloq.	time word, phrase + 起 **qǐ**	n		pre-vb

11.2.2.3 Till (a certain time)

到 **dào**: to, till:

他到天亮时才睡觉。 **tā dào tiānliàng shí cái shuìjiào**
(lit. he cv:till daylight time only then sleep)
He did not go to bed till daybreak.

他一觉睡到大天亮。 **tā yī jiào shuì dào dà tiānliàng**
(lit. he one sleep sleep cv:till daylight) He slept right through to daybreak.

至 **zhì**: to:

事情至此才有了眉目。 **shìqing zhì cǐ cái yǒu le méimu**
(lit. matter cv:till this only then have *le* prospect of solution)
The matter only now has a prospect of solution.

她工作直至深夜。 **tā gōngzuò zhízhì shēnyè**
(lit. she work direct cv:to deep night) She worked deep into the night.

迄 **qì**: till:

失踪人的下落迄今还没有消息。
shīzōng rén de xiàluò qìjīn hái méiyǒu xiāoxi
(lit. lose-track-people *de* whereabouts cv:till now still not have news)
There is still no news of the whereabouts of the missing people.

届 **jiè**: till, at:

这件事届时再跟你详谈。 **zhèi jiàn shì jièshí zài gēn nǐ xiángtán**
(lit. this mw matter cv:at time again cv:with you in detail talk)
I will speak to you again in detail about this matter when the time comes/in
due course.

临 **lín**: at the point of, on the verge of:

他临危不惧。 **tā línwēi bù jù**
(lit. he cv:at the point of danger not afraid) He faced danger without fear.

我临行匆忙，来不及向您告别。
wǒ línxíng cóngmáng | láibují xiàng nín gàobié
(lit. I cv:at the point of leaving in a hurry, no time cv:to you (polite) say
good-bye)
I was very busy before departing and didn't have time to say goodbye to
you [polite].

顶 **dǐng**: until:

顶凌晨四点他才睡觉。 **dǐng língchén sì diǎn tā cái shuìjiào**
(lit. cv:until approach morning four o'clock he only then sleep)
He did not go to bed until 4 o'clock in the early hours of the morning.

coverb	usage	register	collocational	governmental	prosodic	sequential
到 **dào**		neut.	. . . 止 **zhǐ**	n, v, cl	直到 **zhídào**	pre-/post-vb
至 **zhì**		fml.	. . . 为止 **wéi zhǐ**	n, v, cl	直至 **zhízhì**	pre-/post-vb
迄 **qì**		class.	今 **jīn** 'today'	n		pre-vb
届 **jiè**		class.	时 **shí** 'time'	n		pre-vb
临 **lín**		colloq.	时 **shí** 'provisionally' 急 **jí** 'in haste' 危 **wēi** 'in danger' 死 **sǐ** 'die' 行 **xíng** 'travel'	n, adj, v		pre-vb
顶 **dǐng**		dial.		n		pre-vb

11.2.2.4 At the most opportune moment

趁 **chèn**: taking opportunity of, while:

趁热打铁。 **chèn rè dǎtiě**
(lit. cv:while hot strike iron) Strike while the iron is hot.

孩子趁妈妈不在家的时候出去玩儿。
háizi chèn māma bù zài jiā de shíhou chūqu wánr
(lit. child cv:while mother not at home *de* time out-go play)
The child went out to play while his/her mother was not at home.

乘 **chéng**: taking advantage of, while:

右锋乘对方防守不严时射入一球。
yòufēng chéng duìfāng fángshǒu bù yán shí shè rù yī qiú
(lit. right-wing forward cv:taking advantage of opponent defence not tight
time shoot-enter one ball)
The right-wing forward took advantage of the slack defence of the
opposition to score a goal.

就 **jiù**: fitting in with [convenience]:

这本书，请你就便捎给他。
zhèi běn shū | qǐng nǐ jiùbiàn shāo gěi tā
(lit. this mw book, please you cv:fitting in with convenience take cv:giving to him)
Please will you take this book to him while you are about it.

顺 **shùn**: following, along with:

请你顺手把门关上。 **qǐng nǐ shùnshǒu bǎ mén guān shàng**
(lit. please you cv:along with hand cv:grasp door close up)
Would you please as you go out/as you come in/on your way shut the door.

随 **suí**: along with:

你随时可以跟我联系。 **nǐ suíshí kěyǐ gēn wǒ liánxì**
(lit. you cv: along with time may cv:with me contact)
You can get in touch with me any time.

跟 **gēn**: along with:

他一进屋子，跟手就把鞋脱掉。
tā yī jìn wūzi | gēnshǒu jiù bǎ xié tuō diào
(lit. he once enter room, cv:along with hand then cv:grasp shoes take off)
As soon as he came into the room, he straight away took off his shoes.

coverb	usage	register	collocational	governmental	prosodic	sequential
趁 **chèn**		neut.	机 **jī** 'opportunity' 便 **biàn** 'covenience' 势 **shì** 'situation'	n, adj, v, cl		pre-vb
乘 **chéng**		fml.	机 **jī**, 便 **biàn**	n		pre-vb
就 **jiù**		fml.	便 **biàn**	n		pre-vb
顺 **shùn**		colloq.	便 **biàn**, 势 **shì**, 手 **shǒu** 'hand'	n		pre-vb
随 **suí**		colloq.	时 **shí** 'time' 便 **biàn**, 机 **jī**, 手 **shǒu**	n		pre-vb
跟 **gēn**		slang	手 **shǒu**	n		pre-vb

11.2.2.5   Whenever something happens

当 **dāng**: when:

当他回家度假时，我去探望他。 **dāng tā huíjiā dùjià shí | wǒ qù tànwàng tā**
(lit. cv:when he come home have holiday time, I go visit him)
When he comes home on holiday, I'll go to visit him.

逢 **féng**: whenever:

彩票逢星期六开奖。 **cǎipiào féng xīngqī liù kāijiǎng**
(lit. lottery tickets cv:whenever Saturday draw lottery)
The lottery is drawn every Saturday.

遇 **yù**: when, whenever:

球赛遇雨顺延。 **qiúsài yù yǔ shùn yán**
(lit. ball game cv:when rain postpone)
The match was postponed when it rained.

coverb	usage	register	collocational	governmental	prosodic	sequential
当 **dāng**		neut.	. . . 时 **shí** or . . . 的时候 **de shíhou**	clause	每当 **měidāng**	pre-vb
逢 **féng**		neut.		n	每逢 **měiféng**	pre-vb
遇 **yù**		fml.		n	凡遇 **fányù**	pre-vb

11.2.2.6   As soon as possible

赶 **gǎn**: hurrying with:

我们赶快走吧。 **wǒmen gǎnkuài zǒu ba**
(lit. we cv:hurrying with speed go **ba**) Let's go at once.

请你赶紧回去。 **qǐng nǐ gǎnjǐn huíqu**
(lit. please you cv:hurrying with urgency return-go)
Please hurry back straight away.

尽 **jǐn**: as is possible:

请你尽早给我一个答复。 **qǐng nǐ jǐnzǎo gěi wǒ yī ge dáfù**
(lit. please you cv:as is possible early give me one mw reply)
Please let me have a reply as early as possible.

希望你能尽快回答我的问题。 **xīwàng nǐ néng jǐnkuài huídá wǒde wèntí**
(lit. hope you can cv:as is possible fast reply my question)
Hope you can reply to my question as quickly as possible.

coverb	usage	register	collocational	governmental	prosodic	sequential
赶 **gǎn**		colloq.	快 **kuài** 'fast' 紧 **jǐn** 'tight'	adj		pre-vb
尽 **jǐn**		colloq.	快 **kuài**, 早 **zǎo** 'early'	n, adj		pre-vb

11.2.3   WITH, FOR OR BY SOMEONE OR SOMETHING

11.2.3.1   Together with

跟 **gēn**: with:

我跟你说句话。 **wǒ gēn nǐ shuō jù huà**
(lit. I cv:with you speak mw words) I will have a word with you.

我想跟你们合作。 **wǒ xiǎng gēn nǐmen hézuò**
(lit. I like to cv:with you cooperate) I'd like to cooperate with you.

和 **hé**: with:

我可以和你当面谈谈吗? **wǒ kěyǐ hé nǐ dāngmiàn tántán ma**
(lit. I may cv:with you cv:facing face talk-talk *ma*)
May I have a chat with you face to face.

与 **yǔ**: with:

他与她十分要好。 **tā yǔ tā shífēn yàohǎo**
(lit. he cv:with her extremely be on good terms)
He is a very close friend of hers.

他与此事无关。 **tā yǔ cǐshì wúguān**
(lit. he cv:with this matter without connection)
He has nothing to do with this (matter).

同 **tóng**: with:

他同她根本合不来。 **tā tóng tā gēnběn hébulái**
(lit. he cv:with her basically match-not-come) He really doesn't get on with her.

我同小李住在一起。 **wǒ tóng xiǎolǐ zhù zài yīqǐ**
(lit. I cv:with Little Li live cv:at the same place)
I live with Little Li.

coverb	usage	register	collocational	governmental	prosodic	sequential
跟 **gēn**		northern colloq.		n, pron		pre-vb
和 **hé**		neut.		n, pron		pre-vb
与 **yǔ**		class.		n, pron		pre-vb
同 **tóng**		southern colloq.		n, pron		pre-vb

11.2.3.2 For (somebody) – beneficiary

给 **gěi**: for, to:

我给哥哥写了一封回信。 **wǒ gěi gēge xiě le yī fēng huíxìn**
(lit. I cv:to elder brother write **le** one mw reply letter)
I wrote a reply to elder brother.

快给他赔个不是。 **kuài gěi tā péi ge bùshi**
(lit. quickly cv:to him compensate mw not right)
Apologise to him immediately.

你能给我们当翻译吗? **nǐ néng gěi wǒmen dāng fānyì ma**
(lit. you can cv:for us act as interpreter **ma**)
Can you be our interpreter?

替 **tì**: for:

大家都来替她送行。 **dàjiā duō lái tì tā sòngxíng**
(lit. everyone all come cv:for her see-on-way)
Everyone came to see her off.

人人都替你高兴。 **rénrén duō tì nǐ gāoxìng**
(lit. everyone all cv:for you happy) Everyone is happy for you.

同 **tóng**: for:

我同你出个主意。 **wǒ tóng nǐ chū ge zhǔyi**
(lit. I cv:for you come-up-with mw idea)
I'll think up an idea for you.

你去买票，行李我同你看管。
nǐ qù mǎi piào | xíngli wǒ tóng nǐ kānguǎn
(lit. you go buy tickets, luggage I cv:for you look after)
You go and buy the tickets, and I will keep an eye on the luggage for you.

为 **wèi**: for:

让我们为客人们的健康干杯！
ràng wǒmen wèi kèrenmen de jiànkāng gānbēi
(lit. let us cv:for guests *de* health dry glass)
Let's drink a toast to our guests./Let's drink to the health of our guests.

请为我向主人表示谢意。 **qǐng wèi wǒ xiàng zhǔrén biǎoshì xièyì**
(lit. please cv:for me cv:to host express thanks)
Please say thank you to the host for me.

别为这件小事担心。 **bié wèi zhèi jiàn xiǎoshì dānxīn**
(lit. don't cv:for this mw small matter carry worries) Please don't worry
about this small matter.

他为我送来了一份请帖。 **tā wèi wǒ sònglai le yī fèn qǐngtiě**
(lit. he cv:for me send-come *le* one mw invitation letter)
He sent me an invitation.

为安全起见，请勿在机舱使用手提电话。
wèi ānquán qǐjiàn | qǐng wù zài jīcāng shǐyòng shǒutí diànhuà
(lit. cv:for safety sake, please don't cv:in cabin use hand-carry telephones)
For safety reasons, please don't use mobile phones in the cabin.

为了 **wèile**: for sake of, in order to:

为了向顾客提供方便，商店决定周末开门营业。 **wèile xiàng gùkè tígōng
fāngbiàn | shāngdiàn juédìng zhòumò kāimén yíngyè**
(lit. cv:for sake of cv:to customers provide convenience, store decide
weekend open door do business)
For the convenience of customers, the store decided to open for business
at the weekends.

为了维护球场的秩序，警方派出了不少警察。
wèile wéihù qiúchǎng de zhìxù | jǐngfāng pàichū le bùshǎo jǐngchá
(lit. in order to maintain football-ground *de* order, police-side send out not
a few policemen)
To preserve order at the football ground, the police deployed a considerable
number of officers.

coverb	usage	register	collocational	governmental	prosodic	sequential
给 gěi		colloq.		n, pron		pre-vb
替 tì		neut.		n, pron		pre-vb
同 tóng		dial.		pron		pre-vb
为 wèi		neut.	... 起见 qǐjiàn	n, pron, adj	为了 wèile	pre-vb
为了 wèile	always as a sentence beginner	fml.	... 起见 qǐjiàn	n, pron, adj, vb, cl		pre-vb

11.2.3.3   By – be the responsibility of (somebody)

由 **yóu**: by:

这件事由我负责。 **zhèi jiàn shì yóu wǒ fùzé**
(lit. this mw matter cv:by me take responsibility)
This matter is my responsibility.

归 **guī**: by, up to:

这些事全部归你管。 **zhèixiē shì quánbù guī nǐ guǎn**
(lit. these mw matters entirely cv:up to you take charge)
You are in charge of all these matters.

coverb	usage	register	collocational	governmental	prosodic	sequential
由 yóu		fml.		n, pron		pre-vb
归 guī		colloq.		n, pron		pre-vb

11.2.4   INSTRUMENT AND VEHICLE

11.2.4.1   With (a certain instrument or appliance)

用 **yòng**: with, using:

她用梳子梳了梳头发。 **tā yòng shūzi shū le shū tóufa**
(lit. she cv:with comb comb *le* comb hair) She combed her hair.

他用手掠了一下额前的头发。 **tā yòng shǒu lüè le yīxià é qián de tóufa**
(lit. he cv:with hand brush aside *le* one mw:time forehead in front *de* hair)
He brushed the hair from his forehead with his hand.

我用胳膊碰了他一下。 **wǒ yòng gēbo pèng le tā yīxià**
(lit. I cv:with arm nudge *le* him one mw:time) I nudged him with my arm.

你用什么理由来说服她呢? **nǐ yòng shénme lǐyóu lái shuōfú tā ne**
(lit. you cv:using what reason come convince her *ne*)
What reason did you use to convince her (then)?

拿 **ná**: with, taking:

我们拿把尺子量一量。 **wǒmen ná bǎ chǐzi liáng yī liáng**
(lit. we cv:with mw ruler measure one measure) Let's measure it with a ruler.

请你拿几句话概括一下。 **qǐng nǐ ná jǐ jù huà gàikuò yīxià**
(lit. please you cv:with few mw words summarise one mw:time)
Please would you give a summary in a few words.

你帮了我这么多的忙。我拿什么谢你呢?
nǐ bāng le wǒ zhème duō de máng | wǒ ná shénme xiè nǐ ne
(lit. you help *le* me so much *de* help. I cv:with what thank you *ne*)
You've helped me so much. How can I thank you?

你拿什么做标准来衡量呢? **nǐ ná shénme zuò biāozhǔn lái héngliáng ne**
(lit. you cv:with what make criterion come judge *ne*)
What criteria do you adopt to make a judgement?

coverb	usage	register	collocational	governmental	prosodic	sequential
用 **yòng**		neut.	concrete or abstract objects	n, pron		pre-vb
拿 **ná**		colloq.	concrete or abstract objects	n, pron		pre-vb

11.2.4.2 By (a vehicle)

坐 **zuò**: by:

我们打算坐船去。 **wǒmen dǎsuan zuò chuán qù**
(lit. we intend cv:by boat go) We intend to go by boat.

乘 **chéng**: by:

你们乘哪一班飞机来? **nǐmen chéng nǎ/něi yī bān fēijī lái**
(lit. you (plural) cv:by which one mw plane come)
Which flight will you come on?

搭 **dā**: by:

> 他们搭末班车回家。 **tāmen dā mòbānchē huíjiā**
> (lit. they cv:by last mw bus/train return home)
> They went home on the last bus/train.

coverb	usage	registeral	collocational	governmental	prosodic	sequential
坐 **zuò**		colloq.		n		pre-vb
乘 **chéng**		fml.		n		pre-vb
搭 **dā**		neut.		n		pre-vb

11.2.5   BY MEANS OF, IN ACCORDANCE WITH, ETC.

11.2.5.1   Relying on (a person, etc.)

靠 **kào**: relying on:

> 他家里靠他挣钱过活。 **tā jiā li kào tā zhèngqián guòhuó**
> (lit. his home-in cv:relying on him earn money pass life)
> His family relied on his earnings.

仗 **zhàng**: relying on:

> 这件事全仗大家帮忙。 **zhèi jiàn shì quán zhàng dàjiā bāngmáng**
> (lit. this mw matter entirely cv:relying on everyone help)
> This matter is entirely reliant on everyone's help.

> 别仗势欺人。 **bié zhàng shì qī rén**
> (lit. don't cv:relying on power bully people)
> Don't rely on your power to bully people.

指着 **zhǐzhe**: relying on:

> 我们就指着你帮忙哩。 **wǒmen jiù zhǐzhe nǐ bāngmáng li**
> (lit. we just cv:relying on you help *li*) We just rely on your help.

coverb	usage	register	collocational	governmental	prosodic	sequential
靠 **kào**		neut.		n, pron		pre-vb
仗 **zhàng**		class.	势 **shì** 'power'	n, pron		pre-vb
指着 **zhǐzhe**		colloq.		n, pron		pre-vb

11.2.5.2   By means of

凭 **píng**: by means of:

> 凭票入场。**píng piào rùchǎng**
> (lit. cv:by ticket enter stadium/theatre) Admission by ticket only.

> 人类凭借语言互相交流思想。
> **rénlèi píngjiè yǔyán hùxiāng jiāoliú sīxiǎng**
> (lit. mankind cv:relying on language mutually exchange thinking)
> Mankind exchanges ideas by means of language.

借 **jiè**: taking advantage of:

> 我想借此机会向大家表示感谢。
> **wǒ xiǎng jiè cǐ jīhuì xiàng dàjiā biǎoshì gǎnxiè**
> (lit. I want cv:taking advantage of this opportunity cv:towards everyone
> express thanks)
> I want to take this opportunity to thank everyone.

> 他藉着朋友的帮助顺利地回到了家乡。
> **tā jièzhe péngyou de bāngzhù shùnlì de huídào le jiāxiāng**
> (he cv:taking advantage of friends' *de* help successfully *de* return to *le*
> hometown)
> With the help of friends he successfully made it back to his hometown.

通过 **tōngguò**: by means of, through:

> 爱迪生通过各种试验终于发明了电灯。
> **àidíshēng tōngguò gèzhǒng shìyàn zhōngyú fāmíng le diàndēng**
> (lit. Edison cv:through every mw:kind experiment in the end invent *le*
> electric light)
> Edison finally invented the electric light after all kinds of experiments.

coverb	usage	register	collocational	governmental	prosodic	sequential
凭 **píng**		neut.	票 **piào** 'ticket'	n	凭借 **píngjiè**	pre-vb
借 **jiè**		fml.	机会 **jīhuì** 'opportunity'	n	藉着[8] **jièzhe**	pre-vb
通过 **tōngguò**		fml.		n		pre-vb

---

[8] 藉着 **jièzhe** is in fact a more commonly used written form than 借着 **jièzhe**.

11.2.5.3 According to

凭 **píng**: according to:

你凭什么得出这样的结论？ **nǐ píng shénme déchū zhèiyàng de jiélùn**
(lit. you cv:according to what reach this kind *de* conclusion)
How did you reach a conclusion like this?

照 **zhào**: according to:

咱们就照这样办吧。 **zánmen jiù zhào zhèiyàng bàn ba**
(lit. we then cv:according to this way do *ba*)
Let's do it like this then.

按 **àn**: according to:

请按次序发言。 **qǐng àn cìxù fāyán**
(lit. please cv:according to order speak) Please speak in order.

请按时把作业交上来。 **qǐng ànshí bǎ zuòyè jiāo shànglai**
(lit. please cv:according to time cv:grasp assignment hand over-come)
Please hand in your assignment on time.

请大家按照原来的规定去做。 **qǐng dàjiā ànzhào yuánlái de guīdìng qù zuò**
(lit. please everyone cv:according to original *de* stipulation go-do)
Would every please do it/act as originally stipulated.

依 **yī**: according to:

依我看，问题并不复杂。 **yī wǒ kàn | wèntí bìng bù fùzá**
(lit. cv:as I see, problem certainly not complicated)
As I see it, the problem certainly isn't complicated.

请依照情况而定。[9] **qǐng yīzhào qíngkuàng ér dìng**
(lit. please cv:according to circumstances and decide)
Please decide in the light of circumstances.

请大家依次就座！ **qǐng dàjiā yī cì jiùzuò**
(lit. please everyone cv:according to order occupy seat)
Would everyone please sit in proper order.

---

[9] In somewhat more formal statements 而 **ér** 'and (under these circumstances)' is placed between the coverb expression and the verb. This is likely to happen particularly if the verb is monosyllabic.

本着 **běnzhe**: in line with:

我们应该本着互助的精神办事。
wǒmen yīnggāi běnzhe hùzhù de jīngshén bànshì
(lit. we ought to cv:in line with mutual help *de* spirit do things)
We must work in the spirit of mutual assistance.

以 **yǐ**: according to, by means of:

你可以以此类推。 **nǐ kěyǐ yǐ cǐ lèituī**
(lit. you can cv:by this draw analogy) You can draw analogies from this.

你得以理服人。 **nǐ děi yǐ lǐ fúrén**
(lit. you must cv:by means of reason convince people)
You must convince people by reason.

我以个人的名义向您保证。 **wǒ yǐ gèrén de míngyì xiàng nín bǎozhèng**
(lit. I cv:according to individual name cv:towards you (polite) guarantee)
I give you my personal guarantee.

我以老朋友的身份劝你别这样做。
wǒ yǐ lǎo péngyou de shēnfèn quàn nǐ bié zhèyàng zuò
(lit. I cv:according to old friend's *de* capacity urge you don't this way do)
I urge you as an old friend not to do this.

平均每户以四口人计算。 **píngjūn měi hù yǐ sì kǒu rén jìsuàn**
(lit. average every household cv:according to four mw people calculate)
The average household is calculated as four people.

就 **jiù**: according to:

就我来说，还是不去好。 **jiù wǒ lái shuō | háishi bù qù hǎo**
(lit. cv:according to I come-say, still not go good)
In my view it is best not to go.

据 **jù**: according to:

据我推测，他是不会同意的。 **jù wǒ tuīcè | tā shì bùhuì tóngyì de**
(lit. cv:according to I guess, he is not likely agree *de*)
My guess is he won't agree.

根据气象台的预报，明天要下雨。
gēnjù qìxiàngtái de yùbào | míngtiān yào xià yǔ
(lit. cv:according to weather station *de* forecast, tomorrow will rain)
According to the weather forecast, it will rain tomorrow.

据说，他已经出国去了。 **jùshuō | tā yǐjīng chūguó qù le**
(lit. cv:according to say, he already exit country go *le*)
They say he has already left the country.

准 **zhǔn**: according to:

咱们准前例办吧。 **zánmen zhǔn qiánlì bàn ba**
(lit. we cv:according to precedent do *ba*) Let's act according to precedent.

如 **rú**: according to:

请如期完成。 **qǐng rúqī wánchéng**
(lit. please cv:according to schedule complete) Please finish on time.

在此如数归还，请查收。 **zài cǐ rúshù guīhuán | qǐng cháshōu**
(lit. herewith cv:according to original numbers return, please check accept)
Please find the original amount returned herewith.

遵循 **zūnxún**: according to:

这类事情可以遵循常规解决。 **zhèi lèi shìqing kěyǐ zūnxún chángguī jiějué**
(lit. this mw:kind matter can cv:according to common practice resolve)
This matter can be resolved routinely.

基于 **jīyú**: on the basis of:

基于以上的理由，我不赞成你的意见。
jīyú yǐshàng de lǐyóu | wǒ bù zànchéng nǐ de yìjian
(lit. cv:on the basis of the above *de* reasons, I not agree your opinion)
For the reasons above, I do not agree with your opinion.

由于 **yóuyú**: owing to:

由于种种原因，他无法出席这次会议。
yóuyú zhǒngzhǒng yuányīn | tā wúfǎ chūxí zhèi cì huìyì
(cv:owing to all kind of reasons, he no way attend this mw:occasion meeting)
For various reasons, he cannot attend this meeting.

由于工作关系，我未能离开。
yóuyú gōngzuò guānxì | wǒ wèinéng líkāi
(lit. cv:owing to work reasons, I not able leave)
I could not leave because of work [commitments].

出于 **chūyú**: stemming from:

出于好奇，他极力想弄清事实的真相。
chūyú hàoqí | tā jílì xiǎng nòngqīng shìshí de zhēnxiàng
(lit. cv:stemming from curiosity, he extreme strength want make clear facts
de truth)
Out of curiosity, he was intent on getting to the truth of the situation/the
real facts.

针对 **zhēnduì**: in the light of:

请你针对具体情况作出决定吧。
qǐng nǐ zhēnduì jùtǐ qíngkuàng zuòchū juédìng ba
(lit. please you cv:in the light of concrete circumstances make out decision *ba*)
Please come to a decision in the light of concrete conditions.

coverb	usage	register	collocational	governmental	prosodic	sequential
凭 **píng**		colloq.		n		pre-vb
照 **zhào**		colloq.		n		pre-vb
按 **àn**		neut.		n	按照 **ànzhào**	pre-vb
依 **yī**		neut.		n	依照 **yīzhào**	pre-vb
本着 **běnzhe**		neut.	精神 **jīngshén** 'spirit' 原则 **yuánzé** 'principle'	n		pre-vb
以 **yǐ**		class.		n		pre-vb
就 **jiù**		class.		n, cl		pre-vb
据 **jù**	usually as a sentence beginner	fml.		n, v	根据 **gēnjù**	pre-vb
准 **zhǔn**		fml.		n		pre-vb
如 **rú**		class.	期 **qī** 'deadline' 数 **shù** 'amount'	n		pre-vb
遵循 **zūnxún**		fml.		n	遵照 **zūnzhào**	pre-vb
基于 **jīyú**	usually as a sentence beginner	fml.		n		pre-vb
由于 **yóuyú**	usually as a sentence beginner	fml.		n		pre-vb
出于 **chūyú**	usually as a sentence beginner	fml.		n		pre-vb
针对 **zhēnduì**		fml.		n		pre-vb

11.2.5.4 Regarding, about

于 **yú**: regarding:

抽烟于健康有害。 **chōuyān yú jiànkāng yǒu hài**
(lit. smoking cv:regarding health harmful)
Smoking is harmful to health.

这样于你自己不利。 **zhèyàng yú nǐ zìjǐ bùlì**
(lit. this way cv:regarding you self not beneficial)
This is no good to you personally.

至于 **zhìyú**: as regards:

至于其他问题，以后再说。 **zhìyú qítā wèntí | yǐhòu zài shuō**
(lit. cv:as regards other questions, later again speak)
We will talk again about the other questions later.

关于 **guānyú**: concerning:

关于这件事，我没有意见。 **guānyú zhèi jiàn shì | wǒ méiyǒu yìjian**
(lit. cv:concerning this mw matter, I not have opinion)
I don't have an opinion on this matter.

关于这个问题，后面还要详述。
guānyú zhèi ge wèntí | hòumian hái yào xiángshù
(lit. cv:concerning this mw question, afterwards still need detail account)
As regards this question, [I] will go into greater details later on.

讲 **jiǎng**: speaking of:

讲条件，他没有你好。 **jiǎng tiáojiàn | tā méiyǒu nǐ hǎo**
(lit. cv:speaking of qualification, he not have you good)
Speaking of qualifications, he is not as good as you.

论 **lùn**: as regards:

论能力，他比你强。 **lùn nénglì | tā bǐ nǐ qiáng**
(lit. as regards ability, he cv:compared with you strong)
As regards ability, he is better than you.

论打壁球，他数第一。 **lùn dǎ bìqiú | tā shǔ dìyī**
(lit. as regards playing squash, he rank no. 1)
He is ranked number one in squash.

coverb	usage	register	collocational	governmental	prosodic	sequential
于 **yú**		fml.		n		pre-vb
至于 **zhìyú**	usually as a sentence beginner	neut.	问题 **wèntí** 'problem'	n		pre-vb
关于 **guānyú**	usually as a sentence beginner	neut.		n		pre-vb
讲 **jiǎng**	usually as a sentence beginner	colloq.		n, cl		pre-vb
论 **lùn**	usually as a sentence beginner	colloq.		n, vb, cl		pre-vb

11.2.5.5 Besides, except

除 **chú**: besides, apart from:

除持票者以外，谁也不准入场。
chú chípiàozhě yǐwài | shuí yě bùzhǔn rùchǎng
(lit. cv:apart from ticket-holder apart, anyone also not allow enter stadium/hall)
No one is allowed in apart from ticket-holders.

她除了家务之外，什么都不会做。
tā chúle jiāwù zhīwài | shénme duō bùhuì zuò
(lit. she cv:apart from household duties part, anything all not can do)
She can't do anything but housework.

coverb	usage	register	collocational	governmental	prosodic	sequential
除 **chú**		neut.	... 以外 **yǐwài** ... 之外 **zhīwài**	n, pron, adj, vb, cl	除了 **chúle** 除开 **chúkāi**	pre-vb

11.2.5.6 Considering as

为 **wéi**: considering as:

他把这一切都视为自己的责任。 **tā bǎ zhèi yīqiè dōu shì wéi zìjǐ de zérèn**
(lit. he cv:grasping this everything all look upon cv:as own responsibility)
He considers all this his own responsibility.

作 **zuò**: considering as:

可别把这件事当作儿戏！ **kě bié bǎ zhèi jiàn shì dàngzuò érxì**
(lit. really don't cv:grasping this mw matter regard cv:as children's game)
Mind you don't treat this matter as something trifling.

coverb	usage	register	collocational	governmental	prosodic	sequential
为 **wéi**	always as complement	class.	视 **shì** . . . 为 **wéi**	n		post-vb
作 **zuò**	always as complement	colloq.	当 **dàng** . . . 作 **zuò**	n		post-vb

11.2.6 GRAMMATICAL OPERATORS

11.2.6.1 Manipulative

把 **bǎ**: grasping:[10]

不要把事情弄糟了。 **bùyào bǎ shìqing nòngzāo le**
(lit. don't cv:grasping matter make mess **le**)
Don't mess the business up.

快把药吃了。 **kuài bǎ yào chī le**
(lit. quick cv:grasping medicine eat **le**) Hurry up and take the medicine.

将 **jiāng**: grasping:

先将他请来。 **xiān jiāng tā qǐng lái**
(lit. first cv:grasping him invite-come) Invite him here first.

拿 **ná**: taking:

别拿我开玩笑。 **bié ná wǒ kāi wánxiào**
(lit. don't cv:taking me make joke) Don't make fun of me.

谁都拿他没办法。 **shuí dōu ná tā méi bànfǎ**
(lit. anyone all cv:taking him have no way)
No one can do anything with him.

---

[10] See Chapter 12 for a full discussion of the 把 **bǎ** construction.

管 **guǎn**: taking:

> 民间管月蚀叫天狗吃月亮。 **mínjiān guǎn yuèshí jiào tiāngǒu chī yuèliang**
> (lit. people-among cv:taking lunar eclipse call heavenly hound eating the moon)
> According to folklore, lunar eclipse is known as the Heavenly Hound
> Eating the Moon.

> 你管这个叫什么? **nǐ guǎn zhèi ge jiào shénme**
> (lit. you cv:taking this call what) What do you call this?

coverb	usage	register	collocational	governmental	prosodic	sequential
把 **bǎ**		neut.		n, pron		pre-vb
将 **jiāng**		fml.		n, pron		pre-vb
拿 **ná**		colloq.		n, pron		pre-vb
管 **guǎn**		coloq.	. . . 叫 **jiào**	n, pron		pre-vb

11.2.6.2 Passive

被 **bèi**: by:

> 那个拳击手被他的对手打败了。 **nèi ge quánjīshǒu bèi tāde duìshǒu dǎbài le**
> (lit. that mw boxer cv:by his opponent defeat *le*)
> That boxer was beaten by his opponent.

叫 **jiào**: by:

> 谜语叫她(给)猜着了。 **míyǔ jiào tā (gěi) cāizháo le**
> (lit. riddle cv:by her *gei* guess-right *le*) The riddle was guessed by her.

让 **ràng**: by:

> 行李让雨(给)淋湿了。 **xíngli ràng yǔ (gěi) lín shī le**
> (lit. luggage cv:by rain *gei* sprinkle wet *le*)
> The luggage was soaked by the rain.

给 **gěi**: by:

> 车库的门给小偷撬开了。 **chēkù de mén gěi xiǎotōu qiàokāi le**
> (lit. garage *de* door cv:by petty thief prise open *le*)
> The garage door was prised open by a thief.

为 **wéi**: by:

他从来不为别人所左右。 **tā cónglái bù wéi biérén suǒ zuǒyòu**
(lit. he all along not cv:by other people *suo* control)
He was never controlled by other people.

他为大家所尊敬。 **tā wéi dàjiā suǒ zūnjìng**
(lit. he cv:by everyone *suo* respect) He is respected by everyone.

coverb	usage	register	collocational	governmental	prosodic	sequential
被 **bèi**		fml.		n, pron		pre-vb
叫 **jiào**		colloq.	. . . 给 **gěi** (optional)	n, pron		pre-vb
让 **ràng**		infml.	. . . 给 **gěi** (optional)	n, pron		pre-vb
给 **gěi**		colloq.		n, pron		pre-vb
为 **wéi**		class.	. . . 所 **suǒ**	n, pron		pre-vb

11.2.6.3 Comparison

Note that comparative coverbs are more often followed by adjectival phrases rather than by verbal phrases.

象 **xiàng**: similar to:

她象她妈妈一样固执。 **tā xiàng tā māma yīyàng gùzhi**
(lit. she cv:similar to her mother the same stubborn)
She is as stubborn as her mother.

她象她爸爸一样不喜欢吃鱼。 **tā xiàng tā bàba yīyàng bù xǐhuan chī yú**
(lit. she cv:similar to her father the same not like eat fish)
Like her father, she does not like eating fish.

如 **rú**: like:

那儿的夏天如冬天一般寒冷。 **nàr de xiàtiān rú dōngtiān yībān hánlěng**
(lit. there *de* summer cv:like winter the same cold)
Summer there is as cold as winter.

跟 **gēn**: compared with:

这个学期的功课跟上学期一样多。
zhèi ge xuéqī de gōngkè gēn shàng xuéqī yīyàng duō
(lit. this mw term *de* coursework cv:compared with last term the same much)
The coursework this term/semester is just as much as last term/semester.

比 **bǐ**: compared with:

> 这门课比那门容易。 **zhèi mén kè bǐ nèi mén róngyì**
> (lit. this mw discipline/course cv:compared with that mw easy)
> This course/discipline is easier than that one.

较 **jiào**: compared with:

> 今年的成绩较去年为好。 **jīnnián de chéngjì jiào qùnián wéi hǎo**
> (lit. this year *de* results cv:compared with last year be better)
> This year's results are better than last year's.

于 **yú**: than:

> 地球大于月亮。 **dìqiú dà yú yuèliang**
> (lit. earth big cv:than moon) The earth is bigger than the moon.

> 健康的体魄贵于任何财富。 **jiànkāng de tǐpò guì yú rènhé cáifù**
> (lit. healthy *de* physique valuable cv:than any wealth)
> A healthy body is worth more than riches.

coverb	usage	register	collocational	governmental	prosodic	sequential
象 **xiàng**	resemblance	neut.	. . . 一样 **yīyàng**	n, adj, vb, cl	好象 **hǎoxiàng**	pre-vb
如 **rú**	resemblance	fml.	. . . (一)般 **(yī)bān**	n, adj, vb, cl	犹如 **yóurú**	pre-vb
跟 **gēn**[11]	resemblance	infml.	. . . 一样 **yīyàng**	n, adj, vb, cl		pre-vb
比 **bǐ**	comparison	neut.		n, adj, vb, cl		pre-vb
较 **jiào**	comparison	fml.	. . . 为 **wéi**	n, adj, vb, cl		pre-vb
于 **yú**	comparison, always as a complement	fml.		n		post-vb

11.3 COVERBAL POSITIONS

As we have seen above, coverbs can be positioned pre-verbally or post-verbally. A pre-verbal position indicates that the coverbal phrase is being used as an adverbial specifying the background in which the action encoded in the main verb takes place, e.g. location, time, direction taken, instrument used, means employed, principle followed, person involved, and so on. These preliminaries

---

[11] In this context, 跟 **gēn** may be used interchangeably with 和 **hé**, 与 **yǔ**, 同 **tóng**.

or conditions must first be established before the action can be carried out, and the coverbal phrase is therefore placed before the main verb to give it precedence. The pre-verbal coverbal phrase is in fact primarily concerned with the starting position of the subject. For example:

他在图书馆学习。 **tā zài túshūguǎn xuéxí**
(lit. he cv:in library study) He is studying in the library.

*他学习在图书馆。 **tā xuéxí zài túshūguǎn**
*(lit. he study cv:in library)

Here the subject has to locate himself 'in the library' before he 'can begin to study'.[12]

However, there are situations where the actions in the main verb must be carried out first before a particular location or point of time is reached. For example, the verb 放 **fàng** 'to put' and the verb 走 **zǒu** 'to walk' naturally lead to new locations or destinations. At a more abstract level, a meeting may be scheduled at a particular time or something may be regarded in a different light. All these actions of putting, walking, scheduling or regarding must all happen before the new location, time, etc. is reached, and it is therefore logical for the coverbal phrases to come after the main verbs as complements.[13] These post-verbal coverbal phrases are, in most cases, concerned with the end or final position of the object. For example,

他把衣服放在床上。 **tā bǎ yīfu fàng zài chuáng shàng**
(lit. he cv:grasping clothes put cv:on bed-top) He put the clothes on the bed.

Here the location of the subject is not specified, but the important thing is that, as he puts down the clothes, they, the object of the sentence, end up on the bed.

Similarly, in the following example:

他游到对岸。 **tā yóu dào duì'àn**
(lit. he swim cv:reaching opposite shore) He swam to the opposite shore.

---

[12] This precedence rule must be followed in the prose grammar of present-day Chinese, which differs from Classical Chinese where such precedence rules were not made or from Chinese poetry where precedence rules may be violated to give way to rhythm or euphony, e.g. 我们走在大路上。 **wǒmen zǒu zài dà lù shàng** 'We are walking on a main road' should, strictly speaking, be reworded as: 我们在大路上走着。 **wǒmen zài dà lù shàng zǒu zhe**.

[13] It must be understood that the logic behind the precedence between the coverb and the main verb is a prominent feature of present-day Chinese. In Classical Chinese or in a more classical style, the precedence question discussed here is one more of usage than of meaning or logic.

It is obvious that he must start swimming before he can reach the opposite shore.

In some sentences, particularly those with intransitive verbs, a subject may locate itself in a place before the action and remain in the same place afterwards, so that the starting position and the end position of the subject coincide. As far as meaning is concerned, there is no difference between the pre-verbal and post-verbal position of the coverbal phrase in these cases. For example:

他在北京住。 **tā zài běijīng zhù**
(lit. he cv:in Beijing live)

他住在北京。 **tā zhù zài běijīng**
(lit. he live cv:in Beijing) He lives in Beijing.

蝴蝶在花丛中飞舞。 **húdié zài huācóng zhōng fēiwǔ**
(lit. butterflies cv:in flower-clusters middle fly-dance)

蝴蝶飞舞在花丛中。 **húdié fēiwǔ zài huācóng zhōng**
(lit. butterflies fly-dance cv:in flower-clusters middle)
The butterflies flew about among the flowers.

Elsewhere, context and common sense, too, in a meaning-oriented language like Chinese, will rule out any misunderstanding that might arise from pre-verbal or post-verbal positioning of a coverbal phrase. For instance:

他在黑板上写了几个字。 **tā zài hēibǎn shàng xiě le jǐ ge zì**
(lit. he cv:on blackboard write *le* a few mw characters)
He wrote a few Chinese characters on the blackboard.

means very much the same as the following sentence apart from the switch to definite reference for the object 字 **zì** 'characters':

他把那几个字写在黑板上。 **tā bǎ nèi jǐ ge zì xiě zài hēibǎn shàng**
(lit. he cv:grasping those few mw characters write cv: on blackboard-top)
He wrote those few Chinese characters on the blackboard.

In the first sentence, it will still be understood that the subject is standing in front of the blackboard writing Chinese characters on it, and no one of sound mind will think that subject has climbed on to the blackboard before writing.

Sometimes, when a coverbal phrase indicates time or location (particularly with a fairly long expression), scope, basis or purpose, it may come at the beginning of the sentence before the subject:

趁人不注意，他悄悄地离开了。

chèn rén bù zhùyì | tā qiāoqiāo de líkāi le

(lit. cv:taking advantage of people not paying attention, he quietly *de* leave *le*)

He quietly left while people weren't paying attention.

在希马拉亚山的山颠上，空气极其稀薄。

zài xīmǎlāyà shān de shāndiān shàng | kōngqì jíqí xībó

(lit. cv:on Himalaya mountains *de* summit-on, air extremely thin)

The air is extremely thin on the summit of Himalayan mountains.

对于这个问题，他们还没有作出答复。

duīyú zhèi ge wèntí | tāmen hái méiyǒu zuòchū dáfù

(lit. cv:regarding this mw question, they still not-have produce reply)

They still have not replied on this question.

关于青少年的品行问题，学校与家长都应该负责。

guānyú qīngshàonián de pǐnxíng wèntí | xuéxiào yǔ jiāzhǎng dōu yīnggāi fùzé

(lit. cv:concerning young people teenager *de* behaviour question, school and parents both must take responsibility of)

School and parents must both take responsibility for the behaviour of young people and teenagers.

除了法语之外，她还学习汉语。

chúle fǎyǔ zhīwài | tā hái xuéxí hànyǔ

(lit. cv:besides French apart, she also study Chinese)

She is studying Chinese as well as French.

根据最近的研究，记忆的好坏跟年龄无关。

gēnjù zuìjìn de yánjiū | jìyì de hǎohuài gēn niánlíng wúguān

(lit. cv:according to latest *de* research, memory *de* good-bad cv:with age no connection)

According to the latest research, quality of memory/whether memory is good or bad has no relation to age.

为了大家，她宁可牺牲自己的利益。

wèile dàjiā | tā nìngkě xīshēng zìjǐ de lìyì

(lit. cv:for the sake of everyone, she would rather sacrifice own *de* interest)

For everyone's sake, she would rather sacrifice her own interests.

12 把 **bǎ** CONSTRUCTIONS

A 把 **bǎ** construction is a syntactic feature unique to the Chinese language. It is a device which uses the coverb 把 **bǎ** 'to grasp'[1] to move a definite-referenced object to a position before the main verb. This leaves the space after the verb available to elements other than the object, e.g. for a consequential complement to indicate the result inflicted upon the object through the action contained in the verb. This repositioning manouevre arises from the fact that Chinese sentences find it possible, only in very few instances,[2] to hold an object and an additional element together in a position after the same verb, particularly if the additional element is three or more syllables long. Given its association with an action verb, the 把 **bǎ** construction is a regular feature of a narrative sentence.

12.1 THE STRUCTURAL FEATURES OF 把 **bǎ** CONSTRUCTION

A 把 **bǎ** construction must have the following three structural features:

(**a**) the object of the coverb 把 **bǎ** must be of definite reference;
(**b**) the main verb of the sentence must be followed by a complement[3] or, less commonly, by a second noun;
(**c**) the main verb must be an action verb.

If any one of the three conditions is not fulfilled, the construction is not acceptable, as in the following:

*他把一个电视机弄坏了。 ***tā bǎ yī ge diànshìjī nònghuài le**
*He broke a television set.

in which the object of 把 **bǎ** is of indefinite reference;

*他把那个电视机送。 ***tā bǎ nèi ge diànshìjī sòng**
*He gave the televison set.

in which the verb 送 **sòng** 'to give as a present' is not followed by either of the elements listed under (**b**) above;

---

[1] See §11.2.6.
[2] See §11.1.
[3] Sometimes just 了 **le** itself with its underlying notion of 了 **liǎo** 'to finish'.

*他把这件事知道了。 ***tā bǎ zhèi jiàn shì zhīdao le**
*He came to know this matter.

in which the verb 知道 **zhīdao** 'to know' is an involuntary cognitive verb, not an action verb.

12.1.1 DEFINITE-REFERENCED OBJECT

Since the definite reference of the object of the coverb 把 **bǎ** is a requirement of the construction, the object does not need to be specifically marked for definiteness. That is to say, an unmarked noun without any demonstrative adjective will be assumed to be definite:

她自己把药吃了。 **tā zìjǐ bǎ yào chī le**
(lit. she self cv:grasping medicine eat *le*) She took the medicine herself.

12.1.2 THE ELEMENTS AFTER THE MAIN VERB

The extra elements after the verb in a 把 **bǎ** construction may take the form of a complement or an object.

12.1.2.1 Different forms of complement

(**a**) resultative:

大夫把他的病治好了。 **dàifu bǎ tāde bìng zhìhuǎ le**
(lit. doctor cv:grasping his illness cure-well *le*)
The doctor cured his illness.

你把我原来的意思讲走了。 **nǐ bǎ wǒ yuánlái de yìsi jiǎngzǒu le**
(lit. you cv:grasping my original meaning speak-*away le*)
You distorted/did not convey my original meaning.

(**b**) locational:

母亲把孩子搂在怀里。 **mǔqin bǎ háizi lǒu zài huái li**
(lit. mother cv:grasping child hold cv:in bosom-inside)
Mother took the child in her arms.

他把布告贴在最显眼的地方。
tā bǎ bùgào tiē zài zuì xiǎnyǎn de dìfang
lit. he cv:grasping notice stick cv:on most eye-catching place)
He stuck the notice in the most eye-catching/conspicuous place.

(c) directional:

什么风把你刮来了？　**shénme fēng bǎ nǐ guālai le**
(lit. what wind cv:grasping you blow-come *le*)
What wind has blown you here?

她把窗帘放了下来。**tā bǎ chuānglián fàng le xiàlai**
(lit. she cv:grasping window blind let *le* down-come)
She pulled down the blind.

(d) dative:

他把信转交给她。**tā bǎ xìn zhuǎnjiāo gěi tā**
(lit. he cv:grasping letter pass on cv:to her)
He passed on the letter to her.

奶奶把那些故事讲给孩子们听。[4]
nǎinai bǎ nèixiē gùshi jiǎng gěi háizimen tīng
(lit. grandma cv:grasping those stories tell cv:to children listen)
Grandma told those stories to the children.

(e) durational:

警察把小偷关了三天。**jǐngchá bǎ xiǎotōu guān le sān tiān**
(lit. policemen cv:grasping petty thief lock up *le* three days)
The police locked up the petty thief for three days.

姐姐把黄豆浸了两个钟头。
jiějie bǎ huángdòu jìn le liǎng ge zhōngtóu
(lit. elder sister cv:grasping soybean soak *le* two mw hours)
Elder sister soaked the soybeans for two hours.

(f) brief durational:

他把那篇稿子修改了一下。**tā bǎ nèi piān gǎozi xiūgǎi le yīxià**
(lit. he cv:grasping that mw manuscript revise *le* one cv:occasion)
He made some revisions to the draft.

机场的服务员把他的行李称了称。
jīchǎng de fúwùyuán bǎ tāde xíngli chēng le chēng
(lit. airport *de* service people cv:grasping his luggage weigh *le*
weigh)
The airport official weighed his baggage.

---

[4] Here 给 **gěi** is the coverb in the complement and links with another verb 听 **tīng** 'to listen'.

(**g**) frequency:

> 他把那几个生词默写了好几遍。
>
> **tā bǎ nèi jǐge shēngcí mòxiě le hǎo jǐ biàn**
>
> (lit. he cv:grasping those few mw new words write-from-memory *le* very a-few times)
>
> He wrote the new vocabulary out from memory a good many times.

> 老师把那首唐诗朗诵了三次。
>
> **lǎoshī bǎ nèi shǒu tángshī lǎngsòng le sān cì**
>
> (lit. teacher cv:grasping that mw Tang poem recite *le* three times)
>
> The teacher read out/recited that Tang poem three times.

(**h**) descriptive with 得 **de**:

> 她把房间收拾得干干淨淨。
>
> **tā bǎ fángjiān shōushi de gāngānjìngjìng**
>
> (lit. she cv:grasping room tidy *de* dry-dry-clean-clean)
>
> She gave the room a thorough tidying.

> 他把书架上的书放得整整齐齐。
>
> **tā bǎ shūjià shàng de shū fàng de zhěngzhěngqíqí**
>
> (lit. he cv:grasping bookcase-top *de* books place *de* whole-whole-flush-flush)
>
> He placed/arranged the books neatly on the bookcase.

(**i**) evaluative with 得 **de**:

> 律师把问题解释得很清楚。 **lùshī bǎ wèntí jiěshī de hěn qīngchu**
>
> (lit. lawyer cv:grasping problem explain *de* very clear)
>
> The lawyer explained the problem very clearly.

> 爸爸把道理说得十分详细。 **bàba bǎ dàolǐ shuō de shífēn xiángxì**
>
> (lit. father cv:grasping reason say *de* very clear)
>
> Father put the argument in great detail.

(**j**) judgemental with 成 **chéng**, etc.:

> 导演把整个戏剧处理成一个喜剧。
>
> **dǎoyǎn bǎ zhěng ge xìjù chùlǐ chéng yī ge xǐjù**
>
> (lit. director cv:grasping whole mw play treat cv:as one mw comedy)
>
> The director treated the whole play as a comedy.

他们把这件事儿视为无关紧要的事儿。
tāmen bǎ zhèi jiàn shìr shìwéi wúguān jǐnyào de shìr
(lit. they cv:grasping this mw matter look upon cv:as not-concern-
ing-importance *de* matter)
They viewed the business/affair as something of no importance.

老奶奶把小姑娘当作自己的女儿。
lǎo nǎinai bǎ xiǎo gūniang dàngzuò zìjǐ de nǚ'ér
(lit. old granny cv:grasping little girl look upon cv:as her own *de*
daughter)
The old lady looked upon the young girl as her own daughter.

12.1.2.2 A second object in the form of a noun or a number/measure word

妹妹把花浇了水了。 **mèimei bǎ huā jiāo le shuǐ le**
(lit. younger sister cv:grasping flower sprinkle *le* water *le*)
Younger sister has watered the flowers.

妹妹把水浇了花了。 **mèimei bǎ shuǐ jiāo le huā le**
(lit. younger sister cv:grasping water sprinkle *le* flower *le*)
Younger sister has used the water to water the flowers.

弟弟把蛋糕吃了一半。 **dìdi bǎ dàngāo chī *le* yī bàn**
(lit. younger brother cv:grasping cake eat *le* a-half)
Younger brother ate half of the cake.

妈妈把蛋糕切了一块。 **māma bǎ dàngāo qiē *le* yī kuài**
(lit. mother cv:grasping cake cut *le* one piece) Mother cut a slice of cake.

12.1.3 THE MAIN VERB IN A 把 **bǎ** CONSTRUCTION

The main verb in a 把 **bǎ** construction, as we have said, must be an action
verb, most commonly within a narrative sentence. Therefore the non-action
verbs, generally found in expository sentences, would not occur with 把 **bǎ**: 是
shì 'to be'; 有 **yǒu** 'to have', verbs of emotion (喜欢 **xǐhuan** 'to like'; 爱 **ài** 'to
love', etc.) and most cognitive verbs (知道 **zhīdào** 'to know', 懂 **dǒng** 'to understand', etc.). However, a small number of cognitive verbs, which encode a mental
exertion or process rather than result, may still be used with 把 **bǎ** sentences:

请把这件重要的事儿记住！ **qǐng bǎ zhèi jiàn zhòngyào *de* shìr jìzhu**
(lit. please cv:grasping this mw important *de* matter keep-in-mind firmly)
Please remember this important matter.

别把我的电话号码忘了。 **bié bǎ wǒ** *de* **diànhuà hàomǎ wàng** *le*
(lit. don't cv:grasping my telephone number forget *le*)
Don't forget my telephone number.

请你把这一点了解清楚。 **qǐng nǐ bǎ zhèi yī diǎn liǎojiě qīngchu**
(lit. please you cv:grasping this one point understand clear)
Please get a clear understanding of this point.

12.2   INTENTIONALITY IN A 把 **bǎ** CONSTRUCTION

Intentionality is an inherent implication underlying most 把 **bǎ** constructions,
that is to say, a deliberate action is usually involved. However, there are contexts
in which either the outcome of the action of the verb is unintentional or the
question of intentionality simply does not arise:

他没照镜子，把帽子戴歪了。 **tā méi zhào jìngzi | bǎ màozi dài wāi le**
(lit. he did not look at the mirror, cv:grasping hat put-on not-straight *le*)
He didn't look at the mirror and put his hat on crooked.

太阳把大地染红了。 **tàiyáng bǎ dàdì rǎn hóng le**
(lit. sun cv:grasping big-land dye red *le*)
The sun has painted the earth red.

潮水把沙滩上的衣服冲走了。
cháoshuǐ bǎ shātān shàng de yīfu chōng zǒu le
(lit. tide cv:grasping beach-on *de* clothes wash off *le*)
The tide washed away the clothes on the beach.

In other cases the action may be deliberate or not depending on the context:

弟弟把花瓶打破了。 **dìdi bǎ huāpíng dǎpò le**
(lit. younger brother cv:grasping flower vase hit-broken *le*)
Younger brother broke the flower vase.

他把回信耽搁了。 **tā bǎ huíxìn dānge le**
(lit. he cv:grasping reply-letter delay *le*)
He was late with his (letter of) reply.

老师点名的时候，把她的名字漏了。
lǎoshī diǎnmíng de shíhou | bǎ tāde míngzi lòu le
(lit. teacher call roll *de* time, cv:grasping her name leave out *le*)
When the teacher took the register, he left out her name.

However, if 给 **gěi** is inserted between the 把 **bǎ** phrase and the verb, the
implication will invariably be that the action is unintentional:

弟弟(一不小心)把花瓶给打破了。
dìdi (yī bū xiǎoxīn) bǎ huāpíng gěi dǎpò le
(lit. younger brother (one-not-careful) cv:grasping flower vase *gei* hit-broken *le*)
Younger brother broke the flower vase (in a moment of carelessness).

妹妹(无意中)把她那条漂亮的裙子给弄脏了。
mèimei (wúyì zhōng) bǎ tā nèi tiáo piàoliang de qúnzi gěi nòngzāng le
(lit. younger sister (have-no-intention-in) cv:grasping her that mw beautiful skirt *gei* make-dirty *le*)
Younger sister (inadvertently) got that beautiful skirt of hers dirty.

12.3 把 **bǎ** CONSTRUCTION AND IMPERATIVES

Given the emphasis on intention and specific action of the 把 **bǎ** construction, it is only natural that it is often used in imperatives, either to make requests or to give orders:

请你随手把门关上。 **qǐng nǐ suíshǒu bǎ mén guān shàng**
(lit. please you follow-hand cv:grasping door close-up)
Please close the door behind you.

请把窗户打开。 **qǐng bǎ chuānghu dǎkāi**
(lit. please cv:grasping window hit-open) Please open the window.

快把瓶口封严。 **kuài bǎ píngkǒu fēngyán**
(lit. quick cv:grasping bottle-mouth seal tight)
Hurry up and seal (tight) the bottle.

火旺了，快把锅坐上。 **huǒ wàng le | kuài bǎ guō zuò shàng**
(lit. fire burn-bright *le*, quick cv:grasping pot sit-on)
The fire is roaring/burning up, hurry up and put the pot on.

请你把梨皮旋掉。 **qǐng nǐ bǎ lípí xuàn diào**
(lit. please you cv:grasping pear-skin peel off) Please peel the pear.

请把盐递给我。 **qǐng bǎ yán dì gěi wǒ**
(lit. please cv:grasping salt pass cv:to me) Please pass me the salt.

请大家把果皮扔在垃圾桶里。 **qǐng dàjiā bǎ guǒpí rēng zài lājī tǒng li**
(lit. please everybody cv:grasping fruit-skin throw cv:in litter-bin-inside)
Would everyone please put their litter in the rubbish bins.

别把说明书取走！ **bié bǎ shuōmíngshū qǔ zǒu**
(lit. don't cv:grasping explaining-book take off *le*)
Don't go off with the synopsis/manual.

12.4 A PARTICULAR FEATURE OF 把 **bǎ** CONSTRUCTION IN EVALUATIVE SENTENCES

When the 把 **bǎ** construction is used in an evaluative sentence following a modal verb, the necessity for the object of 把 **bǎ** to be of definite reference is removed:

你总不能把什么责任都推给我吧。
nǐ zǒng bùnéng bǎ shénme zérèn dōu tuī gěi wǒ ba
(lit. you after-all not able cv:grasping whatever responsibility all push cv:to me *ba*)
You can't possibly push all the responsibilities on to me.

你可以把字写得好一点儿吗？ **nǐ kěyǐ bǎ zì xiě de hǎo yīdiǎnr ma**
(lit. you can cv:grasping words write *de* a little better *ma*)
Could you write a bit better?

谁都应该把书放回原处。 **shuí dōu yīnggāi bǎ shū fàng huí yuánchù**
(lit. nobody all ought to cv:grasping book place-back original place)
Everyone ought to put books back where they came from.

别／不要⁵把什么罪名都加在我身上。
bié/bùyào bǎ shénme zuìmíng dōu jiā zài wǒ shēnshàng
(lit. don't cv:grasping whatever crime-label all add cv:on my body-on)
Don't level all the charges against me.

Admonitions or admonitory notices may likewise have indefinite-referenced objects after 把 **bǎ**:

不准把车辆停放在进出口！
bùzhǔn bǎ chēliàng tíngfàng zài jìnchūkǒu
(lit. not permit cv:grasping vehicles park-place cv:at enter-exit-opening)
Parking (vehicles/cars) at the entrance and exit is forbidden.

禁止把七岁以下的小孩带入会场！
jìnzhǐ bǎ qī suì yǐxià de xiǎohái dàirù huìchǎng
(lit. forbid cv:grasping seven year old below *de* child bring cv:into assembly hall)
It is not allowed to bring children under 7 into the assembly.

---

⁵ 别 **bié** is the fused form of 不要 **bùyào** and is therefore considered to be the combination of a negator and a modal verb.

严禁把香烟售给十八岁以下的青少年。
yánjìn bǎ xiāngyān shòu gěi shíbā suì yǐxià de qīngshàonián
(lit. strictly forbid cv:grasping cigarettes sell cv:to 18 year below *de* youths and teenagers)
It is strictly forbidden to sell cigarettes to young people under 18.

怎么可以把垃圾扔在这儿呢? **zénme kěyǐ bǎ lājī rēng zài zhèr ne**
(lit. how can cv:grasping rubbish throw cv:at here *ne*)
How can rubbish be dumped here?

12.5 把 **bǎ** VERSUS 将 **jiāng**

In a less colloquial and more formal style, 将 **jiāng** may be used in place of 把 **bǎ**:

特将详细的情况报告如下。 **tè jiāng xiángxì de qíngkuàng bàogào rúxià**
(lit. especially cv:grasping detailed situation report as follows)
I hereby report the detailed situation as follows.

以免将谈判弄僵了。 **yǐmiǎn jiāng tánpàn nòngjiāng le**
(lit. avoid cv:grasping negotiation make-deadlock *le*)
To avoid bringing the negotiation to a deadlock.

13 THE PASSIVE VOICE AND 被 **bèi** CONSTRUCTIONS

It has often been suggested that the passive voice is not as commonly used in Chinese as in European languages. There is certainly some truth in this, in that the Chinese language, being meaning-oriented and not morphologically stringent, seems to rely more heavily on context than on grammatical form. The language avoids the use of formal passive voice markers (e.g. 被 **bèi**) until it is perfectly necessary, but from a broader perspective it is possible to see that the passive voice in Chinese in its various forms, marked or unmarked, does occur widely and, as such, may be just as frequently encountered in Chinese (both in speech and in writing) as in European languages.

13.1 THREE FORMS OF PASSIVE

The passive voice in Chinese may adopt any of the following three forms depending on the required tone and emphasis:

(a) **the notional passive** – where no formal passive marker is employed. This passive normally carries an expository tone.

> 问题 ‖ 解决了。[1] **wèntí ‖ jiějué *le***
> (lit. problem ‖ solve *le*) The problem was/has been solved.

(b) **the formal passive** – where a passive marker like 被 **bèi** is introduced. Here the tone is usually narrative:

> 问题 ‖ 终被解决。 **wèntí ‖ zhōng bèi jiějué**
> (lit. problem ‖ finally ***bei*:by solve) The problem was finally solved.

(c) **the lexical passive** – where a verb, indicating that the subject or the topic is the 'receiver' of the action, is followed by a nominalised verbal object. Whether this passive is built into a narrative or an exposition, the tone tends to be rather formal.

> 问题 ‖ 得到了解决。 **wèntí ‖ dédào *le* jiějué**
> (lit. problem ‖ receive *le* solution)
> A solution was found for the problem.

---

[1] Note that the result expressed in the complement of all notional and formal passive constructions is invariably associated with some kind of change in a situation. The sentence particle 了 *le* is therefore always present.

问题 ‖ 得到解决了。 **wèntí ‖ dédào jiějué** *le*
(lit. problem ‖ receive solution *le*)
A solution has been found for the problem.

We will now look at the specific features of these passive forms.

13.2 THE NOTIONAL PASSIVE

The notional passive is the most common form of passive voice in the language.
The structure is possible only with a non-morphological language like Chinese,
where speakers are accustomed to relying as much on meaning as on form. Take
the following example:

信 ‖ 寄走了。 **xìn ‖ jì zǒu** *le*
(lit. letter ‖ send off *le*) The letter has been put in the post.

Here there is of course no danger of the hearer misinterpreting the statements as
meaning that the letter has initiated the action of sending itself, despite the fact
that there is no indication of a passive voice in the verb.

The notional passive in fact avoids passive markers by relying on the hearer's
common sense or knowledge of the world. It offers (or invites – in the form of
a question) an updated explanation or description of a situation. Essentially what
is happening with a notional passive is that the original object of the verb is now
posed as the topic under discussion and is shifted to the beginning of the sentence. This is clear from the following structural conversion:

我 ‖ 已经寄了信了。 **wǒ ‖ yǐjīng jì** *le* **xìn** *le*
(lit. I ‖ already send *le* letter *le*)
I have (already) put the letter in the post.

where 信 **xìn** 'letter' is the object of the predicate verb 寄 **jì** 'send; post'.

Moving the object in the above sentence to the beginning of the sentence, we
have:

信 ‖‖ 我 ‖ 已经寄了。 **xìn ‖‖ wǒ ‖ yǐjīng jì** *le*
(lit. letter ‖‖ I ‖ already send *le*)
As for the letter, I have already put it in the post.

The original object has now become the topic and occurs before the original
subject while the aspect marker *le* indicating the completion of the action merges
with the sentence particle *le* (for updating the information) to convey both meanings. Apart from these changes, the rest of the original sentence remains intact.
If we leave out the original subject 我 'I', the sentence becomes a notional
passive with the topic alone directly affected by the predicate comment:

信 ‖ 已经寄了。 **xìn ‖ yǐjīng jì** *le*
(*lit.* letter ‖ already send *le*) The letter has already been sent.

The term 'notional passive' derives from the fact that the sentence, though apparently a straightforward 'topic ‖ explanatory comment' structure, is really an 'object (now turned topic) ‖ transitive verb' construction. It is passive in its underlying meaning but without a surface passive marker.

Being a conversion from an originally 'verb + object' construction, the notional passive naturally has a transitive verb in the comment. An intransitive verb gives an unacceptable meaning relationship between the noun and the verb. For example, a sentence like

*信 ‖ 已经走了。 **xìn ‖ yǐjīng zǒu** *le*
(*lit.* letter ‖ already leave *le*) *The letter has already departed.

in which 走 **zǒu** 'leave' is an intransitive verb, could be understood only in a metaphorical sense.

In addition, as the notional passive is an explanatory comment on a situation, the verb, particularly if it is monosyllabic, generally has to incorporate a complement of some kind, which indicates the relevant consequence of the action or the features attributable to the situation under discussion. The complement takes various forms, which are similar to those in the 把 **bǎ** construction, and which most commonly indicate the following:

(**a**) result:

信 ‖ 收到了。 **xìn ‖ shōudào** *le*
(*lit.* the letter ‖ receive-arrive *le*) The letter has been received.

窗户 ‖ 打开了。 **chuànghu ‖ dǎkāi** *le*
(*lit.* the window ‖ hit-open *le*) The window has been opened.

房间 ‖ 收拾好了。 **fángjiān ‖ shōushi hǎo** *le*
(*lit.* the room ‖ tidy-well *le*) The room has been tidied.

桌子 ‖ 抹干淨了。 **zhuōzi ‖ mā gānjìng** *le*
(*lit.* the table ‖ wipe-clean *le*) The table has been wiped clean.

(**b**) direction:

衣服 ‖ 晾出去了。 **yīfu ‖ liàng chūqu** *le*
(*lit.* the clothes ‖ hang out-go *le*) The clothes have been put out to dry.

电话号码 || 抄下来了。 **diànhuà hàomǎ || chāo xiàlai** *le*
(lit. telephone number || copy down-come *le*)
The telephone number has been transcribed.

大箱子 || 放不进去了。 **dà xiāngzi || fàngbujìnqu** *le*
(lit. big case || place not enter-go *le*) The big case can't be fitted in.

(c) location:

招贴画 || 贴在墙上了。 **zhāotiēhuà || tiē zài qiáng shàng** *le*
(lit. the poster || stick cv:on wall-on *le*)
The poster is stuck on the wall.

行李 || 放在行李架上了。 **xíngli || fàng zài xínglijià shàng** *le*
(lit. the luggage || place cv:on the luggage rack-on *le*)
The luggage is (placed) on the luggage rack.

(d) frequency:

这个电影 || 已经放映过两次了。
zhèi ge diànyǐng || yǐjīng fàngyìng guo liǎng cì *le*
(lit. this film || see *guo* two times *le*)
This film has already been shown twice.

那篇文章 || 改了很多次了。
nèi piān wénzhāng || gǎi *le* **hěnduō cì** *le*
(lit. that mw essay || revise *le* very many times *le*)
That essay has been revised many times.

(e) duration:

那场戏 || 演了三个月了。 **nèi chǎng xì || yǎn** *le* **sān ge yuè** *le*
(lit. that mw play || perform *le* three mw months *le*)
That play has been on for three months.

这个菜 || 放了两天了。 **zhèi ge cài || fàng** *le* **liǎng tiān** *le*
(lit. this mw dish || put *le* two days *le*)
This dish has been left/has not been touched for two days running.

(f) manner and appearance:

书 || 放得整整齐齐的。 **shū || fàng de zhěngzhěngqíqí de**
(lit. the books || place *de* whole-whole-flush-flush *de*)
The books have been arranged very neatly.

字 || 写得歪歪斜斜的。 **zì || xiě de wāiwāixiéxié de**
(lit. the characters || write *de* crooked-crooked-slant-slant *de*)
The characters have been written in a crooked fashion.

The complement however may be replaced by an object which relates semantically to the topic often in part for whole terms:

那封信 || 写了三张纸。 **nèi fēng xìn || xiě le sān zhāng zhǐ**
(lit. that mw letter || write *le* three mw:sheet paper)
That letter has been written using three sheets of paper.

那瓶酒 || 喝了一半。 **nèi píng jiǔ || hē le yī bàn**
(lit. that mw:bottle wine || drink *le* a half)
Half of that bottle of wine has been consumed.

土豆 || 削了皮了。 **tǔdòu || xiāo le pí le**
(lit. the potatoes || peel *le* skin *le*) The potatoes have been peeled.

汽车 || 加了油了。 **qìchē || jiā le yóu le**
(lit. the car || add *le* petrol *le*) The car has been refuelled.

Some verbs carry the meaning of result within them:

那件工作 || 完成了。 **nèi jiàn gōngzuò || wánchéng le**
(lit. that mw work || complete *le*) That job has been carried out.

理想 || 实现了。 **lǐxiǎng || shíxiàn le**
(lit. the ideal || realise *le*) The dream has been fulfilled.

Verbs in a notional passive are generally couched in a disyllabic form. If the verb used is monosyllabic, it has to be supported pre-verbally or post-verbally by modals, adverbials or particles, or to be echoed in a rhythmic pattern:

(a) pre-verbal support:

信 || 可以寄了。 **xìn || kěyǐ jì le**
(lit. the letter || can send *le*) The letter can now be sent.

信 || 已经寄了。 **xìn || yǐjīng jì le**
(lit. the letter || already send *le*) The letter has already been sent.

(b) post-verbal support:

信 || 寄了没有？ **xìn || jì le méiyǒu?**
(lit. the letter || send *le* have not) Has the letter been sent or not?

信 || 寄了吗? **xìn || jì le ma?**
(lit. the letter || send *le ma*) Has the letter been sent?

(c) rhythmic pattern:

信 || 寄了，饭 || 煮了，你要我办的事儿 || 都办了。
xìn || jì le | fàn || zhǔ le | nǐ yào wǒ bàn de shìr || dōu bàn le
(lit. the letter || send *le*, the rice || cook *le*, you-want-me-to-do things || all do *le*)
The letter has been sent, the meal has been prepared, everything you want me to do has been done.

As was said earlier, a notional passive is designed to offer or invite an explanatory comment on a situation. The focus or emphasis is therefore often on an observed or foreseen result that has a bearing on the situation. This being the case, modals and/or adverbials in the form of time nouns or referential adverbs often form a natural part of the comment in expository or evaluative sentences. For example:

(a) modal:

你的鞋 || 应该擦一擦。 **nǐde xié || yīnggāi cā yī cā**
(lit. your shoes || should | brush one brush)
Yours shoes should be given a brush.

(b) time adverbial:

我家的阴沟 || 经常堵塞。 **wǒ jiā de yīngōu || jīngcháng dǔsè**
(lit. my home *de* drains || often block)
Drains in my house often get blocked.

(c) referential adverb:

花园里的花儿 || 都浇了水了。
huāyuán li de huār || dōu jiāo le shuǐ le
(lit. the garden-inside *de* flower || all sprinkle *le* water *le*)
All the flowers in the garden have been watered.

On the other hand, adverbials of manner often occur with notional passives in narrative or descriptive sentences:

信 || 胡乱地拆开看了之后，就随随便便地扔在桌子上。
xìn || húluàn de chāikāi kàn le zhīhòu | jiù suísuíbiànbiàn de rēng zài zhuōzi shàng
(lit. the letter || carelessly tear open read *le* after, then casually throw cv:on table-top)
After the letter had been carelessly torn open and read, it was casually thrown on the table.

In sentences like these, the formal passive marker 被 **bèi**,[2] as a standard feature of narrative, can be introduced to give a slightly more vivid picture of the incident or situation being narrated or described. The above sentence, for example, may be converted into a formal passive with the meaning remaining essentially unchanged:

信 ‖ 被胡乱地拆开看了之后，就被随随便便地扔在桌子上。
xìn ‖ bèi húluàn _de_ **chāikāi kàn** _le_ **zhīhòu | jiù bèi suísuíbiànbiàn** _de_ **rēng zài zhuōzi shàng**

If anything, the addition of 被 **bèi** associates the actions of 'tearing the letter open' and 'throwing it down' more closely with the person unspecified who carried them out.

The negation of a notional passive is normally achieved by placing the negator 没(有) **méi(yǒu)** immediately before the verb. For example:

问题 ‖ 还没解决。 **wèntí ‖ hái méi jiějué**
(lit. the problem ‖ still not solve) The problem has not yet been solved.

Once the negator is used, 了 _le_ as either aspect marker or sentence particle can no longer occur. As a result, monosyllabic verbs need to be linked with complements or similar lengthening devices. A positive statement like:

信 ‖ 已经寄了。 **xìn ‖ yǐjīng jì** _le_
(lit. the letter ‖ already send _le_) The letter has already been sent.

will therefore convert to the negative in ways like the following:

(**a**) with the help of a complement

信 ‖ 还没寄走。 **xìn ‖ hái méi jì zǒu**
(lit. the letter ‖ still not send off)
The letter has not been sent off yet.

信 ‖ 还没寄出去。 **xìn ‖ hái méi jì chūqu**
(lit. letter ‖ still not send out) The letter has not been sent yet.

(**b**) with the help of a particle other than 了 _le_ after the verb:

信 ‖ 还没寄呢。 **xìn ‖ hái méi jì** _ne_
(lit. letter ‖ still not send _ne_)
The letter has not been sent off yet. (connotation: I'm sorry to say.)

---

[2] See §13.3 below.

In a more formal written text, 尚未 **shàng wèi** 'not yet' may be used instead of 还没 **hái méi** 'not yet'. For example,

问题 ‖ 尚未解决。 **wèntí ‖ shàng wèi jiějué**
(lit. problem ‖ still not solve) The problem has not yet been solved.

信 ‖ 尚未寄走。 **xìn ‖ shàng wèi jì zǒu**
(lit. letter ‖ still not send off) The letter has not been sent off yet.

Where a sentence is suppositional and refers to a future situation the negative is expressed by 不 **bù** 'not' rather than 没(有) **méi(yǒu)**.

工作 ‖ 不完成，我 ‖ 不睡觉。
gōngzuò ‖ bù wánchéng | wǒ ‖ bù shuìjiào
(lit. the work ‖ not complete, I ‖ not sleep)
If the work is not completed, I won't go to bed.

不 **bù** 'not' is also used in sentences where time adverbs indicate a habit or customary practice:

推销员打来的电话 ‖ 通常不接。
tuīxiāoyuán dǎlai de diànhuà ‖ tōngcháng bù jiē
(lit. salesman make *de* telephone call ‖ usually not receive)
Telephone calls from salesmen usually are not taken.

In all our examples so far of notional passives the topics have been inanimate objects; where the topic is a human or animate being, ambiguity can arise. For example:

他的助手 ‖ 借走了。 **tāde zhùshǒu ‖ jiè zǒu le**
(lit. his assistant ‖ borrow away *le*)
topic ‖ comment: His assistant has been borrowed (by somebody else for another project).
subject ‖ predicate: His assistant has borrowed it (something understood in the given context).

The first interpretation sees the sentence as a notional passive in which as usual an 'unspecified doer' (in this case maybe a boss or professor) has inflicted the action of the verb on the topic (his assistant). In the second interpretation, the verb is in the active voice, and the subject (his assistant) has borrowed something that is unspecified but is clear from the context (a book, computer, etc.).[3]

---

[3] Absence of specification like this, where identification is self-evident from the context, is a feature of the Chinese language (see Chapter 25).

In the great majority of cases, the context makes the meaning perfectly clear, but nonetheless there is the possibility of ambiguity in cases like these.

To avoid this, speakers normally use formal or lexical passive markers. For example, a sentence like:

他的助手 ‖ 救活了。 **tāde zhùshǒu ‖ jiù huó** *le*
(lit. *his assistant ‖ save alive le*)

could be open to two potential interpretations:

topic ‖ comment: His assistant was saved (e.g. by the doctor).
subject ‖ predicate: His assistant has saved the life of somebody else (understood in the context).

To ensure that the passive meaning of 'His assistant was saved' is understood, it would be possible to include either a formal passive marker:

他的助手 ‖ 被救活了。 **tāde zhùshǒu ‖** *bèi* **jiù huó** *le*
(lit. *his assistant ‖* *bei* *save alive le*)

or to adopt, if possible, a lexical passive strategy (see §13.4):

他的助手 ‖ 得救了。 **tāde zhùshǒu ‖ déjiù** *le*
(lit. *his assistant ‖ receive save le*)

13.3 THE FORMAL PASSIVE

13.3.1 SALIENT FEATURES

The most salient feature of a formal passive is the inclusion of the coverb 被 **bèi** as a formal passive marker to indicate that the subject of the sentence, instead of initiating the action specified in the predicate verb, is actually the 'receiver' of the action. The identity of the actual initiator of the action may be revealed immediately after 被 **bèi** or it may remain unstated or vague. For example:

(**a**) identity unstated:

那个警察 ‖ 被打伤了。 **nèi ge jǐngchá ‖ bèi dǎshāng** *le*
(lit. *that mw policeman ‖* *bei*:by hit-wounded *le*)
That policeman was wounded.

(**b**) identity vague:

那个警察 ‖ 被人打伤了。 **nèi ge jǐngchá ‖ bèi rén dǎshāng** *le*
(lit. *that mw policeman ‖* *bei*:by somebody hit-wounded *le*)
That policeman was wounded (by somebody).

(c) initiator revealed:

> 那个警察 ‖ 被流氓打伤了。**nèi ge jǐngchá ‖ bèi liúmáng dǎshāng** *le*
> (lit. that mw policeman ‖ *bei*:by hooligan hit-wounded *le*)
> That policeman was wounded by hooligans.

In speech, the more formal passive marker 被 **bèi** may be replaced by 让 **ràng**, 叫 **jiào**/教 **jiào**, 给 **gěi** or 让 **ràng** . . . 给 **gěi**, 叫 **jiào** . . . 给 **gěi**, etc. In these cases, the initiator is either identified precisely or vaguely. For example, sentences (**b**) or (**c**) above could take any one of the following forms:

让 **ràng**:	那个警察 ‖ 让人/流氓打伤了。
	nèi ge jǐngchá ‖ ràng rén/liúmáng dǎshāng *le*
叫 **jiào**/教 **jiào**:	那个警察 ‖ 叫人/流氓打伤了。
	nèi ge jǐngchá ‖ jiào rén/liúmáng dǎshāng *le*
给 **gěi**:	那个警察 ‖ 给人/流氓打伤了。
	nèi ge jǐngchá ‖ gěi rén/liúmáng dǎshāng *le*
让 **ràng** . . . 给 **gěi**:	那个警察 ‖ 让人/流氓给打伤了。
	nèi ge jǐngchá ‖ ràng rén/liúmáng gěi dǎshāng *le*
叫 **jiào** . . . 给 **gěi**:	那个警察 ‖ 叫人/流氓给打伤了。
	nèi ge jǐngchá ‖ jiào rén/liúmáng gěi dǎshāng *le*

13.3.2 BASIC CHARACTERISTICS

As mentioned earlier, the basic characteristic of a formal passive is its inbuilt narrative stance. Compared with the notional passive, which can occur in any type of sentence, the formal passive is generally more committed to the narration or description of an incident or event which has already taken place. For example, in the following two pairs of sentences, a notional passive (**i**) is felt to be less plausible than the formal passive (**ii**):

(a) (i) + 那天下午门 ‖ 撬开了。 + **nèi tiān xiàwǔ mén ‖ qiào kāi** *le*
     (lit. that day afternoon the door ‖ prize open *le*)
   (ii) 那天下午门 ‖ 被撬开了。 **nèi tiān xiàwǔ mén ‖ bèi qiào kāi** *le*
     (lit. that day afternoon the door ‖ *bei*:by (somebody) prize open *le*)
     That afternoon the door was prised open (by somebody).

(b) (i) + 不久小偷 ‖ 抓住了。 + **bùjiǔ xiǎotōu ‖ zhuā zhù** *le*
     (lit. not long after the thief ‖ catch firm *le*)
   (ii) 不久小偷 ‖ 被抓住了。 **bùjiǔ xiǎotōu ‖ bèi zhuā zhù** *le*
     (lit. not long after the thief ‖ *bei*:by catch firm *le*)
     Not long after, the thief was caught.

A further distinction between formal and notional passives is that, while the latter is normally objective in stance and can accommodate complements of positive or negative meaning, formal passives tend to convey a negative sense. The two sentences below demonstrate the contrasting meanings possible with a notional passive:

(a) 饭 || 煮好了。 **fàn || zhǔ hǎo** *le*
(lit. the rice || cook well *le*) The rice is cooked.

饭 || 煮糊了。 **fàn || zhǔ hú** *le*
(lit. the rice || cook burnt *le*) The rice is burnt.

The expectation that the outcome of a formal passive will be negative means that, if the same two sentences have a passive marker, only the second will be acceptable:

(a) *饭 || 被煮好了。 ***fàn || bèi zhǔ hǎo le**
(lit. the rice || *bei*:by cook well *le*) *The rice has been cooked.

饭 || 被煮糊了。 **fàn || bèi zhǔ hú le**
(lit. the rice || *bei*:by cook burnt *le*) The rice has been burnt.

(b) *饭 || 让我给煮好了。 ***fàn || ràng wǒ gěi zhǔ hǎo** *le*
(lit. the rice || *rang*:by me *gei* cook well *le*)
The rice has been cooked by me.

饭 || 让我给煮糊了。 **fàn || ràng wǒ gěi zhǔ hú** *le*
(lit. the rice || *rang*:by me *gei* cook burnt *le*)
The rice was burnt by me.

Here are a few more examples of the undesirable outcomes of formal passives:

电视机 || 被我弄坏了。 **diànshìjī || bèi wǒ nòng huài** *le*
(lit. the television set || *bei*:by me handle-damaged *le*)
The television was damaged by me.

衣服让我给弄脏了。 **yīfu || ràng wǒ gěi nòng zāng** *le*
(lit. the clothes || *rang*:by me *gei* make-dirty *le*)
The clothes were dirtied by me.

钥匙叫他给弄丢了。 **yàoshi || jiào tā gěi nòng diū** *le*
(lit. the key || *jiao*:by him make-lose *le*) The key was lost by him.

气球被小弟弟戳破了。 **qìqiú || bèi xiǎo dìdi chuōpò** *le*
(lit. the balloon || *bei*:by little younger brother poke-break *le*)
The balloon was burst by younger brother.

那棵树被大风刮倒了。 **nèi kē shù || bèi dà fēng guā dǎo le**
(lit. that mw tree || *bei*:by great wind blow-fall *le*)
That tree was blown down by the gale.

小妹妹被我们笑得不好意思了。
xiǎo mèimei || bèi wǒmen xiào de bù hǎo yìsi le
(lit. little younger sister || *bei*:by us laugh *de* embarrassed *le*)
Little sister was embarrassed by our teasing.

腿上叫蚊子给叮了一下。 **tuǐ shàng || jiào wénzi gěi dīng le yīxià**
(lit. leg-on || *jiao*:by mosquito bite *le* one time)
I/(s)he was bitten on the leg by a mosquito.

绒大衣被虫子蛀了一个窟窿。**róng dàyī || bèi chōngzi zhù le yī ge kūlong**
(lit. the woollen overcoat || *bei*:by moth eat *le* one mw hole)
The woollen overcoat had a hole eaten in it by a moth.

13.3.3 IMPERATIVES

In imperatives, the formal 被 **bèi** cannot be used, but the other more colloquial
alternatives are acceptable:

别让开水给烫着。 **bié ràng kāishuǐ || gěi tàng zhe**
(lit. don't *rang*:by boiling water *gei* scald-reach)
Don't get scalded by the boiling water.

别叫雨把行李给淋湿了。 **bié jiào yǔ bǎ xíngli || gěi línshī le**
(lit. don't *jiao*:by rain *ba*:grasping luggage *gei* soak-wet *le*)
Don't let the luggage get soaked by the rain.

13.3.4 WHOLE–PART RELATIONSHIPS

It is not unusual for a formal passive to incorporate a 把 **bǎ** construction if the
subject of the sentence and the object of 把 **bǎ** have a whole–part relationship.
For example:

新书 || 被小妹妹 | 把封面 | 撕掉了。
xīn shū || bèi xiǎo mèimei | bǎ fēngmiàn | sī diào le
the new book || *bei*:by little sister | *ba*:grasping cover | tear-off *le*
The cover of the new book was torn off by little sister.

in which 新书 **xīn shū** 'the new book' and 封面 **fēngmiàn** 'the cover' have a
whole–part relationship.

In other words, the subject must represent the whole entity while the object of 把 **bǎ** must represent part of it.

Here is another example:

姐姐 ‖ 叫滚水 | 把手 | 给烫伤了。
jiějie ‖ jiào gǔnshuǐ | bǎ shǒu | gěi tàng shāng *le*
elder sister ‖ *jiao*:by boiling water | *ba*:grasping hand | *gei*:by scald-hurt *le*
My elder sister had her hand scalded by boiling water.

13.3.5 A CLASSICAL VARIANT

A classical variant of the formal passive is encoded by 为 **wéi** ... 所 **suǒ**. 为 **wéi**, like 被 **bèi**, is followed by the initiator of the action in the verb, while 所 **suǒ** precedes the verb itself. In this formal passive construction, the verb may be monosyllabic or disyllabic and does not need any complement.

他的讲话 ‖ 为掌声所淹没。 **tāde jiǎnghuà ‖ wéi zhǎngshēng suǒ yānmò**
(lit. his speech ‖ *wei*:by applause *suo* drown)
His speech was drowned by the applause.

这位老师 ‖ 为他的学生所爱戴。
zhèi wèi lǎoshī ‖ wéi tāde xuésheng suǒ àidài
(lit. this mw teacher ‖ *wei*:by his students *suo* love-esteem)
This teacher was loved by his students.

这样的丑事 ‖ 必然为人所笑。**zhèyàng de chǒushì ‖ bìrán wéirén suǒ xiào**
(lit. this kind *de* scandal ‖ inevitably *wei*:by people *suo* laugh)
This kind of scandal is inevitably laughed at by people.

13.4 THE LEXICAL PASSIVE

In a lexical passive, the subject of the sentence is the receiver of an action, which is the formal object of a particular set of verbs such as 得到 **dédào** 'get', 受到 **shòudào** 'receive', 遭到 **zāodào** 'suffer (from)'. The true initiator of the action is identified as an attributive to the formal object. Though the syntactic construction of a lexical passive is a straightforward SVO, the important presence of the initiator modifies this to SV attributive O, where

S = receiver of the action
V = 'receiving' verb
O = action initiated by somebody else
attributive to O = initiator

In other words, the semantic formula of the sentence is:

receiver + verb + initiator (as an attributive) + nominalised verb

For example:

他 || 得到 | 朋友们的支持。 **tā || dédào | péngyoumen de zhīchí**
(lit. he || get | friends' support)
He won the support of his friends./He was supported by his friends.[4]

The formal object of the 'receive' verb is always a nominalised verb. It cannot therefore incorporate a complement and it must adopt a disyllabic form. One cannot say, for example:

*他受到大家的罚。 ***tā shòudào dàjiā de fá**
*He received everyone's punishment.

Nor is the addition of a complement acceptable, as the formal object is now itself a noun:

*他受到大家的罚一次。 ***tā shòudào dàjiā de fá yī cì**
*He received a punishment from everyone.

Also being a nominalised form it does not take an object of its own:

*他受到大家的罚一镑。 ***tā shòudào dàjiā de fá yī bàng**
*He received a penalty of one pound from everyone.

An acceptable formulation can be achieved, however, through the juxtaposition of another monosyllabic verb or through the addition of an attributive:

他受到大家的惩罚。 **tā shòudào dàjiā de chéngfá**
(lit. he received everyone's punishment/penalty)
He was punished/penalised by everyone.

他受到大家的重罚。 **tā shòudào dàjiā de zhòngfá**
(lit. he receive everyone's heavy punishment/penalty)
He was heavily punished/penalised by everyone.

Other examples are:

他的话受到人们的赞赏。 **tāde huà shòudào rénmen de zànshǎng**
(lit. his words receive people's admiration)
His words were admired by people.

---

[4] The alternative English translation is here to show that a lexical passive in Chinese may be a formal passive in English.

她的行为遭到父母的批评。 **tāde xíngwéi zāodào fùmǔ de pīpíng**
(lit. her behaviour suffer parents' criticism)
Her bahaviour met with criticism from her parents/was criticised by her
parents.

我的建议得到我妹妹的支持。 **wǒde jiànyì dédào wǒ mèimei de zhīchí**
(lit. my suggestion get my younger sister's support)
My suggestion gained my younger sister's support/was supported by my
younger sister.

In a notional or a formal passive, the nature of the outcome of an action is
expressed by the complement. The initiator of the action is often not mentioned
since it is the outcome that is important. In a lexical passive, however, the focus
shifts to the initiator of the action or to the degree or extent to which the action
has been carried out. In other words, the emphasis is on the object (the nominalised
verb) with its attributive, and the sentence loses focus without an attributive:

*他 ‖ 得到支持。 ***tā ‖ dédào zhīchí**
(lit. he ‖ get support) *He won support.

The attributive encodes semantically either the initiator and/or the extent to
which the action is carried out:

(**a**) attributive = initiator:

她受到老师的批评。 **tā shòudào lǎoshī de pīpíng**
(lit. she receive teacher's criticism) She was criticised by the teacher.

(**b**) attributive = degree or extent to which the action was carried out:

她受到严厉的批评。 **tā shòudào yánlì de pīpíng**
(lit. she receive severe **de** criticism) She was severely criticised.

(**c**) attributive = initiator + degree or extent to which the action was carried
out:

她受到老师严厉的批评。 **tā shòudào lǎoshī yánlì de pīpíng**
(lit. she receive teacher severe **de** criticism)
She was severely criticised by the teacher.

Similar examples are:

老师得到学生的尊敬。 **lǎoshī dédào xuésheng de zūnjìng**
(lit. the teacher receive students' respect)
The teacher was respected by the students.

经理受到多方的责难。 **jīnglǐ shòudào duōfāng de zénàn**
(lit. the manager receive many parties' censure/blame)
The manager was blamed on all fronts.

来宾受到热烈的欢迎。 **láibīn shòudào rèliè de huānyíng**
(lit. the guests receive warm *de* welcome)
The guests were warmly welcomed.

他遭到沉重的打击。 **tā zāodào chénzhòng de dǎjī**
(lit. he suffer heavy *de* blow) He suffered heavy [psychological] blows.

The three most commonly used verbs in a lexical passive, 得到 **dédào**, 受到
shòudào and 遭到 **zāodào**, have their semantic individualities. While 得到 **dédào**
is usually used in a positive sense and 遭到 **zāodào** in a negative sense, 受到
shòudào is generally neutral, as we can clearly see from the above examples.
Compare the following pairs of sentences:

*学生得到老师的批评。 ***xuésheng dédào lǎoshī de pīpíng**
(lit. the students get teacher's criticism)

学生得到老师的表扬。 **xuésheng dédào lǎoshī de biǎoyáng**
(lit. the students get teacher's praise)
The students were praised by the teacher.

*来宾遭到热烈的欢迎。 ***láibīn zāodào rèliè de huānyíng**
(lit. the guests suffer warm *de* welcome)

来宾遭到主人的冷落。 **láibīn zāodào zhǔrén de lěngluò**
(lit. the guests suffer host's cold-shoulder/neglect)
The guests were cold-shouldered/neglected by the host.

however:

他的建议受到人们的赞赏。 **tāde jiànyì shòudào rénmen de zànshǎng**
(lit. his suggestion receive people's admiration)
His suggestion was admired/well received by people.

他的建议受到人们的反对。 **tāde jiànyì shòudào rénmen de fǎnduì**
(lit. his suggestion receive people's opposition)
His suggestion was opposed by people.

In terms of register, a notional passive is always extremely colloquial while a
formal passive can be made informal by replacing 被 **bèi** with 让 **ràng** or 叫 **jiào**

plus 给 **gěi**. On the other hand, a lexical passive is always extremely formal, having a nominalised verb which is usually more abstract than physical in nature.

In addition, a lexical passive generally has a disyllabic nominalised verb as the formal object of a disyllabic 'receive' verb, which has a V + 到 **dào** structure. There is, however, an alternative form of lexical passive which makes use of a set of disyllabic expressions in a V + N format. This alternative form is unmodifiable in syntactic terms and it is found only in established lexical collocations, for example:

遭殃	**zāoyāng**	to meet with disaster[5]
罹难	**línàn**	to meet with misfortune
受伤	**shòushāng**	to be injured, wounded (lit. receive injury)
得救	**déjiù**	to be saved (lit. get rescue)
惹祸	**rěhuò**	to court disaster
遇险	**yùxiǎn**	to run into danger

As the V + N format is self-sufficient and is itself the focal point, there is no need for an attributive, unlike the syntactically modifiable lexical passive. For example:

孩子受了伤。 **háizi shòu *le* shāng**
(lit. the child receive *le* injury) The child was injured.

人质遇难了。 **rénzhì yùnàn *le***
(lit. the hostage meet calamity *le*) The hostage was killed.

病人得救了。 **bìngrén déjiù *le***
(lit. the patient get-rescue *le*) The patient was saved.

---

[5] The English translations here do not necessarily reflect the passive sense of the Chinese.

14 CHAIN CONSTRUCTIONS

Chinese, unlike English, does not have verb forms like infinitives, participles or gerunds. Such functions are all covered by the bare verbal stem, that is, the uninflected verb. This being the case, these bare verbs are often seen strung together in a series of two or three to form the predicate of a sentence in what we call a chain (or serial) construction. They are arranged in accordance with an intrinsic time sequence. For example:

我 ‖ 骑车 | 到火车站 | 去 | 买票。
wǒ ‖ qí chē | dào huǒchēzhàn | qù | mǎi piào
(lit. I ‖ ride bike | cv: to (i.e. arriving at) railway station | go | buy ticket)
Getting on my bike, I rode to the railway station to get a ticket.

The English translation of the above may also be constructed as, for example: 'To buy a ticket, I went to the railway station by bike', where the presence of the infinitive and the preposition allows for a flexible ordering of the verbal phrases. Without linguistic facilities like these, Chinese can only resort to strict time sequencing in terms of meaning. In this case, for example, one has to get on a bike before starting off in the direction of the railway station, and one has to reach the station before going to the ticket office to buy a ticket. Hence the order of the three verbs or verbal phrases is fixed: first 骑车 **qí chē** 'to ride a bicycle', second 到火车站去 **dào huǒchēzhàn qù** 'to go to the railway station' and third 买票 **mǎi piào** 'to buy a ticket'.

In the following sections, we shall look at the meaning relationships generally found between the verbs in chain constructions.

14.1 THE FIRST VERB INTRODUCING A COVERBAL PHRASE THAT INDICATES LOCATION, ETC.

The first verb in a chain construction can often be a verb, usually a coverb, indicating a location, destination, etc. Location phrases are normally marked by 在 **zài** 'to exist; at; in', destination phrases by 到 **dào** 'to arrive; to', direction phrases by 向 **xiàng** 'in the direction of'.[1]

我妻子在花园里种花。 **wǒ qīzi zài huāyuán li zhònghuā**
(lit. my wife cv:at garden-inside grow flower)
My wife is planting flowers in the garden.

---

[1] See Chapter 11 on coverbs.

孩子们到游乐场去玩儿。**háizimen dào yóulèchǎng qù wánr**
(lit. children cv:to pleasure-park go play)
The children go to play at the funfair.

邻居的狗向我跑来。**línjū de gǒu xiàng wǒ pǎolai**
(lit. neighbour's dog cv:towards me run-come)
The neighbour's dog ran up to me.

Coverbal phrases indicating destination are usually followed by 去 **qù** 'to go' or 来 **lái** 'to come' either as the main verb itself or as part of the main verb. In the case of direction coverbs, 来 **lái** 'to come' or 去 **qù** 'to go' always form part of the main verb. For instance, in the destination sentence above, 孩子们到游乐场去玩儿 **háizimen dào yóulèchǎng qù wánr** 'The children go to play at the funfair', 去 **qù** is juxtaposed with 玩儿 **wánr** 'to play' indicating purpose.

However the sentence could be modified as follows:

(a) 孩子们到游乐场去。**háizimen dào yóulèchǎng qù**
    (lit. children cv: arriving at funfair go)   (where 去 **qù**
    The children went to the funfair.   is the main verb)

(b) 孩子们到游乐场玩儿去。
    háizimen dào yóulèchǎng wánr qù   (where 去 **qù** forms part
    (lit. children cv: arriving at funfair play-go) of the main verb with
    The children went to play at the funfair.   玩儿 **wánr** 'to play')

Similarly with direction coverbs you can have:

警犬朝我扑过来。   (where 过来 **guòlai** 'over
jǐngquǎn cháo wǒ pū guòlai   and towards' forms part
(lit. police dog cv:towards me jump-over-come) of the main verb with
The police dog jumped at me.   扑 **pū** 'to jump at')

海鸥向海面飞去。   (where 去 **qù** forms part
hǎi'ōu xiàng hǎimiàn fēi qù   of the main verb with
(lit. seagull cv:towards sea-surface fly-go)   飞 **fēi** 'to fly')
The seagull flew down to the sea.

14.2 THE SECOND VERB INDICATING PURPOSE

In English, adverbials expressed in terms of infinitives often indicate purpose. In Chinese, purpose is expressed simply by a second verb in a chain construction.

我买了一个礼物送给她。**wǒ mǎi le yī ge lǐwù sòng gěi tā**
(lit. I buy *le* one mw present give cv:to her)
I bought a present to give to her.

孩子们都回家来过圣诞节。 **háizimen dōu huíjiā lái guò shèngdànjié**
(lit. children all return home come pass Christmas)
The children all come home for Christmas.

救火车赶到现场去救火。 **jiùhuǒchē gǎn dào xiànchǎng qù jiùhuǒ**
(lit. fire engine rush cv:arriving at scene go fight fire)
The fire engine rushed to the scene (to fight the fire).

我们到电影院去看电影。 **wǒmen dào diànyǐngyuàn qù kàn diànyǐng**
(lit. we cv:arriving at cinema go see film)
We went to the cinema (to see a film).

It should be noted that, in encoding purposes, there are often cultural differences between Chinese and European languages, as can be seen from the last two examples above. In English, when a fire engine comes to a scene or somebody goes to the cinema, the purpose is self-evident and to express it might be felt to be tautological. In Chinese, however, purpose is generally spelled out whether self-explanatory or not.

Another point to note is that 来 **lái** 'to come' and 去 **qù** 'to go' are often used in connection with purpose, and are usually placed before the second verb. More colloquially, they may also be found after the second verb or even both before and after it. Compare the following sets of sentences:

(**a**) 姐姐进城去买东西了。 **jiějie jìnchéng qù mǎi dōngxi le**
(lit. elder sister enter town go buy things *le*)

姐姐进城买东西去了。 **jiějie jìnchéng mǎi dōngxi qù le**
(lit. elder sister enter town buy things go *le*)

姐姐进城去买东西去了。 **jiějie jìnchéng qù mǎi dōngxi qù le**
(lit. elder sister enter town go buy things go *le*)

which all mean 'Elder sister has gone shopping in town'.

(**b**) 我明天上剑桥去赴约。 **wǒ míngtiān shàng jiànqiáo qù fùyuē**
(lit. I tomorrow cv: to Cambridge go keep appointment)

我明天上剑桥赴约去。 **wǒ míngtiān shàng jiànqiáo fùyuē qù**
(lit. I tomorrow cv: to Cambridge keep appointment go)

我明天上剑桥去赴约去。 **wǒ míngtiān shàng jiànqiáo qù fùyuē qù**
(lit. I tomorrow cv: to Cambridge go keep appointment go)

which all translate as 'I am going for an appointment in Cambridge tomorrow'.

Here are some more colloquial examples using 来 **lái** 'to come' or 去 **qù** 'to go':

大家快来看。 **dàjiā kuài lái kàn**
(lit. everyone quick come look)
Everyone come and have a look straight away.

你来帮帮忙。 **nǐ lái bāngbang máng**
(lit. you come help-help busy) Come and give me a hand.

爸爸，你来出出主意。 **bàba | nǐ lái chūchu zhǔyi**
(lit. father, you come express-express opinion)
Dad, come and tell us what you think (about it).

你去歇歇吧。 **nǐ qù xiēxie ba**
(lit. you go rest-rest *ba*) Go and have a rest.

我们贺喜来了。 **wǒmen hèxǐ lái le**
(lit. we congratulate-come *le*) We've come to say congratulations.

他来看我来了。 **tā lái kàn wǒ lái le**
(lit. he come see me come *le*) He came to see me.

我去找他去。 **wǒ qù zhǎo tā qù**
(lit. I go seek him go) I'll go and look for him.

However, when 来 **lái** 'to come' or 去 **qù** 'to go' occur with verbs that have an inherent meaning of direction, they can only follow these verbs:

妈妈进城去了。 **māma jìnchéng qù le**
(lit. mother enter town go *le*) Mother has gone into town.

爸爸回家来了。 **bàba huíjiā lái le**
(lit. father return home come *le*) Father has come home.

姐姐出门去了。 **jiějie chūmén qù le**
(lit. elder sister exit door go *le*) Elder sister is away.

The following would not normally be acceptable:

*妈妈去进城了。 **māma qù jìnchéng le*
*爸爸来回家了。 **bàba lái huíjiā le*
*姐姐去出门了。 **jiějie qù chūmén le*

There are some explicit indicators of purpose such as 以 **yǐ** 'so as to', 免得 **miǎndé** 'to avoid':[2]

他在那几个字下面画了一条红线，以引起读者的注意。

tā zài nèi jǐ ge zì xiàmiàn huà le yī tiáo hóngxiàn | yǐ yǐnqǐ dúzhě de zhùyì

(lit. he cv:at those few mw characters-below draw *le* one mw:line red line, so as to attract readers' attention)

He put a red line under those characters (so as) to attract the readers' attention.

请你到了之后，马上打个电话来，免得大家记挂。

qǐng nǐ dào le zhīhòu | mǎshàng dǎ ge diànhuà lái | miǎndé dàjiā jìguà

(lit. please you arrive *le* after, immediately make mw telephone call come, to avoid everyone be concerned)

Please phone immediately you arrive to avoid everyone getting worried.

请把盖子拧紧，以免里面的饼干受潮。

qǐng bǎ gàizi nǐng jǐn | yǐmiǎn lǐmiàn de bǐnggān shòucháo

(lit. please cv:grasping lid twist tight, to avoid inside *de* biscuits receive damp)

Please fasten the lid tight to stop the biscuits inside getting damp.

When one verb simply follows another, the action and purpose relationship between them tends to be more implicit than explicit, in contrast with the more explicit relationship when 来 **lái** or 去 **qù** or indicators like 以 **yǐ** or 免得 **miǎndé** are present:

大家一起鼓掌表示欢迎。 **dàjiā yīqǐ gǔzhǎng biǎoshì huānyíng**

(lit. everyone together applaud show welcome)

Everyone applauded in welcome.

我请了几天假回家探望我父母。

wǒ qǐng le jǐ tiān jià huíjiā tànwàng wǒ fùmǔ

(lit. I request *le* few days holiday return home visit my parents)

I requested a few days' leave to visit my parents.

他坐在河边钓鱼。 **tā zuò zài hébiān diàoyú**

(lit. he sit cv:at riverside fish fish) He sat fishing on the river bank.

---

[2] Note that 为了 **wèile** 'in order to' never introduces a second-verb phrase, but is always placed at the beginning of a sentence: e.g. 为了不让妈妈知道，她撒了一个谎。 **wèile bù ràng māma zhīdao | tā sǎ le yī ge huǎng**, 'In order not to let mother know (what has happened), she told a lie'.

我在客厅里腾出个地方放钢琴。
wǒ zài kètīng li téngchū ge dìfang fàng gāngqín
(lit. I cv:at drawing-room-inside clear out mw place put piano)
I cleared a space in the drawing-room for a piano.

孩子站在秋千上来回悠荡。
háizi zhàn zài qiūqiān shàng láihuí yōudàng
(lit. child stand cv:on swing-top to and fro swing)
The child stood swinging back and forth on the swing.

他走累了，坐下来休息休息。 **tā zǒu lèi le | zuò xiàlai xiūxi xiūxi**
(lit. he walk tired *le*, sit down-come rest-rest)
He was tired with walking and sat down for a rest.

她闭上眼睛养养神。 **tā bì shàng yǎnjing yǎngyǎng shén**
(lit. she close-up eyes repose-repose spirit) She closed her eyes in relaxation.

To indicate briefness or casualness, the verb of purpose may be repeated as in
the last two examples above. Similarly, in making suggestions or requests, the
purpose verb is often reduplicated[3] to convey a feeling of tentativeness:

我们找个安静的地方好好地聊一聊。
wǒmen zhǎo ge ānjìng de dìfang hǎohāo de liáo yī liáo
(lit. we find mw quiet *de* place well-well *de* chat-one-chat)
Let's find a quiet place to have a good chat.

请把窗户打开透透气。 **qǐng bǎ chuānghu dǎkāi tòutòu qì**
(lit. please cv:grasping window thrust-open let in-let in air)
Please open the window to let in some air.

讲个笑话给大家听听吧。 **jiǎng ge xiàohua gěi dàjiā tīngtīng ba**
(lit. tell mw joke cv:for everyone hear-hear *ba*)
Tell a joke for everyone to hear.

咱们聚在一起商量商量。 **zánmen jù zài yīqǐ shāngliang shāngliang**
(lit. we gather cv:at together discuss-discuss)
Let's get together for a discussion.

---

[3] In any instance of reduplication, where the verb reduplicated is a monosyllabic verb, there are two
possible formulations: VV or V 一 V, e.g. 看看 **kànkàn** or 看一看 **kàn yī kàn** 'to have a look'; if
the verb is disyllabic and has an internal juxtapositional structure (i.e. VV), the reduplication
can only be VV VV and the insertion of 一 **yī** is not possible, e.g. 学习学习 **xuéxí xuéxí** 'to
learn from' and not *学习一学习 ***xuéxí yī xuéxí**; if it is a disyllabic verb with an internal 'verb +
object' structure, only the verb is reduplicated and not the object, e.g. 散步 **sànbù** 'to take a walk'
> 散散步 **sànsàn bù** or 散一散步 **sàn yī sàn bù** and not *散步散步 ***sànbù sànbù**.

To emphasise this tentativeness, a reduplicated main verb is often followed by the monosyllabic 看 **kàn** 'to see what happens':

你先试试看。 **nǐ xiān shìshì kàn**
(lit. you first try-try to see what happens) (You) have a try first.

你尝尝看。 **nǐ chángcháng kàn**
(lit. you taste-taste to see what happens) Have a taste.

穿穿看。 **chuānchuān kàn**
(lit. put on-put on and see what happens) Try it on.

Sometimes the purpose is expressed succinctly with a monosyllabic verb, single or reduplicated, which more often than not shares the object of the previous verb:

哥哥倒了杯茶喝。 **gēge dào le bēi chá hē**
(lit. elder brother pour *le* (one) cup tea drink)
Elder brother poured out a cup of tea to drink.

妹妹要出席舞会，向姐姐借了一条裙子穿。
mèimei yào chūxí wǔhuì | xiàng jiějie jiè le yī tiáo qúnzi chuān
(lit. younger sister want attend dance, cv:from elder sister borrow *le* one mw skirt wear)
Younger sister wanted to go to a dance and borrowed a skirt from her elder sister to wear.

你去买份报纸瞧瞧。 **nǐ qù mǎi fèn bàozhǐ qiáoqiáo**
(lit. you go buy (one) mw newspaper look-look)
You go and buy a paper to have a look.

咱们租辆自行车骑骑。 **zánmen zū liàng zìxíngchē qíqí**
(lit. we hire (one) mw bicycle ride-ride) Let's hire a bike to have a ride.

我可以搭下一班飞机走。 **wǒ kěyǐ dā xià yī bān fēijī zǒu**
(lit. I can take next one mw:flight plane leave) I can go on the next flight.

14.3 THE FIRST VERB INDICATING REASON OR CAUSE

The first verb may state the reason why the action in the second verb should be or has been carried out:

人家正在睡觉，别去打搅。 **rénjiā zhèngzài shuìjiào | bié qù dǎjiǎo**
(lit. other people at-this-very-moment sleep, don't go disturb)
(S)he is just asleep, (so) don't disturb him/her.

我能见到您，感到十分荣幸。

wǒ néng jiàn dào nín | gǎndào shífēn róngxìng

(lit. I can see you [polite], feel extremely honoured)

I will be deeply honoured to meet you./I was deeply honoured to have met you.

水管坏了，射了他一身的水。 **shuǐguǎn huài le | shèle tā yī shēn de shuǐ**

(lit. waterpipe broke *le*, spurt *le* him one mw:body *de* water)

The (water)pipe burst and spurted water all over him.

行李没打好，都散开了。 **xíngli méi dǎ hǎo | dōu sǎn kāi le**

(lit. luggage not pack well, all scatter *le*)

The luggage was not fastened properly and everything spilled out.

花瓶掉在地上，摔破了。 **huāpíng diào zài dì shàng | shuāi pò le**

(lit. flower-vase fall cv:on ground-top, fall-break *le*)

The vase fell on the floor/ground and broke.

他着了凉，病了几天。 **tā zháo le liáng | bìngle jǐ tiān**

(lit. he catch *le* cold, sick *le* few days)

He caught a cold and was sick/ill for a few days.

老张说了个笑话，把大家都逗乐了。

lǎozhāng shuō le ge xiàohua | bǎ dàjiā dōu dòulè le

(lit. old Zhang tell *le* (one) mw joke, cv:grasping everyone all amuse-happy *le*)

Old Zhang told a joke and amused everyone.

The first-verb phrase can be an adjective or adjectival expression:

孩子太小，还怕生。 **háizi tài xiǎo | hái pà shēng**

(lit. child too small, still afraid stranger)

The child was very small and still shy with strangers.

她的脾气好，很容易跟人相处。

tāde píqì hǎo | hěn róngyì gēn rén xiāngchǔ

(lit. her temper good, very easy cv:with people get along)

She is good-tempered/has a pleasant disposition and gets on well with people.

Explanations or causes (or their lack) are expressed by an opening verb phrase consisting of 有 **yǒu** 'to have' (or 没有 **méiyǒu** 'to have not') and a noun. In many cases, the noun is abstract, like 理由 **lǐyóu** 'reason', 责任 **zérèn** 'responsibility', 权力 **quánlì** 'power or authority', 资格 **zīgé** 'qualification'.

你没由理由怀疑他的动机。 **nǐ méiyǒu lǐyóu huáiyí tāde dòngjī**
(lit. you don't have reason doubt his motive)
You have no reason to question his motive.

世界各国都有责任反对恐怖主义。
shìjiè gè guó dōu yǒu zérèn fǎnduì kǒngbù zhǔyì
(lit. world every country all have responsibility oppose terrorism)
All the countries in the world have a responsibility to fight terrorism.

老师有病请两天假。 **lǎoshī yǒu bìng qǐng liǎng tiān jià**
(lit. teacher has illness request two days leave)
The teacher is ill and asks for two days' leave.

秘书有事不能来上班。 **mìshū yǒu shì bù néng lái shàngbān**
(lit. secretary has business not able come work)
The secretary has something on and can't come to work.

你有信心写好这篇文章吗？ **nǐ yǒu xìnxīn xiě hǎo zhèi piān wénzhāng ma**
(lit. you have confidence write-well this mw essay **ma**)
Do you have the confidence to write this essay?

她有没有勇气克服这个困难？ **tā yǒu méiyǒu yǒngqì kèfú zhèi ge kùnnan**
(lit. she has-not-has courage overcome this mw difficulty)
Does she have the courage to overcome this difficulty?

他没有能力帮助你们。 **tā méiyǒu nénglì bāngzhù nǐmen**
(lit. he not have ability help you) He doesn't have the ability to help you.

你没有必要去跟他们纠缠。 **nǐ méiyǒu bìyào qù gēn tāmen jiūchán**
(lit. you not have necessity go cv:with them bicker)
There's no need for you to go and bicker with them.

我实在没有时间来考虑这个问题。
wǒ shízài méiyǒu shíjiān lái kǎolù zhèi ge wèntí
(lit. I in fact not have time come consider this mw problem)
I really don't have time to think about this problem.

Other abstract nouns which can collocate with 有 **yǒu** (or 没有 **méiyǒu**) include: 办法 **bànfǎ** 'resource', 本事 **běnshì** 'ability', 力量 **lìliàng** 'strength', 把握 **bǎwò** 'certainty', 机会 **jīhuì** 'opportunity', 条件 **tiáojiàn** 'condition', 可能 **kěnéng** 'possibility'.

14.4 THE FIRST VERB EXPRESSING ACCOMPANYING MANNER OR CIRCUMSTANCES

The accompanying manner or circumstances of an action, which is usually conveyed by a participial phrase in English, is commonly expressed in Chinese by a verbal phrase with the manner indicator 着 *zhe* attached to the verb. A verbal phrase like this always comes before the main verb. For example:

她笑着跟我谈了几句。 **tā xiàozhe gēn wǒ tán le jǐ jù**
(lit. she laugh *zhe* cv:with me talk *le* few sentences)
Smiling, she had a few words with me.

他怀着满腔的热情接受了这个任务。
tā huáizhe mǎnqiāng de rèqíng jiēshòu le zhèi ge rènwu
(lit. he embrace *zhe* full breast *de* enthusiasm accept *le* this mw task)
He took on this job filled with enthusiasm.

我带着所有的文件去见律师。 **wǒ dàizhe suǒyǒu de wénjiàn qù jiàn lǜshī**
(lit. I carry *zhe* all documents go see lawyer)
I went to see the lawyer, taking all the documents.

母亲哼着歌儿哄孩子睡觉。 **mǔqin hēngzhe gēr hǒng háizi shuìjiào**
(lit. mother hum *zhe* tune/song coax child sleep)
Mother humming a tune, coaxed the child to sleep.

孩子们扒着窗台看游行队伍。
háizimen bāzhe chuāngtái kàn yóuxíng duìwu
(lit. children hold *zhe* window-sill watch parade procession)
The children watched the parade leaning on the window-sill.

他抄着手站在一边看热闹。 **tā chāo zhe shǒu zhàn zài yībiān kàn rènào**
(lit. he fold *zhe* arms stand cv: at one side watch excitement)
Standing to one side with arms folded, he watched the excitement.

两个小学生跳着跑过来。 **liǎng ge xiǎo xuésheng tiào zhe pǎo guòlai**
(lit. two mw primary school pupils jump *zhe* run across-come)
Two primary schoolchildren came jumping across.

两个中国老师争着付钱。 **liǎng ge zhōngguó lǎoshī zhēng zhe fù qián**
(lit. two mw Chinese teachers vie *zhe* pay money)
The two Chinese teachers vied (with each other) to pay.

小李红着脸说了几句。 **xiǎolǐ hóng zhe liǎn shuō le jǐ jù**
(lit. little Li red *zhe* face say *le* few sentences)
Little Li with a red face said a few words.

别背着人说别人的坏话。 **bié bèi zhe rén shuō biérén de huàihuà**
(lit. don't behind-back *zhe* someone speak other person *de* unpleasant talk)
Don't talk ill of someone behind his/her back.

A 着 *zhe* phrase with a monosyllabic verb may be reduplicated to indicate repetitiveness. A phrase like this may be placed after the subject or at the beginning of the sentence before the subject:

我们说着说着已经走到了湖边。
wǒmen shuō zhe shuō zhe yǐjīng zǒu dào le húbiān
(lit. we talk *zhe* talk *zhe* already walk cv:arriving at *le* lake side)

or:

说着说着我们已经走到了湖边。
shuō zhe shuō zhe wǒmen yǐjīng zǒu dào le húbiān
(lit. talk *zhe* talk *zhe* we already walk cv:arriving at *le* lakeside)
Talking endlessly, we had already arrived at the lakeside.

哭着哭着她晕了过去。 **kū zhe kū zhe tā yūn le guòqu**
(lit. weep *zhe* weep *zhe* she faint le pass-go)
She wept and wept until she fainted.

他们吵着吵着打起架来。 **tāmen chǎo zhe chǎo zhe dǎ qǐ jià lai**
(lit. they argue *zhe* argue *zhe* fight begin-come)
They argued and argued until they began to fight.

Accompanying actions in some cases do not need 着 *zhe* if there are verbal complements with balanced rhythm. For example:

护士放轻脚步屏住气走近病人床前。
hùshi fàng qīng jiǎobù píngzhu qì zǒujìn bìngrén chuángqián
(lit. nurse place light footstep hold-fix breath walk near patient bed-front)
The nurse, with light steps and holding her/his breath, approached the patient's bed.

compare:

护士踮着脚屏着呼吸走近病人床前。
hùshi diǎn zhe jiǎo píng zhe hūxī zǒujìn bìngrén chuángqián
(lit. nurse tip-toe *zhe* hold *zhe* breath walk near patient bed-front)
The nurse, on tiptoe and holding his/her breath, approached the patient's bed.

14.5 CONSECUTIVE ACTIONS

A sentence expressing consecutive action regularly takes the form in Chinese of a completed action verb phrase or its negative alternative followed by the most commonly used referential adverbs 就[4] **jiù** 'then' or 才 **cái** 'only then' before the main verb:

他下了课就回家去了。 **tā xiàle kè jiù huíjiā qù le**
(lit. he finish *le* class, then return home go *le*)
He went home when class was finished.

客人进了门就把鞋脱下来。 **kèren jìn le mén jiù bǎ xié tuō xiàlai**
(lit. guests enter *le* door then cv:grasping shoes take-off down-come)
The guests took off their shoes when they came in.

哥哥吃了饭才开始复习功课。 **gēge chī le fàn cái kāishǐ fùxí gōngkè**
(lit. elder brother eat *le* food, only then begin revise schoolwork)
Elder brother didn't begin to revise his schoolwork until he had eaten.

我没有吃饭就去打网球了。 **wǒ méiyǒu chīfàn jiù qù dǎ wǎngqiú le**
(lit. I not have eat food then go play tennis *le*)
Without eating, I went to play tennis.

A series of completed action verbs may precede the main verb:

他洗了脸，刷了牙，脱了衣服，就上床睡觉去了。
tā xǐ le liǎn | shuā le yá | tuō le yīfu | jiù shàng chuáng shuìjiào qù le
(lit. he wash *le* face, brush *le* teeth, take-off *le* clothes, then get on bed sleep go *le*)
After washing his face, brushing his teeth and undressing, he went to bed.

他戴上眼镜，拿起书本，翻到第三页，便大声朗诵起来。
tā dài shàng yǎnjìng | náqǐ shūběn | fān dào dì sān yè | biàn dàshēng lǎngsòng qǐlai
(lit. he put on spectacles, pick up book, turn cv:to third page, then loud voice read aloud begin)
After putting on his glasses, picking up the book and turning to page three, he began to read it out in a loud voice.

In making requests and suggestions relating naturally to projected rather than completed action, the referential adverb 再 **zài** 'only then' is often used to mark consecutive sequence to the final verb:

这个问题咱们好好地研究研究再说。
zhèi ge wèntí zánmen hǎohāo de yánjiū yánjiū zài shuō
(lit. this mw question we well-well *de* study-study then talk)
Let's give this question some thought before we talk further.

[4] 便 **biàn** 'then, as soon as' is used as an alternative to 就 **jiù**, particularly in written style.

这件事搁一搁再办吧。 **zhèi jiàn shì gē yī gē zài bàn ba**
(lit. this mw matter put aside-one-put aside then deal with *ba*)
Let's put this matter aside for a while before we deal with it.

茶刚泡上，闷一会儿再喝。 **chá gāng pào shàng | mēn yīhuìr zài hē**
(lit. tea just made, brew a while then drink)
The tea is just made. Let it brew for a moment before (you) drink it.

请你等一等再走。 **qǐng nǐ děng yī děng zài zǒu**
(lit. please you wait-one-wait then leave) Please wait a bit before you go.

我先给你垫上，等你取了款再还我。
wǒ xiān gěi nǐ diàn shàng | děng nǐ qǔle kuǎn zài huán wǒ
(lit. I first cv:for you advance (money), wait you draw *le* money (from
bank) then return me)
I will give you an advance, and you can pay me back when you draw
money out (of the bank).

A consecutive sequence of actions may also include a coverbal or 着 **zhe** phrase
or both before the final verb, with or without a referential adverb:

他扭过头来冲我笑了笑。 V + CoV + V
tā niǔ guò tóu lai chōng wǒ xiàole xiào
(lit. he twist-over head come, cv:towards me, laugh *le* laugh)
He turned (his head) round and gave a smile in my direction.

他抽出一支香烟凑着鼻子闻了闻。 V + Vzhe + V
tā chōuchū yī zhī xiāngyān còuzhe bízi wénle wén
(lit. he take out one mw cigarette, press-close *zhe* nose smell *le* smell)
He took out a cigarette, held it close to his nose and smelled it.

她用两手支着头在想什么？ CoV + Vzhe + V
tā yòng liǎng shǒu zhīzhe tóu zài xiǎng shénme
(lit. she cv:using two hands support *zhe* head thinking what)
What is she thinking about, holding her head in her hands?

外宾学着用筷子吃饭。 Vzhe + CoV + V
wàibīn xuézhe yòng kuàizi chīfàn
(lit. foreign guests learn *zhe* cv:using chopsticks eat food)
The foreign visitors are learning to eat with chopsticks.

老爷爷停了一下，皱了皱眉头，又接着往下说。
V + V + refA + Vzhe + CoV + V
lǎo yéye tíngle yīxià | zhòule zhòu méitóu | yòu jiēzhe wǎng xià shuō

(lit. grandpa stop *le* one moment, furrow *le* furrow brow, then again
continue *zhe* cv:going ahead speak)
Grandpa stopped for a moment, frowned, and then continued speaking.

Two consecutive actions may of course be carried out by the same person or by
two different people. If one action follows the other very quickly, the two verbs
are often linked by a pair of referential adverbs 一 yī . . . 就 jiù 'as soon as'
placed respectively before them. For example:

老师一走进教室，就拿出点名簿点名。

lǎoshī yī zǒujìn jiàoshì | jiù náchū diǎnmíngbù diǎnmíng
(lit. teacher once walk-into classroom, then take out register call roll)
As soon as the teacher came into the classroom, (s)he took out the register
to do the roll-call.

校长一走进礼堂，大家就安静下来。

xiàozhǎng yī zǒujìn lǐtáng | dàjiā jiù ānjìng xiàlai
(lit. head teacher once walk-into auditorium, everyone then quiet
down-come)
As soon as the head teacher entered the auditorium, everyone went quiet.

比赛一开始，利兹联队就进了一球。

bǐsài yī kāishǐ | lìzī liánduì jiù jìn le yī qiú
(lit. game once begin, Leeds United then enter *le* one ball)
As soon as the game started, Leeds United scored a goal.

太阳一出来，鸟儿就在树上叽叽喳喳地叫起来。

tàiyáng yī chūlai | niǎor jiù zài shù shàng jījīzhāzhā de jiào qǐlai
(lit. sun once out-come, birds then cv:at tree-top chirp-chirp *de* call-begin)
As soon as the sun came out, the birds in the trees began to chatter.

爸爸一进门就把鞋脱掉，把大衣挂在衣架上。

bàba yī jìn mén jiù bǎ xié tuōdiào | bǎ dàyī guà zài yījià shàng
(lit. father once enter door then cv:grasping shoes take off, cv:grasping
overcoat hang cv:at clothes stand-top)
As soon as father comes, he takes off his shoes and hangs up his overcoat.

弟弟一放下刀叉就跑去看电视。

dìdi yī fàng xià dāochā jiù pǎo qù kàn diànshì
(lit. younger brother once put down knife fork then run-go watch
television)
As soon as younger brother puts down his knife and fork, he rushes off to
watch television.

14.6 SIMULTANEOUS ACTIONS

Simultaneous actions are linked by a pair of adverbials 一边 **yībiān** . . . 一边 **yībiān** 'while; whilst; at the same time'[5] which are placed respectively before the two verbs. For example:

他一边看书，一边听音乐。 **tā yībiān kàn shū | yībiān tīng yīnyuè**
(lit. he one-side read book, one-side listen to music)
He was reading and listening to music (at the same time).

售货员一边跟我谈话，一边把我买的东西包好。
shòuhuòyuán yībiān gēn wǒ tánhuà | yībiān bǎ wǒ mǎi de dōngxi bāo hǎo
(lit shop-assistant one-side cv:with me chat, one-side cv:grasping I bought *de* things wrap well)
The shop assistant chatted to me as (s)he wrapped up the things I had bought.

14.7 AN EMPHATIC CHAIN CONSTRUCTION

An idiomatic and emphatic chain construction can be formulated by using in sequence two verbs with contrasting meanings, one in the affirmative and the other in the negative. Generally, the affirmative verb comes first:

她拽住他不放。 **tā zhuài zhù tā bù fàng**
(lit. she hold-firm him not let go)
She caught hold of him and would not let him go.

你坐着别动！ **nǐ zuò zhe bié dòng**
(lit. you sit *zhe* don't move) You sit (where you are) and don't move.

小孙丢下工作不管。 **xiǎosūn diū xià gōngzuò bù guǎn**
(lit. little Sun throw-down work not care)
Little Sun abandoned the work and didn't bother about it.

老李板起脸孔不笑。 **lǎolǐ bǎnqǐ liǎnkǒng bù xiào**
(lit. old Li made serious face not smile)
Old Li gave a stern look and didn't smile.

孩子看到橱窗里的玩具，赖着不肯走。
háizi kàn dào chúchuāng li de wánjù | làizhe bùkěn zǒu

---

[5] 一面 **yīmiàn** . . . 一面 **yīmiàn** 'at the same time' are used in the same way but more by southern speakers.

(lit. child see shop-window-inside de toys, drag on *zhe* not willing leave)
Seeing the toys in the shop window, the child hung back and would not
move.

你怎么能撂下这件事儿不办呢?
nǐ zénme néng liàoxia zhèi jiàn shìr bù bàn ne
(lit. you how able put down this mw matter not deal with *ne*)
How can you put down this work and not deal with it?

The follow-up negatives in the above examples all indicate intentional actions.
If the negative is an expression of something unintentional, it may take the form
of a potential complement[6] instead:

邮票已经粘住了，撕不下来。 **yóupiào yǐjīng niānzhù le | sībuxiàlai**
(lit. stamp already stick-firm *le*, tear not off-come)
The stamps have already stuck (to the envelope) and cannot be taken off.

我饱了，一点儿也吃不下了。 **wǒ bǎo le | yīdiǎnr yě chībuxià le**
(lit. I full *le*, one bit even eat not down *le*)
I'm full and I can't eat a bit more.

14.8 AN ARTICULATED CHAIN CONSTRUCTION[7]

It is extremely common in Chinese to use the object of a first verb to be the
subject of a following verb without having to reiterate the nominal or pronominal
item, the formula being:

N1 + V1 + N2, V2 (+ N3, V3) . . .

我说'大家'自然包括你在内。 **wǒ shuō 'dàjiā' zìrán bāokuò nǐ zàinèi**
(lit. I say 'everyone' naturally include you within)
When I say everyone, I naturally include you.

你掂一掂这条鱼有多重? **nǐ diān yī diān zhèi tiáo yú yǒu duō zhòng**
(lit. you weigh-one-weigh (in your hand) this mw fish have how heavy)
Weigh this fish in your hand (and see how heavy it is).

那天我在公园里遇见他，在一旁看着他六岁的小女儿，从滑梯上滑下来。
nèi tiān wǒ zài gōngyuán li yùjiàn tā | zài yīpáng kànzhe tā liù suì de
xiǎo nǚ'er | cóng huátī shàng huá xiàlai

---

[6] A potential complement (see §10.2) tends to imply that the ability (or inability) to carry out the
action is beyond the control of the speaker.

[7] See Chapter 25 on abbreviation.

(lit. that day I cv:at park-inside met him, cv:at one side watch *zhe* his 6-years-old *de* little daughter, cv:from slide-top slide down-come)
That day I bumped into him in the park as he was watching his little 6-year-old daughter sliding down a slide.

他在报上发表了一篇文章，攻击那些官僚主义者，只看所谓调查报告，不顾事实真相。
tā zài bào shàng fābiǎo le yī piān wénzhāng | gōngjī nèixiē guānliáozhǔyìzhě | zhǐ kàn suǒwèi diàochá bàogào | bùgù shìshí zhēnxiàng
(lit. he cv:in newspaper-on publish *le* one mw article, attack those bureaucrats, only read so-called findings report, not care facts truth)
He published an article in the paper, attacking those bureaucrats who read only reports of findings and pay no attention to the real state of affairs.

我最喜欢吃古老肉，又甜又酸，容易送饭。
wǒ zuì xǐhuan chī gǔlǎoròu | yòu tián yòu suān | róngyì sòng fàn
(lit. I most like eat 'gulao' meat, both sweet and sour, easy goes with rice)
I like 'gulao' pork because it's sweet and sour and goes well with rice.

As we can see from the last example, a predicate having the object of a preceding verb as its notional subject may be either verbal or adjectival.

15   THE VERB 是 shì

是 shì 'to be' is a versatile verb, which is used for a variety of purposes. One is similar to the verb 'to be' in English to introduce an explanatory predicative. However, 是 shì is a very different verb from the English link verb, and in the following sections, its various uses will be spelled out. By definition, all sentences with 是 shì are expository in nature.

15.1   是 shì INTRODUCING A PREDICATIVE

是 shì 'to be' introduces a predicative, which generally takes the form of a nominal or pronominal. This predicative serves as an explanatory equivalent to the topic under discussion. In other words, 是 shì equates the two items on either side of it. For example:

我弟弟是中学生。 **wǒ dìdi shì zhōng xuésheng**
My younger brother is a secondary school student.

我是大学生。 **wǒ shì dà xuésheng**
I am a university student.

她是我们的邻居。 **tā shì wǒmende línjū**
She is our neighbour.

他是谁? **tā shì shéi**
Who is he?

这是泰山。 **zhè shì tàishān**
This is Mount Tai.

Verbs functioning in a similar equative way include: 姓 **xìng** 'to have the surname of . . .', 叫 **jiào** 'to have the name of . . .', 象 **xiàng** 'to resemble'. For example, 他姓李 **tā xìng lǐ** 'His surname is Li'; 她象她母亲 **tā xiàng tā mǔqin** 'She looks like her mother'.

One salient feature of the equation is that the nominal or pronominal expression on the right-hand side tends to be more general (i.e. less specific) in reference or meaning than that on the left-hand side. One cannot say, for example,

*中学生是我弟弟。 **zhōng xuésheng shì wǒ dìdi**
*A secondary school student is my younger brother.

*大学生是我。 **dà xuésheng shì wǒ**
*A university student is I.

*我们的邻居是她。 **wǒmende línjū shì tā**
*Our neighbour is she.

*谁是他? **shéi shì tā**
*Who is he?

However, it is possible for the words or expressions on either side of the equation to be equally specific and for them to be of a nominal nature. In these cases they are generally reversible without any significant change in the meaning:

王老师是我们的语法老师。 **wáng lǎoshī shì wǒmen de yǔfǎ lǎoshī**
Mr Wang is our grammar teacher.

我们的语法老师是王老师。 **wǒmen de yǔfǎ lǎoshī shì wáng lǎoshī**
Our grammar teacher is Mr Wang.

李明是我的男朋友。 **lǐ míng shì wǒde nán péngyou**
Li Ming is my boyfriend.

我的男朋友是李明。 **wǒde nán péngyou shì Lǐ Míng**
My boyfriend is Li Ming.

If one item is pronominal, then it is generally placed on the left-hand side while the nominal item for explanation is placed on the right-hand side. This is because pronominal items generally indicate given information, which is then posed as the topic:

这是泰山。 **zhè shì tàishān** This is Mount Tai.
他是李明。 **tā shì lǐ míng** He is Li Ming.

One does not say:

*泰山是这。 **tàishān shì zhè** *Mount Tai is this.
*李明是他。 **lǐ míng shì tā** *Li Ming is he.

The predicative may also take the form of a 的 **de** expression attached to a pronoun, adjective, verb or subject–predicate clause. For example,

(a) pronoun + 的 **de** as predicative:

这件羊毛衫是我的。 **zhèi jiàn yángmáoshān shì wǒ de**
This woollen sweater is mine.

(**b**) adjective + 的 *de* as predicative:

> 玫瑰花是<u>最美的</u>。 **méiguì huā shì <u>zuì měi de</u>**
> The roses are the most beautiful flowers.

(**c**) verb expression + 的 *de* as predicative:

> 我弟弟是<u>学汉语的</u>。 **wǒ dìdì shì <u>xué hànyǔ de</u>**
> My younger brother studies Chinese.

(**d**) clause + 的 *de* as predicative:

> 这些礼物是<u>我送给你的</u>。 **zhèixiē lǐwù shì <u>wǒ sòng gěi nǐ de</u>**
> These are presents for you from me./These are presents I am giving to you.

The two sides of such an equation can often be reversed, without any change in the overall meaning of the sentence, although there is some shift in focus. For example:

(**a**) pronoun + 的 *de* as topic:

> <u>我的</u>是羊毛衫。 **<u>wǒ de</u> shì yángmáoshān**
> Mine is a woollen sweater.

(**b**) adjective + 的 *de* as topic:

> <u>最美的</u>是玫瑰花。 **<u>zuì měi de</u> shì méiguì huā**
> The most beautiful are roses.

(**c**) verb + 的 *de* as topic:

> <u>学翻译的</u>是高年级学生。 **<u>xué fānyì de</u> shì gāo niánjí xuésheng**
> Those who study translation are upper-year students.

(**d**) clause + 的 *de* as topic:

> <u>我叫的</u>是大虾。 **<u>wǒ jiào de</u> shì dàxiā**
> What I have ordered are prawns.

的 *de* expressions may, of course, occupy both sides of the equation:

<u>我叫的</u>是<u>我最喜欢的</u>。 **<u>wǒ jiào de</u> shì <u>wǒ zuì xǐhuan de</u>**
What I have ordered is what I like most.

你的是蓝的，我的是红的。 **nǐ de** shì **lán de, wǒ de** shì **hóng de**
Yours is blue, mine is red.

An interesting footnote to this section is perhaps the extensive use of 的
de expressions as topics with 是 **shì** predicatives where English would more
normally have adverbials (e.g. fortunately, unfortunately, more importantly,
strangely enough, etc.). The predicatives under such circumstances have to be in
the form of clauses. For example:

幸运的是那天没有下雨。 **xìngyùn de | shì | nèi tiān méiyǒu xià yǔ**
Fortunately, it did not rain that day./What was fortunate was that it did not
rain that day.

倒霉的是我不会开车。 **dǎoméi de | shì | wǒ bù huì kāichē**
Unfortunately, I do not know how to drive./What is unfortunate is that I do
not know how to drive.

奇怪的是大家都不赞成。 **qíguài de | shì | dàjiā dōu bù zànchéng**
Strangely enough, nobody agreed./What was strange was that nobody
agreed.

更重要的是态度要认真。 **gèng zhòngyào de | shì | tàidù yào rènzhēn**
More importantly, one must adopt a conscientious attitude./What is more
important is that one's attitude must be conscientious.

Apart from introducing explanatory/expository predicatives, 是 **shì** 'to be' may,
of course, also be used to introduce evaluative predicatives with adjectival expressions that incorporate degree adverbs such as 多么 **duōme** 'to an immeasurable
extent', 那么 **nàme** 'to that degree'. Sometimes exclamatory particles such as 啊
ā, 呀 **yā**, etc., occur at the end of such sentences. For example:

他的诗是多么奔放啊！ **tā de shī shì duōme bēnfàng a**
(lit. his poems are how unrestrained *a*) How unrestrained his poems are!

女主人是那么热情。 **nǚ zhǔrén shì nàme rèqíng**
The hostess is so cordial and friendly.

This use of 是 **shì** as a predicative introducer may be modified by an adverb.
For example,

这件羊毛衫好象是我的。[1] **zhèi jiàn yángmáoshān hǎoxiàng shì wǒ de**
This woollen sweater seems to be mine.

---

[1] Please note that 好象 **hǎoxiàng** 'likely' is used here as an adverb.

女主人总是那么热情。 **nǔ zhǔrén zǒng shì nàme rèqíng**
The hostess is always so cordial and friendly.

15.2 PREDICATIVES WITH AN OPTIONAL 是 **shì**

If the predicative is an item which indicates **time**, **date**, **age**, **height**, **weight**, etc., 是 **shì** is often omitted. For example:

现在(是)几点钟? **xiànzài (shì) jǐ diǎn zhōng**
What time is it now?

今天(是)十月二号。 **jīntiān (shì) shí yuè èr hào**
Today is 2 October.

这个孩子今年(是)五岁。 **zhèi ge háizi jīnnián (shì) wǔ suì**
The child is 5 years old.

小李(是)一米七。 **xiǎolǐ (shì) yī mǐ qī**
Little Li is 1 metre and 7 centimetres tall.

是 **shì** cannot, of course, be omitted from the negative forms of these sentences:

今天不是十月二号。 **jīntiān bù shì shí yuè èr hào**
Today is not 2 October.

现在不是五点钟。 **xiànzài bù shì wǔ diǎn zhōng**
It is not five o'clock now.

Arithmetical conversion within the same system from a bigger unit to a smaller unit more often than not results in an equation without 是 **shì**:

一年(是)十二个月。 **yī nián (shì) shí'èr ge yuè**
There are twelve months in a year.

一天(是)二十四小时。 **yī tiān (shì) èrshí sì xiǎoshí**
There are twenty-four hours in a day.

However, if the conversion takes place between different systems, 是 **shì** cannot be omitted:

一吨是一千公斤。 **yī dūn shì yī qiān gōngjīn**
A ton is equal to one thousand kilograms.

一米是多少英尺? **yī mǐ shì duōshǎo yīngchǐ**
How many feet are there in a metre?

When asking or talking about the cost or price of something, omission of 是 **shì** is the standard form, and the order of the equation is generally reversible:

一本多少钱? **yī běn duōshǎo qián**

or:

多少钱一本? **duōshǎo qián yī běn**
How much per copy?

一盒五十便士。 **yī hé wǔshí biànshì**

or:

五十便士一盒。 **wǔshí biànshì yī hé**
Fifty pence for a box.

There is, of course, a set of verbs that express measurements more specifically:

这条绳子长二十米。 **zhèi tiáo shéngzi cháng èrshí mǐ**
(lit. this mw rope is long 20 metres) This rope is 20 metres long.

那栋房子值一百万元。 **nèi dòng fángzi zhí yī bǎiwàn yuán**
(lit. that mw house is worth one million **yuan**)
That house is worth a million yuan.

Other verbs in this category are: 高 **gāo** 'to have the height of . . .', 重 **zhòng** 'to have the weight of . . .', 卖 **mài** 'to sell for . . .', 等于 **děngyú** 'to be equal to', 合 **hé** 'to be the same as'.

15.3　是 **shì** INDICATING EXISTENCE

是 **shì** 'to be' may also be used to indicate existence and in this case it resembles 有 **yǒu** 'to have, there is/are'. However, the kind of existence expressed by 是 **shì**, in comparison with 有 **yǒu**, tends to be more permanent than incidental and to indicate the occupation of the whole specified area rather than part of it.

The structural formula for both 是 **shì** and 有 **yǒu** existential sentences is the same:

Time or location + 是 **shì** or 有 **yǒu** + item(s) that exist(s)

but their underlying meanings are different:

桌子上有书。 **zhuōzi shàng yǒu shū**
There are books on the table. (i.e. other things may be there too)

桌子上都是书。 **zhuōzi shàng dōu shì shū**
The whole table was covered with books. (i.e. the only things on the table are books)

Clearly, 有 **yǒu** seems to imply that the existence of an item or items in a particular place or time, from the speaker's perspective (i.e. as an onlooker), is probably more casual than intentional. The item or items happen to be there and the onlooker senses their presence. Nouns following 有 **yǒu** are therefore invariably of indefinite reference.

Because of this, 有 **yǒu** is more likely to be associated with multiple items or used for making queries:

冰箱里有鱼，有肉，有蔬菜，有水果。
bīngxiāng li yǒu yú, yǒu ròu, yǒu shūcài, yǒu shuǐguǒ
There are fish, meat, vegetables and fruit in the fridge.

屋子里有人吗？ **wūzi li yǒu rén ma?**
Is there anybody inside?

是 **shì** on the other hand implies that the existence of an object or objects in a particular place or time, from what can be seen or understood, is either more deliberate than incidental. In other words, the impression seems to be that the item or items are there because of some design or plan or that they have apparently become the sole and dominating occupants of the location in question. That is what is there. This being the case, the noun after 是 **shì** can have either definite or indefinite reference depending on the context:

后边是诊所。 **hòubian shì zhěnsuǒ**
At the back is a/the clinic.

cf. 后边有诊所。 **hòubian yǒu zhěnsuǒ**
At the back there is a clinic.

大学对面是一家银行。	**dàxué duìmiàn shì yī jiā yínháng**	Opposite the university is a bank.
cf. 大学对面有一家银行。	**dàxue duìmiàn yǒu yī jiā yínháng**	There is a bank opposite the university.
楼上是三间卧室。	**lóu shàng shì sān jiān wòshì**	Upstairs are three bedrooms.
cf. 楼上有三间卧室。	**lóu shàng yǒu sān jiān wòshì**	There are three bedrooms upstairs.

是 **shì** is therefore often associated with a single category of items and commonly occurs with adverbs like 都 **dōu** 'wholly', 全 **quán** 'completely'.

到处是人。	**dàochù shì rén**	There were people everywhere.
满地是水。	**mǎndì shì shuǐ**	There is water all over the ground.
屋子里都是烟。	**wūzi li dōu shì yān**	The room was filled with smoke.

It is interesting to note that the idiom 有的是 **yǒude shì** 'there's plenty of . . .', which employs both 有 **yǒu** and 是 **shì**, is used to indicate the profusion of a particular item in a place:

礼堂里还有座位吗? **lǐtáng li hái yǒu zuòwèi ma**
Are there any more vacant seats in the auditorium?

有的是。 **yǒu de shì**
Yes, there are plenty of them there.

礼堂里有的是座位。 **lǐtáng li yǒu de shì zuòwèi**
There are plenty of seats in the auditorium.

冰箱里有的是冰激凌。 **bīngxiāng li yǒu de shì bīngjīlíng**
There is plenty of ice-cream in the fridge.

15.4 是 shì EXPRESSING EMPHASIS

Similar to cleft sentences in English (e.g. 'It was yesterday that we arrived'), 是 **shì** in Chinese is also used to express emphasis (with 的 **de** being present or not present depending on the situation), and it is placed in front of the word or phrase where emphasis is being sought. In other words, the word or phrase preceded by 是 **shì** will naturally receive sentence stress. We may call this kind of sentence stress pattern **confirmatory emphasis**. Let us look at the following narrative Chinese sentence that recounts something that has already happened:

我去年从美国坐飞机到英国去探望王先生。
wǒ qùnián cóng měiguó zuò fēijī dào yīngguó qù tànwàng wáng xiānsheng
Last year I went by plane from America to Britain to visit Mr Wang.

Different emphasis can be achieved in this sentence by placing 是 **shì** directly before the subject or any adverbial phrase coming before the main verb, with 的 *de* added at the end:[2]

---

[2] In spoken English this kind of confirmatory emphasis may often be achieved by giving sentence stress to the word to be emphasised rather than by using a cleft structure. While sentence stress like this can be used in Chinese, emphasis with 是 **shì** is more common in Chinese than the cleft structure in English.

是<u>我</u>去年从美国坐飞机到英国去探望王先生的。
**shì <u>wǒ</u> qùnián cóng měiguó zuò fēijī dào yīngguó qù tànwàng
wáng xiānsheng de**
[It was] **I** [who] last year went by plane from America to visit
Mr Wang.

我是<u>去年</u>从美国坐飞机到英国去探望王先生的。
**wǒ shì <u>qùnián</u> zuò fēijī cóng měiguó dào yīngguó qù tànwàng
wáng xiānsheng de**
[It was] **last year** [that] I went by plane from America to visit
Mr Wang.

我去年是<u>从美国</u>坐飞机到英国去探望王先生的。
**wǒ qùnián shì <u>cóng měiguó</u> zuò fēijī dào yīngguó qù tànwàng
wáng xiānsheng de**
It was from **America** that I went last year by plane to Britain to visit
Mr Wang.

我去年从美国是<u>坐飞机</u>到英国去探望王先生的。
**wǒ qùnián cóng měiguó shì <u>zuò fēijī</u> dào yīngguó qù tànwàng
wáng xiānsheng de**
It was **by plane** that I went last year from America to Britain to visit
Mr Wang.

我去年从美国坐飞机是<u>到英国去</u>探望王先生的。
**wǒ qùnián cóng měiguó zuò fēijī shì <u>dào yīngguó qù</u> tànwàng
wáng xiānsheng de**
It was **to Britain** that I went last year by plane from America to visit
Mr Wang.

When the main predicate verb itself is to be emphasised, 是 **shì** is still placed
before it, but 的 **de** will have to be shifted to a position in front of the object of
the verb:[3]

---

[3] Some speakers omit 的 *de* as in sentences like these:

我去年从美国坐飞机到英国是<u>去探望</u>王先生。
wǒ qùnián cóng měiguó zuò fēijī dào yīngguó shì <u>qù tànwàng</u> wáng xiānsheng

or

我去年从美国坐飞机到英国去是<u>探望</u>王先生。
wǒ qùnián cóng měiguó zuò fēijī dào yīngguó qù shì <u>tànwàng</u> wáng xiānsheng
It was to visit Mr Wang that I went last year by plane from America to Britain.

我去年从美国坐飞机到英国是<u>去探望</u>的王先生。

wǒ qùnián cóng měiguó zuò fēijī dào yīngguó shì <u>qù tànwàng</u> de wáng xiānsheng

It was to go and visit Mr Wang that I flew last year from America to Britain.

or:

我去年从美国坐飞机到英国去是<u>探望</u>的王先生。

wǒ qùnián cóng měiguó zuò fēijī dào yīngguó qù shì <u>tànwàng</u> de wáng xiānsheng

It was to visit Mr Wang that I went last year by plane from America to Britain.

我去年从美国坐飞机到英国去探望的是<u>王先生</u>。

wǒ qùnián cóng měiguó zuò fēijī dào yīngguó qù tànwàng de shì <u>wáng xiānsheng</u>

It was Mr Wang that I went last year by plane from America to Britain to visit. (The person I went last year by plane from America to Britain to visit was Mr Wang.)

The sentence can be reversed to create a different emphasis, but it remains in line with Chinese syntax:

去年从美国坐飞机到英国去探望王先生的是我。

qùnián cóng měiguó zuò fēijī dào yīngguó qù tànwàng wáng xiānsheng de shì wǒ

The person who went last year by plane from America to Britain to visit Mr Wang was me. (I was the one who went last year by plane from America to Britain to visit Mr Wang.)

However, if the statement refers to the future rather than the past, the particle 的 *de* is not included unless the object is to be emphasised. For example:

我是<u>明年</u>从美国坐飞机到英国去探望王先生。

wǒ shì <u>míngnián</u> cóng měiguó zuò fēijī dào yīngguó qù tànwàng wáng xiānsheng

It is next year that I will go by plane from America to Britain to visit Mr Wang.

我明年从美国是<u>坐飞机</u>到英国去探望王先生。

wǒ míngnián cóng měiguó shì <u>zuò fēijī</u> dào yīngguó qù tànwàng wáng xiānsheng

It is by plane that I will go next year from America to Britain to visit Mr Wang.

我明年从美国坐飞机到英国去探望的是<u>王先生</u>。

wǒ míngnián cóng měiguó zuò fēijī dào yīngguó qù tànwàng de shì <u>wáng xiānsheng</u>

It is Mr Wang that I will go next year by plane from America to Britain to visit.

Corresponding negative sentences are couched in a similar way, again with 的 *de* for past actions but without it for future actions. For example:

不是<u>我</u>(而是<u>我弟弟</u>)去年从美国坐飞机到英国去探望王先生的。

bù shì <u>wǒ</u> (ér shì <u>wǒ dìdì</u>) qùnián cóng měiguó zuò fēijī dào yīngguó qù tànwàng wáng xiānsheng de

It was not I (but my younger brother) who went last year by plane from America to Britain to visit Mr Wang.

我不是<u>去年</u>(而是<u>前年</u>)从美国坐飞机到英国去探望王先生的。

wǒ bù shì <u>qùnián</u> (ér shì <u>qiánnián</u>) cóng měiguó zuò fēijī dào yīngguó qù tànwàng wáng xiānsheng de

It was not last year (but the year before) that I went by plane from America to Britain to visit Mr Wang.

我不是<u>明年</u>(而是<u>后年</u>)从美国坐飞机到英国去探望王先生。

wǒ bù shì <u>míngnián</u> (ér shì <u>hòunián</u>) cóng měiguó zuò fēijī dào yīngguó qù tànwàng wáng xiānsheng

It is not next year (but the following year) that I will go by plane from America to Britain to visit Mr Wang.

We have so far confined our examples to simple sentences. In fact, emphasis can also be introduced into a subordinate clause beginning with 因为 **yīnwèi** 'because' to indicate cause or reason. The word order has to be modified under such circumstances.

For instance, if we take the sentence:

因为昨天天气不好，所以我没出去。

yīnwèi zuótiān tiānqì bù hǎo | suǒyǐ wǒ méi chūqù

I did not go out yesterday because the weather was not good.

the emphatic transformation with 是 **shì** would be:

我昨天没出去是因为天气不好。

wǒ zuótiān méi chūqù shì yīnwèi tiānqì bù hǎo

It was because the weather was not good that I did not go out yesterday.

or:

我昨天之所以没出去是因为天气不好。
wǒ zuótiān zhī suǒyǐ méi chūqù shì yīnwèi tiānqì bù hǎo
The reason why I did not go out yesterday was because the weather was
not good.

We have called the sentence stress patterns illustrated above **confirmatory emphasis**, since they confirm a particular point through the combined workings of
是 **shì** and sentence stress. However, if the sentence stress does not fall on the
word or phrase that follows 是 **shì** but on 是 **shì** itself, then the emphasis will
focus on the whole sentence. We may call this kind of sentence stress pattern
concessionary emphasis, which in English would be conveyed by tone of voice
or by the addition of something like 'It is true that . . .'. As the emphasis falls on
the whole sentence, it is only natural for 是 **shì** to come between the subject and
the predicate. For example:

我昨天是没来上课。 **wǒ zuótiān shì méi lái shàngkè**
[It is true that] I did not turn up for class yesterday.

我是喝了三杯啤酒。 **wǒ shì hē le sān bēi píjiǔ**
[I must confess that] I did down three glasses of beer.

我是没有钱。 **wǒ shì méiyǒu qián**
[You are right,] I don't have any money.

他是在学习英语。 **tā shì zài xuéxí yīngyǔ**
[Yes,] he is studying English.

Additional remarks to contradict the concession may refer back to any element
in the sentence:

我昨天是没来上课，可是预先请了假 。
wǒ zuótiān shì méi lái shàngkè | kěshì yùxiān qǐng le jià
[It is true that] I did not turn up for class yesterday, but I had asked for
leave in advance.

我昨天是没来上课，可是在家自学。
wǒ zuótiān shì méi lái shàngkè | kěshì zài jiā zìxué
[It is true that] I did not turn up for class yesterday, but I did study on my
own at home.

我昨天是没来上课，可是前天来了。
wǒ zuótiān shì méi lái shàngkè | kěshì qiántiān lái le
[It is true that] I did not turn up for class yesterday, but I did come the day
before yesterday.

我是喝了三杯啤酒，可是并没有喝醉。
wǒ shì hē le sān bēi píjiǔ | kěshì bìng méiyǒu hē zuì
[I must confess that] I did down three glasses of beer, but I certainly did not get drunk.

我是喝了三杯啤酒，可是我没喝葡萄酒啊。
wǒ shì hē le sān bēi píjiǔ | kěshì wǒ méi hē pútao jiǔ a
[I must confess that] I did down three glasses of beer, but I did not touch any wine.

Whether the emphasis is confirmatory or concessionary, the presence of 是 **shì** as the core verb in all these sentences makes them expository, even though they can have any type of sentence – narrative (most commonly), descriptive, evaluative or expository – embedded in them.

The negation of either a confirmatory or concessionary emphatic sentence is by the addition of the negator 不 **bù** before 是 **shì**:

我不是没有钱。 **wǒ bù shì méiyǒu qián**
It is not that I don't have any money.

她不是不会说英语。 **tā bù shì bù huì shuō yīngyǔ**
It is not that she doesn't know how to speak English.

15.5 是 **shì** ASSESSING AN OVERALL SITUATION

是 **shì** may also be used loosely to refer to or to make an overall assessment of a situation, rather like its function as a marker of emphasis.[4] Under these circumstances, 是 **shì** is not usually stressed, and it is followed by a verbal phrase or a clause. The subject or topic of the sentence can be any part of speech or it can be left out if 是 **shì** is modified by an adverb. For example:

她是不会来了。 **tā shì bù huì lái le**
(lit. she *shi* not probable come *le*)
I don't think she will come./She is unlikely to come.

那是说起来容易，做起来难。 **nà shì shuōqǐlái róngyi | zuòqǐlái nán**
(lit. that *shi* say up-come easy, do up-come difficult)
That is easier said than done.

如今是什么办法都试过了。 **rújīn shì shénme bànfǎ dōu shì guò le**
(lit. till now *shi* any method all try *guo le*)
So far we have tried whatever methods we could think of.

---

[4] See §16.3.

这儿是天无三日晴，地无三尺平。
zhèr shì tiān wú sān rì qíng | dì wú sān chǐ píng
(lit. here *shi* sky has not three days fine, land has not three feet level)
Here there aren't three fine days in succession or three square feet of land
that are level.

都是你不好。 **dōu shì nǐ bù hǎo**
(lit. all *shi* you not good) It was entirely your fault.

不是我不愿意。 **bù shì wǒ bù yuànyì**
(lit. not *shi* I not willing) It is not that I am/was unwilling.

This use of 是 **shì** is most susceptible to modification by adverbs. For example:

他<u>简直</u>是疯了。 **tā <u>jiǎnzhí</u> shì fēng le**
(lit. he simply *shi* mad *le*) He is simply crazy.

她<u>照例</u>是不发表意见。 **tā <u>zhàolì</u> shì bù fābiǎo yìjiàn**
(lit. she as usual *shi* not express opinion)
As usual, she did not express an opinion.

<u>其实</u>是你没有弄明白。 **qíshí shì nǐ méiyǒu nòng míngbái**
(lit. in fact *shi* you not have achieve comprehension)
In fact you have not got a clear understanding of it.

15.6 是 shì FORMING PART OF A CONNECTOR

Precisely because of the particular uses of 是 **shì** discussed in the above sections,
many 是 **shì** expressions with their adverbial modifications have become established as conjunctions often used to introduce subordinate or coordinate clauses:

<u>要是</u>你不愿意，我就请别人帮忙。
<u>yàoshì</u> nǐ bù yuànyì | wǒ jiù qǐng biérén bāngmáng
If you are unwilling, I will ask others to help.

你想去看电影<u>还是</u>去听音乐?
nǐ xiǎng qù kàn diànyǐng <u>háishì</u> qù tīng yīnyuè
Would like to go to the cinema or [to go to] a concert.

我很喜欢这件衣服，<u>可是</u>太贵了。
wǒ hěn xǐhuan zhèi jiàn yīfu | <u>kěshì</u> tài guì le
I like this piece of clothing very much, but it is too expensive.

Other such connectors include: 于是 **yúshì** 'then', 但是 **dànshì** 'but', 尤其是 **yóuqíshì** 'especially'.

15.7 是 **shì** AS A PIVOT

是 **shì** can also be used as a pivot between two identical words or expressions for emphatic reiteration. The emphasis is confirmed by the presence of an adverbial pre-modifier. For example:

事实总是事实。 **shìshí zǒng shì shìshí**
(lit. facts always are facts.) Facts are facts.

好就是好。 **hǎo jiù shì hǎo**
(lit. good then is good.) What is good is good.

不懂就是不懂。 **bù dǒng jiù shì bù dǒng**
(lit. not understand then is not understand)
If you don't understand, you don't understand.

When there is no adverb, two similar pivotal sentences are needed to make the statement sound complete. For example:

一是一，二是二。 **yī shì yī | èr shì èr**
(lit. one is one, two are two) That's how it is [and that's that].

好是好，坏是坏。 **hǎo shì hǎo | huài shì huài**
(lit. good is good, bad is bad)
What is good is good; and what is bad is bad.

Where there is only one such pivotal sentence, it becomes a concessionary statement and needs to be completed by a further comment. For example:

这件衣服漂亮是漂亮，就是贵了点儿。
zhèi jiàn yīfu piàoliang shì piàoliang | jiù shì guì le diǎnr
(lit. this mw: piece clothing beautiful is beautiful, then is expensive *le* a little)
This piece of clothing may be beautiful, but it is a little too expensive.

我有是有，可是一下子找不到。 **wǒ yǒu shì yǒu | kěshì yī xiàzi zhǎobudào**
(lit. I have is have, but one mw: occasion find-not-reach)
I am sure I have this, but I cannot lay my hands on it at the moment.

好是好，可是我还是不去。 **hǎo shì hǎo | kěshì wǒ háishì bù qù**
(lit. good is good, but I still not go)
It's all very well, but I am still not going.

16 THE VERB 有 yǒu

有 **yǒu** 'to have', like 是 **shì**, is also extremely versatile, and its grammatical function far exceeds its partial counterpart 'to have' in English. It not only expresses possession, but it also indicates existence, characteristics, condition, degree, comparison, and so on. In the following sections, we shall discuss the multiple uses of 有 **yǒu** in different contexts, syntactic as well as lexical. Statements of possession or existence are by definition explanatory and therefore most sentences that incorporate 有 **yǒu** either are or become expository in nature.[1]

16.1   有 **yǒu** INDICATING POSSESSION

The primary meaning of 有 **yǒu** 'to have' is to indicate possession. The subject of a 有 **yǒu** sentence, that is, the possessor, is usually a living being, but it can also be an inanimate object that contains or consists of component parts:

我有两个妹妹。 **wǒ yǒu liǎng ge mèimei**
I have two younger sisters.

他有不少词典。 **tā yǒu bùshǎo cídiǎn**
He has quite a lot of dictionaries.

哥哥有一辆摩托车。 **gēge yǒu yī liàng mótuōchē**
(My) elder brother has a motorbike.

每个人都有两只手。 **měi ge rén dōu yǒu liǎng zhī shǒu**
Everyone has two hands.

那本书有个很漂亮的封面。 **nèi běn shū yǒu ge hěn piàoliang de fēngmiàn**
That book has a very beautiful cover.

这种锅有两个把柄。 **zhèi zhǒng guō yǒu liǎng ge bǎbǐng**
This kind of pot has two handles.

有 **yǒu** is negated by 没 **méi** (and not 不 **bù**). Once negated, it is generally followed by a generic noun, which is not restricted or modified by numeral and measure word phrases or by other attributives unless the restriction or modification itself is the focus of attention or argument:

---

[1] See Chapter 20 on different sentence types.

我没有妹妹。 **wǒ méiyǒu mèimei**
I haven't got/don't have a younger sister.

哥哥没有摩托车。 **gēge méiyǒu mótuōchē**
(My) elder brother hasn't got/doesn't have a motorbike.

这样的戏没有观众。 **zhèyàng de xì méiyǒu guānzhòng**
A play like this doesn't get an audience.

One does not say:

*我没有两个妹妹。 **wǒ méiyǒu liǎng ge mèimei**
*I don't have two younger sisters.

*这样的戏没有五百个观众。 **zhèyàng de xì méiyǒu wǔ bǎi ge guānzhòng**
*A play like this doesn't get an audience of five hundred.

unless the specific number is the focus of contrast:

他只有一个妹妹，没有两个。 **tā zhǐyǒu yī ge mèimei | méiyǒu liǎng ge**
He has only one younger sister, not two.

那种锅没有两个把柄，只有一个。
nèi zhǒng guō méiyǒu liǎng ge bǎbǐng | zhǐyǒu yī ge
This kind of pot doesn't have two handles, but only one.

The negation can be made more emphatic by reversing the order of the object noun and 有 **yǒu**, with the noun qualified by 一 **yī** 'a single' or 半 **bàn** 'half' and the appropriated measure word, and with 有 **yǒu** modified by 也 **yě** or 都 **dōu**:[2]

我一个妹妹也没有。 **wǒ yī ge mèimei yě méiyǒu**
I don't even have one younger sister.

他半本词典都没有。 **tā bàn běn cídiǎn dōu méiyǒu**
He doesn't even have half a dictionary.

16.2 有 **yǒu** INDICATING EXISTENCE

有 **yǒu** indicates existence, if the subject of the sentence is a time or location expression. The object of 有 **yǒu** naturally refers to the person or thing that exists in that particular location or at that particular time.

---

[2] See also §1.2.3.

明天晚上有个音乐会。 **míngtiān wǎnshang yǒu yī ge yīnyuèhuì**
Tomorrow evening there's a concert.

书架上有很多杂志。 **shūjià shàng yǒu hěn duō zázhì**
There are many magazines on the bookcase.

商店里有不少顾客。 **shāngdiàn li yǒu bùshǎo gùkè**
There are quite a few customers in the store/shop.

The negation of the existential verb 有 **yǒu** is either 没有 **méiyǒu** or 没 **méi**:

那时候，街上没有一个行人。[3] **nèi shíhou | jiē shàng méiyǒu yī ge xíngrén**
At that time, there wasn't one pedestrian on the street.

屋子里没人。 **wūzi li méi rén**
There is no one in the room.

楼下没有电话。 **lóu xià méiyǒu diànhuà**
There isn't a telephone downstairs.

The negation of an existential sentence, as with a possession sentence, can be made more insistent by moving the object noun before 有 **yǒu** and by adding 也 **yě** or 都 **dōu**:

那时候，街上一个行人也没有。
nèi shíhou | jiē shàng yī ge xíngrén yě méiyǒu
At that time, there wasn't [even] one pedestrian on the street.

天上半朵云也没有。 **tiān shàng bàn duǒ yún yě méiyǒu**
There isn't/wasn't (half) a cloud in the sky.

屋子里一点声音都没有。 **wūzi li yīdiǎn shēngyīn dōu méiyǒu**
There wasn't the slightest sound in the room.

There is often a fine line between 有 **yǒu** indicating possession and 有 **yǒu** meaning existence, which can invite alternative translations in English:

图书馆有很多中文书。 **túshūguǎn yǒu hěnduō zhōngwén shū**
The library has a lot of Chinese books.
There are a lot of Chinese books in the library.

---

[3] The object of a non-existential 没有 **méiyǒu**, like non-possession, cannot be associated with numerals and measures: e.g. *那时候，街上没有两个行人 *'At that time, there weren't two pedestrian on the street'. However, the numeral 一 **yī** plus a measure is possible because in a sentence like this it does not literally indicate a number but emphasises the idea of 'none' or 'not a single one'.

这座楼一个电梯也没有。 **zhèi zuò lóu yī ge diàntī yě méiyǒu**
This building doesn't have one lift/elevator.
There isn't one lift/elevator in this building.

The semantic difference between 有 **yǒu** and 是 **shì** when indicating existence
has been explained in the previous chapter (§15.3). As we saw, 是 **shì** can be
followed by nouns of either definite or indefinite reference, but 有 **yǒu** takes
nouns of only indefinite reference. For example:

前面是两座大山。 **qiánmiàn shì liǎng zuò dà shān** (indefinite)
In front are two big mountains.

对面就是我家。 **duìmiàn jiùshì wǒ jiā** (definite)
Opposite is my home.

but:

沿路有很多商店。 **yánlù yǒu hěn duō shāngdiàn**
Along the road there are many shops.

靠床有一个衣柜。 **kào chuáng yǒu yī ge yīguì**
There is a wardrobe next to the bed.

桌子上没有书。 **zhuōzi shàng méiyǒu shū**
There aren't any books on the table.

*马路对面有那家商店。 **mǎlù duìmiàn yǒu nèi jiā shāngdiàn**
Opposite the main road there is that store/shop.

16.3 有 **yǒu** INTRODUCING SUBJECTS AND TIME OR LOCATION EXPRESSIONS OF INDEFINITE REFERENCE

Chinese, unlike English, lacks definite and indefinite articles, and definite and
indefinite reference is often decided simply by context. However, in narrative
sentences, it is usually the position of a noun in relation to the verb that indicates
its reference. A noun in a pre-verbal position, that is, the subject of a sentence,
generally encodes known or old information and is therefore of definite reference; whereas a noun in a post-verbal position and the object of a verb, tends to
encode unknown or new information and is consequently of indefinite reference.
The English translations below illustrate this:

那时候客人来了。 **nèi shíhou kèrén lái le**
At that moment <u>the</u> guest(s) arrived.

那时候来了一个客人。 **nèi shíhou lái le yī ge kèren**
At that moment <u>a</u> guest arrived.

However, 有 **yǒu** is used as a dummy verb when an indefinitely referenced noun is moved to a subject, that is, pre-verbal position. The presence of 有 **yǒu** before the noun ensures that the noun retains its post-verbal position and its indefinite reference:

那时候有(一)[4]个医生进来了。 **nèi shíhou yǒu (yī) ge yīshēng jìn lái le**
At that moment a doctor came in.

*那时候一个医生进来了。 **nèi shíhou yī ge yīshēng jìn lái le**
At that moment a doctor came in.

In this case the other and perhaps more natural option would remain:

那时候进来了一个医生。 **nèi shíhou jìn lái le yī ge yīshēng**
At that moment a doctor came in.

However, this last option is possible only with an intransitive verb (like the one in the example). If the verb in the sentence has an object or a complement, the 有 **yǒu** construction becomes obligatory. For example:

(外面)有人在敲门。 **(wàimian) yǒu rén zài qiāo mén**
There is someone (outside) knocking at the door.

(这时候)有辆车在路口停了下来。
(zhè shíhou) yǒu liàng chē zài lùkǒu tíng le xiàlai
(At this moment) a car stopped at the intersection.

花丛中有很多蜜蜂在采蜜。 **huācóng zhōng yǒu hěn duō mìfēng zài cǎi mì**
There were lots of bees gathering nectar from the flowers.

Time and location expressions are of definite reference and are naturally placed at the beginning of a sentence or very early in a sentence in a pre-verbal position:

那天我去找他。 **nèi tiān wǒ qù zhǎo tā**
That day I went to look for him.

---

[4] 一 **yī** 'one' is usually omitted for reasons of rhythm. 一个 **yī ge** is disyllabic, but when 有 **yǒu** is added, the phrase becomes awkwardly trisyllabic. To return to the more comfortable disyllabic rhythm, 一 **yī** is therefore generally left out (see Chapter 26 on prosody).

火车站里挤满了人。 **huǒchēzhàn li jǐ mǎn le rén**
The railway station was packed with people.

However, if the time or location expression is intentionally indefinite, 有 **yǒu** will once again have to be introduced:

有一天我去找他。 **yǒu yī tiān wǒ qù zhǎo tā**
One day I went to look for him.

有个火车站不停普通客车。 **yǒu ge huǒchēzhàn bù tíng pǔtōng kèchē**
There is one railway station where ordinary passenger trains don't stop.

Other examples are:

有一次/有一回我在城里遇见他。
yǒu yī cì | yǒu yī huí wǒ zài chéng li yùjiàn tā
On one occasion, I met him in the town.

有时候他也上我家来。 **yǒu shíhou tā yě shàng wǒ jiā lái**
Sometimes he came to my home too.

16.4   有 **yǒu** SPECIFYING DEGREE OR EXTENT

有 **yǒu** is used with adjectives like 大 **dà** 'big', 高 **gāo** 'tall', 重 **zhòng** 'heavy', to specify how big, tall, heavy, etc., something or somebody is.

他的屋子有多大? **tāde wūzi yǒu duō dà**
How big is his room?

他的屋子有三米长,两米宽。 **tāde wūzi yǒu sān mǐ cháng | liǎng mǐ kuān**
His room is 3 metres long and 2 metres wide.

你弟弟有多高? **nǐ dìdi yǒu duō gāo**
How tall is your younger brother?

我弟弟有一米九高。 **wǒ dìdi yǒu yī mǐ jiǔ gāo**
My younger brother is 1.9 metres tall.

这个包裹有两公斤重。 **zhèi ge bāoguǒ yǒu liǎng gōngjīn zhòng**
This parcel weighs 2 kilos. (lit. 2 kilos heavy)

The phrases 有点 **yǒudiǎn** or 有些 **yǒuxiē** meaning 'a little; a bit' may be used before adjectives or verbs in the predicate to indicate 'to a certain extent or degree':

我有点紧张。 **wǒ yǒudiǎn jǐnzhāng**
I'm a bit nervous.

他有些害怕。 **tā yǒuxiē hàipà**
He's a bit afraid.

大家都有点舍不得他离开这儿。 **dàjiā dōu yǒudiǎn shěbude tā líkāi zhèr**
Everyone was a little sorry he was leaving here.

16.5 有 **yǒu** INTRODUCING COMPARISON[5]

The capacity of 有 **yǒu** to specify degree or extent leads on naturally to its
function of introducing comparisons. Often 那么 **nàme** or 那样 **nàyàng** 'so, like
that' is present, and the basic formula is N1 + (没)有 **(méi)yǒu** + N2 + (那么)
(nàme) + adjective + (吗) **(ma)**:

你弟弟有你(那么)高吗？ **nǐ dìdi yǒu nǐ (nàme) gāo ma**
Is your younger brother as tall as you?

我弟弟没有我(这么)高。 **wǒ dìdi méiyǒu wǒ (zhème) gāo**
My younger brother isn't as tall as me.

这个包裹有那个(那么)重吗？ **zhèi ge bāoguǒ yǒu nèi ge (nàme) zhòng ma**
Is this parcel as heavy as that one?

这个包裹真的有那个(那么)重。
zhèi ge bāoguó zhēnde yǒu nèi ge (nàme) zhòng
This parcel really is as heavy as that one.

那条狗有一只小老虎(那样)大。
nèi tiáo gǒu yǒu yī zhī xiǎo lǎohǔ (nàyàng) dà
That dog is as big as a small tiger.

这棵树有一个人(那么)高。 **zhèi kē shù yǒu yī ge rén (nàme) gāo**
This tree is as tall as a man.

16.6 有 **yǒu** AS AN ADJECTIVAL FORMATIVE

有 **yǒu** is also a most versatile element in the formation of an almost unlimited
number of adjectives or adjectival phrases in the lexicon. It does this by incorporating nominal objects. For example:

---

[5] See Chapter 11 on the coverb 比 **bǐ** and comparisons.

有 **yǒu**	to have	+ 钱 **qián**	money	= rich; wealthy
有 **yǒu**	to have	+ 利 **lì**	profit; benefit	= profitable; beneficial
有 **yǒu**	to have	+ 能力 **nénglì**	ability	= capable; able
有 **yǒu**	to have	+ 办法 **bànfǎ**	method	= resourceful

Here are some more examples in sentences:

这个人有信用吗? **zhèi ge rén yǒu xìnyòng ma**
(lit. does this person have credit) Is this person trustworthy?

那个孩子很有礼貌。 **nèi ge háizi hěn yǒu lǐmào**
(lit. that child very much has courtesy) That child is very polite.

我今晚没(有)空。 **wǒ jīnwǎn méi(yǒu) kòng**
(lit. I tonight don't have spare time) I am busy tonight.

16.7 有 **yǒu** EXPRESSING IDEAS OF DEVELOPMENT AND CHANGE

有 **yǒu** is often used with verbal nouns like 提高 **tígāo** 'improvement', 发展 **fāzhǎn** 'development', 变化 **biànhuà** 'change', 进步 **jìnbù** 'progress', 增长 **zēngzhǎng** 'increase', to express ideas of development and change.

她的中文有了显著的提高。 **tāde zhōngwén yǒu le xiǎnzhù de tígāo**
Her Chinese has seen marked improvement.

人们的思想有了很大的变化。
rénmen de sīxiǎng yǒu le hěn dà de biànhuà
People's thinking has undergone a huge change.

16.8 有 **yǒu** INTRODUCING A CONDITIONAL CLAUSE

只有[6] **zhǐyǒu** 'only when; only if' is used in a full or abbreviated clause[7] to form a conditional clause. The main clause that follows incorporates the monosyllabic adverb 才 **cái** 'only then' before the predicate verb to echo the condition posed by 只有 **zhǐyǒu**. The main clause will have a full form if the conditional clause is abbreviated, and an abbreviated form if the conditional clause is in its full form. Both the conditional clause and the main clause need of course to be full if their respective subjects are different.

---

[6] See Chapter 22 on conjunctions and conjunctives.
[7] A full clause is defined as one with subject and predicate; and an abbreviated clause is one where the subject of the clause is omitted, but appears in the main clause later on.

只有懂得这一点，你才能进步。
zhǐyǒu dǒngde zhèi yīdiǎn | nǐ cái néng jìnbù
Only if you understand this point will you be able to make progress.

你只有懂得这一点，才能进步。
nǐ zhǐyǒu dǒngde zhèi yīdiǎn | cái néng jìnbù
Only if you understand this point will you be able to make progress.

只有你懂得这一点，我才能帮助你。
zhǐyǒu nǐ dǒngde zhèi yīdiǎn | wǒ cái néng bāngzhù nǐ
Only if you understand this point will I be able to help you.

只有有人献血，我们才能救活他。
zhǐyǒu yǒu rén xiàn xuè/xiě | wǒmen cái néng jiùhuó tā
Only if people donate blood will we be able to save him.

16.9 没(有) **méi(yǒu)** AS NEGATOR OF ACTION VERBS

16.9.1 NEGATOR OF PAST ACTION/EXPERIENCE

没(有) **méi(yǒu)** is the negator of past action (in a narrative sentence) and of past experience (in an expository sentence). Notice that in the case of the former the completed action aspect marker 了 *le* is not present, while in the latter the experiential verbal suffix 过 *guo* is retained:

他没(有)去北京。 **tā méi(yǒu) qù běijīng**   (narrative)
He did not go to Beijing.

他没(有)去过北京。 **tā méi(yǒu) qù guo běijīng**   (expository)
He has never been to Beijing.

16.9.2 AFFIRMATIVE–NEGATIVE QUESTIONS AND PAST ACTION/EXPERIENCE

Affirmative–negative questions relating to past action and experience are also constructed with 没有 **méiyǒu**, though for these 有 **yǒu** is usually retained. Note that in past-action questions the aspect marker 了 *le* has to be present because the completion of the action has to be expressed as the affirmative alternative.

他去了北京没有? **tā qù le běijīng méiyǒu**   Did he go to Beijing?
他去过北京没有? **tā qù guo běijīng méiyǒu**   Has he been to Beijing?

16.9.3   ANOTHER FORM OF THE QUESTION

These alternative questions may also be expressed by putting 有没有 **yǒu méiyǒu** before the verb (in past action questions) or the verb + 过 **guo** (in enquiries about experience). This form of the question is used throughout China, but it is perhaps more characteristic of the speech of people in the south of the country.

他有没有去北京？	**tā yǒu méiyǒu qù běijīng**	Did he go to Beijing?
他有没有去过北京？	**tā yǒu méiyǒu qù guo běijīng**	Has he been to Beijing?

16.10   有 **yǒu** TO INDICATE 'PART OF'

In these constructions, a topic is first posed and is then followed by 有的 **yǒude** to indicate different elements or parts. 的 *de* may be positioned after 有 **yǒu** or it can be left till the end of the construction, and the predicate that comes after 有 **yǒu** may be adjectival or verbal:

我的领带，有的贵，有的便宜。 **wǒde lǐngdài | yǒude guì | yǒude piányi**
Some of my ties are expensive, some cheap.

我的领带，有贵的，也有便宜的。
wǒde lǐngdài | yǒu guì de | yě yǒu piányi de
As for my ties, there are expensive ones and cheap ones.

这儿的学生，有的会说法语，有的会说德语，有的会说西班牙语。
zhèr de xuésheng | yǒude huì shuō fǎyǔ | yǒude huì shuō déyǔ | yǒude huì shuō xībānyáyǔ
Some of the students here can speak French, some German and others Spanish.

这儿的学生，有会说法语的，有会说德语的，也有会说西班牙语的。
zhèr de xuésheng | yǒu huì shuō fǎyǔ de | yǒu huì shuō déyǔ de | yě yǒu huì shuō xībānyáyǔ de
As for the students here, there are some that can speak French, some German and others Spanish.

A more emphatic version links 的 *de* to the adjectival or verbal predicate and leaves the verb 有 **yǒu** until the end of the clause:

我的领带，贵的有，便宜的也有。
wǒde lǐngdài | guì de yǒu | piányi de yě yǒu
As for ties, I've got expensive ones and cheap ones too.

这儿的学生，会说法语的有，会说德语的有，会说西班牙语的也有。
zhèr de xuésheng | huì shuō fǎyǔ de yǒu | huì shuō déyǔ de yǒu | huì shuō xībānyáyǔ de yě yǒu
As for the students here, there are some that can speak French, some German and others Spanish too.

If a nominal predicate is intended, then 是 **shì** must be incorporated after 有的 **yǒude**:

展出的书，有的是原著，有的是译本。
zhǎnchū de shū | yǒude shì yuánzhù | yǒude shì yìběn
Of the books on display, some are original books and some are translations.

In this case, however, 的 **de** may be left out altogether, and 有 **yǒu** then becomes the main verb:

展出的书，有原著，也有译本。
zhǎnchū de shū | yǒu yuánzhù | yě yǒu yìběn
Of the books on display, there are original books and there are also translations.

16.11 有 **yǒu** AS THE FIRST VERB IN A SEQUENCE

有 **yǒu** is frequently used in a serial sequence following the pattern of subject + 有 **yǒu** + verb . . . For example:

谁有时间帮我一下忙吗？ **shuí yǒu shíjiān bāng wǒ yīxià máng ma**
Who has time to give me some help?

你有没有钱买一盒巧克力？ **nǐ yǒu méiyǒu qián mǎi yī hé qiǎokèlì**
Do you have the money to buy a box of chocolates?

我没有办法解决这个问题。 **wǒ méiyǒu bànfǎ jiějué zhèi ge wèntí**
I have no way to solve this problem.

17 VERBS THAT TAKE VERBAL OR CLAUSAL OBJECTS

This chapter deals with cognitive verbs and verbs of emotion. Though some of them take noun objects, they tend to be followed by verbal or clausal objects and are more expository than narrative in nature. They are in fact not unlike modal verbs, which, as we shall see in Chapter 18 take verbal objects but which can be categorised as evaluative rather than expository. These cognition or emotion verbs convey a range of meaning covering intention, disposition, knowledge, etc., and because of their expository nature they are more likely to be associated with the negator 不 **bù** rather than 没有 **méiyǒu**.

她不喜欢吃面。 **tā bù xǐhuan chī miàn**
She does not like (eating) noodles.

*她没喜欢吃面。 **tā méi xǐhuan chī miàn**

As we have already seen, 不 **bù** 'not' negates actions that are or were not intended to be carried out while 没(有) **méi(you)** 'not' refers to actions that were or have not been carried out.

昨天上午她故意不去上班。 **zuótiān shàngwǔ tā gùyì bù qù shàngbān**
Yesterday morning, she deliberately would not go to work.

昨天上午她没去上班。 **zuótiān shàngwǔ tā méi qù shàngbān**
Yesterday morning, she did not go to work.

For the same reason, these emotion or sense verbs cannot be used with the aspect-marker 了 **le**, even if they refer to the past:

他以前喜欢喝咖啡。 **tā yǐqián xǐhuan hē kāfēi**
He used to like drinking coffee (in the past).

One cannot say, for example:

*他以前喜欢了喝咖啡。 *tā yǐqián xǐhuan le hē kāfēi

Most verbs in this category, as we have said, may take either verbal or clausal objects. The distinction between a verbal and a clausal object lies in whether the action expressed in the object verb or clause is initiated by the subject of the sentence. If it is, the object will be a verbal expression; if it is not, the object takes the form of a clause:

你希望什么时候休假? (a verbal object)
nǐ xīwàng shénme shíhou xiūjià
(lit. you hope what time take holiday)
When do you hope to go on holiday?

你希望你太太什么时候休假? (a clausal object)
nǐ xīwàng nǐ tàitai shénme shíhou xiūjià
(lit. you hope wife what time take holiday)
When do you hope that your wife will take her holiday?

We will now list the verbs in semantic groups.

17.1 INTENTION AND ASPIRATION

17.1.1 POSITIVE INTENTIONS AND ASPIRATIONS

准备 **zhǔnbèi** 'to prepare, plan', 打算 **dǎsuan** 'to prepare', 决定 **juédìng** 'to decide', 试图 **shìtú** 'to try', 企图 **qìtú** 'to attempt', 设法 **shèfǎ** 'to design', 要求 **yāoqiú** 'to request', 希望 **xīwàng** 'to hope', 盼望 **pànwàng** 'to long', 渴望 **kěwàng** 'to yearn', 期望 **qíwàng** 'to expect', 指望 **zhǐwàng** 'to look forward', 立志 **lìzhì** 'to be determined', 热心 **rèxīn** 'to be eager', 忍不住 **rěnbuzhù** 'cannot help but'.

你打算几时走? **nǐ dǎsuan jǐshí zǒu**
(lit. you intend what time go) When do you intend to go?

我带了一筒饼干和几包薯片，准备在路上吃。
wǒ dàile yī tǒng bǐnggān hé jǐ bāo shǔpiàn | zhǔnbèi zài lù shàng chī
(lit. I bring *le* one mw:tube biscuits and a few mw: packets potato crisps, prepare cv:on road-top eat)
I have brought a tube of biscuits and few packets of potato crisps to eat on the way.

他们准备下午四点钟开个讨论会。
tāmen zhǔnbèi xiàwǔ sì diǎn zhōng kāi ge tǎolùn huì
(lit. they plan afternoon four mw: dot clock hold mw seminar/symposium)
They plan to hold a seminar/symposium at 4 o'clock in the afternoon.

他决定下个月动身去欧洲旅游。
tā juédìng xià ge yuè dòngshēn qù ōuzhōu lǚyóu
(lit. he decide next mw month set out go Europe travel)
He has decided to go travelling in Europe next month.

朋友们都希望他早日恢复健康。
péngyoumen dōu xīwàng tā zǎorì huīfù jiànkāng
(lit. friends all hope he early days recover health)
His friends all hope he will soon recover his health.

计划 **jìhuà** 'to plan', 考虑 **kǎolǜ** 'to consider', 琢磨 **zuómo** 'to ponder', 衡量 **héngliáng** 'weigh the pros and cons', etc., also belong to this group. They often incorporate interrogatives in the verbal or clausal object:

你琢磨琢磨这里面还有什么问题。
nǐ zuómo zuómo zhè lǐmiàn hái yǒu shénme wèntí
(lit. you ponder-ponder this-inside still have what problems)
You ponder whether there are still any problems here/in this.

请你考虑一下怎么教育这个孩子。
qǐng nǐ kǎolǜ yīxià zěnme jiàoyù zhèi ge háizi
(lit. please you consider one mw:occasion how educate this mw child)
Please give some consideration to how this child might be educated.

17.1.2 NEGATIVE INTENTIONS

懒得 **lǎndé** 'to save oneself the trouble', 免得 **miǎndé** 'to avoid', 以免 **yǐmiǎn** 'to avoid', 省得 **shěngdé** 'to evade', 舍不得 **shěbudé** 'cannot bear', 后悔 **hòuhuǐ** 'to regret', 讨厌 **tǎoyàn** 'to hate', 不屑 **bùxiè** 'to disdain', 反对 **fǎnduì** 'to oppose', 犯不着 **fànbuzháo** 'to be not worth one's while'.

我后悔没有学会开车。 **wǒ hòuhuǐ méiyǒu xué huì kāi chē**
(lit. I regret did not learn-able drive car)
I regret that I never learned to drive.

我到达之后马上给他发了一个电子邮件，免得他记挂。
wǒ dàodá zhīhòu mǎshàng gěi tā fā le yī ge diànzǐ yóujiàn | miǎndé tā jìguà
(lit. I arrive afterwards immediately cv: to him send *le* one mw email to avoid he be concerned)
When I arrived, I immediately sent him an email to avoid making him anxious.

她不该这么说，但是你犯不着跟她生气。
tā bùgāi zhème shuō | dànshì nǐ fànbuzháo gēn tā shēngqì
(lit. she not ought like this speak, but you not worth while cv:with her get angry)
She ought not to have said this, but it is not worth your getting angry with her.

17.1.3   UNCERTAIN ASPIRATIONS

幻想 **huànxiǎng** 'to dream', 妄想 **wàngxiǎng** 'to hope vainly', 恨不得 **hènbudé** 'to wish very much', 巴不得 **bābudé** 'to wish earnestly'.

> 孩子们都幻想当电脑专家。
> **háizimen dōu huànxiǎng dāng diànnǎo zhuānjiā**
> (lit. children all dream be computer expert)
> Children all dream of becoming computer experts.

> 那个北方人恨不得自己马上能说广东话。
> **nèi ge běifāng rén hènbudé zìjǐ mǎshàng néng shuō guǎngdōng huà**
> (lit. that mw northern man very much wish himself immediately be able speak Cantonese)
> That northerner very much wants to be able to speak Cantonese straight away.

17.1.4   GROUP INTENTIONS

研究 **yánjiū** 'to study, consider, give thought to', 讨论 **táolùn** 'to discuss', 商量 **shāngliang** 'to consult', 酝酿 **yùnniàng** 'to discuss informally', 策划 **cèhuà** 'to plan', 合计 **héjì** 'to put heads together'.[1]

Sentences with these verbs often incorporate an adverb like 怎样 **zényàng** 'how' or 如何 **rúhé** 'in what fashion' within the object verb expression or clause. They may also often be reduplicated to express urgency.

> 请大家研究研究如何救济这些难民。
> **qǐng dàjiā yánjiū yánjiū rúhé jiùjì zhèixiē nànmín**
> (lit. please everyone study-study how relieve these mw refugees)
> Please would everyone give thought to how to get relief to these refugees.

> 咱们商量一下这个会议怎么开。
> **zánmen shāngliang yīxià zhèi ge huìyì zénme kāi**
> (lit. we consult one mw:occasion this mw meeting how hold)
> Let's consult about how to hold this meeting.

17.1.5   VOICED INTENTIONS

建议 **jiànyì** 'to suggest', 主张 **zhǔzhāng** 'to propose', 宣怖 **xuānbù** 'to announce', 说明 **shuōmíng** 'to explain', 强调 **qiángdiào** 'to emphasise', 发誓 **fāshì** 'to vow', 保证 **bǎozhèng** 'to guarantee', 扬言 **yángyán** 'to declare', 叫嚣 **jiàoxiāo** 'to clamour'.

---

[1] 研究 **yánjiū** 'to study, consider, give thought to' and 策划 **cèhuà** 'to plan' in this group of verbs may, of course, also be used with individual subjects.

我建议坐长途汽车去。 **wǒ jiànyì zuò chángtú qìchē qù**
(lit. I suggest cv:travel by long distance bus go)
I suggest going by coach/long-distance bus.

谁都主张把问题先搁一搁。 **shuí dōu zhǔzhāng bǎ wèntí xiān gē yī gē**
(lit. everyone all propose cv:grasping question first shelve-one-shelve)
Everyone proposes that the question be shelved for a while now.

他宣布辞职。 **tā xuānbù cízhí**
(lit. he announce resign) He announced his resignation.

17.1.6 INTENTIONS PUT INTO PRACTICE

开始 **kāishǐ** 'to begin', 继续 **jìxù** 'to continue', 着手 **zhuóshǒu** 'to tackle', 抓紧 **zhuājǐn** 'to make haste', 负责 **fùzé** 'to be responsible'.

新生已经开始报到。 **xīnshēng yǐjīng kāishǐ bàodào**
(lit. new students already begin register)
The new students have already begun to register.

冷空气正继续向南移动。 **lěng kōngqì zhèng jìxù xiàng nán yídòng**
(lit. cold air just continue cv:towards south move)
Cold air is continuing to move south.

17.1.7 FRUSTRATION AND COMPULSION

停止 **tíngzhǐ** 'to stop', 不堪 **bùkān** 'cannot bear', 不宜 **bùyí** 'be unsuitable', 不便 **bùbiàn** 'be inconvenient', 不致 **bùzhì** 'to fail, not to result in', 不禁 **bùjīn** 'cannot help', 不甘 **bùgān** 'be unwilling, not resigned to', 不屑 **bùxiè** 'to disdain', 不由得 **bùyóudé** 'cannot help, cannot but', 禁不住 **jīnbuzhù** 'cannot bear'.

那家商店已经停止营业。 **nèi jiā shāngdiàn yǐjīng tíngzhǐ yíngyè**
(lit. that mw shop already stop business)
That shop has already gone out of business.

一阵海风吹来，我禁不住打了一个寒颤。
yī zhèn hǎifēng chuīlai | wǒ jīnbuzhù dǎ le yīge hánchàn
(lit. one mw:blast sea wind blow-come, I cannot help give *le* one mw shiver)
There was a blast/gust of sea breeze, and I could not help giving a shiver.

17.2 ATTITUDES

爱 **ài** 'to love', 喜欢 **xǐhuan** 'to like', 乐意 **lèyì** 'to be willing', 害怕 **hàipà** 'to fear', 敢于 **gǎnyú** 'to be brave enough', 勇于 **yǒngyú** 'to be courageous enough',

甘于 **gānyú** 'to consign oneself', 急于 **jíyú** 'to be anxious', 善于 **shànyú** 'to be good at', 习惯 **xíguàn** 'to be accustomed', 假装 **jiǎzhuāng** 'to pretend', 适合 **shìhé** 'to be suitable for'.

These verbs are often modified by a degree adverb (e.g. 很 **hěn** 'very much'), and a number have the suffix 于 **yú**. They normally take verbal rather than clausal objects because the actions in the verbal objects are generally initiated by the subject of the sentence.

他很乐意帮助大家。 **tā hěn lèyì bāngzhù dàjiā**
(lit. he very willing help everyone) He is very willing to help everyone.

那个人真喜欢开玩笑。 **nèi ge rén zhēn xǐhuan kāi wánxiào**
(lit. that mw man really like make jokes)
That man really likes making jokes.

我爱听中国传统音乐。 **wǒ ài tīng zhōngguó chuántǒng yīnyuè**
(lit. I love listen to China traditional music)
I love listening to traditional Chinese music.

铁爱生锈。 **tiě ài shēng xiù** [a metaphorical extension]
(lit. iron love rust) Iron is apt to get rusty.

要敢于提出自己的见解。 **yào gǎnyú tíchū zìjǐ de jiànjiě**
(lit. must be brave enough to raise self *de* opinions)
You must be brave enough to put forward your own opinions.

别急于求成。 **bié jíyú qiú chéng**
(lit. don't be anxious achieve success) Don't be anxious to achieve success.

17.3 KNOWING AND THINKING

记得 **jìdé** 'to remember', 忘记 **wàngjì** 'to forget', 知道 **zhīdao** 'to know', 相信 **xiāngxìn** 'to believe', 觉得 **juéde** 'to feel', 感到 **gǎndào** 'to feel', 认为 **rènwéi** 'to think', 以为 **yǐwéi** 'to suppose', 估计 **gūjì** 'to surmise', 肯定 **kěndìng** 'to be sure', 担心 **dānxīn** 'to be worried', 怕 **pà** 'to be afraid', 怀疑 **huáiyí** 'suspect', 同意 **tóngyì** 'to agree', 证明 **zhèngmíng** 'to prove', 断定 **duàndìng** 'to conclude'.

你离开的时候，请记得把窗户关上。
nǐ líkāi de shíhou | qǐng jìdé bǎ chuānghu guān shàng
(lit. you leave *de* time, please remember cv:grasping window close-to)
Please remember to shut the window(s) when you leave.

对不起，我忘记把你要的书带来了。
duìbuqǐ | wǒ wàngjì bǎ nǐ yào de shū dàilai le

(lit. sorry, I forgot cv:grasping you want *de* book bring-come *le*)
Sorry, I forgot to bring the book(s) you want.

很多人都相信英国球队一定能打赢。
hěn duō rén dōu xiāngxìn yīngguó qiúduì yīdìng néng dǎ yíng
(lit. very many people all believe England football team definitely can win)
Many people believe that the English (football) team will certainly
(be able to) win.

我觉得他说的话是很对的。 **wǒ juéde tā shuō de huà shì hěn duì de**
(lit. I feel he said *de* words are very correct *de*)
I feel that what he said was quite right.

这件事我认为应该先跟他商量一下。
zhèi jiàn shì wǒ rènwéi yīnggāi xiān gēn tā shāngliang yīxià
(lit. this mw matter I think must first cv:with him consult one mw:occasion)
I think that this matter ought to be discussed with him first.

17.4 APPEARANCE AND VALUE

好象 **hǎoxiàng** 'to seem', 显得 **xiǎnde** 'to appear', 不如 **bùrú** 'to be better', 值得 **zhíde** 'to be worth', 不足 **bùzú** 'to be not enough', 不见得 **bù jiàn de** 'to be not necessarily so', 看起来 **kàn qǐlai** 'to look as if', 在于 **zàiyú** 'to rest on', 有待 **yǒudài** 'to wait for'.

These verbs tend to make comments or judgement about happenings, and the person making the judgement is often unstated.

她好象有什么心事。 **tā hǎoxiàng yǒu shénme xīnshì**
(lit. she seem have what worries)
She seems to have something on her mind.

这本书值得一读。 **zhèi běn shū zhíde yī dú**
(lit. this mw book worth one read) This book is worth a read.

这样的问题不值得争论。 **zhèyàng de wèntí bù zhíde zhēnglùn**
(lit. this kind *de* questions not worth debate)
A question like this is not worth arguing about.

那个问题有待解决。 **nèi ge wèntí yǒudài jiějué**
(lit. that mw problem need resolve) That problem waits to be resolved.

口说不足为凭。 **kóu shuō bù zú wéi píng**
(lit. mouth say not sufficient as proof)
Verbal statements are not enough for proof.

17.5   DUMMY VERBS

There are circumstances when a plain verb is felt to be rhythmically or stylistically inadequate and a dummy or make-weight verb is introduced before the original verb, making it the verbal object of the dummy verb. Such linguistic manoeuvres are similar to dichotomies in English, like 'consider' and 'give consideration to', 'solve' and 'provide a solution to', and so on. Unlike some of the categories of verbs above, these dummy verbs may be negated by either 不 **bù** or 没(有) **méi(yǒu)**.

There are three common dummy verbs in the language:

(**a**) 加以 **jiāyǐ** 'to provide (an envisaged result)', which is often found with verbal objects like:

> 解决 **jiějué** 'to resolve', 分析 **fēnxi** 'to analyse' and 考虑 **kǎolǜ** 'to consider'.

> 我们对这种情况应该加以分析。
> **wǒmen duì zhèzhǒng qíngkuàng yīnggāi jiāyǐ fēnxi**
> (lit. we cv:towards this mw:kind situation ought to dv: provide analyse)
> We ought to make an analysis of circumstances like these.

> 这样的问题必须及时加以解决。
> **zhèyàng de wèntí bìxū jíshí jiāyǐ jiějué**
> (lit. this kind *de* questions ought to in time dv: provide resolve)
> A question like this ought to be resolved promptly.

(**b**) 进行 **jìnxíng**[2] 'to start or carry out (an indicated process)' which is followed by verbal objects like:

> 研究 **yánjiū** 'to study', 探讨 **tàntǎo** 'to explore', etc.

> 我们能否碰一碰头对这件事进行认真的研究?
> **wǒmen néng fǒu pèng yī pèng tóu duì zhèi jiàn shì jìnxíng rènzhēn de yánjiū**
> (lit. we can or not bump-one-bump head cv:towards this mw matter dv: carry out serious study)
> Can we put our heads together and carry out a serious study of this?

---

[2] 进行 **jìnxíng** and 给予 **gěiyǔ** (see (c) below) are the only two verbs in this category that may take the aspect marker 了 *le*.

生物学家对遗传基因进行了广泛的探讨。

shēngwùjiā duì yíchuán jīyīn jìnxíng le guǎngfàn de tàntǎo

(lit. biologist cv:towards hereditary genes dv: carry out *le* extensive exploration)

Biologists carried out/pursued a wide-ranging exploration of hereditary genes.

(c) 给予 **gěiyǔ**[3] 'to grant (action as necessary)', which links with:

照顾 **zhàogù** 'care', 同情 **tóngqíng** 'sympathy' and 关注 **guānzhù** 'attention'.

对死难者的家属，我们必须给予照顾。

duì sǐnànzhě de jiāshǔ | wǒmen bìxū gěiyǔ zhàogù

(lit. cv:towards die-killed-in-an-accident-person *de* relatives, we must dv: grant care)

We must provide care for the families of those who have died.

世界人权组织对人权问题给予了极大的关注。

shìjiè rénquán zǔzhī duì rénquán wèntí gěiyǔ *le* jídà de guānzhù

(lit. world human rights organisation cv:towards human rights questions dv: grant *le* extreme great concern)

World human rights organisations paid the greatest attention to human rights issues.

---

[3] Alternative verbs synonymous in meaning and function to 给予 **gěiyǔ** are 给以 **gěiyǐ**, 予以 **yǔyǐ** and 致以 **zhìyǐ**, the last of which is used more often with 敬礼 **jìnglǐ** 'salute'.

18 MODAL VERBS

Modal verbs are a closed set of verbs that are used immediately before the main verb in a sentence to reflect the mood or attitude of either the speaker or the subject of the sentence from the perspective of the speaker. This speaker-oriented stance makes all utterances that incorporate modal verbs evaluative in nature,[1] which means that these verbs, like those in expository sentences, do not occur with aspect markers.

In the first section below, we review all the modal verbs in the language in their semantic categories.

18.1 SEMANTIC CATEGORIES OF MODAL VERBS

18.1.1 PERMISSION

可以 **kěyǐ** 'may; be allowed to' or 能 **néng** 'can; be able to':

你可以走了。 **nǐ kěyǐ zǒu le**
(lit. you may leave *le*) You may leave now.

他也可以回家了。 **tā yě kěyǐ huíjiā le**
(lit. he also may return-home *le*) He may go home as well.

能 **néng** is used interchangeably with 可以 **kěyǐ**, particularly in questions:

我能走了吗? **wǒ néng zǒu le ma**
(lit. I can leave *le ma*) May I leave now?

他可以回家了吗? **tā kěyǐ huíjiā le ma**
(lit. he may return-home *le ma*) Can he go home?

来宾可(以)不可以[2]在这儿停车? **láibīn kě(yǐ) bù kěyǐ zài zhèr tíng chē**
(lit. guest may-not-may cv:at here stop-car)
May guests park here?

---

[1] See Chapter 20 on different sentence types.
[2] The affirmative–negative question format of a disyllabic modal verb like 可以 **kěyǐ** can be either 可以不可以 **kěyǐ bù kěyǐ** or increasingly 可不可以 **kě bù kěyǐ**, with the second syllable of the modal omitted before the repetition.

In negative statements, 不能 **bù néng**, probably for rhythmic reasons, is colloquially more often used than 不可以 **bù kěyǐ**:

你不能走。 **nǐ bù néng zǒu**
(lit. you not can leave) You can't go now.

In set expressions with a classical tone, 可 **kě** or 以 **yǐ** may be used as individual
modal verbs:

无可奉告 **wú kě fènggào** or 无以奉告 **wú yǐ fènggào**
(lit. nothing can respectfully tell)
No comment. (i.e. there is nothing that I may tell you)

千万不可掉以轻心。 **qiānwàn bù kě diào yǐ qīng xīn**
(lit. by all means not may let-drop light-heart)
Don't under any circumstances lower your guard!

18.1.2 POSSIBILITY

能 **néng** or 能够 **nénggòu** 'can' and 可以 **kěyǐ** 'be possible' also express possibility
in the sense of someone being able to do something on a particular occasion:

你能帮我把这个箱子抬起来吗?
nǐ néng bāng wǒ bǎ zhèi ge xiāngzi tái qǐlai ma
(lit. you can help me cv:grasping this mw box/case (two-people-)lift-up *ma*)
Can you help me lift this case?

你能(够)不能够替我翻译一下这句话?
nǐ néng(gòu) bù nénggòu tì wǒ fānyì yīxià zhèi jù huà
(lit. you can-not-can cv:for me translate one mw:occasion this mw:sentence
words)
Can you translate this sentence for me?

Generally, 能 **néng** or 能够 **nénggòu** 'can' and 可以 **kěyǐ** 'be possible' are used
in the sense of permission in questions with first person or third person subjects,
and in the sense of possibility in questions with second person or inanimate
subjects. As far as statements are concerned, context usually disambiguates any
confusion that may arise between possibility and permission:

你能把胡椒粉递给我吗? **nǐ néng bǎ hújiāofěn dì gěi wǒ ma**
(lit. you can cv:grasping pepper-powder pass-give me *ma*)
Can you pass me the pepper, please?

你明天可以在会上发言吗? **nǐ míngtiān kěyǐ zài huì shàng fāyán ma**
(lit. you tomorrow be-possible cv:at meeting-on give-speech *ma*)
Is it possible for you to give a speech at tomorrow's meeting?

这种病能治好吗? **zhèi zhǒng bìng néng zhì hǎo ma**
(lit. this kind illness can cure-recover *ma*)
Can this kind of illness be cured?

他的感冒已经好了，可以参加比赛了。
tāde gǎnmào yǐjīng hǎo le | kěyǐ cānjiā bǐsài le
(lit. his flu already well *le*, can take-part-in race *le*)
He has already recovered from his flu and can take part in the race.

18.1.3 PROBABILITY

会 **huì** 'is likely to, may', which usually invites the presence of the particle 的 *de* at the end of the sentence:

她会来的。 **tā huì lái de**
(lit. she probable come *de*) She will probably come.

他不会骗我的。 **tā bùhuì piàn wǒ de**
(lit. he not probable deceive me *de*) He won't lie to me.

Where another particle like 吗 *ma* or 了 *le* is used, it replaces 的 *de*:

明天会下雨吗? **míngtiān huì xià yǔ ma**
(lit. tomorrow probable fall-rain *ma*) Is it likely to rain tomorrow?

她会来吗? **tā huì lái ma**
(lit. she probable come *ma*) Will she come?

她不会来了。 **tā bùhuì lái le**
(lit. she not probable come *le*) Probably she won't turn up now.

Probability or likelihood, that is not simply chance, but imminent or planned, is expressed by 要 **yào** 'about to', often with a monosyllabic adverb such as 就 **jiù** 'soon' and 快 **kuài** 'quickly' preceding it and the particle 了 *le* at the end of the sentence to confirm the sense of change of circumstances:

(天)要下雨了。 **(tiān) yào xià yǔ le**
(lit. sky about-to fall-rain *le*) It is about to rain.

火车就要开了。 **huǒchē jiùyào kāi le**
(lit. train soon about-to start *le*) The train is just about to leave.

工程快要结束了吗？ **gōngchéng kuàiyào jiéshù le ma**
(lit. engineering project quickly about-to finish *le ma*)
Will the project soon be finished?

If the probability is based on scientific findings or is within human control, 可能
kěnéng 'be possible' is used:

北极的冰山可能融化吗？ **běijí de bīngshān kěnéng rónghuà ma**
(lit. North Pole *de* iceberg possible melt *ma*)
Are the icebergs at the North Pole going to melt?

全球可能出现经济萧条。 **quánqiú kěnéng chūxiàn jīngjì xiāotiáo**
(lit. whole globe possible appear economic depression)
The whole world is likely to go into an economic depression.

你可能出席这次会议吗？ **nǐ kěnéng chūxí zhèi cì huìyì ma**
(lit. you possible be-present-at this mw:time meeting *ma*)
Are you going to be able to attend this meeting?

18.1.4 ABILITY OR SKILL

能 **néng** 'can' and 能够 **nénggòu** 'be able to' convey general and physical
capability, and are often used with a quantitative measurement:

我一次能喝三杯啤酒。 **wǒ yī cì néng hē sān bēi píjiǔ**
(lit. I at-one-time can drink three glasses beer)
I can drink three glasses of beer at one go.

你能够一只手把这个杠铃举起来吗？
nǐ nénggòu yī zhī shǒu bǎ zhèi ge gànglíng jǔ qǐlai ma
(lit. you can one mw hand cv:grasping this mw barbell lift-up *ma*)
Can you lift this barbell with one hand?

会 **huì**, on the other hand, indicates acquired skills:

她会打太极拳。 **tā huì dǎ tàijíquán**
(lit. she can hit *taiji* boxing) She can do shadow-boxing.

你会游泳吗？ **nǐ huì yóuyǒng ma**
(lit. you can swim *ma*) Can you swim?

我不会说法语。 **wǒ bùhuì shuō fǎyǔ**
(lit. I not can speak French) I can't speak French.

18.1.5 OBLIGATION

Moral obligation is usually expressed by 应该 **yīnggāi** 'ought to' or its alternatives 应当 **yīngdāng** (more emphatic), 应 **yīng** (classical), 该 **gāi** (colloquial) and 当 **dāng** (in parallelisms):

你应该支持她。 **nǐ yīnggāi zhīchí tā**
(lit. you ought-to support her) You ought to support her.

你应当好好地对待他。 **nǐ yīngdāng hǎohāo de duìdài tā**
(lit. you ought-to well-well *de* treat him) You ought to treat him well.

你应记住这点。 **nǐ yīng jìzhù zhèi diǎn**
(lit. you should remember-firmly this point)
You must always remember this point.

我该走了。 **wǒ gāi zǒu le**
(lit. I should leave *le*) I must be off now.

当说就得说。 **dāng shuō jiù děi shuō**
(lit. should say then should say) What should be said should be said.

这件事我应(该)不应该告诉他?
zhèi jiàn shì wǒ yīng(gāi) bù yīnggāi gàosu tā
(lit. this mw matter I should-not-should tell him)
Should I tell him about this?

这件事你不该怪他。 **zhèi jiàn shì nǐ bù gāi guài tā**
(lit. this mw matter you not should blame him)
You should not (have) blame(d) him for this.

Compulsory obligation, on the other hand, is expressed by 必须 **bìxū** 'must' or 须要 **xūyào** 'have to':

你必须服从命令。 **nǐ bìxū fúcóng mìnglìng**
(lit. you must obey command) You must obey orders.

我们必须马上离开。 **wǒmen bìxū mǎshàng líkāi**
(lit. we must immediately leave)
We must [i.e. we are supposed to] leave immediately.

他必须准时赶到。 **tā bìxū zhǔnshí gǎn dào**
(lit. he must punctually hurry-arrive) He must get there in time.

这个问题须要仔细考虑。 **zhèi ge wèntí xūyào zǐxì kǎolǜ**
(lit. this mw problem has to carefully consider)
This problem has to be carefully considered.

To negate compulsory obligation 不 **bù** is not used with 必须 **bìxū**, but in the following formulations:

不得	**bùdé**	not supposed to
不准	**bùzhǔn**	forbidden to
不要	**bùyào**	don't
不可以	**bù kěyǐ**	not allowed to; may not
不可	**bù kě**	not permitted
不能够	**bù nénggòu**	cannot

In emphatic warnings or exhortations, 不可 **bù kě** 'not permitted' occurs as a sentence terminal in conjunction with 非 **fēi** 'not' or 非得 **fēiděi** 'have got to',[3] which is placed before the main verb. The two negative expressions convey a strongly positive meaning:

你非来不可。 **nǐ fēi lái bù kě**
(lit. you not come not possible) You have to come.

这篇文章非看不可。 **zhèi piān wénzhāng fēi kàn bù kě**
(lit. this mw essay not look not possible) You have to read this essay.

这件事你非得去处理不可。[4] **zhèi jiàn shì nǐ fēiděi qù chùlǐ bù kě**
(lit. this mw matter you not must go deal-with not possible)
You have to go and sort this matter out.

18.1.6 WISHING

A mild wish is usually expressed by 想 **xiǎng** 'would like' or 'to be thinking of' while a strong desire is conveyed by 要 **yào** 'want'. Compare the following:

今晚我想去看电影。 **jīnwǎn wǒ xiǎng qù kàn diànyǐng**
(lit. tonight I would-like go see film)
I would like to go and see a film tonight.

今晚我要去看电影。 **jīnwǎn wǒ yào qù kàn diànyǐng**
(lit. tonight I want go see film) I want to go and see a film tonight.

---

[3] See §18.1.8 below.
[4] In fact, 非得 **fēiděi** may sometimes go before the subject to highlight it, e.g.: 这件事非得你去处理不可。 **zhèi jiàn shì fēiděi nǐ qù chùlǐ bù kě** (lit. this mw matter not must you go deal-with not possible) 'It's you who'll have to go and sort this matter out'.

In questions, 想 **xiǎng** and 要 **yào** are virtually interchangeable:

你想喝点儿什么？ **nǐ xiǎng hē diǎnr shénme**
(lit. you would-like drink mw:some what) What would you like to drink?

你要喝点儿什么？ **nǐ yào hē diǎnr shénme**
(lit. you want drink mw:some what) What do you want to drink?

For more explicit intentions, verbs like 打算 **dǎsuàn** 'to plan to', 准备 **zhǔnbèi** 'to prepare, plan to', and 决定 **juédìng** 'to decide to' are used:[5]

今晚你打算做什么？ **jīnwǎn nǐ dǎsuàn zuò shénme**
(lit. this evening you plan do what) What are you planning to do tonight?

今晚你准备去看电影吗？ **jīnwǎn nǐ zhǔnbèi qù kàn diànyǐng ma**
(lit. this evening you prepare go see film *ma*)
Are you planning to go and see a film tonight?

今晚我决定待在家里。 **jīnwǎn wǒ juédìng dāi zài jiā li**
(lit. this evening I decide stay cv:at home-inside)
I have decided to stay at home tonight.

The negatives of 想 **xiǎng** and 要 **yào** carry the flavour of disinclination for the former and refusal for the latter:

今晚我不想吃鱼。 **jīnwǎn wǒ bù xiǎng chī yú**
(lit. tonight I not like eat fish)
I don't want (to eat) fish tonight. [I don't fancy the prospect]

今晚我不要吃鱼。 **jīnwǎn wǒ bù yào chī yú**
(lit. tonight I not want eat fish)
I don't want (to eat) fish tonight. [I am against the idea]

One feature of 想 **xiǎng** 'would like' is that like 愿意 **yuànyì** 'be willing to' (see below) it may be modified by degree adverbs like 很 **hěn** 'very much', 正 **zhèng** 'at this very moment, just', or 不大 **bùdà** 'not really', 只 **zhǐ** 'only':

我很想去见见他。 **wǒ hěn xiǎng qù jiànjian tā**
(lit. I very-much like go see-see him) I'd very much like to go and see him.

我正想去找您。 **wǒ zhèng xiǎng qù zhǎo nín**
(lit. I just want go look-for you) I was just thinking of going to find you.

---

[5] See §17.1 (**a**).

今晚我不大想出去。 **jīnwǎn wǒ bù dà xiǎng chūqu**
(lit. tonight I not very-much want out-go)
I don't really want to go out tonight.

我只想好好地休息休息。 **wǒ zhǐ xiǎng hǎohāo de xiūxi xiūxi**
(lit. I only want well-well *de* rest-rest) I just want to have a good rest.

18.1.7 WILLINGNESS

愿意 **yuànyì** 'be willing' or 肯 **kěn** 'be willing (after some persuasion or with some reluctance)':

我愿意帮助你。 **wǒ yuànyì bāngzhù nǐ**
(lit. I willing help you) I am willing to help you.

他肯参加吗? **tā kěn cānjiā ma**
(lit. he willing take-part *ma*) Is he willing to take part?

Like 想 **xiǎng** 'would like' (see above), 愿意 **yuànyì** may also be modified by degree adverbs:

她很愿意帮你的忙。 **tā hěn yuànyì bāng nǐde máng**
(lit. she very willing help your busy) She is very willing to help you.

他不大愿意坐火车去。 **tā bù dà yuànyì zuò huǒchē qù**
(lit. he not very-much willing cv: travel-by train go)
He is not really willing to go by train.

18.1.8 NECESSITY

得 **děi** 'to have to, must' is used in colloquial speech to indicate necessity, and is often interchangeable with the modal verbs of moral or compulsory obligation:

我得走了。 **wǒ děi zǒu le**
(lit. I have to leave *le*) I'll have to go/I must be off.

有意见得说出来。 **yǒu yìjiàn děi shuō chūlai**
(lit. have opinion have to say out-come)
If you have an opinion, you must speak.

得 **děi** is never used in the negative, but it does appear with 不 **bù** in more formal statements, notices, etc., when it is pronounced **dé**:

闲人不得入内。**xiánrén bùdé rùnèi**
(lit. outsiders not have-to enter inside)
No admittance./Private [i.e. outsiders should not enter the premises]

The negative for necessity is expressed by 不必 **bùbì**, 不用 **bù yòng**, 无须 **wúxū** 'need not':

你不必去了。**nǐ bù bì qù le**
(lit. you not necessary go *le*) You don't have to go.

你不用等我了。**nǐ bùyòng děng wǒ le**
(lit. you not need wait-for me *le*) You needn't wait for me.

你无须出席。**nǐ wúxū chūxí**
(lit. you not must be-present)
There's no need for you to be present./You're not obliged to be there.

需要 **xūyào** 'need' is originally a full verb, but it may also take on a modal function before the verb 有 **yǒu** to indicate 'necessity':

人人都需要有社会公德。**rénrén duō xūyào yǒu shèhuì gōngdé**
(lit. everybody all need have society public-morality)
Everybody needs to have a public spirit.

18.1.9 BOLDNESS

敢 **gǎn** 'dare'.

你敢打人吗？**nǐ gǎn dǎ rén ma**
(lit. you dare hit people *ma*) How dare you hit people?

我不敢走黑路。**wǒ bù gǎn zǒu hēilù**
(lit. I not dare walk dark roads) I dare not walk in the dark.

18.2 SPEAKER PERSPECTIVE OF MODAL VERBS

The speaker-oriented nature of modal verbs can be seen clearly in the case of 要 **yào** 'to want'. When used with a first person subject (who is naturally the speaker), it indicates a wish on the part of the speaker:

我要喝点儿水。**wǒ yào hē diǎnr shuǐ**
(lit. I want drink mw:some water) I'll have/I'd like some water.

But it takes on a different meaning if the subject is in the second person:

你要喝点儿水。**nǐ yào hē diǎnr shuǐ**
(lit. you must drink mw:some water) You should drink some water.

Here the speaker is not voicing the listener's wish, but his or her own, and is advising or urging the listener to take the action.

However, if the two sentences are expressed as questions, the meanings of 'want' and 'should' may be reversed:

你要喝点儿水吗？ **nǐ yào hē diǎnr shuǐ ma**
(lit. you want drink mw:some water *ma*) Do you want to drink some water?

我要喝点儿水吗？ **wǒ yào hē diǎnr shuǐ ma**
(lit. I must drink mw:some water *ma*) Should I drink some water?

The interrogative has naturally switched the roles of the speaker and the listener, and the emphasis is on the listener's attitude rather than the speaker's.

18.3 NEGATION OF MODAL VERBS

Because the function of a modal verb is to indicate mood or attitude, its negator is always 不 **bù** 'not' (or the more classical 无 **wú** 'not' in some cases) and never 没 **méi** or 没有 **méiyǒu** even if it is referring to a mood or attitude in the past.

不 **bù** 'not' is most commonly placed before the modal verb, but it can also be used after the modal verb (and before the main verb), where it conveys a different meaning:

你不可以走。 **nǐ bù kěyǐ zǒu**
(lit. you not may leave)
You may not go. [i.e. you are not allowed to go]

你可以不走。 **nǐ kěyǐ bù zǒu**
(lit. you may not leave)
You may stay. [i.e. you are allowed not to leave]

他不肯去。 **tā bù kěn qù**
(lit. he not willing go) He is not willing to go.

他肯不去。 **tā kěn bù qù**
(lit. he willing not go)
He is willing not to go. [i.e. he is willing to stay behind]

她不敢来。 **tā bù gǎn lái**
(lit. she not dare come) She dare not come. [a statement]

她敢不来？ **tā gǎn bù lái**
(lit. she dare not come) Dare she not turn up! [a threat]

However, sentences with the negative after the modal verb sometimes need a degree of modification in order to be acceptable:

他不要喝牛奶。**tā bùyào hē niúnǎi**
(lit. he not want drink milk) He doesn't want to drink (any) milk.

*他要不喝牛奶。**tā yào bù hē niúnǎi**
*(lit. he want not drink milk) *He wants not to drink milk.

but:

他要三天不喝牛奶。 **tā yào sān tiān bù hē niúnǎi**
(lit. he want three days not drink milk)
He wants to stop drinking milk for three days.

and:

她不应该抽烟。 **tā bù yīnggāi chōuyān**
(lit. she not should suck cigarette) She shouldn't smoke.

*她应该不抽烟。 **tā yīnggāi bù chōuyān**
*(lit. she should not suck cigarette)

but:

她应该从此不抽烟。 **tā yīnggāi cóngcǐ bù chōuyān**
(lit. she should from now not suck cigarette)
She should stop smoking from now on.

不 **bù** can, of course, be used both before the modal verb and before the main verb to indicate a double negative:

你不可以不走。**nǐ bù kěyǐ bù zǒu**
(lit. you not may not leave)
You must go. [i.e. you are not allowed to stay]

他不肯不去。**tā bù kěn bù qù**
(lit. he not willing not go) He insists on going.

18.4 GRAMMATICAL ORIENTATION OF MODAL VERBS

The incorporation of a modal verb in a sentence automatically makes the sentence evaluative,[6] since it expresses a subjective observation on the part of a

---

[6] See Chapter 20 in particular.

named or unnamed speaker. The sentence takes the form of a topic + comment structure with the modal verb introducing the comment:

你 || 应该帮助他。 **nǐ || yīnggāi bāngzhù tā**
(lit. you ought to help him) You ought to help him.

Here 你 **nǐ** 'you' is not the subject of a narrative sentence initiating the action of 'helping', and there is no certainty that 你 **nǐ** will ever carry out the action. Instead 你 **nǐ** 'you' is the topic and 应该帮助他 **yīnggāi bāngzhù tā** 'must help him' is the comment. The speaker's intention is to comment on what 你 **nǐ** 'you' should do.

Because of this topic–comment relationship, a sentence like the following is possible:

药 || 应该准时吃。 **yào || yīnggāi zhǔnshí chī**
(lit. medicine must on-time eat) Medicine should be taken at the right time.

In this case 药 **yào** 'medicine' obviously does not initiate the action of 'taking', but it is a topic followed by a comment relating to it.

In addition to being a noun or pronoun, the topic can naturally take any syntactic form:

懒惰 || 会妨碍你的进步。 (topic = adjective)
lǎnduò || huì fáng'ài nǐde jìnbù
(lit. lazy mv: may hamper your progress)
Being lazy may hamper your progress./If you're lazy, it may hamper your progress.

经常锻炼身体 || 能增进健康。 (topic = verb phrase)
jīngcháng duànliàn shēntǐ || néng zēngjìn jiànkāng
(lit. regularly exercising body mv:can improve health)
Regular exercises can improve health.

大家都坐经济舱 || 可以节省不少开支。(topic = clause)
dàjiā dōu zuò jīngjì cāng || kěyǐ jiéshěng bùshǎo kāizhī
(lit. everyone all sit-in economy cabin mw:can save not a little expenses)
Everyone can save a lot of expense travelling economy.

19 TELESCOPIC CONSTRUCTIONS

By telescopic constructions, we mean constructions where one subject–predicate or topic–comment sentence is seen to be embedded in or interwoven with another.

In the next chapter, we discuss the distinctive features of different sentence types such as narrative, descriptive, expository and evaluative. Telescopic constructions, though they may take the form of any of these sentence types, are themselves generally expository or evaluative. In other words, the first part of a telescopic construction, whatever its formulation, is by definition, a topic presented for explanation or comment.

In the following sections, we will describe the different kinds of telescopic construction commonly encountered in the language.

19.1 TOPIC AND SUB-TOPIC

The typical format of a topic and sub-topic construction is that the topic once stated is immediately followed by a sub-topic, which semantically has a part–whole relationship with the topic. The comment that follows is of course closely related to the sub-topic, which is its immediate focus of interest. However because of the part–whole meaning relationship between the topic and the sub-topic, the comment relates to the topic and the sub-topic together.

> 她脾气很坏。 **tā píqì hěn huài**
> (lit. she temper very bad) She has a bad temper.

> 这两个孩子身体都很好。 **zhèi liǎng ge háizi shéntǐ dōu hěn hǎo**
> (lit. these two mw children body both very good)
> These two children are in good health.

In these examples 脾气 **píqì** 'temperament' is clearly part of 她 **tā** 'her' and 身体 **shēntǐ** 'body; health' is part of 孩子 **háizi** 'the children'. There may be multiple and varied parts to a whole:

> 这件衣服，领子太大，袖子太短。
> **zhèi jiàn yīfu | lǐngzi tài dà | xiùzi tài duǎn**
> (lit. this mw clothes, collar too big, sleeves too short)
> The collar on this suit is too big and the sleeves too short.

他妻子仪表端庄， 谈吐文雅， 举止大方。
tā qīzi yíbiǎo duānzhuāng | tántǔ wényǎ | jǔzhǐ dàfang
(lit. his wife bearing dignified, conversation refined, manner poised)
His wife's bearing is dignified, her conversation refined and her manner poised.

这些水果， 一半给你， 一半给你弟弟。
zhèixiē shuǐguǒ | yī bàn gěi nǐ | yī bàn gěi nǐ dìdi
(lit. these mw fruit, one half give you, one half give your younger brother)
Half of these fruit are for you and half for your brother.

来这儿度假的游客， 大部分是英国人， 小部分是法国人。
lái zhèr dùjià de yóukè | dà bùfen shì yīngguó rén | xiǎo bùfen shì fǎguó rén
(lit. come here pass holiday *de* tourists, majority are English, minority are French)
The majority of the tourists who come here for holidays are British and the minority French.

我们花园里的水仙花， 有的是黄的， 有的是白的。
wǒmen huāyuán li de shuǐxiānhuā | yǒude shì huáng de | yǒude shì bái de
(lit. our garden-inside *de* narcissus, some are yellow *de*, some are white *de*)
Some of the narcissus in our garden are yellow and some white.

A common relationship between topic and sub-topic is that of initiator and activity. The comment that follows may refer to the initiator-topic or the sub-topic activity. Such flexibility broadens the choice of comment:

他学习很出色。 **tā xuéxí hěn chūsè**
(lit. he study very outstanding) He is an outstanding student.

他学习很认真。 **tā xuéxí hěn rènzhēn**
(lit. he study very conscientious) He is a conscientious student.

It is obvious that 出色 **chūsè** 'outstanding' refers to the sub-topic 学习 **xuéxí** 'studies' while 认真 **rènzhēn** 'conscientious' describes the topic 他 **tā** 'him'.

The sub-topic activity may again be multiple:

小黄不但学习认真， 而且工作积极。
xiǎo huáng bùdàn xuéxí rènzhēn | érqiě gōngzuò jījí
(lit. little Huang not only study conscientious but also work vigorous)
Little Huang not only studies conscientiously, but he also works hard.

这个球员，进攻勇猛，防守稳健。
zhèi ge qiúyuán | jìngōng yǒngměng | fángshǒu wěnjiàn
(lit. this mw player attack bold defend firm)
This player is bold in attack and firm in defence.

19.2   TOPIC AND SUBJECT

It is not uncommon in a *le*-expository sentence[1] for a topic and subject to appear
together. For example:

信 ‖ 我 | 早就寄走了。 **xìn ‖ wǒ | zǎo jiù jì zǒu le**
(lit. letter I early then send-go *le*) I've sent the letter some time ago.

我的论文 ‖ 导师 | 已经看过了。 **wǒde lùnwén ‖ dǎoshī | yǐjīng kàn guo le**
(lit. my thesis supervisor/tutor already see *guo le*)
My supervisor/tutor has already read through my thesis.

In the first example, 信 **xìn** 'the letter' is the topic whereas 我 **wǒ** 'I' is the
subject that initiates the action of 寄 **jì** 'sending' in the predicate; and in
the second, 论文 **lùnwén** 'the dissertation' is the topic while 导师 **dǎoshī** is the
subject initiating the action of 看 **kàn** 'reading' in the predicate. Semantically
speaking, 信 **xìn** 'the letter' and 论文 **lùnwén** 'the dissertation' are respectively
the notional object of the verbs 寄 **jì** 'to send' and 看 **kàn** 'to read'.

This being the case, these *le*-expository sentences are easily reconvertible to
their narrative originals, with end-of-sentence 了 *le* as an expository indicator
changing to aspect indicator 了 *le* to mark that the actions have been completed:

我早就寄走了那封[2]信。 **wǒ zǎo jiù jì zǒu le nèi fēng xìn**
(lit. I early then send-go *le* that mw letter) I had long since sent that letter.

导师已经看过[3]了我的论文。 **dǎoshī yǐjīng kàn guo le wǒde lùnwén**
(lit. supervisor/tutor already read *guo le* my thesis)
The supervisor/tutor had already read through my thesis.

In fact *le*-expository sentences are conversions from corresponding narrative
sentences, topicalising the original object, dismantling the straight-forward
'initiator + action + target' narrative format or its 把 **bǎ** or 被 **bèi** derivatives,

---

[1]   See Chapter 21, where *le*-expository sentences are discussed in greater detail.
[2]   那封 **nèi fēng** 'that + measure word for a letter' are added here to counteract the post-verbal
indefinite reference of a narrative sentence and also to provide rhythmic balance.
[3]   Note the difference between 过 **guò** 'to have read through' as a resultative complement in this
sentence and 过 **guo** 'to have had the experience of' as an expository indicator in a sentence like
导师看过我的论文 **dǎoshī kàn guo wǒde lùnwén** 'The tutor has read my thesis'.

and shifting the perspective from recounting a past action to explaining a present situation with the addition of an end-of-sentence 了 *le* or other relevant particles. Here are some more examples:

这件事 ‖ 大家 | 都知道了。 **zhèi jiàn shì ‖ dàjiā | dōu zhīdao le**
(lit. this mw matter everyone all know *le*) Everyone knows about this.

八点钟的火车 ‖ 我 | 赶不上了。
bā diǎn zhōng de huǒchē ‖ wǒ | gǎnbushàng le
(lit. eight o'clock *de* train I catch not up *le*)
I can't catch the eight o'clock train.

那条裙子 ‖ 妹妹 | 送给她的朋友了。
nèi tiáo qúnzi ‖ mèimei | sòng gěi tāde péngyou le
(lit. that mw skirt younger sister present-give her friend *le*)
Younger sister has given that skirt to her friend.

那场大火 ‖ 消防队员 | 很快就扑灭了。
nèi chǎng dàhuǒ ‖ xiāofáng duìyuán | hěn kuài jiù pū miè le
(lit. that mw big fire fire brigade very fast then extinguish *le*)
The fire brigade very quickly put out that blaze.

圣诞礼物 ‖ 我 | 早就买了。 **shèngdàn lǐwù ‖ wǒ | zǎo jiù mǎi le**
(lit. Christmas presents I early then buy *le*)
I bought my Christmas presents a long time ago.

There are also topics derived from nominal items taken as the main focus of interest in multi-valency sentences. This is to say that the comment on the topic may take the form of a subject and verb–object predicate. For example:

花儿 ‖ 我 | 浇了水了。 **huār ‖ wǒ | jiāo le shuǐ le**
(lit. flowers I sprinkle *le* water *le*) I have watered the flowers.

水 ‖ 我 | 浇了花儿了。 **shuǐ ‖ wǒ | jiāo le huār le**
(lit. water I sprinkle *le* flowers *le*)
I have watered the flowers with the water.

车库的门 ‖ 我 | 上了漆了。 **chēkù de mén ‖ wǒ | shàng le qī le**
(lit. garage *de* door I put on *le* paint *le*) I have painted the garage door.

漆 ‖ 我 | 用来油了车库的门了。 **qī ‖ wǒ | yòng lái yóu le chēkù de mén le**
(lit. paint I use-come paint *le* garage *de* door *le*)
I have used the paint to paint the garage door.

19.3 'SUBJECT + PREDICATE' AS TOPIC

A subject + predicate clause can also act as the topic of a topic + comment evaluative sentence[4] with the predicate verb being unmarked. This plain structure contrasts with the variety of grammatical patterns required by English translations:

老年人少吃盐对身体有好处。
lǎoniánrén shǎo chī yán duì shēntǐ yǒu hǎochu
(lit. old people little eat salt cv:for body have benefit)
If old people eat less salt, it is good for their health.
It is good for the health of old people to eat less salt.

你这么做太不象话了。 **nǐ zhème zuò** tài bù xiànghuà le
(lit. you like this do too shocking/unreasonable *le*)
It was really shocking/unreasonable for you to have done this.

这个小伙子当翻译真行。 **zhèi ge xiǎohuǒzi dāng fānyì** zhēn xíng
(lit. this young man be interpreter really good)
It is really good that this young man is the interpreter.

If the subject of this topical 'subject + predicate' structure is of a general or universal nature, it may be left out. What remains of the topic will now be an unmarked, unmodified verb predicate. For example:

下雨天划艇没有什么意思。 **xiàyǔtiān huà tǐng** méiyǒu shénme yìsi
(lit. fall rain day row boat have not any interest)
There is no interest at all in going rowing on a rainy day.

到国外去度假可以增进见闻。 **dào guówài qù dùjià** kěyǐ zēngjìn jiànwén
(lit. cv:to country-outside go pass holiday can promote see-hear)
Going on holidays abroad can add to one's knowledge.

19.4 '(SUBJECT) + PREDICATE' INSERTED BETWEEN 'TOPIC' AND 'COMMENT'

In this structure, a subject + predicate clause is placed between the topic and the comment usually to create an expository or evaluative sentence. In many cases, the subject is absent or understood, and the predicate is always complemented by the descriptive indicator 着 *zhe* or a directional indicator 来 **lái** or 起来 **qǐlai**. The clause carries an underlying conditional meaning.

---

[4] See next chapter.

这双鞋你穿着正合适。 **zhèi shuāng xié <u>nǐ chuān zhe</u> zhèng héshì**
(lit. this mw:pair shoes <u>you wear *zhe*</u> just suit)
These shoes fit you beautifully/well.

那双鞋太紧， <u>穿着</u>不舒服。 **nèi shuāng xié tài jǐn | <u>chuān zhe</u> bù shūfu**
(lit. that mw:pair shoes too tight, <u>wear *zhe*</u> not comfortable)
Those shoes are too tight and would be uncomfortable to wear.

这个人看着很面熟。 **zhèi ge rén <u>kàn zhe</u> hěn miànshú**
(lit. this mw person <u>look *zhe*</u> very face-familiar)
This man looks very familiar.

这个箱子提着有些沉。 **zhèi ge xiāngzi <u>tí zhe</u> yǒuxiē chén**
(lit. this mw case <u>carry/lift *zhe*</u> has some heavy)
This case is a bit heavy (to carry).

这种药吃下去就见效。 **zhèi zhǒng yào <u>chī xiàqu</u> jiù jiànxiào**
(lit. this mw:kind medicine <u>eat down-go</u> then become effective)
Taking this medicine will do the trick/be effective.

那个老人看上去还很健壮。 **nèi ge lǎoren <u>kàn shàngqu</u> hái hěn jiànzhuàng**
(lit. that mw old man <u>look as if</u> still very robust)
That old man looks as though he is still very robust.

这篇文章念起来不顺口。 **zhèi piàn wénzhāng <u>niàn qǐlai</u> bù shùnkǒu**
(lit. this mw essay <u>begin to read</u> not smooth for mouth)
This essay does not read smoothly.

这种游戏看起来很简单， 其实并不简单。
zhèi zhǒng yóuxì <u>kàn qǐlai</u> hěn jiǎndān | qíshí bìng bù jiǎndān
(lit. this mw:kind game <u>look as if</u> very simple, in fact certainly not simple)
This game looks simple, but in fact it isn't.

20 NARRATION, DESCRIPTION, EXPOSITION AND EVALUATION

Chinese syntax follows the universal differentiation of sentences along the line of function into four major types: declarative, imperative, interrogative and exclamatory. However, being less morphologically oriented but more functionally disposed than some other languages, Chinese syntax may further differentiate its declarative sentences into the following four subtypes: narrative, descriptive, expository[1] and evaluative. Inevitably, there is blurring at the boundaries between subtypes since the vagaries of language will always defy absolute demarcations. Nonetheless, this differentiation is of extreme importance because it highlights other essential grammatical distinctions which need to be made.

In this chapter, we will concentrate on the most distinctive features of each of these subtypes. However, before we go into greater detail on them, we will first of all give a very brief description of the grounds on which such a sub-categorisation is based.

A narrative sentence sets out to recount an incident or tell a story, and it therefore follows a 'subject + predicate' format, where the subject is the initiator or recipient of the action specified in the predicate. A narrative sentence is thus a stage in a sequence, encoding one action in a chain of actions, which comprise an overall event.

A descriptive sentence, though it follows a 'subject + predicate' format like a narrative, is nevertheless an objective depiction of an action that is ongoing at a particular time. The focus is on the continuous action.

An expository sentence aims to give an explanation. It may adopt either a 'subject + predicate' or 'topic + comment' format. In its 'subject + predicate' form, it makes a statement of what somebody does or can do out of habit, experience or nature, and so on, or intends to do in the future. In a 'topic + comment', the comment consists of either the verb 是 **shì** 'to be' or 有 **yǒu** 'to

---

[1] Expository sentences, as we shall see in the next chapter, have an associated category that we label *le*-expository.

have' or an unmodified verb or adjective. An expository sentence states either a fact or an intention.

An evaluative sentence, on the other hand, conveys an observation, an opinion, a subjective criticism or assessment. It always takes a 'topic + comment' format. If an action verb is used in the comment, it is preceded by a modal verb or followed by a *de*-complement; and if an adjective is present in the comment, it is modified by a degree adverb or followed by a degree complement. These modifications represent the element of evaluation or judgement in the statement.

In the following sections, the distinctive features of each of these four subtypes will be discussed in detail.

20.1 NARRATIVE SENTENCES

A narrative sentence reports an event or incident that has already taken place, and it generally recounts that somebody (or something) carried out (or caused) an action or that something happened to someone (or something) on some past occasion. If we define the 'subject + predicate' format as a typical syntactic representation of the concept of an initiator who initiates an action or a recipient who receives an action, then this format naturally comprises a narrative.

There are two prominent features of a narrative sentence in Chinese. First, since Chinese syntax lacks the category of definite and indefinite articles, nouns in the language depend either on context or their position in sentence for the specification of definite or indefinite reference. In a Chinese narrative sentence, all nouns in a pre-verbal position take on definite reference. Second, the verb in the predicate, being part of a narrative, and naturally indicating a completed action, is therefore generally marked by 了 *le*. Both these features are illustrated in the example below:

孩子从屋子里跑了出来。 **háizi cóng wūzi li pǎo le chūlai**
The child came out of the room.

The English translation makes clear that the noun 孩子 **háizi**, despite being unmarked and without any referential indication, is nevertheless of definite reference, and the action of coming out by the child, as indicated by the aspect marker 了 *le*, was obviously completed.

The corollary to this tendency of pre-verbal nouns to be definite-referenced is the fact that all nouns positioned post-verbally are liable to be of indefinite reference. Post-verbal nouns are in fact generally marked by a 'numeral + measure' phrase to confirm this indefiniteness:

屋子里跑出来(了)一个孩子。² **wūzi li pǎo chūlai (le) yī ge háizi**
Out of the room came **a** child.

The two sentences above therefore demonstrate the standard referential properties required for nouns by narrative syntax: pre-verbal definite, and post-verbal
indefinite, but usually marked as such.

However, the subject of narrative sentences can have indefinite reference, even
if marked by a 'numeral + measure' phrase, provided *either*:

(a) the dummy verb 有 **yǒu** 'to have' is placed before it, so that it is still, in
a sense, post-verbal:

有两个陌生人走了进来。 **yǒu liǎng ge mòshēngrén zǒu le jìnlai**
(lit. have two mw stranger walk *le* in-come)
Two strangers walked in.

有一辆轿车在门口停了下来。
yǒu yī liàng jiàochē zài ménkǒu tíng le xiàlai
(lit. have one mw sedan cv:at entrance stop *le* down-come)
A sedan stopped at the door.

or:

(b) it is moved to a post-verbal position, where indefinite-reference nouns
are normally found:³

那时候进来了两个陌生人。 **nèi shíhou jìn lái le liǎng ge mòshēngrén**
(lit. that time come in *le* two mw stranger)
At that moment two strangers walked in/in walked two strangers.

门口开来了一辆轿车。 **ménkǒu kāi lái le yī liàng jiàochē**
(lit. entrance drive-come *le* one mw sedan)
A sedan drove up to the door.

The same applies to a subject noun that is modified by a descriptive, i.e.
adjectival attributive, since this modification automatically makes the noun
indefinite:

---

² 了 *le* in this sentence is optional for reasons of prosody (see Chapter 26). The sentence may also be
reworded as 屋子里跑出一个孩子来。
³ This is only possible if the action verb used is intransitive.

有(一)个面孔圆圆的孩子从屋子里跑了出来。
yǒu (yī) ge miànkǒng yuányuán de háizi cóng wūzi li pǎo le chūlai

or:

屋子里跑出来了一个面孔圆圆的孩子。
wūzi li pǎo chūlai le yī ge miànkǒng yuányuán de háizi
A chubby-faced child came (running) out of the room.

If definite reference has to be expressed, this can be achieved in this case and in all cases by the addition of a 'demonstrative + measure' phrase:

那个面孔圆圆的孩子从屋子里跑了出来。
nèi ge miànkǒng yuányuán de háizi cóng wūzi li pǎo le chūlai
That chubby-faced child came out of the room.

It should be noted that subject nouns that are marked as indefinite, but which are followed by the referential adverbs 都 **dōu** 'all; both' and 也 **yě** 'also', are perfectly acceptable in a pre-verbal position, since they are made definite in reference by the presence of the adverbs:

两个陌生人都走了进来。 **liǎng ge mòshēngrén dōu zǒu le jìnlai**
(lit. two mw strangers both walk *le* in-come)
The two strangers both walked in.

三辆轿车也在门口停了下来。
sān liàng jiàochē yě zài ménkǒu tíng le xiàlai
(lit. three mw sedan also cv:at entrance stop *le* down-come)
The three sedans also stopped at the door.

On the other hand, a post-verbal noun may be given definite reference by either:

(**a**) introducing the standard 'demonstrative + measure' phrase before the noun:

我看了那个电影。 **wǒ kàn le nèi ge diànyǐng**
I saw that film.

他们讨论了这个问题。 **tāmen tǎolùn le zhèi ge wèntí**
They discussed this problem.

or:

(**b**) leaving the noun unmarked and adding a new clause begun with 就 **jiù** 'then' or 才 **cái** 'only then' to make the sentence sound complete:

我看了电影⁴就去赶最后一班车。
wǒ kàn le diànyǐng jiù qù gǎn zuì hòu yī bān chē
(lit. I see *le* film then go catch last one mw:run bus)
I went to catch the last bus as soon as I had seen **the** film.

她做完(了)功课才上楼去睡觉。
tā zuò wán (le) gōngkè cái shàng lóu qù shuìjiào
(lit. she do-finish *le* homework only-then step upstairs go sleep)
She did not go upstairs to bed until she had finished **the/her**
homework.

From the above examples, we can also see that point-of-time and location expressions with their specifying capacities are naturally of definite reference as are personal pronouns, which refer to previously mentioned nouns. All of these are likewise generally found in pre-verbal positions in a narrative sentence:

<u>上个星期</u>我收到了几十封电子邮件。
<u>**shàng ge xīngqī**</u> **wǒ shōudào le jǐ shí fēng diànzǐ yóujiàn**
(lit. last week I receive *le* few ten mw emails)
Last week I received dozens of emails.

我们<u>在花园里</u>种了不少⁵玫瑰花。
wǒmen <u>**zài huāyuán li**</u> **zhòng le bùshǎo méiguìhuā**
(lit. we cv:in garden-inside plant *le* not few roses)
We planted a good number of/quite a few roses in the garden.

<u>他们</u>下了两盘棋。 <u>**tāmen**</u> **xià le liǎng pán qí**
(lit. they play *le* two mw games chess) They played two games of chess.

Narrative sentences with time or location beginners often indicate 'emergence' or 'disappearance' relating to the noun in question:

昨天我家来了许多客人。 **zuótiān wǒ jiā lái le xǔduō kèrén**
(lit. yesterday my home come *le* many guests)
A lot of guests came to our place yesterday.

上午下了一场大雨。 **shàngwǔ xià le yī chǎng dà yǔ**
(lit. before noon fall *le* one mw big rain)
There was a heavy rain in the morning.

---

⁴ All unmarked nouns as the object of an action verb aspect-marked by 了 *le* are of definite reference, but, as we saw in §6.8.1, a statement with this formulation is felt to be incomplete.
⁵ 不少 **bùshǎo** 'quite a few' is an adjective which naturally indicates indefiniteness.

天边出现了一团乌云。 **tiān biān chūxiàn le yī tuán wūyún**
(lit. sky edge appear *le* one mw:mass black clouds)
There appeared a mass of black clouds on the horizon.

羊圈里跑了一只羊。 **yángjuàn li pǎo le yī zhī yáng**
(lit. sheep-pen-in run *le* one mw sheep) A sheep was missing from the pen.

海面上飞来了很多海鸥。 **hǎimiàn shàng fēi lái le hěn duō hǎi'ōu**
(lit. sea surface-on fly come *le* many gulls)
Many gulls came flying over the surface of the sea.

Apart from these prototypical narratives with noun phrases followed by 了 *le*-aspected action verbs, which are in turn followed by noun phrases or complements, there are other narrative formats such as the 把 **bǎ** construction and the passive voice with 被 **bèi**[6] and sentences with dative or causative verbs. They may all be regarded as narrative sentences, as they normally indicate actions or events which have already taken place, and the above-mentioned referential requirements apply to them in the same way. However, these narrative sentences do not necessarily require the presence of 了 *le* since the notion of completion is very often conveyed by the complement following the verb.

In a 把 **bǎ** sentence, not only does the subject have definite reference, as in other narrative sentences, but the noun following the coverb 把 **bǎ** must also be definite in reference as it is still positioned pre-verbally. For example:

爸爸把稿子扔进了字纸篓。 **bàba bǎ gǎozi rēng jìn le zìzhǐlǒu**
(lit. father cv:grasping manuscript throw enter *le* wastepaper basket)
Father threw **the** manuscript into the wastepaper basket.

妈妈把洗好的[7]衣服晾在晾衣绳上。
māma bǎ xǐ hǎo de yīfu liàng zài liàngyīshéng shàng
(lit. mother cv:grasping wash well *de* clothes dry cv:on clothesline-top)
Mother put **the** washing out on the clothesline (to dry).

in the first sentence, both 爸爸 **bàba** 'father' and 稿子 **gǎozi** 'manuscript', and in the second, both 妈妈 **māma** 'mother' and 衣服 **yīfu** 'clothes' are of definite reference.

In a 被 **bèi** sentence, the noun following the coverb 被 **bèi** can be either definite or indefinite in reference depending on the context:

---

[6] See Chapters 12 and 13.
[7] The noun after 把 **bǎ** marked or unmarked always remains definite.

弟弟被老师训了一顿。 **dìdi bèi lǎoshī xùn le yī dùn**
(lit. younger brother cv:by teacher lecture *le* one mw:time)
Younger brother was given a lecture by **the** teacher.

Here 弟弟 **dìdi** 'younger brother' and 老师 **lǎoshī** 'teacher' are both of definite
reference; on the other hand in a sentence like:

箱子被老鼠咬了一个洞。 **xiāngzi bèi lǎoshǔ yǎo le yī ge dòng**
(lit. box cv:by rat gnaw *le* one mw hole)
A hole was gnawed in the box by rats.

箱子 **xiāngzi** 'box' is of definite reference, but 老鼠 **lǎoshǔ** 'rat' can be of
indefinite reference.

In dative and causative sentences, all unmarked nouns, that is, all nouns unmodified by a 'numeral + measure' phrase are of definite reference.

In a dative sentence, for example, the indirect object, being the personal target of
the action of giving or rendering, is generally regarded as of definite reference
and remains unmarked, and the direct object, which usually comes after the
indirect object, is usually marked by a 'numeral + measure' phrase as indefinite:

老太太给了小姑娘一个苹果。 **lǎo tàitai gěi le xiǎo gūniang yī ge píngguǒ**
The old granny gave **the** young girl an apple.

流氓踢了警察一脚。 **liúmáng tī le jǐngchá yī jiǎo**
(lit. hooligan kick *le* policeman one foot)
The hooligan kicked **the** policeman.

In a causative sentence, the pivotal noun, i.e. the object-and-subject-in-one,
when unmarked,[8] is usually of definite reference:

教练鼓励运动员坚持到底。 **jiàoliàn gǔlì yùndòngyuán jiānchí dào dǐ**
(lit. coach encourage athlete persist till bottom/end)
The coach encouraged **the** athlete(s) to persist till the end.

老师指导学生做了一个实验。 **lǎoshī zhǐdǎo xuésheng zuò le yī ge shíyàn**
The teacher taught **the** students how to carry out a particular experiment.

One exceptional feature of a causative narrative is that the causative action verb
may never take the completed action aspect marker 了 *le*.

---

[8] It must, however, be noted that a few commonly used pivotal nouns like 人 **rén** 'people', 别人
biéren 'others', etc., which are indefinite, are exceptions to this.

*老师指导了学生做了一个实验。
*lǎoshī zhǐdǎo le xuésheng zuò le yī ge shíyàn
*The teacher taught the students how to carry out a particular experiment.

Finally, with regard to completed action, it is of course possible for the aspect marker 了 *le* to be used with an intransitive action verb, which is not followed by a noun or which has a noun built into it:

她2000年就去世了。 **tā èrlínglínglíng nián jiù qùshì le**
She passed away in (the year) 2000.

建筑计划都批准了。 **jiànzhù jìhuà dōu pīzhǔn le**
The building plans were all approved.

The verbs in these sentences essentially point to some form of termination and in varying degrees they may carry some implication of assumed change which is characteristic of the *le*-expository sentences to be discussed in the next chapter. In fact there are clearly cases where 了 *le* following a verb at the end of a sentence is almost certainly performing the two functions of being both an aspect marker and indicator of change.[9]

20.2 DESCRIPTIVE SENTENCES

A descriptive sentence differs from a narrative sentence in many respects, although it is also objective in stance. Rather than recounting what has already happened, it describes either: (**a**) what is going on through the action of the verb at the moment of speaking; or (**b**) a state that has resulted from the action of the verb. As with a narrative sentence, its structure is subject–predicate, though in the case of (**b**) the subject is more a recipient of the action, as in passive *bei* structures in narrative sentences. The time reference depends on the context, and, while it is mostly the present, it can also be past and, sometimes, future.

The main syntactic feature of a descriptive sentence is that, as in narrative sentences, the verb tends to be marked. This is achieved through the association of the verb with the 'ongoing' aspect marker 在 **zài**[10] (or its emphatic alternative 正在 **zhèngzài**) and the persistent manner indicator 着 *zhe*. 在 **zài** and 着 *zhe* in general terms represent respectively the alternative (**a**) and (**b**) forms of the descriptive sentence. However, as we shall see below, they can both occur in the same sentence.

---

[9] See §21.5.

[10] See Chapter 6. The ongoing aspect may be indicated by 在 **zài** on its own or as part of an adverbial location phrase, e.g. 在树上 **zài shùshàng** 'on/in the tree'.

As regards reference, the subject of a narrative sentence must be of definite reference whereas the subject/topic of a descriptive sentence may be either definite or indefinite. The post-verbal noun of a descriptive sentence, however, whether marked by a 'numeral + measure' phrase or left unmarked, always remain indefinite unless it is preceded by a 'demonstrative + measure' phrase. Here are some examples:

王老师在备课。 **wáng lǎoshī zài bèikè**
(lit. teacher Wang marker:*zai* prepare lesson)
Teacher Wang is preparing [his/her] lessons.

姑娘们在舞台上跳舞。 **gūniangmen zài wǔtái shàng tiàowǔ**
(lit. (young) girls cv:on stage-top dance) The girls are dancing on the stage.

小鸟在树上歌唱。 **xiǎoniǎo zài shù shàng gēchàng**
(lit. (little) birds cv: on tree-top sing) Birds are singing in the trees.

他在草地上躺着。 **tā zài cǎodì shàng tǎng zhe**
(lit. he cv:on grass-land-top lie *zhe*) He is lying on the grass.

鱼在锅里煎着。 **yú zài guō li jiān zhe**
(lit. fish cv:in pan-inside fry *zhe*) The fish is/are frying in the pan.

In the first example, 在 **zài** indicates ongoing action on the part of the subject. In the second and third, 在 **zài** as part of a coverbal location phrase again registers the ongoing action. The subjects of the first two examples are of definite reference, but the subject of the third is most likely to be of indefinite reference. In the fourth and fifth examples, 着 **zhe** is incorporated to indicate the persistent manner in which the action is being carried out.[11] In the last example, the subject 鱼 **yú** 'fish' is the recipient of the action of the verb 煎 **jiān** 'to fry'.

Sometimes, as we have seen in Chapter 8, a location phrase with 在 **zài** may come after the verb. These constructions are similarly descriptive sentences. For example:

伤员躺在担架上。 **shāngyuán tǎng zài dānjià shàng**
The wounded are lying on the stretcher.

商品陈列在橱窗里。 **shāngpǐn chéngliè zài chúchuāng li**
Goods are being displayed in the shop window.

---

[11] It is a prosodic requirement in Chinese syntax that in descriptive sentences 在 **zài** phrases of location cannot be followed by monosyllabic verbs. The speaker either chooses a disyllabic verb or a multi-syllabic verbal expression or suffixes 着 *zhe* to a monosyllabic verb to make it disyllabic.

Location expressions in a sentence are of course always of definite reference wherever they occur.

In a 着 *zhe* sentence, any verb marked by 着 *zhe* calls attention to the action itself, and therefore carries a descriptive flavour. As was suggested above, a descriptive sentence indicating a state that has resulted from the action of the verb often includes 着 **zhe**. The usual layout of the sentence is location phrase + action verb + 着 **zhe** + noun:

墙上挂着一幅画儿。 **qiáng shàng guà zhe yī fú huàr**
(lit. wall-on hang *zhe* one mw picture) A picture is hanging on the wall.

书架上放着很多中文书。 **shūjià shàng fàng zhe hěnduō zhōngwén shū**
(lit. bookshelf-on place *zhe* many Chinese books)
There are many Chinese books on the bookshelf.

樱桃树上长着密密麻麻的樱花。
yīngtáo shù shàng zhǎng zhe mìmìmámá de yīnghuā
(lit. cherry tree-on grow *zhe* dense-dense-motley-motley *de* cherry blossoms)
There grow countless cherry blossoms on the cherry tree.

玫瑰园里散发着一股清香。 **méiguì yuán li sànfā zhe yī gǔ qīngxiāng**
(lit. rose garden-in diffuse *zhe* one mw delicate fragrance)
There came a faint scent from the rose garden.

A variant of this descriptive format makes use of the completion aspect marker 了 *le* with or without the verbal complement 满 **mǎn** 'full'[12] instead of 着 *zhe*. These sentences are regarded as descriptive rather than narrative because the verb with 了 *le* calls attention to the resultant state and not the action:

大门上贴了一副对联。 **dàmén shàng tiē le yī fù duìlián**
(lit. big door-on stick *le* one mw:pair couplets)
On the door was (posted) a couplet.

屋檐下挂了两个灯笼。 **wūyán xià guà le liǎng ge dēnglóng**
(lit. house eve-under hang *le* two mw lanterns)
Under the eves were hanging two lanterns.

桌子上摆满了餐具。 **zhuōzi shàng bǎi mǎn le cānjù**
(lit. table-on put full *le* meal instruments) The table was laid.

---

[12] When 满 **mǎn** 'full' is used, the post-verbal noun cannot be marked by a 'numeral + measure' phrase.

礼堂里坐满了听众。**lǐtáng li zuò mǎn le tīngzhòng**
(lit. auditorium-in sit full *le* listening crowd) The auditorium was full.

车里挤满了乘客。**chē li jǐ mǎn le chéngkè**
(lit. bus-in squeeze full *le* passengers) The bus was full of passengers.

20.3 EXPOSITORY SENTENCES

Expository sentences are factual statements that offer some form of explanation relating to actual situations or experiences. The aspect markers 了 *le* and 在 **zài** and the persistent manner indicator 着 *zhe* do not occur in them, and there are no rules or restrictions for the pre-verbal and post-verbal positioning of nouns for definite and indefinite reference. Their range of meaning covers: (**a**) definition and identification, and possession and existence; and (**b**) experience, objective potential, the factual and the habitual, cognition and intention. They may be either topic–comment or subject–predicate in format, and the categories of meaning under (**a**) above are generally the former and those under (**b**) the latter.

20.3.1 TOPIC–COMMENT EXPOSITORY SENTENCES

20.3.1.1 'To be' and 'to have'

Two verbs that have a dominant presence are 是 'to be' and 有 'to have, there is/are'. In addition the near-synonymous or hyponymous counterparts of 是 **shì** (象 **xiàng** 'to resemble', 姓 **xìng** 'to be called'), also have a place:

他是我叔叔。	**tā shì wǒ shūshu**	He is my uncle.
昆虫有六只脚。	**kūnchóng yǒu liù zhī jiǎo**	Insects have six legs.
她象她妈妈。	**tā xiàng tā māma**	She looks like her mother.
我姓张。	**wǒ xìng zhāng**	My surname is Zhang.

As well as being nouns of definite or indefinite reference, topics may also adopt different parts of speech or take various forms:

地球是圆的。 **dìqiú shì yuán de**   (noun: definite reference)
The earth is round.

蜘蛛有八只脚。 **zhīzhū yǒu bā zhī jiǎo**   (noun: indefinite reference)
Spiders have eight legs.

月亮是地球的卫星。   (noun: definite reference)
yuèliang shì dìqiú de wèixīng
The moon is a satellite of the earth.

这副眼镜是我的。 **zhèi fù yǎnjìng shì wǒ de**   (noun: definite reference)
This pair of spectacles are mine.

打太极拳是他的爱好之一。

dǎ tàijíquán shì tāde àihào zhī yī   (verbal phrase)

(lit. hit *taiqi* boxing is his favourite *zhi* one)

One of his favourite sports is taiqi/shadow-boxing.

严格有很多好处。 **yángé yǒu hěnduō hǎochù**   (adjective)

(lit. strict has many benefits)

Being strict can be very productive.

办事认真是她的一个特点。

bànshì rènzhēn shì tāde yī ge tèdiǎn   (clause)

(lit. handle matters serious is her one mw characteristic)

One of her characteristics is that she handles things seriously.

In addition to indicating definition, possesion, etc., 是 **shì** or 有 **yǒu** are also used to express emphasis or to make comparisons,[13] and remain expository when performing this function:

他是两年前结的婚。 **tā shì liǎng nián qián jié de hūn**   (emphasis)

It was two years ago that he got married.

妹妹是不喜欢喝啤酒。 **mèimei shì bù xǐhuan hē píjiǔ**   (emphasis)

It's true that younger sister doesn't like beer.

这件外套没有那件那么暖。

zhèi jiàn wàitào méiyǒu nèi jiàn nàme nuǎn   (comparison)

This jacket isn't as warm as that one.

20.3.1.2 Adjectival predicates and complements

These constitute another form of comment. It must, however, be remembered that an unmodified adjective always implies a contrast.

谁不累？大家都累。 **shéi/shuí bù lèi | dàjiā dōu lèi**

Who's not tired? Everybody's tired.

苹果贵，香蕉也贵。 **píngguǒ guì | xiāngjiāo yě guì**

Apples are expensive and so are bananas.

昨天冷，今天也冷。 **zuótiān lěng | jīntiān yě lěng**

It was cold yesterday and it's cold today as well.

---

[13] See Chapters 13 and 14 on 是 **shì** and 有 **yǒu** sentences.

她可长得漂亮。 **tā kě zhǎng de piàoliang**
But she is/has grown beautiful.

他比我讲得清楚。 **tā bǐ wǒ jiǎng de qīngchu**
He explains [it] more clearly than I.

20.3.2 SUBJECT–PREDICATE EXPOSITORY SENTENCES

Both action and cognitive verbs are used in these sentences:

20.3.2.1 Statements of past action

Statements of past action indicated by presence of the verb suffix 过 *guo*:[14]

我吃过蜗牛。	**wǒ chī guo wōniú**	I have tried snails before.
他听过中国歌曲。	**tā tīng guo zhōngguó gēqǔ**	He has heard Chinese songs.
她说她见过鬼。	**tā shuō tā jiàn guo guǐ**	She said that she once saw a ghost.
我去过中国。	**wǒ qù guo zhōngguó**	I have been to China.
他们到过长城。	**tāmen dào guo chángchéng**	They have been to the Great Wall.

20.3.2.2 Potential complements

Potential complements[15] as positive or negative statements of capability, possibility, likelihood, etc.:

他一辈子也学不会中文。 **tā yībèizi yě xuébuhuì zhōngwén**
(lit. he whole life also learn-cannot-master Chinese)
He will never in his life be able to learn/master Chinese.

这么贵的衣服我买不起。 **zhème guì de yīfu wǒ mǎibuqǐ**
(lit. such expensive *de* clothes I buy-cannot-afford)
I can't afford such expensive clothes.

这辆车坐得下五个人。 **zhèi liàng chē zuòdexià wǔ ge rén**
(lit. this mw car seat-can-hold five mw people)
This car can seat five people.

---

[14] See Chapter 6.
[15] See Chapter 10. Note the distinction made there between statements of capability by potential complements and by modal verbs. The latter as will be seen are elements in evaluative sentences.

这个人一顿饭吃得下二十片面包。
zhèi ge rén yī dùn fàn chīdexià èrshī piàn miànbāo
(lit. this mw person one mw meal eat-can-down twenty slices bread)
This person can eat twenty slices of bread in one meal.

20.3.2.3   Factual statements and habitual action

马吃草。	**mǎ chī cǎo**	Horses eat grass.
太阳从东方升起。	**tàiyáng cóng dōngfāng shēngqǐ**	The sun rises in the east.
我每天买报纸。	**wǒ měitiān mǎi bàozhǐ**	I buy a paper every day.

20.3.2.4   Cognition and preference

我知道他是中国人。	**wǒ zhīdao tā shì zhōngguórén**	I know he is Chinese.
我明白你的意思。	**wǒ míngbái nǐde yìsi**	I understand what you mean.
他喜欢看外国电影。	**tā xǐhuan kàn wàiguó diànyǐng**	He likes watching foreign films.
我爱花鸟。	**wǒ ài huā niǎo**	I love flowers and birds.

20.3.2.5   Intentions and plans

我打算去旅行。	**wǒ dǎsuan qù lǚxíng**	I intend to go travelling.
我们买这个。	**wǒmen mǎi zhèi ge**	We'll buy this one.
他的儿子明天来。	**tāde érzi míngtiān lái**	His son is coming tomorrow.
我们去帮他的忙。	**wǒmen qù bāng tāde máng**	We are going to help him.

20.3.3   NEGATION OF EXPOSITORY SENTENCES

It is perhaps appropriate to point out here that all negative sentences with 不 **bù** (to negative habitual or intentional action) or 没(有) **méi(yǒu)** (to negate non-completed action with reference to a current situation)[16] are expository. Their function is not to narrate or describe but to explain.

我不去。**wǒ bù qù**
I won't go.

她不是我的女朋友。**tā bù shì wǒde nǚpéngyou**
She is not my girlfriend.

---

[16] This use of 没有 **méiyǒu** must be distinguished from its use to negate past actions, which will then be narrative.

大家都不理他。 **dàjiā dōu bù lǐ tā**
Everybody ignored him.

他还没(有)来。 **tā hái méi(yǒu) lái**
He still hasn't come.

她从来不吃大蒜。 **tā cónglái bù chī dàsuàn**
She never touches garlic.

她从来没(有)吃过大蒜。 **tā cónglái méi(yǒu) chī guo dàsuàn**
She has never touched garlic.

20.4   EVALUATIVE SENTENCES

Evaluative sentences are in fact expository, but they present a judgemental stance
on the part of the speaker, so that they are not necessarily factual. They invariably
have a topic–comment structure and the comment voices the opinion of the
speaker. Like expository sentences, they never include an aspect marker at their
core. They take two forms, one focusing on a modal verb, and the other on a
modified adjective or complement.

20.4.1   THE MODAL VERB EVALUATIVE

Take the following example,

他应该马上开始工作。 **tā yīnggāi mǎshàng kāishǐ gōngzuò**
He must start work immediately.

It is obviously the speaker's view that the man referred to 'must start work
immediately'. 他 **tā** 'he', in fact, is not the initiator of the action in the verb, but
he is the topic on which the speaker is commenting in relation to the action, and
is the focus of the speaker's concern and attention.

A major feature of an evaluative sentence is that, as with an expository topic–
comment, the topic posed for comment can be of either definite or indefinite
reference, can be any part of speech, and can be of any structural format. For
example:

一个人不能不讲理。 **yī ge rén bùnéng bù jiǎnglǐ**
(lit. one mw person not can not talk reason)
A person has to listen to reason.

两个人能办很多事情。 **liǎng ge rén néng bàn hěnduō shìqing**
(lit. two mw people can do many things) Two hands can make light work.

办事情要有计划。 **bàn shìqing yào yǒu jìhuà**
(lit. do things must have plan) One needs a plan to do things.

懒惰会毁坏他的一生。 **lǎnduò huì huǐhuài tāde yīshēng**
(lit. lazy possible ruin his one life)
Laziness is likely to ruin his whole life.

他不下场会影响球赛的胜负。
tā bù xià chǎng huì yǐngxiǎng qiúsài de shèngfù
(lit. he not come on to the pitch will affect match *de* victory-defeat)
His not taking part in the match will affect its outcome.

In the first and second examples, the noun topics are of indefinite reference; in the third, the topic takes the form of a verb; in the fourth, it is an adjective; in the last example, it is a clause.

20.4.2 THE MODIFIED ADJECTIVE/COMPLEMENT EVALUATIVE

The presence in the comment of a degree adverbial or complement registers the evaluative force of these sentences:

他办事情非常认真。 **tā bàn shìqing fēicháng rènzhēn**
He runs/does things extremely seriously/conscientiously.

这儿的风景好极了。 **zhèr de fēngjǐng hǎo jí le**
The scenery here is really beautiful.

他跑得真快。 **tā pǎo de zhēn kuài**
He runs really fast.

这件事儿他处理得好得很。 **zhèi jiàn shìr tā chǔlǐ de hǎo de hěn**
(lit. this mw matter he handle *de* good *de* very much)
He handled this matter very well.

20.5 COMPARISONS BETWEEN SENTENCE TYPES

The following pairs of similar sentences illustrate the distinctions that can be made between sentence types:

(a) 我们去了上海。 **wǒmen qù le shànghǎi**   (narrative)
We went to Shanghai.

我们去过上海。 **wǒmen qù guo shànghǎi**   (expository)
We've been to Shanghai

The contrast here is plain: 了 *le* in the first sentence indicating the completion of an action implies a past event and is therefore narrative, whereas 过 *guo* in the second stating a past experience serves as an explanation and is therefore expository.

    (**b**) 他在墙上挂了一幅画儿。   (narrative)
           tā zài qiáng shàng guà le yī fú huàr
           He hung a picture on the wall.

           墙上挂了一幅画儿。 **qiáng shàng guà le yī fú huàr**   (descriptive)
           On the wall hangs a picture.

The first sentence is clearly narrative completed action, while in the second the action verb with 了 *le* following the location phrase creates a resultant state and is therefore descriptive.

    (**c**) 爸爸在花园里看我给他买的报纸。[17]
           bàba zài huāyuán li kàn wǒ gěi tā mǎi de bàozhǐ   (descriptive)
           Father is in the garden reading the newspaper I bought for him.

           爸爸在花园里看了我给他买的报纸。
           bàba zài huāyuán li kàn le wǒ gěi tā mǎi de bàozhǐ   (narrative)
           Father read the newspaper I bought for him in the garden.

In the first sentence the location phrase 在花园里 **zài huāyuán lǐ** establishes the basis for the ongoing action of a descriptive sentence, but in the second it provides the setting for the completed action of a narrative sentence.

    (**d**) 我去找他。 **wǒ qù zhǎo tā**   (expository)
            I'll go and look for him.

           我去找了他。 **wǒ qù zhǎo le tā**   (narrative)
            I went to look for him.

The first sentence expresses an intention and is therefore expository; the second with aspect marker 了 *le* is obviously a completed action narrative.

    (**e**) 筑路工人在路上挖了一个洞。   (narrative)
           zhù lù gōngrén zài lù shàng wā le yī ge dòng
           The road workers dug a hole in the road.

---

[17] It is possible to further insert the persistent-manner indicator 着 **zhe** in this sentence to enhance its descriptive effect: e.g. 爸爸在花园里看着我给他买的报纸。 **bàba zài huāyuán li kàn zhe wǒ gěi tā mǎi de bàozhǐ** 'Father is in the garden reading the newspaper I bought for him'.

筑路工人在路上挖洞。
zhù lù gōngrén zài lù shàng wā dòng (descriptive)
Road workers were digging a hole/holes in the road.

These sentences are obviously narrative and descriptive, but notice that in the first the subject has to be of definite reference, while in the second it can be either definite or indefinite depending on the context.

(**f**) 他很快地跑着。 **tā hěn kuài de pǎo zhe** (descriptive)
He is/was running very quickly.

他跑得很快。 **tā pǎo de hěn kuài** (expository)
He runs very quickly.

The adverbial phrase 很快地 **hěn kuài de** in the first sentence describes the way in which he is running. The verb-complement in the second sentence 跑得很快 **pǎo de hěn kuài** explains the fact that he runs very fast.

(**g**) 他昨天到了北京。 **tā zuótiān dào le běijīng** (narrative)
He arrived in Beijing yesterday.

他是昨天到的北京。 **tā shì zuótiān dào de běijīng** (expository)
He arrived in Beijing <u>yesterday</u>.

The first sentence narrates the fact that he arrived, but the emphatic 是 **shì** ... 的 **de** construction in the second makes the sentence an explanation focusing on the time of his arrival and is therefore expository.

(**h**) 我不能喝那么多的酒。 **wǒ bùnéng hē nàme duō de jiǔ** (evaluative)
I cannot drink so much wine.

我喝不了那么多的酒。 **wǒ hēbùliǎo nàme duō de jiǔ** (expository)
I cannot drink so much wine.

The use of the modal verb 能 **néng** in the first sentence means that the speaker is making a subjective judgement, perhaps on the level of principle or diet. The second sentence with its potential complement 喝不了 **hēbùliǎo** is more object-ive and most likely indicates that he does not have the physical capacity to down any more liquor.

(**i**) 他在北京住。 **tā zài běijīng zhù** He lives in Beijing. (expository)
他住在北京。 **tā zhù zài běijīng** He is living in Beijing. (descriptive)

The first sentence using an unmarked verb simply states the fact that he lives in Beijing and is therefore expository. The second with a 在 **zài** phrase as a complement clearly sets out to highlight a persistent state (i.e. he is living in Beijing) and is therefore descriptive.

(j) 妈妈把房间收拾干净。
māma bǎ fángjiān shōushi gānjìng
Mother tidied up the room.   (narrative)

妈妈把房间收拾得真干净。
māma bǎ fángjiān shōushi de zhēn gānjìng
Mother tidied up the room really well.   (evaluative)

The first sentence is a narrative report. The focus in the second is on 真 **zhēn** 'really', which makes the statement evaluative, despite the presence of 把 **bǎ**.

20.6 CONCLUDING REMARKS

The categorisation of sentences into sentence types attempts to provide a function-based framework to analyse the peculiarities of Chinese syntax. As we pointed out at the beginning of this chapter, it is difficult, not to say impossible, to establish any such watertight framework, and our analysis of Chinese sentence structure demonstrates that we have not lost sight of other approaches, including structural, semantic, stylistic and elemental, which of course are equally valid.

Imperatives, interrogatives and exclamations[18] are used very much for their respective functions and there is little need therefore to subject them to the kind of minute differentiation discussed above. However, since they are all based on corresponding statements, their characteristic features are derivable from their declarative counterparts.

There remains one further exceedingly important sentence type to be discussed. We have called this type *le*-expository, since it involves the addition of the particle 了 *le* at the end of the sentence and in function it provides a particular style of exposition. It can, in fact, be added to any of the four sentence types analysed above and its impact on them will be examined in detail in the next chapter.

---

[18] See Chapters 23 and 24.

21 了 *le*-EXPOSITORY SENTENCES

了 *le*-expository sentences are formed by putting the particle 了 *le* at the end of virtually any statement. Like expository sentences they offer an explanation, but they add to this explanation the implication of some form of change or a reversal of a previous situation. They suggest that what is stated represents a change from what existed or what was happening before. In expressing him/herself in this way, the speaker is giving updated information, and (s)he will often back it with some degree of personal endorsement. Much of the time the change asserted in 了 *le*-expository sentences is simply factual, but it also regularly counters an assumption or expectation in the mind of the person addressed. The context, in which the statement is made, is extremely important, and, as we will see, the implications of a particular sentence can vary significantly depending on the situation in which it is used. Not surprisingly, the construction is very much a feature of spoken language and the social interaction among Chinese people. It is therefore important to understand how it works, but its subtleties have been notoriously challenging for non-native speakers. We hope that the explanations and examples given below may throw some light on it.

This use of 了 *le* is of course separate from its role as an aspect marker. However, etymologically, the particle derives from the classical verb 了 **liǎo** 'to end', and a semantic link can clearly be seen between its two functions, one being the completion of an action, and the other the termination of a previous situation.

Consider the following two sentences:

她生了一个孩子。 **tā shēng le yī ge háizi**
She had a baby.

她生了一个孩子了。 **tā shēng le yī ge háizi** *le*
She's had a baby.

The first is a flat statement and the meaning implied by 了 *le* is that the action of 生 **shēng** 'to give birth to' has been completed. In other words, the action of giving birth to a child has already taken place. The sentence thus encodes a narrative. The second, on the other hand, is much more animated with almost certainly stress on the word 'baby', and the end-of-sentence 了 *le* conveys the sense that a new situation of 'giving birth to a child' has happened for someone who probably has not had a baby before. The speaker could of course have a range of different ideas in mind, depending on the circumstances, and the event could be happy, worrying, unexpected, thought to have been impossible, and so on, but the fundamental notion is that there has been a change. If the first example resembles a past tense in English, the second example is more like a present perfect. The aspect indicator 了 *le* in the former belongs to the realm of narration while the end-of-sentence 了 *le* in the latter is a pointer to exposition.[1]

In the following sections we will focus, each at a time, on the various semantic and syntactic properties of end-of-sentence 了 *le*, where necessary in comparison with the aspect 了 *le*.

21.1 CHANGE OR REVERSAL OF A PREVIOUS SITUATION

Let us look at two more examples of change of circumstances, as described above. The first is a straightforward change:

我妹妹会说日文了。 **wǒ mèimei huì shuō rìwén** *le*
My younger sister can speak Japanese [now].

This implies that my sister did not know how to speak Japanese before but now she does, and this is something I think deserves some attention.

他看电影了。 **tā kàn diànyǐng** *le*
He has gone to the cinema [after all].

The suggestion here is that perhaps the person referred to as *he* used to be against cinema-going, or did not like going to the cinema at all, or something else. However, what used to be the case is not important. What *is* important for the speaker who cares to impart this piece of information is that the person referred to has now changed or reversed his former attitude: he is now doing what he would not do before.

Everyday situations also invite this kind of emphasis:

病人吃饭了。 **bìngrén chīfàn** *le*
This patient is eating. [(s)he has been unable to eat before]

天晴了。 **tiān qíng** *le*
The weather has cleared up. [it has been raining up till now]

时间不早了。 **shíjiān bù zǎo** *le*
Time's getting on. [lit. the time is not early any more]

[1] See Chapter 20.

All these examples describe an emerging situation that has turned the prior situation on its head.

Adjectives, being situation rather than action indicators, are regularly core elements in *le*-expository sentences indicating reversals. They may be used either independently as predicatives (as the first three examples below show) or as complements to verbs (as in the last three):

东西贵了。 **dōngxi guì** *le*
Things have become expensive/gone up.

他有点醉了。 **tā yǒudiǎn zuì** *le*
He's a bit drunk.

你的茶快凉了。 **nǐde chá kuài liáng** *le*
Your tea will soon be cold.

孩子的玩具摔坏了。 **háizi de wánjù shuāi huài** *le*
The children's toy has been/is broken.

我吃饱了。 **wǒ chī bǎo** *le*
I've eaten my fill./I am full.

这个字你写错了。 **zhèi ge zì nǐ xiě cuò** *le*
You have written this character wrongly.

Some expressions, which clearly signal new situations, past or future, are naturally linked with end-of-sentence 了 *le*: time adverbs like 已经 **yǐjīng** 'already', 快 **kuài** 'is about to', 要 **yào** 'will soon'; modal verbs, which indicate future possibilities, obligations or necessities; and all sentences with resultative complements signifying that something has 'already' been or will soon be accomplished or brought about:

(a) time adverbs:

我的病已经治好了。 **wǒde bìng yǐjīng zhì hǎo** *le*
My illness is already cured.

截止的日期快到了。 **jiézhǐ de rìqī kuài dào** *le*
The deadline is soon.

电影马上就要开演了。 **diànyǐng mǎshàng jiùyào kāiyǎn** *le*
The film is just about to start.

(b) modal verbs:

我该走了。 **wǒ gāi zǒu** *le*
I must be off.

他不肯再捐款了。 **tā bù kěn zài juānkuǎn** *le*
He's not willing to donate any more money.

你可以回去了。 **nǐ kěyǐ huíqu** *le*
You may go back.

(c) resultative complements:

壶里的水煮开了。 **hú li de shuǐ zhǔ kāi** *le*
(The water in) the pot has boiled.

来宾快到齐了。 **láibīn kuài dào qí** *le*
The guests are almost all here.

电灯安好了。 **diàndēng ān hǎo** *le*
The electric light has been installed.

It is clear from all the above examples that, though 了 *le* is unstressed, the speaker who is using it is very much making a point. By tagging 了 *le* to the statement (s)he wants to affirm the message and make the listener aware of its importance or relevance to the immediate situation. This immediate situation, while commonly located in the present, may also relate to events in the past or posed for the future:

去年九月底已经开始下雪了。 **qùnián jiǔyuè dǐ yǐjīng kāishǐ xià xuě le**
By the end of September last year it had already started snowing.

你明天九点钟才来的话，他可能已经离开这儿了。
nǐ míngtiān jiǔ diǎn zhōng cái lái de huà | tā kěnéng yǐjīng líkāi zhèr le
If you don't come tomorrow till 9 o'clock, he will probably already have left.

A hypothetical future can also be relevant:

我如果再有机会上大学，我一定不会象以前那样懒惰了。
wǒ rúguǒ zài yǒu jīhuì shàng dàxué | wǒ yīdìng bù huì xiàng yǐqián nàyàng lǎnduò le
If I had the chance to go to university again, I certainly would not be as lazy as I was before.

This underlying attitude, the enthusiasm and willingness to put the listener in the picture, explains why native speakers make particular use of 了 *le* when they are trying to explain a situation or to sum it up.

21.2 SUBJECTIVE ENDORSEMENT BEHIND THE OBJECTIVE EXPLANATION

A speaker's response to a situation that is markedly better or worse than expected is regularly couched in a 了 *le*-expository form. (S)he is, in fact, voicing feelings about the impact of the new situation on him (or her) and (s)he expresses appreciation or displeasure, often vehemently. This explains why sentence 了 *le* is a common adjunct to hyperbole. Consider the following:

(我们)太幸运了。 **(wǒmen) tài xìngyùn** *le*
We are really lucky.

(这)真是再好不过了。 **(zhè) zhēn shì zài hǎo bùguò** *le*
You can't do better than this.

(这条裙子)漂亮极了。 **(zhèi tiáo qúnzi) piàoliang jí** *le*
This skirt is extremely pretty.

这个人坏透了。 **zhèi ge rén huài tòu** *le*
This man is thoroughly bad.

屋子里闷死了。 **wūzi li mēn sǐ** *le*
It's really stuffy in the room.

The structure holds good too for gentle imperatives or urgent requests where some form of immediate reversal of the existing situation is being urged or cautioned against:

好了，好了，别胡闹了。 **hǎo** *le* | **hǎo** *le* | **bié húnào** *le*
OK, OK, stop the racket.

走了，走了，时间不早了。 **zǒu** *le* | **zǒu** *le* | **shíjiān bù zǎo** *le*
Let's go, let's go, time's getting on.

不要哭了。 **bù yào kū** *le*
Stop crying.

大家都坐好了。 **dàjiā dōu zuò hǎo** *le*
Would everyone sit down.

请别谈话了，会议开始了。 **qǐng bié tánhuà** *le* | **huìyì kāishǐ** *le*
Please stop talking. The meeting is starting.

快浇点儿水，别让花儿蔫了。
kuài jiāo diǎnr shuǐ | bié ràng huār niān *le*
Hurry up and water them and don't let the flowers droop.

多穿点儿衣服，别着凉了。 **duō chuān diǎnr yīfu | bié zháoliáng** *le*
Put a bit more on and don't catch cold.

A similarly committed response can also be expected from the listener when a speaker asks questions demanding immediate indication as to whether a reversal of the existing situation can be expected or brought about:

情况究竟怎么样了？ **qíngkuàng jiūjìng zénmeyàng** *le*
What's the situation really like?

这么晚了。他到底来不来了？ **zhème wǎn** *le* **| tā dàodǐ lái bù lái** *le*
It's so late. Is he really coming or not?

Sometimes the speaker may even explicitly indicate that the new situation is counter to his/her expectation:

我<u>以为</u>他回家去了。 **wǒ <u>yǐwéi</u> tā huí jiā qù le**
I <u>thought</u> he had gone home.

<u>想不到</u>在这儿见到你了。 **<u>xiǎngbudào</u> zài zhèr jiàn dào nǐ le**
[I] <u>didn't realise</u> that I would bump into you here.

It is often the case that it is the impact of change or reversal as much as the change itself that is in the mind of the speaker:

我们看过那个电影了。 **wǒmen kàn guo nèi ge diànyǐng le**
We have seen that film. [we don't want to see it again]

儿子偷了父亲的钱了。 **érzi tōu le fùqīn de qián le**
The son stole his father's money. [that is unthinkable]

21.3 SUMMING UP AFTER A SERIES OF ACTIONS

A narrative account in Chinese usually consists of the description of a sequence of actions or events, marked as appropriate by the aspect marker 了 *le*, which is terminated by some form of summing up ending with sentence 了 *le*. This last summing up naturally presents a picture of the new circumstances at the end of the preceding sequence:

他洗了脸，刷了牙，脱了衣服，上床睡觉去了。

tā xǐ le liǎn | shuā le yá | tuō le yīfu | shàngchuáng shuìjiào qù *le*

He washed his face, brushed his teeth, undressed and went to bed.

爸爸吃了早饭，翻了翻报纸，披上衣服，就开车去上班了。

bàba chī le zǎofàn | fān le fān bàozhǐ | pī shàng yīfu | jiù kāichē qù shàngbān *le*

Father had breakfast, looked through the paper, put on his coat and drove off to work.

There are cases where there is a need to stress new circumstances at every step and these naturally invite end-of-sentence/clause 了 *le*:

天黑了，路上的行人越来越少了，商店也一家接一家地关门了，她觉得饿了，可是钱却花完了，走着走着，她哭起来了。

tiān hēi *le* **| lù shàng de xíngrén yuè lái yuè shǎo** *le* **| shāngdiàn yě yī jiā jiē yī jiā de guānmén** *le* **| tā juéde è** *le* **| kěshì qián huā wán** *le* **| zǒu zhe zǒu zhe | tā kū qǐlai** *le*

It went dark, people on the street grew fewer and fewer, (and) the shops closed one after another. She felt hungry, but she had spent all her money. She walked and walked, and began to cry.

This sense of summing up a situation or bringing a particular topic to a close before going on to a new one by the use of end-of-sentence/clause 了 *le* may also be found with nominal comments. Compare the following pairs of sentences:

孩子今年五岁。 **háizi jīnnián wǔ suì**
孩子今年五岁了。 **háizi jīnnián wǔ suì** *le*
The child is 5 years old.

今天星期六。 **jīntiān xīngqī liù**
今天星期六了。 **jīntiān xīngqī liù** *le*
It's Saturday today.

The first example of each pair only expresses a fact: 'the child is 5 years old' or 'today is Saturday'. The addition of end-of-sentence 了 *le* conveys the sense of eventually reaching the present situation or position: the child is (now) 5, and today is (finally) Saturday.

21.4 A RHYTHMIC NECESSITY FOR MONOSYLLABIC VERBS OR VERBALISED ADJECTIVES

Syntactic constructions in Chinese are not only governed by structural and lexical validity, but are also shaped by rhythmic patterns. This applies to

end-of-sentence 了 *le* (as well as aspect 了 *le*) which may sometimes be optional
with disyllabic verbs or adjectives, but is obligatory with monosyllabic verbs or
verbalised adjectives. Compare the following sets of sentences:

(a) 客人早已离开了。 **kèren zǎo yǐ líkāi** *le*
客人早已离开。 **kèren zǎo yǐ líkāi**

客人早已走了。 **kèren zǎo yǐ zǒu** *le*
*客人早已走。 ***kèren zǎo yǐ zǒu**
The guests have long since left.

(b) 事情已经办妥了。 **shìqing yǐjīng bàn tuǒ** *le*
事情已经办妥。 **shìqing yǐjīng bàn tuǒ**

事情已经办了。 **shìqing yǐjīng bàn** *le*
*事情已经办。 ***shìqing yǐjīng bàn**
The matter has already been settled.

(c) 他的病即将痊愈了。 **tāde bìng jíjiāng quányù** *le*
他的病即将痊愈。 **tāde bìng jíjiāng quányù**

他的病快要[2]好了。 **tāde bìng kuàiyào hǎo** *le*
*他的病快要好。 ***tāde bìng kuàiyào hǎo**
He will soon recover from his illness.

It can be seen from the three sets of sentences that the last one in each case is
unacceptable, because a monosyllabic verb or verbalised adjective coming at the
end of a sentence can be regarded as valid only if it is accompanied by an extra
syllable for rhythm. 了 *le* here fulfils this function ideally, as it also serves as an
end-of-sentence marker.[3]

In many cases, these end-of-sentence 了 *le* serves as a rhythmic filler as well as
an indicator of the reversal of circumstances. Common examples are:

天晴了。	**tiān qíng** *le*	It has cleared up.
天黑了。	**tiān hēi** *le*	It's gone dark.
天亮了。	**tiān liàng** *le*	It's light now.
雨停了。	**yǔ tíng** *le*	It's stopped raining.
你胖了。[4]	**nǐ pàng** *le*	You've put on weight.

---

[2] The difference between 即将 **jíjiāng** 'soon' and 快要 **kuàiyào** 'soon' is one of register and style. It
does not affect structural validity of the sentence.

[3] Resultative complements like 妥 **tuǒ** 'settled' often act as rhythmic fillers, as does the descriptive
indicator 着 **zhe**, e.g. *他在树荫下躺 versus 他在树荫下躺着 **tā zài shùyìn xià tǎng zhe** 'He is lying
in the shade of the tree'.

[4] This is under most circumstances a compliment rather than a critical comment.

我的孩子都大了。	**wǒde háizi dōu dà** *le*	My children are all grown up.
我们赢了。	**wǒmen yíng** *le*	We won.
谁输了？	**shuí shū** *le*	Who lost?

21.5 TWO OR THREE FUNCTIONS IN ONE

As was said earlier in the chapter, end-of-sentence 了 *le* is isomorphic with aspectual 了 *le*, with both of them deriving from 了 **liǎo** 'to end'. This being the case, an end-of-sentence 了 *le* following a verb may often represent the completion of the action indicated by the verb as well as the emergence of a new situation. This two-in-one role is apparent in most of the above examples at the end of §22.4.

In some cases, even the meaning of the isomorphic 了 **liǎo** 'to end' may be implied in an end-of-sentence 了 *le*, thus giving it a three-in-one function. For example:

请把剩下的酒喝了！ **qǐng bǎ shèngxia de jiǔ hē** *le*
Please finish off the remaining wine.

垃圾我已经倒了。 **lājī wǒ yǐjīng dào** *le*
I have already tipped out the rubbish.

她把不要的衣服全扔了。 **tā bǎ bùyào de yīfu quán rēng** *le*
She threw out all the clothes she did not want.

This three-in-one function is confirmed if we rewrite the above three sentences, incorporating the resultative complement 掉 **diào** 'to be finished' (which is itself co-morphogenic with 了 **liǎo** 'to finish'). In each case the meaning remains the same:

请把剩下的酒喝掉了！ **qǐng bǎ shèngxia de jiǔ hē diào** *le*
Please finish off the remaining wine.

垃圾我已经倒掉了。 **lājī wǒ yǐjīng dào diào** *le*
I have already tipped out the rubbish.

她把不要的衣服全扔掉了。 **tā bǎ bùyào de yīfu quán rēng diào** *le*
She threw out all the clothes she did not want.

21.6 *le*-EXPOSITORY SENTENCES AND THE FOUR BASIC SENTENCE TYPES

We said at the beginning of this chapter that 了 *le* could be added to any sentence to form a *le*-expository sentence. To sum up our discussion of *le*-expository sentences, we will here illustrate in a sequence of paired examples the impact end-of-sentence 了 *le* has on the other sentence types. We will start off with expository sentences:

21.6.1   EXPOSITORY SENTENCES

我哥哥是工程师。 **wǒ gēge shì gōngchéngshī**   (expository)
My elder brother is an engineer.

我哥哥是工程师了。 **wǒ gēge shì gōngchéngshī le**   (*le*-expository)
My elder brother is now an engineer. [he wasn't before]

她有孩子。 **tā yǒu háizi**   (expository)
She has got children.

她有孩子了。 **tā yǒu háizi le**   (*le*-expository)
She has a child/children now. [she didn't before]

妈妈吃素。 **māma chī sù**   (expository)
(lit. mother eat vegetarian food)
Mother is a vegetarian.

妈妈吃素了。 **māma chī sù le**   (*le*-expository)
(lit. mother eat vegetarian food)
Mother has become a vegetarian. [she wasn't one before]

她拉小提琴。 **tā lā xiǎotíqín**   (expository)
She plays the violin.

她拉小提琴了。 **tā lā xiǎotíqín le**   (*le*-expository)
She plays the violin now. [she did not use to]

这个人不怕鬼。 **zhèi ge rén bù pà guǐ**   (expository)
(lit. this mw person not afraid-of ghosts)
This person is not afraid of ghosts.

这个人不怕鬼了。 **zhèi ge rén bù pà guǐ le**   (*le*-expository)
(lit. this mw person not afraid-of ghosts *le*)
This person is no longer afraid of ghosts. [he was before]

21.6.2   NARRATIVE SENTENCES

他在钢琴上弹了两个曲子。
tā zài gāngqín shàng tán le liǎng ge qǔzi   (narrative)
He played two pieces of music on the piano.

他在钢琴上弹了两个曲子了。
tā zài gāngqín shàng tán le liǎng ge qǔzi le   (*le*-expository)
He has [already] played two pieces of music on the piano.
[that's enough; someone else can play, etc.]

他当了父亲。 **tā dāng le fùqin**   (narrative)
He became a father.

他当了父亲了。 **tā dāng le fùqin le**   (*le*-expository)
He is now a father. [he wasn't one before and now he has a child]

我学了三年英文。 **wǒ xué le sān nián yīngwén**   (narrative)
I studied English for three years.

我学了三年英文了。 **wǒ xué le sān nián yīngwén le**   (*le*-expository)
I have studied English for three years.
[this is the point I have reached in the learning process]

他喝了十杯啤酒。 **tā hē le shí bēi píjiǔ**   (narrative)
He drank ten glasses of beer.

他喝了十杯啤酒了。 **tā hē le shí bēi píjiǔ le**   (*le*-expository)
He's drunk ten glasses of beer.
[he should not have any more; that is why he can't stand up, etc.]

我在这儿等了半个钟头。 **wǒ zài zhèr děng le bàn ge zhōngtou**   (narrative)
I waited here for half an hour.

我在这儿等了半个钟头了。   (*le*-expository)
wǒ zài zhèr děng le bàn ge zhōngtou le
I have been waiting here for half an hour. [I won't wait any longer]

21.6.3 DESCRIPTIVE SENTENCES

外面下着大雪。 **wàimian xià zhe dà xuě**   (descriptive)
(lit. outside fall *zhe* big snow) It is snowing heavily outside.

外面下着大雪了。 **wàimian xià zhe dà xuě le**   (*le*-expository)
(lit. outside fall *zhe* big snow *le*)
It is now snowing heavily outside. [it wasn't a moment ago]

她在生气。 **tā zài shēngqì**   (descriptive)
She is sulking.

她在生气了。 **tā zài shēngqì le**   (*le*-expository)
She is now sulking. [that wasn't the case before]

他在准备他的功课。 **tā zài zhǔnbèi tāde gōngkè**   (descriptive)
He is preparing/doing his homework.

他在准备他的功课了。**tā zài zhǔnbèi tāde gōngkè le**   (*le*-expository)
He is preparing/doing his homework. [this is something he ought to do]

车子在外面等着。 **chēzi zài wàimian děng zhe**   (descriptive)
The car is waiting outside.

车子在外面等着了。 **chēzi zài wàimian děng zhe le**   (*le*-expository)
The car is now waiting outside.
[it's just arrived and I think you ought to go)

21.6.4 EVALUATIVE SENTENCES

你应该感谢他。 **nǐ yīnggāi gǎnxiè tā**   (evaluative)
You should thank him.

你应该感谢他了。 **nǐ yīnggāi gǎnxiè tā le**   (*le*-expository)
You should now thank him.
[it might not have been necessary to do so before]

我能去。 **wǒ néng qù**   (evaluative)
I can go.

我能去了。 **wǒ néng qù le**   (*le*-expository)
I can go now. [I couldn't before]

我今天必须画完这幅画儿。   (evaluative)
wǒ jīntiān bìxū huà wán zhèi fú huàr
I must finish this painting today.

我今天必须画完这幅画儿了。
wǒ jīntiān bìxū huà wán zhèi fú huàr le   (*le*-expository)
Now I must finish this painting today. [I should have finished it already]

这朵花儿很香。 **zhèi duǒ huār hěn xiāng**   (evaluative)
This flower has a beautiful scent.

这朵花儿很香了。 **zhèi duǒ huār hěn xiāng le**   (*le*-expository)
This flower (now) has a beautiful scent.
[it didn't before; I did not expect it to be so fragrant]

Though 了 *le* can be added to any sentence to make it *le*-expository, there are cases where the result would require exceptional circumstances. However, no matter how infrequent or strange a situation might be on the face of it, a possible reading can always be found. For example:

他们在谈天了。 **tāmen zài tántiān le**
(lit. they *zai* chat *le*)
They are chatting now. [it was not the case a moment ago]

The implication can of course be retrieved only from the context: e.g. they were working very hard and had not had the time to sit down for a chat before, or they had quarrelled and now seem to be getting on better.

Stranger still might be an example like the following:

他在等人了。 **tā zài děng rén le**
He is now waiting for somebody. [it was not the case a while ago]

Possible interpretations of this might be that he had been busy doing something else and had forgotten he should be waiting for somebody or that it is usually the case that somebody else is waiting for *him* and now the situation is reversed, and so on.

Whatever the prior situation may be, it is only retrievable from the context. The prime syntactic function of 了 *le* in all *le*-expository sentences is to indicate a reversal: a declaration that what is the case now is not what it was before.

22 CONJUNCTIONS AND CONJUNCTIVES

Conjunctions in Chinese may be divided into two major types: those coupling words or phrases, and those linking clauses. Conjunctives, on the other hand, are a set of monosyllabic referential adverbs, which generally are found at the beginning or towards the beginning of the second (or main) clause of a sentence. They refer back to the preceding (or subordinate) clause, which may itself include a conjunction or, in a limited number of cases, another conjunctive.

Clauses in a sentence can also be brought together without any form of connective marker (conjunction or conjunctive). This happens when correlative or parallel constructions are employed, or where two clauses are set in apposition, where the meaning of the second clause is in some way consequential on that of the first.

In the following sections, we will discuss conjunctions which join words and phrases, conjunctions and conjunctives that link clauses, correlatives that introduce parallel structures, and clauses set in apposition to each other.

22.1 CONJUNCTIONS THAT LINK WORDS OR PHRASES

22.1.1 THE FOUR CONJUNCTIONS

There are four conjunctions that join nouns or nominal expressions. These conjunctions, which all mean 'and', may often be used interchangeably, the difference between them being one of style:

和 **hé**	[neutral]
跟 **gēn**	[northern colloquial]
同 **tóng**	[southern colloquia]
与 **yǔ**	[formal]

For example:

爸爸和妈妈　都出去了。 **bàba hé māma dōu chūqù le**
Mother and father have both gone out.

城市跟农村　我都住过。 **chéngshì gēn nóngcūn wǒ dōu zhùguo**
I have lived in towns and villages.

你同我都是南方人。 **nǐ tóng wǒ dōu shì nánfāng rén**
You and I are both Southerners.

白天与黑夜他都在工作。 **báitiān yǔ hēiyè tā dōu zài gōngzuò**
He works day and night.

If there are more than two nominal items, the conjunction comes between the last two, the rest being separated by *dun*-commas / 、/, which are enumerative commas. These *dun*-commas are unique to Chinese and are written in the reverse direction of a standard comma / , /:

哥哥、姐姐、妹妹和弟弟 **gēge | jiějie | mèimei hé dìdi**
Elder brother, elder sister, younger sister and younger brother.

物理、化学、数学和哲学 **wùlǐ | huàxué | shùxué hé zhéxué**
Physics, chemistry, maths and philosophy.

22.1.2 而 **ér** 'also'

This is often used to join two adjectives or adjectival expressions, which are either both affirmative or an affirmative followed by a negative. In the former case, the two adjectives must be of similar length, either both monosyllabic or both disyllabic. In the latter case, the affirmative adjective is always monosyllabic and the negative disyllabic with 不 **bù** 'not' as the first syllable, in a rhythmic, antithetical sequence:

这个人坚定而勇敢。 **zhèi ge rén jiāndìng ér yǒnggǎn**
This man is steadfast and brave.

他是个认真而严谨的科学家。 **tā shì ge rènzhēn ér yánjǐn de kēxuéjiā**
He is a serious and rigorous scientist.

这篇文章长而空。 **zhèi piān wénzhāng cháng ér kōng**
This essay is long and vacuous/devoid of content.

长而不空 **cháng ér bù kōng**
long but not vacuous

艳而不俗 **yàn ér bù sú**
gaudy but not vulgar

这个西瓜大而不甜。 **zhèi ge xīguā dà ér bù tián**
This watermelon is large but not sweet.

22.1.3 并 **bìng** 'also'

This can link two predicate verbs which are transitive and share the same object:

会上讨论并通过了这项提案。
huì shàng tǎolùn bìng tōngguòle zhèi xiàng tí'àn
The meeting discussed and passed this motion.

大家都同意并拥护我的提议。 **dàjiā dōu tóngyì bìng yōnghū wǒde tíyì**
Everyone agreed with and supported my proposal.

The lexical conjunctions cited above are the standard connectives for the three word categories of nouns, adjectives and verbs. However, as we shall see from the clausal conjunctions below, they have disyllabic variants: e.g. 以及 **yǐjí** 'also' for 和 **hé**, etc., 而且 **érqiě** 'but also' for 而 **ér**, and 并且 **bìngqiě** 'and also' for 并 **bìng**.

22.2 CLAUSAL CONJUNCTIONS AND CONJUNCTIVES

Clausal conjunctions in Chinese form a large closed set. They display the following distinctive features:

(**a**) some have monosyllabic and disyllabic variants depending on rhythmic requirements:

但是 **dànshì** 'but' > 但 **dàn** 'but'
虽然 **suīrán** 'though' > 虽 **suī** 'though'
如果 **rúguǒ** 'if' > 如 **rú** 'if'

(**b**) some occur in pairs, others individually or in pairs, and others with conjunctives:

不但 **bùdàn** 'not only' ... 而且 **érqiě** 'but also'   (a pair)
不过 **bùguò** 'but'   (individual)
(因为 **yīnwèi** 'because') ... 所以 **suǒyǐ** 'therefore' (individual/a pair)
只有 **zhǐyǒu** 'only' ... 才 **cái** 'then'   (with conjunctive)

(**c**) they may be positioned either before the subject/topic or before the predicate/comment depending on the scope of meaning they govern in the sentence:

他不但会说英文，而且会说中文。
tā bùdàn huì shuō yīngwén | érqiě huì shuō zhōngwén
He cannot only speak English, but he can speak Chinese too.

不但大人会说中文，而且连小孩也会说中文。

bùdàn dàrén huì shuō zhōngwén | érqiě lián xiǎohái yě huì shuō zhōngwén

Not only can the adults speak Chinese, but even the children can too.

Clausal conjunctives are monosyllabic referential adverbs. They are limited in number, with the most common being: 就 **jiù** 'then', 才 **cái** 'only then', 都 **dōu** 'both or all', 也 **yě** 'also' (or its classical counterpart 亦 **yì** 'also'), 还 **hái** 'as well', 却 **què** 'but', etc. They are used mainly in the second clause of a sentence:[1]

(a) to echo a conjunction in the first clause:

今天<u>虽然</u>出太阳，气温<u>却</u>很低。

jīntiān <u>suīrán</u> chū tàiyáng | qìwēn <u>què</u> hěn dī

<u>Although</u> the sun is out today, the temperature is (however) very low.

他<u>如果</u>喝醉了，我们<u>就</u>送他回家。

tā <u>rúguǒ</u> hē zuì le | wǒmen <u>jiù</u> sòng tā huíjiā

<u>If</u> he is drunk, we will (then) take him home.

(b) to enhance the second of a pair of conjunctions:

<u>要是</u>你不舒服，<u>那(么)就</u>别来了。

<u>yàoshi</u> nǐ bù shūfu | <u>nà(me) jiù</u> bié lái le

<u>If</u> you aren't well, <u>in that case</u> don't come (then).

他<u>不但</u>骂人，<u>而且还</u>打人呢。

tā <u>bùdàn</u> mà rén | <u>érqiě hái</u> dǎ rén ne

He <u>not only</u> swears at people, <u>but also</u> (<u>in addition</u>) hits them.

22.3 CLAUSAL CONJUNCTIONS AND CONJUNCTIVES IN SEMANTIC CATEGORIES

In each subset the meaning is more or less similar, but in style they can range from the formal to the colloquial.

22.3.1 GIVING REASONS: BECAUSE, BECAUSE OF, THEREFORE

(a) 因为 **yīnwèi** 'because' . . . 所以 **suǒyǐ** 'therefore' paired conjunctions in pre-subject/topic positions:

---

[1] See Chapter 17 on adverbials for a full list of these monosyllabic referential adverbs.

因为天气不好，所以比赛暂停。
yīnwèi tiānqì bù hǎo | suǒyǐ bǐsài zàntíng
<u>Because</u> the weather was bad, the match was (<u>therefore</u>) suspended.

(b) 因为 **yīnwèi**/因 **yīn** 'because', on its own as a first-clause conjunction with flexible positioning:[2]

因为有些事情没办完，我在广州多停留了四天。
yīnwèi yǒuxiē shìqing méi bàn wán | wǒ zài guǎngzhōu duō tíngliúle sì tiān
<u>Because</u> there was some unfinished business, I stayed on for four days in Guangzhou.

因年代久远，这件事已无法考查。
yīn niándài jiǔyuǎn | zhèi jiàn shì yǐ wúfǎ kǎochá
<u>Because</u> it was in the remote past, there is no way to check this matter.

我刚到广州的时候，因为不懂广州话，闹了不少笑话。
wǒ gāng dào guǎngzhōu de shíhou | yīnwèi bù dǒng guǎngzhōu huà | nàole bùshǎo xiàohua
When I first arrived in Guangzhou, <u>because</u> I did not understand Cantonese, I made a lot of funny mistakes.

(c) 由于 **yóuyú** 'because', first-clause conjunction in a pre-subject/topic position:

由于腿部受伤，他没参加比赛。
yóuyú tuǐbù shòushāng | tā méi cānjiā bǐsài
<u>Because</u> he had a leg injury, he did not play in the match.

(d) 因而 **yīn'ér** or 因此 **yīncǐ** 'therefore', second-clause conjunctions in a pre-subject/topic position:

天气不好，因而比赛暂停。 **tiānqì bù hǎo | yīn'ér bǐsài zàntíng**
The weather was bad, <u>so</u> the match was suspended.

他腿部受了伤，因此没参加比赛。
tā tuǐ bù shòule shāng | yīncǐ méi cānjiā bǐsài
He had a leg injury, <u>so</u> he did not play in the match.

---

[2] What is meant by 'flexible positioning' is that it may be used either in a pre-subject/topic position or in a pre-predicate/comment position, depending on the context.

她非常和气，<u>因而</u>大家都喜欢她。
tā fēicháng héqì | <u>yīn'ér</u> dàjiā dōu xǐhuan tā
She was extremely kind, <u>therefore</u> everyone liked her.

他们来得很晚，<u>因此</u>没有饭吃。
tāmen lái de hěn wǎn | <u>yīncǐ</u> méiyǒu fàn chī
They came very late, <u>and so</u> there was nothing to eat.

(e) 所以 **suǒyǐ** 'therefore', second-clause conjunction, with flexible positioning:

这条路我常走，<u>所以</u>很熟。
zhèi tiáo lù wǒ cháng zǒu | <u>suǒyǐ</u> hěn shú
I often go this way, <u>and so</u> (I) know it well.

我知道你口重，<u>所以</u>多放了点儿盐。
wǒ zhīdao nǐ kǒuzhòng | <u>suǒyǐ</u> duō fàng le diǎnr yán
I know you are fond of salty food, <u>and therefore</u> I have added a bit more salt.

22.3.2 MAKING INFERENCES: SINCE

既然 **jìrán** 'since' ... (那么 **nàme**) 就 **jiù** 'then', 'conjunction + (conjunction) conjunctive' pair. (The first-clause conjunction is flexible in positioning, but the second-clause conjunctive may only be used pre-verbally. 那么 **nàme** 'then' as the second conjunction is often omitted or abbreviated to 那 **nà**):

他<u>既然</u>认错了，你<u>就</u>原谅他吧。 **tā <u>jìrán</u> rèncuò le | nǐ <u>jiù</u> yuánliàng tā ba**
<u>Since</u> he's admitted his mistake, you (<u>then</u>) forgive him.

<u>既然</u>两(个)人的看法不一样，这项合作<u>就</u>只好作罢了。
<u>jìrán</u> liǎng (ge) rén de kànfǎ bù yīyàng | zhèi xiàng hézuò <u>jiù</u> zhǐhǎo zuòbà le
<u>Since</u> the two of them have different views, cooperation on this must (<u>then</u>) be abandoned.

<u>既然</u>她不理你，<u>那么</u>你<u>就</u>别理她吧。
<u>jìrán</u> tā bùlǐ nǐ | <u>nàme</u> nǐ <u>jiù</u> bié lǐ tā ba
<u>Since</u> she is ignoring you, (<u>in that case</u>) don't you (<u>then</u>) take any notice of her.

<u>既然</u>她不愿意，<u>那就</u>算了。 **<u>jìrán</u> tā bù yuànyi | <u>nà jiù</u> suàn le**
<u>Since</u> she is unwilling, (<u>in that case</u>) (<u>then</u>) forget about it.

22.3.3 EXPRESSING SUPPOSITION: IF

(a) 如(果) **rú(guǒ)** / 要(是) **yào(shi)** (colloquial) . . . (那么 **nàme**) 就 **jiù** 'then', a 'conjunction + (conjunction) conjunctive' pair, with the second conjunction optional. (The position of the first-clause conjunction is flexible while the second-clause conjunctive is always pre-verbal):

> 翻译<u>如果</u>不顾本国语的特点，<u>就</u>会使人看不懂。
> **fānyì <u>rúguǒ</u> bù gù běnguóyǔ de tèdiǎn | <u>jiù</u> huì shǐ rén kàn bù dǒng**
> (lit. translation if not consider native language *de* characteristics | then may cause people read not understand)
> <u>If</u> translation ignores the characteristics of the original language, (<u>then</u>) people may not understand.

> <u>如果</u>你认为这样办比较好，<u>那么</u>咱们<u>就</u>这么办吧。
> **<u>rúguǒ</u> nǐ rènwéi zhèyàng bàn bǐjiào hǎo | <u>nàme</u> zánmen <u>jiù</u> zhème bàn ba**
> <u>If</u> you think doing it this way is better, <u>in that case</u> /<u>then</u> let's do it this way.

> 我今晚没空，你<u>要是</u>想去，<u>那就</u>请便吧。
> **wǒ jīnwǎn méi kòng | nǐ <u>yàoshi</u> xiǎng qù | <u>nà jiù</u> qǐngbiàn ba**
> I am busy this evening, and <u>if</u> you want to go, <u>then</u> please yourself/ go ahead.

> <u>要</u>把这篇文章写好，<u>就</u>得多参考一些有关的资料。
> **<u>yào</u> bǎ zhèi piān wénzhāng xiě hǎo | <u>jiù</u> děi duō cānkǎo yīxiē yǒuguān de zīliào**
> <u>If</u> you want to write this essay well, <u>then</u> (you) will have to do a bit more consulting of relevant materials/data.

(b) 如(果) **rú(guǒ)**/要(是) **yào(shì)** (colloquial), individual first-clause conjunction, with flexible positioning:

> <u>如果</u>你一时手头不便，我可以先给你垫上。
> **<u>rúguǒ</u> nǐ yīshí shǒutóu bùbiàn | wǒ kěyǐ xiān gěi nǐ diànshang**
> <u>If</u> you are short of money for the moment, I can lend you some.

> 你<u>如</u>有困难，我可以帮助你。
> **nǐ <u>rú</u> yǒu kùnnan | wǒ kěyǐ bāngzhù nǐ**
> <u>If</u> you have a problem, I can help you.

你要是见到他，请你把这封信交给他。
nǐ yàoshi jiàn dào tā | qǐng nǐ bǎ zhèi fēng xìn jiāo gěi tā
If you see him, please give him this letter.

要是我忘了，请你提醒我。 **yàoshi wǒ wàng le | qǐng nǐ tíxǐng wǒ**
If I forget, please remind me.

The first-clause conjunction 如果 **rúguǒ** 'if' is generally replaceable by the following:

假如 **jiǎrú** 'supposing' (or its variants 假若 **jiǎruò**, 假使 **jiǎshǐ**)
假如明天不下雨，我一定去。 **jiǎrú míngtiān bù xià yǔ | wǒ yīdìng qù**
If it doesn't rain tomorrow, I'll definitely go.

倘若 **tǎngruò** 'in case'
他倘若不信，就让他亲自去看看。
tā tǎngruò bù xìn | jiù ràng tā qīnzì qù kànkan
In case he does not believe (it), (then) let him see for himself.

若是 **ruòshì** 'if'
我若是³你，我就绝不会答应他。 **wǒ ruòshì nǐ | wǒ jiù jué bùhuì dāying tā**
If I were you, (then) I certainly would not comply with his request.

万一 **wànyī** 'in the event of'
万一出问题，咱们怎么办? **wànyī chū wèntí | zánmen zénme bàn**
In the event of a problem arising, what are we to do?

A more rhetorical supposition which must be negative in meaning is encoded by (要)不是 **(yào)bushì** or 若非 **ruòfēi** 'if (it were) not (the case) that', or 莫非 **mòfēi** 'unless':

(要)不是你提醒我，我差点儿把这件事忘了。
(yào)bushì nǐ tíxǐng wǒ | wǒ chā diǎnr bǎ zhèi jiàn shì wàng le
If you had <u>not</u> reminded me, I could well have forgotten it/could have come close to forgetting.

若非意见分歧，合同早就签订了。
ruòfēi yìjian fēnqí | hétóng zǎo jiù qiāndìng le
If there were <u>not</u> a difference of opinion, (then) the agreement would have long since been signed.

---

³ Note that a conjunction like 若是 **ruòshì**, which has 是 **shì** as a constituent element, does not need to be followed by the verb 是 **shì** 'to be' in a sentence like this.

她原先答应来的，可是现在还没来，<u>莫非</u>她病了(不成)⁴。
tā yuánxiān dāying lái de | kěshì xiànzài hái méilai | <u>mòfēi</u> tā bìng le (bùchéng)
She originally agreed to come, but she still hasn't arrived, and <u>so</u> could she be ill.

22.3.4 STATING CONDITIONS: ONLY IF, ONLY WHEN

(**a**) 只要 **zhǐyào** 'only if, provided', a first-clause conjunction, with flexible positioning, which may or may not be linked with a conjunctive:

<u>只要</u>你努力，你一定能取得优良的成绩。
<u>zhǐyào</u> nǐ nǔlì | nǐ yīdìng néng qǔdé yōuliáng de chéngjì
<u>Only if</u> you put in an effort will you be sure of achieving a good result.

书旧点儿没关系，<u>只要</u>不缺页<u>就</u>行。⁵
shū jiù diǎnr méi guānxi | <u>zhǐyào</u> bù quē yè <u>jiù</u> xíng
It doesn't matter if the book is a bit old, <u>provided</u> no pages are missing (<u>then</u> it will be all right).

<u>只要</u>认真学，什么都能学会。
<u>zhǐyào</u> rènzhēn xué, shénme dōu néng xuéhuì
(You) can master anything, <u>provided</u> you study seriously.

<u>只要</u>肯动脑筋，中文的语法一点儿也不难。
<u>zhǐyào</u> kěn dòng nǎojīn | zhōngwén de yǔfǎ yīdiǎnr yě bù nán
Chinese grammar is not difficult at all, <u>provided</u> you put your mind to it/use your brains.

(**b**) 只有 **zhǐyǒu** 'only when, only if' ... 才 **cái** 'only then', a 'conjunction + conjunctive' pair, the first-clause conjunction being flexible in positioning while the second-clause conjunctive may only be pre-verbal:

<u>只有</u>乐观，你的病<u>才</u>能恢复得快。
<u>zhǐyǒu</u> lèguān | nǐde bìng <u>cái</u> néng huīfù de kuài
<u>Only</u> by being optimistic could you (<u>then</u>) be able to have a speedy recovery (from your illness).

---

⁴ Note that 莫非 **mòfēi** can colloquially have a shift of meaning to 'could (it) be (the case) that' or 'it must be (the case) that', and that, when used in this way, it is often paired with 不成 **bùchéng** 'it will not do' at the end of the sentence.

⁵ The second clause here in fact consists of two clauses: the first clause being 只要不缺页, and the second 就行.

只有保持冷静，你才能赢得最后的胜利。
zhǐyǒu bǎochí lěngjìng | nǐ cái néng yíng de zuìhòu de shènglì
<u>Only</u> by keeping calm will you (<u>then</u>) be able to win the final victory.

(c) 除非 **chúfēi** 'unless' . . . 不然 **bùrán**/否则 **fǒuzé** 'or, otherwise' . . . a conjuction + conjunction pair, with pre-subject positioning:

除非你保持冷静，不然你得不到最后的胜利。
chúfēi nǐ bǎochí lěngjìng | bùrán nǐ débudào zuìhòu de shènglì
<u>Unless</u> you keep calm <u>otherwise</u> you won't be able to win the final victory.

除非天气不好，否则我们下午去看他们。
chúfēi tiānqì bù hǎo | fǒuzé wǒmen xiàwǔ qù kàn tāmen
<u>Unless</u> the weather is bad, (<u>otherwise</u>) we will go to see them this afternoon.

22.3.5   OFFERING CONCESSIONS: THOUGH, ALTHOUGH, YET

虽然 **suīrán** or 虽 **suī** 'although', depending on required rhythm, as first-clause conjunction, with flexible positioning, followed by a second-clause conjunction like 但(是) **dàn(shì)** or 可(是) **kě(shì)** 'yet' or a conjunctive such as 却 **què** 'yet', 倒 **dào** 'nevertheless' or 可 **kě** 'despite all':

他虽然身体不好，但是很少请假。
tā suīrán shēntǐ bù hǎo | dànshì hěn shǎo qǐngjià
<u>Although</u> he wasn't well/strong, (<u>yet</u>) he rarely requested leave.

大家虽然很累，可是心情都很愉快。
dàjiā suīrán hěn lèi | kěshì xīnqíng dōu hěn yúkuài
<u>Although</u> everyone was tired, (<u>yet</u>) their mood was cheerful.

文章虽短，却很有力。 **wénzhāng suī duǎn | què hěn yǒulì**
<u>Although</u> the essay is short, (<u>yet</u>) it is very forceful.

商店虽然很小，货物倒很齐全。
shāngdiàn suīrán hěn xiǎo | huòwù dào hěn qíquán
<u>Although</u> the shop is small, (<u>nevertheless</u>) it is well-stocked.

这孩子年龄虽然不大，说话可十分老练。
zhèi háizi niánlíng suīrán bù dà | shuōhuà kě shífēn lǎoliàn
<u>Although</u> this child isn't old, (<u>yet</u>) (s)he speaks with a voice of experience.

虽然冬天已经到了，可是玫瑰花仍然开着。
suīrán dōngtiān yǐjīng dào le | kěshì méiguìhuā réngrán kāi zhe
<u>Although</u> winter has already arrived, (<u>yet</u>) the roses are still blooming.

The concession, as we can see from the above examples, is usually featured in the first clause and is often negative in nature. If the concession is more positive, i.e. making allowances instead of offering concessions, the conjunctive in the second clause will be 还(是) **hái(shi)** or 仍(然) **réng(rán)** 'still' or 也 **yě** 'nevertheless' to provide a (negative) contrast:

他的病虽然好了，身体还(是)很虚弱。
tāde bìng suīrán hǎo le | shēntǐ hái(shi) hěn xūruò
<u>Although</u> he is better, he is <u>still</u> very weak.

虽然道理已经讲清楚了，可是他仍然不听。
suīrán dàoli yǐjīng jiǎng qīngchu le | kěshì tā réngrán bù tīng
<u>Although</u> the reasons have been made clear, he <u>still</u> won't listen.

For more forceful expressions of concession 虽然 **suīrán** can be replaced by the following adverbial-like conjunctions:

诚然 chéngrán 'it is true that':
建议诚然很好，但时机还不成熟。
jiànyì chéngrán hěn hǎo | dàn shíjī hái bù chéngshú
<u>It's true that</u> it's a good suggestion/idea, <u>but</u> the time is <u>still</u> not ripe.

固然 gùrán 'admittedly':
你的办法固然有很多优点，可是缺点仍然不少。
nǐde bànfǎ gùrán yǒu hěnduō yōudiǎn | kěshì quēdiǎn réngrán bùshǎo
Your method <u>admittedly</u> has many good points, <u>but</u> it <u>still</u> has quite a few defects/weaknesses.

就是 jiùshì/就算 jiùsuàn 'even if':
就算他表面上已经同意，他心里仍然不服。
jiùsuàn tā biǎomiàn shàng yǐjīng tóngyì | tā xīn li réngrán bùfú
<u>Even if</u> he (already) outwardly agrees, he is <u>still</u> not convinced in his heart.

就是你已得到导师的支持，你还得听取校外考官的意见。
jiùshì nǐ yǐ dédào dǎoshī de zhīchí | nǐ hái děi tīngqǔ xiàowài kǎoguān de yìjiàn
<u>Even if</u> you've already got the support of your tutor, you <u>still</u> need to hear the views of the external examiner.

即使 **jíshǐ 'even if'**:

即使你做得很好，也不能骄傲自满。

jíshǐ nǐ zuò de hěn hǎo | yě bùnéng jiāo'ào zìmǎn

<u>Even if</u> you've done very well, you (<u>still</u>) can't be arrogant and smug.

哪怕 **nǎpà 'even if'**:

哪怕天再冷，他还是只穿着一件衬衫。

nǎpà tiān zài lěng | tā háishi zhǐ chuān zhe yī jiàn chènshān

<u>Even if</u> it is even colder, he'll <u>still</u> be wearing only a shirt.

22.3.6 DEFYING SETBACKS: NO MATTER

(a) 无论 **wúlùn** (formal), 不管 **bùguǎn** (colloquial), or 凭 **píng** 'no matter what', first-clause conjunction, with choice depending on style or rhythm, and 都 **dōu**, or 也 **yě** 'still', or 还是 **háishi** 'still', etc., as second-clause conjunctive:

不管天气怎么冷，他还是坚持洗冷水澡。

bùguǎn tiānqì zénme lěng | tā háishi jiānchí xǐ lěngshuǐzǎo

<u>No matter</u> how cold the weather is, he <u>still</u> insists on having a cold bath.

无论语法(的)问题多么复杂，我们都能解释。

wúlùn yǔfǎ (de) wèntí duóme fùzá | wǒmen dōu néng jiěshì

No matter how complicated the grammatical problems are, we can always explain them.

无论情况如何，请您打电话告知。

wúlùn qíngkuàng rúhé | qǐng nín dǎ diànhuà gàozhī

<u>No matter</u> how things are, please telephone to say.

凭你走得怎么快，我也/都赶得上。

píng nǐ zǒu de zénme kuài | wǒ yě/dōu gǎn de shàng

<u>No matter</u> how fast you go, I can <u>still</u> catch up.

(b) 反正 **fǎnzhèng** 'under whatever circumstances, anyway' may be used individually as either a first or second clause adverbial-like conjunction:

别着急，反正不是什么了不起的事儿。

bié zháojí | fǎnzhèng bùshì shénme liǎobuqǐ de shìr

Don't worry, it is not anything exceptional/special <u>anyway</u>.

反正今天没有什么要紧的事儿，咱们出去遛哒遛哒。
fǎnzhèng jīntiān méiyǒu shénme yàojǐn de shìr | zánmen chū qù liūda liūda
<u>Anyway</u>, there is nothing important on today, and we'll go out for a stroll.

22.3.7 CLARIFYING TIME: WHEN, AS SOON AS, AFTER, BEFORE, ETC.

(a) ... 时 **shí** or ... 的时候 **de shíhou** 'when ...' is in fact a noun (phrase) employed as a pseudo-conjunction to introduce a time phrase or clause. 当 **dāng** is sometimes placed at the beginning of such a time clause.[6] This usage, however, is dying out.

(当)太阳出来<u>的时候</u>，我<u>就</u>把衣服晾出去。
(dāng) tàiyáng chūlái de shíhou | wǒ jiù bǎ yīfu liàng chūqu
<u>When</u> the sun came out, I put the clothes out to dry.

(当)他进来<u>时</u>，我正在写信。
(dāng) tā jìnlái shí | wǒ zhèngzài xiě xìn
<u>When</u> he came in, I was just writing a letter.

行车<u>的时候</u>，请大家不要把手伸出窗外。[7]
xíng chē de shíhou | qǐng dàjiā bùyào bǎ shǒu shēnchū chuāngwài
<u>When</u> the train is moving, please would everyone not put your hands out of the window.

(b) ... 后 **hòu** or 以后 **yǐhòu** or 之后 **zhīhòu** 'after ...' and ... 前 **qián** or 以前 **yǐqián** or 之前 **zhīqián** 'before ...' are likewise used to introduce time phrases or clauses. These time phrases or clauses are echoed by the conjunctive 就 **jiù** 'then' in the second clause in declarative sentences:

病人吃药<u>后</u>，烧<u>就</u>退了。 **bìngrén chī yào hòu | shāo jiù tuì le**
<u>After</u> the patient took the medicine, the fever (<u>then</u>) subsided.

他回伦敦<u>以后</u>，<u>就</u>再也没有来过信。
tā huí lúndūn yǐhòu | jiù zài yě méiyǒu láiguo xìn
<u>After</u> he went back to London, he (<u>then</u>) never wrote again/he didn't send any more letters.

---

[6] 当 **dāng** can only be attached to a time clause, but not a time phrase: e.g. 当你回来时 **dāng nǐ huí lái shí** 'When you come back ...', but not *当回来时 **dāng huí lái shí** 'When coming back ...'.

[7] Note that a conjunctive is not needed in the second clause of an imperative or interrogative sentence.

下车<u>前</u>，请乘客检查自己的行李。
xià chē <u>qián</u> | qǐng chéngkè jiǎnchá zìjǐ de xíngli
<u>Before</u> getting off the bus/train, would passengers please check their (own) luggage.

开会<u>之前</u>，让我们为受难者默哀一分钟。
kāihuì <u>zhīqián</u> | ràng wǒmen wèi shòunànzhě mò'āi yī fēnzhōng
<u>Before</u> the meeting starts, let us have a moment's silence for the victims.

(c)   一 **yī** . . . 就 **jiù** . . . 'as soon as . . .' may be regarded as a pair of conjunctives placed respectively before the verb in the first and second clause:

我<u>一</u>说他<u>就</u>明白了。
wǒ <u>yī</u> shuō tā <u>jiù</u> míngbai le
<u>As soon as</u> I said it, he (<u>then</u>) understood.

秋天<u>一</u>到，树上的叶子<u>都</u>掉下来了。
qiūtiān <u>yī</u> dào | shù shàng de yèzi <u>dōu</u> diào xiàlai le
<u>As soon as</u> autumn arrived, the leaves on the trees (<u>all</u>) began to fall.

(d)   于是 **yúshì** 'thereupon, and so', 然后 **ránhòu** 'after that, then', 接着 **jiēzhe** 'following that', conjunctions positioned at the beginning of the second of a pair of clauses or sentences:

我们等了一会儿，他还没来。<u>于是</u>我们就离开了。
wǒmen děngle yīhuìr | tā hái méi lái | <u>yúshì</u> wǒmen jiù líkāi le
We waited a while, (but) he still didn't come, <u>and so</u> we (then) left.

他在银行自动提款机那儿取了款，<u>然后</u>(就)到酒巴间去喝酒了。
tā zài yínháng zìdòng tíkuǎnjī nàr qǔle kuǎn | <u>ránhòu</u> (jiù) dào jiǔbājiān qù hē jiǔ le
He withdrew some money from the automatic machine at the bank, and <u>after that</u> (<u>then</u>) went to drink in a bar.

她先搽点儿胭脂，涂上口唇膏，<u>接着</u>(便)戴上项链和戒指。
tā xiān chá diǎnr yānzhi | tú shàng kǒuchúngāo | <u>jiēzhe</u>(biàn) dài shàng xiàngliàn hé jièzhi
She first applied a bit of rouge and lipstick, and <u>following that</u> (<u>then</u>) put on a necklace and ring.

(e)   The verb 等 **děng** 'to wait for' often serves as a pseudo-conjunction in the first clause meaning 'wait until'. It is often echoed by the conjunctive, 再 **zài** 'then' or 才 **cái** 'only then', in the second clause:

等雨停了再走吧。 **děng yǔ tíng le zài zǒu ba**
Wait until the rain stops and then go.

咱们等下了班再详细谈吧。
zánmen děng xià le bān zài xiángxì tán ba
Let's wait until after office hours and then talk in detail.

他们等春天到了才把种子撒在地里。
tāmen děng chūntiān dàole cái bǎ zhǒngzi sà zài dì li
They waited until spring arrived before [lit. only then] they
scattered the seeds on the soil.

22.3.8   INDICATING PREFERENCE: WOULD RATHER

宁可 **nìngkě** or 宁愿 **nìngyuàn** 'would rather' pre-verb, first-clause conjunction
with 也不 **yě bù** as a pre-verb conjunctive in the second clause:

我宁可吃素，也不吃蜗牛。 **wǒ níngkě chīsù | yě bù chī wōniú**
I would rather be a vegetarian than eat snails.

If the negative is in the first clause, then the second may be either negative with
也不 **yě bù** or positive with 也 **yě** on its own:

我宁愿不睡觉，也要把这个报告写完。
wǒ níngyuàn bù shuìjiào | yě yào bǎ zhèi ge bàogào xiě wán
I would rather not sleep, than [lit. and want to] not finish writing this
report.

今天我宁可不喝酒，也不能酒后驾车。
jīntiān wǒ níngkě bù hē jiǔ | yě bùnéng jiǔhòu jià chē
I would rather not drink, than [lit. and be unable to] drive after drinking.

Preference may be expressed rather more objectively with the linked conjunctions 与其 **yǔqí** 'instead of' . . . and 倒不如 **dàobùrú** 'it's better' . . . :

与其出去看电影，倒不如在家看电视。
yǔqí chūqu kàn diànyǐng | dàobùrú zài jiā kàn diànshì
Instead of going out to see a film, it would be better to stay home and
watch television.

Finally, choice may also be conveyed by pairing the negative 不 **bù** 'not' with
the conjunction, 而 **ér** 'but':

他不开汽车而骑自行车上班。 **tā bù kāi qìchē ér qí zìxíngchē shàngbān**
He doesn't drive but cycles to work.

她<u>不用</u>筷子<u>而</u>用刀叉吃饭。 **tā <u>bù</u> yòng kuàizi <u>ér</u> yòng dāo chā chīfàn**
She doesn<u>'t</u> use chopsticks <u>but</u> a knife and fork to eat.

22.3.9 ELUCIDATING ONE'S PURPOSE: IN ORDER TO, SO AS TO, SO AS NOT TO

为了 **wèile** 'in order to' pre-verb first-clause conjunction, with a relatively serious or forceful tone:

<u>为了</u>锻炼身体，他买了一副哑铃。
<u>wèile</u> duànliàn shēntǐ | tā mǎile yī fù yǎlíng
<u>In order to</u> get fit, he bought a pair/set of dumbbells.

<u>为了</u>保护生态环境，他决定不开汽车，而骑自行车上班。
<u>wèile</u> bǎohù shēngtài huánjìng | tā juédìng bù kāi qìchē | ér qí zìxíngchē shàngbān
<u>In order to</u> protect the (ecological) environment, he decided not to drive but to cycle to work.

Unstressed purpose is expressed by one verb following another:[8]

妈妈到市场去买菜。 **māma dào shìchǎng qù mǎi cài**
Mother goes to the market to buy vegetables.

One does not normally say:

+<u>为了</u>买菜，妈妈到市场去了。+**<u>wèile</u> mǎi cài | māma dào shìchǎng qù le**

An alternative is 以便 **yǐbiàn** 'so as to', pre-verb conjunction in the second clause:

他来看我，<u>以便</u>了解我对这个问题的看法。
tā lái kàn wǒ | <u>yǐbiàn</u> liǎojiě wǒ duì zhèi ge wèntí de kànfǎ
He came to see me <u>so as to</u> understand my view of this question.

Negative purpose is expressed by 以免 **yǐmiǎn** or 免得 **miǎnde** 'so as to avoid', also a pre-verb conjunction in the second clause:

我们提前出发，<u>以免</u>迟到。 **wǒmen tíqián chūfā | <u>yǐmiǎn</u> chídào**
We set out beforehand/early, <u>to avoid</u> arriving late.

他把收音机的音量开得很小，<u>免得</u>干扰隔壁的邻居。
tā bǎ shōuyīnjī de yīnliàng kāi de hěn xiǎo | <u>miǎnde</u> gānrǎo gébì de línjū
He turned down the radio, <u>to avoid</u> disturbing the neighbours next door.

---

[8] See Chapter 14 on verb chains.

22.3.10 ENCODING MISCELLANEOUS RELATIONAL CONCEPTS: APART FROM, LET ALONE, OTHERWISE

除了 **chúle** 'apart from' . . . 以外 **yǐwài** or 之外 **zhīwài** 'to exclude', paired conjunctions in the first clause, surrounding a nominal, an adjectival or verbal expression or even a clause:

除了辣椒之外，什么蔬菜我都喜欢吃。
<u>chúle</u> làjiāo <u>zhīwài</u> | shénme shūcài wǒ dōu xǐhuan chī
<u>Apart from</u> chilli/hot pepper, I like any kind of vegetable.

这次旅行，除了天气不好之外，其他一切都很好。
zhèi cì lǚxíng | <u>chúle</u> tiānqì bù hǎo <u>zhīwài</u> | qítā yīqiè dōu hěn hǎo
On this trip, <u>apart from</u> the weather being bad, everything else was fine.

22.4 CORRELATIONS AND PARALLELS

In correlative or parallel constructions, the first clause and the second clause of a sentence share a lexical item, usually, but not necessarily, placed in the same position in each of the clauses. Sentences of this kind express coordination, continuation, progression, option, contrast, part–whole relationship, and so on.

谁弄坏，谁赔偿。 **shuí nòng huài | shuí péicháng**
(lit. who/anyone breaks, who/anyone pays) Breakages must be paid for.

谁犯规就罚谁。 **shuí fànguī jiù fá shuí**
(lit. who/anyone break rules, then punish who/anyone)
Anyone breaking the rules will be punished.

哪里有火灾，救火车就开到哪里去。
nǎli yǒu huǒzāi | jiùhuǒchē jiù kāi dào nǎli qù
(lit. wherever there is a fire, fire engine then drive to wherever)
Wherever there's a fire, the fire-engine will go.

从哪里拿来就放回到哪里去。 **cóng nǎli nálai jiù fànghuí nǎli qù**
(lit. from <u>wherever</u> take then put back to <u>wherever</u>)
Put (things) back where they came from.

说明书上怎么说，我就怎么装。
shuōmíngshū shàng zénme shuō | wǒ jiù zénme zhuāng
(lit. manual-on how say, I then how assemble)
I assemble it how the manual says.

他们一边喝酒，一边聊天。 **tāmen yībiān hējiǔ | yībiān liáotiān**
(lit. they one-side drink wine one-side chat) They chatted as they drank.

气球越升越高。 **qìqiú yuè shēng yuè gāo**
(lit. balloon the more rose the more high)
The balloon rose higher and higher.

天气越来越热。[9] **tiānqì yuèlái yuè rè**
(lit. weather the more become the more hot)
The weather grew hotter and hotter.

这种苹果又硬又酸。 **zhèi zhǒng píngguǒ yòu yìn yòu suān**
(lit. this kind apple also hard also sour)
This kind/variety of apple is both hard and sour.

或者这样，或者那样，总得有个结论。
huòzhě zhèyàng | huòzhě nèiyàng | zǒngděi yǒu ge jiélùn
(lit. either this mw:way, or that mw:way, must have (**a**) mw conclusion)
Whether this way or that, there must be a conclusion.

要么去，要么不去，你得拿定主意。
yàome qù | yàome bù qù | nǐ děi nádìng zhǔyi
(lit. either go, or not go, you must make up your mind)
You must make up your mind whether you are going or not.

她不是唱歌，就是跳舞，一刻也不停。
tā bùshì chànggē | jiùshì tiàowǔ | yīkè yě bù tíng
(lit. she is not sing, then is dance, one moment even not stop)
She was either singing or dancing without a moment's stop.

有的学生学得好，有的学生学得不好，程度参差不齐。
**yǒude xuésheng xué de hǎo | yǒude xuésheng xué de bù hǎo | chéngdù
cēncī bù qí**
(lit. some students study *de* well, some students study *de* not well, standard
uneven)
Some students studied well and others didn't, and the standard was uneven.

22.5 ZERO CONNECTIVES

Clauses in Chinese also come together without any explicit connective marker
(conjunction or conjunctive) to link them. This happens when the two clauses
are set in apposition to each other and the meaning of the second clause is in
some way sequential on the meaning of the first. These meanings cover the
whole range of those listed in §22.3 for conjunctions and conjunctives:

---

[9] In 越 **yuè** . . . 越 **yuè** 'the more . . . the more' parallel construction, if a meaningful verb is lacking
after the first 越 **yuè**, the gap is filled by the dummy verb 来 **lái** 'become'.

十几年没见了，她还是那么年轻。
shí jǐ nián méi jiàn *le* | **tā háishi nàme niánqīng** (concession)
(lit. ten and more years not see *le*, she still like that young)
Though (I) have not seen (her) for ten or more years, she is still the same as she was.

时间不早了，咱们走吧。 **shíjiān bù zǎo le** | **zánmen zǒu ba** (cause)
(lit. time not early *le*, we go *ba*) As time is getting on, let's go.

你稍等一会儿，我马上就来。
nǐ shāo děng yīhuìr | **wǒ mǎshang jiù lái** (condition)
(lit. you a little wait a moment, I immediately then come)
If you will wait a moment, I will be with you shortly.

他刚想出去，忽然下起大雪来了。
tā gāng xiǎng chūqù | **hūrán xià qǐ dà xuě lai le** (time)
(lit. he just think out-go, suddenly fall begin heavy snow come *le*)
When he was just thinking of going out it suddenly began to snow heavily.

Many formalised or proverbial sayings adopt zero-connective constructions:

欲知后事如何，且听下回分解。
yù zhī hòushì rúhé | **qiě tīng xiàhuí fēnjiě** (supposition)
(lit. want know afterwards matters like what, then listen next chapter recounting)
If you want to know what happens next, listen to the next chapter.
[a storyteller's expression]

前人种树，后人乘凉。 **qiánrén zhòng shù** | **hòurén chéng liáng** (cause)
(lit. previous people plant trees, latter people take advantage of cool)
Because earlier people planted trees, those who came later could enjoy the cool.

不打不相识。 **bù dǎ bù xiāngshí** (cause)
(lit. not fight not mutually know) No discord, no concord.

人不可貌相，海水不可斗量。
rén bùkě mào xiàng | **hǎishuǐ bùkě dǒu liáng** (comparison)
(lit. people not able judge from appearance, sea water not able measure with a cup in bushels)
People can't be judged from appearances as the sea can't be measured in bushels.
(Still waters run deep/great minds can't be fathomed.)

说到曹操，曹操就到。 **shuō dào cáocāo** | **cáocāo jiù dào** (coincidence)
(lit. talk about **Cao Cao**, **Cao Cao** then comes) Talk of the devil.

23 INTERROGATIVE SENTENCES

There are various ways of asking questions in Chinese, but a common feature of all of them is that there is no inversion of word order, which remains the same as in corresponding statements. To formulate a question, you can add an interrogative particle at the end of a statement, introduce a question word at the point in the sentence where the answer would come, or pose alternatives, in particular in the form of an affirmative–negative verb.

In the following sections we shall discuss in detail the various types of questions.

23.1 YES–NO QUESTIONS

Yes–no questions are based on some form of assumption on the part of the questioner, who is generally expecting a yes–no answer. They are formulated by adding the question particle 吗 *ma* at the end of a statement. For example:

statement: 这辆是开往上海的火车。
zhèi liàng shì kāiwǎng shànghǎi de huǒchē
(lit. this mw is bound for Shanghai *de* train)
This is the train to Shanghai.

question: 这辆是开往上海的火车吗?
zhèi liàng shì kāiwǎng shànghǎi de huǒchē ma
Is this the train to Shanghai?

statement: 她买了两张火车票。 **tā mǎi le liǎng zhāng huǒchēpiào**
She bought two railway tickets.

question: 她买了两张火车票吗? **tā mǎi le liǎng zhāng huǒchēpiào ma**
Did she buy two railway tickets?

If the focus of a yes–no question is on the predicate, the answer is usually expressed by repeating the verb or adjective in the affirmative or negative. Where a modal verb is present, the response repeats the modal verb rather than the main verb. Here are some examples:

question	answer		
你是英国人吗? **nǐ shì yīngguó rén ma** Are you English?	是 **shì** Yes.	or	不是 **bù shì** No.
你有证明吗? **nǐ yǒu zhèngmíng ma** Have you got any proof/identity?	有 **yǒu** Yes, I have.	or	没有 **méiyǒu** No, I haven't.
你吃了早饭了吗? **nǐ chī le zǎofàn le ma** Have you had your breakfast?	吃了 **chī le** Yes, I have.	or	还没(有) **hái méi(yǒu)** Not yet.
你去过中国吗? **nǐ qù guo zhōngguó ma** Have you ever been to China?	去过 **qù guo** Yes, I have.	or	没(有)去过 **méi(yǒu) qù guo** No, I haven't.
你累吗? **nǐ lèi ma** Are you tired?	累(呀) **lèi (ya)** Yes, I am.	or	不累 **bù lèi** Not, I am not.
她送你的领带漂亮吗? **tā sòng nǐ de lǐngdài piàoliang ma** Is the tie she gave you attractive?	很[1]漂亮 **hěn piàoliang** Yes, it is.	or	不漂亮 **bù piàoliang** No, it isn't.
我可以进来吗? **wǒ kěyǐ jìnlai ma** May I come in?	可以 **kěyǐ** Yes. (lit. may)	or	不可以 **bù kěyǐ** No. (lit. not may)

If the focus of such a question is shifted to anything other than the predicate, e.g. the subject, object, adverbial or complement in the sentence, the reply is likely to be 是(的) **shì (de)** 'Yes, it is' or 不(是) **bù (shì)** 'No, it isn't'.

你<u>姐姐</u>也来吗? **nǐ jiějie yě lái ma** Is your sister coming too?	是的。 **shì de** Yes, she is.	or	不是。 **bù shì** No, she isn't.
他<u>明天</u>上北京去吗? **tā míngtiān shàng běijīng qù ma** Is he going to Beijing tomorrow?	是的 **shì de** Yes, he is.	or	不是。 **bù shì** No, he isn't.
你同意<u>我的</u>意见吗? **nǐ tóngyì wǒde yìjian ma** Do you agree with my opinon?	是的。 **shì de** Yes	or	不是。 **bù shì** No

---

[1] Normally a degree adverb is built into the affirmative answer to take away implication of contrast.

question	answer		
这儿冬天很冷吗？	是的。	or	不是。
zhèr dōngtiān hěn lěng ma	**shì de**		**bù shì**
Is it very cold here in winter?	Yes		No
你天天都锻炼身体吗？	是的。	or	不是。
nǐ tiāntiān dōu duànliàn shēntǐ ma	**shì de**		**bù shì**
Do you do physical exercises every day?	Yes		No
你去见你的导师吗？	是的。	or	不是。
nǐ qù jiàn nǐde dǎoshī ma	**shì de**		**bù shì**
Are you going to see your supervisor?	Yes		No
他喝醉了吗？	是的。	or	不是。
tā hē zuì le ma	**shì de**		**bù shì**
Is he drunk?	Yes		No

23.2 SURMISE QUESTIONS

If the question has the particle 吧[2] **ba** rather than 吗 **ma**, it embodies a presumption rather than an assumption, and it conveys a surmise with the speaker presuming that what is stated in the question must or must not be the case.

你是李教授吧？ **nǐ shì lǐ jiàoshòu ba**
You must be Professor Li?

你不是李教授吧？ **nǐ bùshì lǐ jiàoshòu ba**
You aren't Professor Li, are you?

Here are some more examples:

他大概不来了吧？ **tā dàgài bù lái le ba**
He probably isn't coming, is he?

你是吃素的吧？ **nǐ shì chīsù de ba**
You are a vegetarian, aren't you?

这是你新买的吧？ **zhè shì nì xīn mǎi de ba**
You have just bought this, haven't you?

这个消息靠得住吧？ **zhèi ge xiāoxi kào de zhù ba**
This news is reliable, isn't it?

---

[2] For the use of 吧 **ba** in imperatives, see Chapter 24.

A negative question with 吗 *ma* in fact also expresses a degree of positive surmise:[3]

你不是李教授吗？ **nǐ bùshì lǐ jiàoshòu ma**
Aren't you Professor Li?

你下星期不来吗？ **nǐ xià xīngqī bù lái ma**
Aren't you coming next week?

23.3   SUGGESTIONS IN THE FORM OF QUESTIONS

Suggestions are often couched in the form of questions. The usual formulation is for a statement of intent to be followed by a question such as 好吗 **hǎo ma**, 行不行[4] **xíng bù xíng** and 怎么样 **zénmeyàng**.

咱们一起去看电影，好吗？ **zánmen yīqǐ qù kàn diànyǐng | hǎo ma**
(lit. we together go see film, all right *ma*) Let's go and see a film together.

你帮一下我的忙，行不行？ **nǐ bāng yīxià wǒde máng | xíng bù xíng**
(lit. you help one mw:time my busy, will do or not)
Can you give me some help?

咱们今晚去喝杯啤酒，怎么样？
zánmen jīnwǎn qù hē bēi píjiǔ | zénmeyàng
(lit. we this evening go drink (one) mw:glass beer, how about that)
Let's go and have a beer tonight./How about going to have a beer tonight?

23.4   ALTERNATIVE QUESTIONS

Alternative questions pose two alternative possibilities expressed in the same format with the pivotal interrogative 还是 **háishi** '. . . or . . .' between them:

question	answer
你要红茶还是要绿茶？	我要红茶。
nǐ yào hóngchá háishi yào lǜchá	**wǒ yào hóngchá**
Do you want black tea or green tea?	I want black tea.

你想喝红茶还是想喝绿茶？ **nǐ xiǎng hē hóngchá háishi xiǎng hē lǜchá**
Would you like (to drink) black tea or green tea?

咱们坐汽车去还是坐火车去？ **zánmen zuò qìchē qù háishi zuò huǒchē qù**
Shall we go by car or by train?

---

[3] See §23.8 on rhetorical questions.
[4] On affirmative–negative expressions like 好不好 **hǎo bù hǎo** 'OK?', 行不行 **xíng bù xíng** 'Will that do?', and so on, see §23.5 below.

他今天走还是明天走？　**tā jīntiān zǒu háishi míngtiān zǒu**
Is he going/leaving today or tomorrow?

今年圣诞节是星期四还是星期五？ [5]
jīnnián shèngdànjié shì xīngqī sì háishi xīngqī wǔ
Is Christmas this year on Thursday or Friday?

他给钱还是我们给钱？　**tā gěi qián háishi wǒmen gěi qián**
Is he paying or are we?

Answers to affirmative–negative questions are usually given in full with the verb as the first example shows.

23.5　AFFIRMATIVE–NEGATIVE QUESTIONS

General enquiries are also expressed by affirmative–negative questions, which suggest a yes or no alternative to the listener by using the affirmative and negative form of the verbal phrase in an alternating sequence:

question	answer			
你去不去看球赛？	去。 **qù**	or	不去。 **bù qu**	
nǐ qù bù qù kàn qiúsài				
(lit. you go not go see game)	Yes, I am.		No, I am not.	
Are you going to the game?				

你吃不吃羊肉？　**nǐ chī bù chī yángròu**
(lit. you eat not eat lamb) Do you eat lamb?

我们打球，你来不来？　**wǒmen dǎ qiú | nǐ lái bù lái**
(lit. we hit ball, you come not come)
We are going for a game, are you coming?

这个问题你清楚不清楚？　**zhèi ge wèntí nǐ qīngchu bù qīngchu**
(lit. this mw question you clear not clear)
Are you clear about this question?

我有个办法，你们大家看行不行？
wǒ yǒu ge bànfǎ | nǐmen dàjiā kàn xíng bù xíng
(lit. I have mw way, you everybody see work not work)
I have a plan. Do you all think it will work?

---

[5] If the verb used in an alternative question is 是 **shì**, it does not need to be repeated in the alternative part. For example, one does not say: *今年圣诞节是星期四还是是星期五？　*jīnnián shèngdànjié shì xīngqī sì háishi shì xīngqī wǔ**.

你冷不冷？ **nǐ lěng bù lěng**
(lit. you cold not cold) Are you cold?

这双球鞋是不是你的？ **zhèi shuāng qiúxié shì bù shì nǐde**
(lit. this pair ball-shoes is not is yours)
Is this pair of trainers/sneakers yours?

你身上有没有零钱？ **nǐ shēnshang yǒu méiyǒu língqián**
(lit. your body-on have not have change)
Do you have any change on you?

If there is a modal verb before the main verb, it is the modal verb that takes the affirmative and negative form:

你想不想去看球赛？ **nǐ xiǎng bù xiǎng qù kàn qiúsài**
(lit. you like not like go see game) Would you like to go to the game?

你会不会滑冰？ **nǐ huì bù huì huábīng**
(lit. you can not can skate ice) Can you skate?

If the verb or modal verb used in the question is disyllabic, the second syllable of the affirmative verb may be omitted:

你打不打算在这儿待下去？ **nǐ dǎ bù dǎsuan zài zhèr dāi xiàqu**
Do you intend to stay here?

instead of:

你打算不打算在这儿待下去？ **nǐ dǎsuan bù dǎshuan zài zhèr dāi xiàqu**

你喜不喜欢看电视剧？ **nǐ xǐ bù xǐhuan kàn diànshìjù**
Do you like (watching) television plays?

instead of:

你喜欢不喜欢看电视剧？ **nǐ xǐhuan bù xǐhuan kàn diànshìjù**

Answers to affirmative–negative questions are simply repetitions of the verb in the positive or negative, similar to those given to yes–no questions (see §23.1 above).

23.6 QUESTION-WORD QUESTIONS

The common question words in Chinese are:

who/ whom	what	which	how/by what means	when	where	why	how (+ adj.)	how many	how long (of time)
谁 shéi/ shuí	什么 shénme	哪 + mw něi	怎么 zénme 怎样 zényàng 怎么样 zénmeyàng	什么时候 shénme shíhou 几时 jǐshí	哪儿/ nǎr/ 哪里 nǎli 什么地方 shénme dìfang	为什么 wèi shénme 干吗 gàn má	多 duō	多少 + mw duōshǎo 几 + mw jǐ	多少时间 duōshǎo shíjiān 多长时间 duōcháng shíjiān 多久 duōjiǔ

The question word is normally placed in the sentence at the point where the required information would be provided in the corresponding statement, and there is no change of word order. Take a statement like the following:

小张昨天在商场买了两件衬衫。
xiǎozhāng zuótiān zài shāngchǎng mǎile liǎng jiàn chènshān
Little Zhang yesterday bought two shirts in the market.

A number of questions can be constructed on the basis of this sentence.

谁昨天在商场买了两件衬衫?
shuí zuótiān zài shāngchǎng mǎile liǎng jiàn chènshān
Who bought two shirts yesterday in the market?

小张什么时候在商场买了两件衬衫?
xiǎozhāng shénme shíhou zài shāngchǎng mǎile liǎng jiàn chènshān
When did Little Zhang buy two shirts in the market?

小张昨天在哪儿买了两件衬衫?
xiǎozhāng zuótiān zài nǎr mǎile liǎng jiàn chènshān
Where did Little Zhang buy two shirts yesterday?

小张昨天在商场做什么?   **xiǎozhāng zuótiān zài shāngchǎng zuò shénme**
What did Little Zhang do yesterday in the market?

小张昨天在商场买了几件衬衫?
xiǎozhāng zuótiān zài shāngchǎng mǎile jǐ jiàn chènshān
How many shirts did Little Zhang buy yesterday in the market?

小张昨天在商场买了两件什么?
xiǎozhāng zuótiān zài shāngchǎng mǎile liǎng jiàn shénme
What two things did Little Zhang buy yesterday in the market?

It is clear from these examples that, while the English word order of the translation is adjusted in each case, the Chinese sentence retains the same format with the question word inserted at the appropriate point.

The only exceptions to this are 为什么 **wèi shénme** and 干吗 **gàn má** 'why', which are placed anywhere in front of the verb, depending on emphasis.

为什么小张昨天在商场买了两件衬衫?
wèi shénme xiǎozhāng zuótiān zài shāngchǎng mǎile liǎng jiàn chènshān
Why did <u>Little Zhang</u> buy two shirts yesterday in the market?

小张为什么昨天在商场买了两件衬衫?
xiǎozhāng wèi shénme zuótiān zài shāngchǎng mǎile liǎng jiàn chènshān
Why did Little Zhang buy two shirts <u>yesterday</u> in the market?

小张昨天为什么在商场买了两件衬衫?
xiǎozhāng zuótiān wèi shénme zài shāngchǎng mǎile liǎng jiàn chènshān
Why did Little Zhang buy two shirts yesterday <u>in the market</u>?

小张昨天在商场为什么买了两件衬衫?
xiǎozhāng zuótiān zài shāngchǎng wèi shénme mǎile liǎng jiàn chènshān
Why <u>did</u> Little Zhang buy two shirts yesterday in the market?

Some general examples of question-word questions:

你是谁? **nǐ shì shuí**
Who are you?

你的导师是谁? **nǐde dǎoshī shì shuí**
Who is your supervisor/tutor?

谁是你的导师? **shuí shì nǐde dǎoshī**
Who is your supervisor/tutor?

你打算跟谁一起去? **nǐ dǎsuan gēn shuí yīqǐ qù**
Who do you intend to go with?

你姓什么? **nǐ xìng shénme**
What is your (sur)name?

你去哪国旅行? **nǐ qù nǎ/něi guó lǚxíng**
Which country are you going to on your travels?

哪个是你的? **nǎ/něi ge shì nǐde**
Which one is yours?

你准备怎么去? **nǐ zhǔnbèi zénme qù**
How do you plan to go?

那儿的气候怎么样? **nàr de qìhòu zěnmeyàng**
What is the weather like there?

你几时上班? **nǐ jǐshí shàngbān**
When do you go to work?

今年什么时候开学? **jīnnián shénme shíhou kāixué**
When does school start this year'?

下星期几举行毕业典礼? **xià xīngqī jǐ jǔxíng bìyè diǎnlǐ**
What day next week is the graduation ceremony being held?

这个图书馆有多少书? **zhèi ge túshūguǎn yǒu duōshao shū**
How many books does this library have?

你去哪儿? **nǐ qù nǎr**
Where are you going?

你是什么地方(的)人? **nǐ shì shénme dìfang (de) rén**
Where are you from?

你为什么不去参加舞会? **nǐ wèi shénme bù qù cānjiā wǔhuì**
Why didn't you go to the party?

埃菲尔铁塔有多高? **āifēi'ěr tiětǎ yǒu duō gāo**
How high is the Eiffel Tower?

你准备在那儿待多久? **nǐ zhǔnbèi zài nàr dāi duōjiǔ**
How long do you plan to stay there?

If the particle 呢 *ne* is added to the end of these question-word questions, the enquiry tends to become more of a query as though the questioner may need to be convinced.

你准备怎么去呢? **nǐ zhǔnbèi zénme qù ne**
How are you planning to go then?

你准备在那儿待多少时间呢? **nǐ zhǔnbèi zài nàr dāi duōshǎo shíjiān ne**
So how long are you planning to stay there?

你打算跟谁一起去呢？ **nǐ dǎsuan gēn shuí yīqǐ qù ne**
Who do you intend to go with then?

那儿的气候怎么样呢？ **nàr de qìhòu zénmeyàng ne**
So what is the weather like there?

23.7 FOLLOW-UP QUERIES WITH 呢 *ne*

Questions like 'and how about . . .', 'and what about . . .', etc., which are asked
in a given situation or context, are expressed by simply placing the particle 呢
ne after the object, person, etc., that is of concern. For example:

(她喝咖啡。 **tā hē kāfēi**) 你呢？ **nǐ ne**
(She's having coffee.) What about you?

(明天不行。 **míngtiān bù xíng**) 后天呢？ **hòutiān ne**
(Tomorrow's no good.) How about day after tomorrow?

(大家都来了。 **dàjiā dōu lái le**) 李先生呢？ **lǐ xiānsheng ne**
(Everyone has come.) What about Mr Li?

(我同意。 **wǒ tóngyì**) 你的朋友呢？ **nǐde péngyou ne**
(I agree.) What about your friend?

(开门吧。 **kāi mén ba**) 钥匙呢？ **yàoshi ne**
(Open the door!) Where's the key?

(真奇怪。 **zhēn qíguài**) 我的大衣呢？ **wǒde dàyī ne**
(This is really strange!) Where is my overcoat?

23.8 RHETORICAL QUESTIONS

Rhetorical questions with their challenge to the hearer to disagree are often
marked in Chinese by the presence of the sentence adverb 难道 **nándào** 'is it
possible to say',[6] which is used in conjunction with the end-of-sentence interrogative particle, 吗 *ma*.

这件事儿难道你不知道吗？ **zhèi jiàn shìr nándào nǐ bù zhīdao ma**
Do you mean you don't know about this?

---

[6] Being an adverb, 难道 **nándào** may be placed anywhere before the verb. For example:

这件事儿难道你不知道吗？ **zhèi jiàn shìr nándào nǐ bù zhīdao ma**
难道这件事儿你不知道吗？ **nándào zhèi jiàn shìr nǐ bù zhīdao ma**
这件事儿你难道不知道吗？ **zhèi jiàn shìr nǐ nándào bù zhīdao ma**

那么重要的事儿难道你忘了吗？
nèime zhòngyào de shìr nándào nǐ wàngle ma
Do you mean to say you have forgotten about something so important?

妈妈难道还不懂得孩子的脾气吗？
māma nándào hái bù dǒngde háizi de píqì ma
Does mother still not understand a child's temper?

难道世界上真有这样的事儿吗？
nándào shìjiè shàng yǒu zhèyàng de shìr ma
Can there really be something like this in the world?

难道天上真的有上帝吗？　**nándào tiānshang zhēn de yǒu shàngdì ma**
Is there really a god in heaven?

In fact, all questions couched in the negative have a rhetorical effect:

你不怕她生气吗？　**nǐ bù pà tā shēngqì ma**
Aren't you afraid she'll get angry?

他不会不守信用吧？　**tā bùhuì bù shǒu xìnyòng ba**
She is bound to keep her promise, isn't she?

这样说岂非自相矛盾？　**zhèyàng shuō qǐfēi zì xiāng máodùn**
Isn't it self-contradictory to say this?

23.9　EXCLAMATORY QUESTIONS

Exclamatory questions, expressing surprise, doubt, insistence, etc., generally have a particle like 啊 **ā**, 呀 **yā**, 啦 **lā**, etc.[7] at the end of the sentence and they often include an adverb like 究竟 **jiūjìng**, 到底 **dàodǐ** 'after all'.

这是怎么回事啊？　**zhè shì zénme huí shì ā**
What's going on?

你究竟吃不吃呀？　**nǐ jiūjìng chī bù chī yā**
Are you going to eat (it) (after all) or not?

你干吗不早说呀？　**nǐ gàn má bù zǎo shuō yā**
Why on earth didn't you say earlier?

---

[7] The particles in these questions like those in exclamations have phonetic and graphemic variants depending on the preceding vowel or consonant (see Chapter 24).

他是不是回去啦？　**tā shì bùshì huíqu lā**
Is it true that he's gone back home?

到底是哪一天哪？　**dàodǐ shì něi yī tiān na**
What day is it then?

24 IMPERATIVES AND EXCLAMATIONS

Similar to questions, imperatives and exclamations in Chinese are also very much based on notional corresponding statements for their word order. For an imperative, the obvious major difference is the regular addition of a 'request' or 'hope' expression at the beginning and a different set of particles at the end. For example:

(a) A 'request' word at the beginning:

> 请坐！ **qǐng zuò**
> Please sit.

(b) A particle at the end:

> 坐下吧！ **zuòxia ba**
> Sit down.

(c) A 'request' word at the beginning as well as a particle at the end:

> 请坐下吧！ **qǐng zuòxia ba**
> Please sit down.

An exclamation is likely to have an interjection at the beginning and a particle at the end of the sentence:

啊！真好哇！ **ā | zhēnhǎo wa**
Hey, it's really good.

Both imperatives and exclamations belong to the realm of topic–comment constructions: the former, where it is present, making explicit the speaker's authoritative attitude to the situation in hand, and the latter, the speaker's emotional response. The employment of end-of-sentence particles, as on all other occasions reveals the committed and emotional nature of what is being said.

In the following sections, we will discuss the various types of imperatives and exclamations.

24.1 VERBS IN IMPERATIVES RESTRICTED TO VOLUNTARY ACTIONS

Not every verb in the language can be used in imperatives, only verbs express-ing voluntary actions which are controllable. In other words, they are requests for action that is achievable or possible. For example:

请把窗户打开！ **qǐng bǎ chuānghu dǎkāi**
Please open the window.

别锁门！ **bié suǒ mén**
Don't lock the door.

*请晕倒！ **qǐng yūn dǎo**
*Please faint!

24.2 IMPERATIVES: BEGINNERS AND END-PARTICLES

Imperatives are generally face-to-face interlocutions, and the person addressed is usually left out. For example:

请喝茶！ **qǐng hē chá**
Please have some tea.

不要打搅他！ **bùyào dǎjiǎo tā**
Don't disturb him!

请别¹说话！ **qǐng bié shuōhuà**
Please shut up.

The addressee must obviously be identified, if there is more than one person present, or ambiguity might arise:

请您回答这个问题！ **qǐng nín huídá zhèi ge wèntí**
Please would you answer the question!

你过来！ **nǐ guòlai**
You come over here.

If a request is made to everybody present, the expression used is 大家 **dàjiā** or 各位 **gèwèi**:

请大家保持安静！ **qǐng dàjiā bǎochí ānjìng**
Would everyone please keep quiet.

---

¹ 别 **bié** 'don't' is the monosyllabic fusion of the original disyllabic expression 不要 **bùyào** 'don't'.

请各位不要离开自己的座位！ **qǐng gèwèi bùyào líkāi zìjǐ de zuòwèi**
Please would you all not leave your seats.

Opening 'request' words like 请 **qǐng** 'please', 别 **bié** 'don't', etc., are usually included if the instruction is initiated by the speaker. If it is a response to a move or request initiated by the addressee, the end-of-sentence particle 吧 **ba** is used:

进来吧！ **jìnlai ba**
Come in!

你先走吧！ **nǐ xiān zǒu ba**
You go ahead!

好吧！ **hǎo ba**
All right.

甭 **béng** 'don't', which is a phonetic fusion of the disyllabic 不用 **bùyòng** 'there's no need to' corresponds to 别 **bié** 'don't':

你甭管！ **nǐ béng guǎn**
(lit. you no-need look-after) Mind your own business!

这件事，你甭操心！ **zhèi jiàn shì | nǐ béng cāoxīn**
(lit. this mw matter, you no-need worry-about) Don't worry about this!

Such imperatives, being responses to the actions and attitudes of others, will usually have to include the addressee, and 甭 **béng** 'there's no need to' would therefore not normally be used on its own:

*甭担心！ *****béng dānxīn**
*Don't worry!

A further point on 吧 **ba** is that, as well as giving consent, it is also commonly used to make suggestions:

咱们走吧！ **zánmen zǒu ba**
Let's go.

让我来跟你做个伴儿吧。 **ràng wǒ lái gēn nǐ zuò ge bànr ba**
Let me be your companion.

我替你满上这杯吧。 **wǒ tì nǐ mǎn shàng zhèi bēi ba**
Let me fill your glass./Let me fill this glass for you.

In addition to 吧 **ba** with its meaning of consent or suggestion, there are three other end-of-imperative particles: 啊 **ā** (and its phonetic variants), which conveys eagerness or impatience for an action to be carried out, or a general state of urgency; 着 *zhe*, which urges the addressee to persist in a state he or she is already in or about to get into; and 了 *le*, which presses for the cessation or change of activity. Here are some detailed examples

(a) 啊 **ā** (and its variants 呀 **ya**, 哪 **na**, 啦 **la**, 嘞 **lēi**, 喽 **lōu**, etc. which all link phonetically with the previous syllable)[2] express urgency on the part of the speaker:

救命啊！ **jiùmìng ā**
Help!/Save me!

来人哪！ **lái rén na**
(lit. come someone) Come and help!

别说啦！ **bié shuō la**
Don't say anything any more!

快来呀！ **kuài lái ya**
(lit. quick come) Hurry!

走嘞！ **zǒu lēi**
Let's go!

大家都坐好喽！ **dàjiā dōu zuò hǎo lōu**
Everyone sit down, please!

(b) 着 *zhe* may only be used with verbs which do not involve movement. In other words, the request is made to the addressee to maintain a certain state or position. 着 *zhe* imperatives are usually extremely brief so as to drive the point home:

(i) maintaining a situation:

坐着！（别站起来！） **zuò zhe (bié zhàn qǐlai)**
Stay sitting! (Don't stand up!)

请等着！（不要离开！） **qǐng děng zhe (bùyào líkāi)**
Please keep waiting! (Don't leave!)

穿着！（别脱下来！） **chuān zhe (bié tuō xiàlai)**
Keep it on! (Don't take it off!)

(ii) holding on to something:

拿着！ **ná zhe**
Keep hold (of it)!

---

[2] See §24.5 below.

放着！ **fàng zhe**
Leave (it) where it is!

记着！ **jì zhe**
Remember!

Verbs indicating continuous movement naturally do not occur as imperatives with 着 *zhe*:

*走着！ *zǒu zhe**
*说着！ *shuō zhe**

(c) 了 *le* imperatives urge an immediate stop or change:

好了，好了，别吵了！ **hǎo le | hǎo le | bié chǎo le**
Enough is enough. Stop arguing!

不要哭了！ **bùyào kū le**
Stop crying!

吃饭了！ **chī fàn le**
Food's up!

集合了！ **jíhé le**
Fall in!

Because of the advisory nature of 了 *le* imperatives, they are more often than not prohibitions or suggestions to put a stop to less desirable actions or conditions. They are therefore mostly negative imperatives with 别 **bié**, etc.:

你别骗我了！ **nǐ bié piàn wǒ le**
Stop cheating/deceiving me!

别开他的玩笑了！ **bié kāi tāde wánxiào le**
Don't tease him!

不要生气了！ **bùyào shēngqì le**
Don't get angry!

The end-of-imperative particle 呗 **bei** 'then' is generally used after some form of a condition has been established:

不懂，就好好学呗！ **bù dǒng | jiù hǎohāo xué bei**
If you don't understand, then study hard!

你既然知道他的脾气，就别再去惹他呗！
nǐ jìrán zhīdao tāde píqì | jiù bié zài qù rě tā bei
As you know what he's like, don't provoke him again!

An imperative without a 'request' beginner or a terminating particle sounds extremely harsh or rude, and is usually either a command or a threat:

立正！**lìzhèng**
Attention!

坐下！**zuòxia**
Sit (down)!

滚出去！**gǔn chūqu**
Get out!

别动！**biédòng**
Don't move!

A **reiterated** or **reduplicated imperative** with or without a beginner or a particle has the tone of a gentle invitation or plea. Such imperatives are never couched in the negative:

坐，坐，坐！**zuò | zuò | zuò**
Sit down, sit down.

帮帮我吧！**bāngbāng wǒ ba**
Give me a hand./Help me.

你好好地想(一)想吧！**nǐ hǎohāo de xiǎng (yī) xiǎng ba**
Think about it!

请你再等一等吧！**qǐng nǐ zài děng yī děng ba**
Please wait a bit longer!

24.3 SPOKEN AND WRITTEN REQUESTS

'Request' beginners, apart from 请 **qǐng** 'please', and end-of-imperative particles are not used in written requests or prohibitions. Public notices about laws and regulations are generally brief and blunt and do not require the emotional colouring provided by particles, etc. In addition, prohibitions are expressed by the more classical 勿 **wù** 'do not', 莫 **mò** 'not to', 不准 **bù zhǔn** 'not allowed', etc. rather than 别 **bié** 'don't':

闲人莫进 **xiánrén mò jìn**
(lit. casual people don't enter) Staff only.

勿触展品 **wù chù zhǎnpǐn**
Don't touch the exhibits!

请勿在此停车 **qǐng wù zàicǐ tíng chē**
No parking (please here).

不准乱丢果皮纸屑 **bùzhún luàn diū guǒpí zhǐxiè**
(lit. not allow indiscriminately drop fruit skin paper scraps) No litter.

禁止吸烟 **jìnzhǐ xīyān**
(lit. forbid smoke) No smoking.

请遵守会场秩序 **qǐng zūnshǒu huìchǎng zhìxù**
Please respect the rules of the premises.

请勿携带儿童入场 **qǐng wù xiédài értóng rùchǎng**
No children./Please don't bring children in.

In letters, imperatives do not normally incorporate particles. They may begin with 请 **qǐng** 'please', or perhaps more often with 希 **xī** or 望 **wàng** 'hope':

请原谅。 **qǐng yuánliàng**
Please forgive me.

万望光临指导。 **wàn wàng guānglín zhǐdǎo**
(lit. ten-thousand hope honour-us-with-your-presence advise)
I/We very much hope you will come and advise me/us.

务希拨冗出席。 **wù xī bōrǒng chūxí**
(lit. earnestly hope set-aside busy-schedule attend)
Your presence is cordially requested.

敬请来信指教。 **jìng qǐng lái xìn zhǐjiào**
You are respectfully invited to write and instruct (me/us).

24.4 INTERJECTIONS AND EXCLAMATORY EXPRESSIONS

The shortest exclamations are simply interjections. Long exclamatory expressions tend to take the form of established expletives relating to specific situations.

Some interesting features of interjections in Chinese are:

(a) they are mostly monosyllabic:

哎 **āi**   Look out!   哎，前面有车！ **āi | qiánmiàn yǒu chē**
Look out, there's a car coming!

哼 **hng**   Humph!   哼，有什么了不起！
hng | yǒu shénme liǎobuqǐ
Humph, what's so wonderful!

(b) the few disyllabic ones all have level tones: e.g.:

嗨哟 **hāiyō**   Heave ho!   嗨哟，加油哇！
hāiyō | jiāyóu wa Go! Go!

哼唷 **hēngyō**   Heave ho!

哎呀 **āiyā**   Gosh; Damn it!   哎呀，电脑坏了。
āiyā | diànnǎo huài le
Damn it, the computer is broken.

哎哟 **āiyō**   Ouch!   哎哟，疼死我啦！
āiyō | téng sǐ wǒ la
Ouch, it hurts!

喔唷 **ōyō**   Ouch!

(c) monosyllabic interjections are extremely tone-sensitive. A syllable, represented by the same grapheme in writing, may adopt different tones for different emotions, e.g.:

啊 **ā**   expressing surprise   啊，下雪啦！ **ā | xià xuě la**
Oh. It's snowing.

啊 **á**   pressing a point   啊？你说什么？ **á | nǐ shuō shenme**
Eh? What did you say?

啊 **ǎ**   expressing query   啊？这是怎么回事啊？
ǎ | zhè shì zénme huí shì á
Eh? What's going on?

啊 **à**   [shorter fall]
agreement   啊，好吧。 **à | hǎo ba** Oh, OK.
[longer fall]
sudden revelation   啊，原来是你。 **à | yuánlái shì nǐ**
Oh, it's you.

(d) some interjections take different graphemes, e.g.:

嗳/唉 **ài**   **If only . . .**   嗳/唉，早知如此，我就不去了。
ài | zǎo zhī rúcǐ | wǒ jiù bù qù le
If only I'd known earlier, I wouldn't
have gone.

嚄/嚯 **huò**   Wow!   嚄/嚯，好大的雪！ **huò | hǎo dà de xuě**
Wow, it's snowing like mad.

Here is a list of interjections in semantic categories:

(**a**) calling somebody's attention:

喂 **wèi**   Hello!   喂，你上哪儿去？ **wèi | nǐ shàng nǎr qù**
Hello, where are you off to?

喴 **wāi**   Hi!   喴，早上好！ **wāi | zǎoshàng hǎo**
Hi, good morning.

喴 **wāi**   Hey!   喴，好久不见了。 **wāi | hǎojiǔ bù jiàn le**
Hey, long time no see.

嘿 **hēi**   Hey!   嘿，快点儿呀！ **hēi | kuài diǎnr ya**
Hey, hurry up!

哎 **āi**   Look out!   哎，小心点儿！ **āi | xiǎoxīn diǎnr**
Be careful!

喏 **nuò**   There!   喏，那不就是你的雨伞？
nuò | nà bù jiùshì nǐde yǔsǎn nuò
There. Isn't that your umbrella?

(**b**) responding to a call:

啊 **à**   All right.   啊，好吧。 **à | hǎo ba** OK.

唉 **āi**   All right.   唉，就这样吧。 **āi | jiù zhèyàng ba**
All right, we'll do it this way.

呣 **m**   H'm; I see.   呣，我就来。 **m wǒ jiù lái**
H'm, I'm coming.

嗯 **ng**   H'm; yes.   嗯，就这么办。 **ng jiù zhème bàn**
Yes, we'll do it like this then.

嗯 **ng**   OK.   嗯，行！ **ng xíng** Fine!

(**c**) expressing doubt or query:

嗯 **ng**   What?   嗯，你说什么？ **ng | nǐ shuō shénme**
What, what did you say?

呣 **m**   Pardon?   呣，什么？ **m | shénme** H'm, what?

啊 **á**   Yes? Well?   啊，你到底去不去呀？
á | nǐ dàodǐ qù bù qù ya
Well, are you going or not?

哦 **ó**   What?   哦，这是真的吗？ **ó | zhè shì zhēnde ma**
What, is this true?

(**d**) expressing sudden revelation:

喔/噢 **ō**   Oh, so it is!   喔/噢，我想起来了。 **ō | wǒ xiǎng qǐlai le**
Oh, I've remembered.

哦 ò   Oh (I see.)   哦，我懂了。 **ò | wǒ dǒng le**
Oh, I understand.

(e) expressing contradiction:

嗳 **ǎi**   Come on; No, no.   嗳，不是这样的。
ǎi | bù shì zhèyàng de
Come on, it's not like this.

欸 **ě**   No, no.   欸，不能这么说！
ě | bùnéng zhème shuō
No, you can't say that.

(f) expressing surprise:

嘻 **xī**   Oh/Gosh!   嘻，多美呀！ **xī | duō měi ya**
Oh, how beautiful!

啊 **ǎ**   What!   啊，不可能吧？ **ǎ | bù kěnéng ba**
What, it isn't possible, is it?

嘿 **hēi**   Why!   嘿，原来是你！ **hēi | yuánlái shì nǐ**
Why, it's you!

嚄 **huō**   Wow!   嚄，这么大的西瓜！
huō | zhème dà de xīguā
Wow, such a big watermelon.

嗬 **hē**   Ah!   嗬，你真行！ **hē | nǐ zhēnxíng**
Ah, you're really good.

哟 **yō**   Oh!   哟，快十二点了。 **yō | kuài shí èr diǎn le**
Oh, it's nearly 12 o'clock.

呀 **yā**   Oh!   呀，下大雨了。 **yā | xià dà yǔ le**
Oh, it's raining very hard.

呦 **yōu**   Hey!   呦，怎么你也来了。 **yōu | zénme nǐ yě lái le**
Hey, how come you're here too.

(g) expressing satisfaction:

嘿 **hēi**   Hey!   嘿，我们赢了。 **hēi | wǒmen yíng le**
Hey, we've won.

哈 **hā**   Aha!   哈，我猜着了。 **hā | wǒ cāizháo le**
Aha, I guessed right.

(h) expressing disgust or dissatisfaction:

哼 **hng**   Humph!   哼，他撒谎！ **hng | tā sāhuǎng**
Humph, he's lying!

噷 **hm**	Humph!	噷，胡说八道！ **hm | húshuō bā dào**	
		Humph, rubbish!	
吓 **hè**	Tut-tut!	吓，你敢？ **hè | nǐ gǎn**	
		Tut-tut, how dare you!	
好 **hǎo**	Well!	好，你真有能耐！	
	[sarcastically]	**hǎo | nǐ zhēn yǒu néngnài**	
		Well, you're really clever.	
呸 **pēi**	Pooh!	呸，他算老几？ **pèi | tā suàn lǎojǐ**	
		Pooh, he's a nobody.	

(i) expressing disappointment:

咦 **yí**	Hey!	咦，这是怎么回事？ **yí | zhè shì zénme huí shì**	
		Hey, what's all this about?	
欸 **é**	Eh? Why?	欸，她怎么走了？ **é | tā zénme zǒu le**	
		Eh, why's she gone?	
哎 **āi**	But why?	哎，为什么不早点说呢？	
		āi | wèi shénme bù zǎo diǎn shuō ne	
		But, why didn't you say earlier?	

(j) expressing regret:

嗳/唉 **ài**	Oh [dejected]	嗳/唉，真可惜！ **ài | zhēn kěxī**	
		Oh, what a shame!	
咳 **hāi**	Huh!	咳，谁知道？ **hāi | shuí zhīdao**	
		Huh, who knows?	
嗐 **hài**	Huh!	嗐，天晓得！ **hài | tiān xiǎode**	
		Huh, heaven knows!	

Exclamatory expressions, on the other hand, are generally situation-specific. The following is a sample list:

(a) for phatic exchanges:

你好！	**nǐ hǎo**	Hello!
你早！	**nǐ zǎo**	Morning!
请进！	**qǐng jìn**	Come in!
慢走！	**màn zǒu**	Take it easy!
再见！	**zàijiàn**	Goodbye!
谢谢！	**xièxie**	Thank you!
不谢	**bù xiè**	Don't mention it!
好说，好说！	**hǎo shuō | hǎo shuō**	You're too kind!
哪里，哪里！	**nǎli nǎli**	It's very kind of you to say so.
见笑，见笑！	**jiànxiào | jiànxiào**	I'm hopeless.

(**b**) introductory phrases:

对不起	**duìbuqǐ**	Sorry . . .
请问	**qǐng wèn**	May I ask . . .
劳驾	**láo jià**	Excuse me . . .
依我看	**yī wǒ kàn**	In my view . . .
一般来说	**yībān lái shuō**	Generally speaking . . .

(**c**) angry and abusive:

活该！	**huógāi**	Serves you right!
滚蛋！	**gǔndàn**	Scram!
他妈的！	**tāmāde**	Damn it!
混帐！	**hùnzhàng**	Bastard!
岂有此理！	**qǐ yǒu cǐ lǐ**	Nonsense!

(**d**) 真 **zhēn** 'really' as an opener:

真糟糕	**zhēn zāogāo**	What a mess./Too bad.
真该死	**zhēn gāisǐ**	Damn it.
真要命	**zhēn yàomìng**	What a nuisance!/It's terrible.
真奇怪	**zhēn qíguài**	Very odd.

(**e**) foregrounding a descriptive term with 的 **de** for emphasis:

好端端的，为什么生起气来了？
hǎoduānduān de | wèishénme shēng qǐ qì lái le
Everything is fine, and so why are you getting angry?

无缘无故的，你怎么骂起人来了？
wúyuán wú gù de | nǐ zénme mà qǐ rén lái le
For no reason at all, why did you start swearing at people?

糊里糊涂的，我把那件事全忘了。
húlihútū de | wǒ bǎ nèi jiàn shì quán wàng le
In my confusion, I entirely forgot about that.

(**f**) 了 *le* voicing an interruption:

好了，好了，别提了。 **hǎo le | hǎo le | bié tí le**
OK, OK, leave it out.

得了，不要再说了。 **dé le | bùyào zài shuō le**
Enough, don't say any more.

算了。 **suàn le**
That's it. [there's nothing we can do about it]

24.5 EXCLAMATIONS: PARTICLES AND DEGREE ADVERBIALS OR COMPLEMENTS

啊 ā is the archi-phonemic indicator for most exclamations. Its phonetic and graphemic variants depend on the last vowel or consonant preceding it. The following table gives a rough guide to the possible phonetic and graphetic variations of 啊 ā:

endings of the previous word	final phonetic and graphemic realisations
a e i (non-alveolar) o ü + 啊 ā	= 呀 **yā**
u ao ou	+ 啊 ā = 哇 **wā**
n	+ 啊 ā = 哪 **nā**
(end-of-sentence) le	+ 啊 ā = 啦 **lā**
ng i (alveolar)	+ 啊 ā = 啊 **ā**

啊 ā is normally preceded in the exclamatory sentence or phrase by a degree adverb or complement, such as 多(么) 'how . . .', etc. Here are some examples:

这里的风景多美呀！ **zhèli de fēngjǐng duō měi ya**
How beautiful the scenery is here.

这项工作多么有意义呀！ **zhèi xiàng gōngzuò duōme yǒu yìyì ya**
This work is really meaningful.

今年夏天的天气真好哇！ **jīnnián xiàtiān de tiānqì zhēnhǎo wa**
The weather this summer is really good.

我的天哪！ **wǒ de tiān na**
Heavens (above)!

什么都安排好啦！ **shénme dōu ānpái hǎo la**
Everything is sorted out/settled.

爷爷病啦！ **yéye bìng la**
Grandpa's ill!

多棒啊！ **duō bàng a**
Wonderful!

屋子里多么安静啊！ **wūzi li duōme ānjìng a**
How quiet it is in the room!

我说的都是真人真事啊！ **wǒ shuōde dōushì zhēnrén zhēnshì a**
I'm talking about real people and events.

啊 **ā** is a direct and instinctive exclamation. However, if the exclamation is a response[3] intended to contradict an apparent assumption, other exclamatory particles are used, which each have specific implications.

呢 **ne** asserts what is truly the case and not what others might have imagined it to be. It features in complaints, contradictions and rejections of criticism and it is often used with adverbs such as 才 **cái** 'only then . . .', 正在 **zhèngzài** 'right at this moment' and 怎么**zénme** 'how can . . .'.

英国队不赢才怪呢！ **yīngguóduì bù yíng cáiguài ne**
It will be odd if the English team does not win.

大家正在想念你呢！ **dàjiā zhèngzài xiǎngniàn nǐ ne**
Everyone's missing you.

你怎么能这样说呢！ **nǐ zénme néng zhèyàng shuō ne**
How could you say that?

嘛 **ma** is also used to retort in a mild way to what seems to be an unreasonable suggestion:

这不是很清楚嘛！ **zhè bù shì hěn qīngchu ma**
Isn't this very clear?

这件事不能怪他。他还小嘛！ **zhèi jiàn shì bùnéng guài tā | tā hái xiǎo ma**
You can't blame him for this. He's still young/only a child.

喽 **lōu**, a variant of 了 **le**, conveys a degree of urgency about something that has to be done or is about to happen:

比赛开始喽！ **bǐsài kāishǐ lōu**
The match is about to begin. [please settle down and watch!]

吃饭喽！ **chī fàn lōu**
The dinner is ready! [please take your seat at the table!]

---

[3] Corresponding to the responsive type in imperatives.

25 ABBREVIATIONS AND OMISSIONS

A highly significant feature of Chinese sentence and discourse structure is the avoidance of repetition wherever possible. Sentences are abbreviated and words omitted where context and co-text make the meaning clear. Pronouns in particular are regularly omitted and the third person neuter 它 **tā** 'it' occurs quite rarely, since it is by definition a reference back to something already identified. Questions with their answers give clear examples of this feature.

25.1 ABBREVIATIONS IN ANSWERS TO QUESTIONS

In answers to questions only essential information is given, and the response to yes–no questions almost invariably focuses on the verb as the core element. In the examples below, we give literal translations to indicate the structure of the responses. There are standard translations in brackets.

question:	你去看电影吗？ **nǐ qù kàn diànyǐng ma**
	You go see film *ma*? (Are you going to the cinema/to see a film?)
answer:	去啊。 **qù ā**
	Go *a*. (Yes.)

question:	那本书你看完了吗？ **nèi běn shū nǐ kàn wán le ma**
	That mw book you read finish *le ma*?
	(Have you finished reading that book?)
answer:	还没有。 **hái méiyǒu**
	Still not have. (Not yet.)

question:	你喜欢这幅画儿吗？ **nǐ xǐhuan zhèi fú huàr ma?**
	You like this mw picture *ma*? (Do you like this picture?)
answer:	我喜欢，可是我妻子不喜欢。
	**wǒ xǐhuan	kěshì wǒ qīzi bù xǐhuan**
	I like, but my wife not like. (I do but my wife doesn't.)

Even in answers to question-word questions where the focus is elsewhere, verbs still tend to be repeated:

question:	谁去帮帮他的忙？ **shuí qù bāngbāng tāde máng**
	Who go help-help his busy? (Who is going to help him?)
answer:	我去。 **wǒ qù**
	I go. (I am.)

question: 什么时候去？[1] **shénme shíhou qù**
What time go? (When are you going?)

answer: 明天去。 **míngtiān qù**
Tomorrow go. (Tomorrow.)

Note that in the last question, while 'you' is required in the English translation, the Chinese has no need for the pronoun since it is clear that it must be the person addressed.[2]

25.2 ABBREVIATIONS IN FACE-TO-FACE EXCHANGES

The omission of 'you' mentioned immediately above is naturally a feature of orders or requests made face to face, since the addressee is in the same way normally obvious:

请进！ **qǐng jìn**
Please come in.

快把东西收拾好！ **kuài bǎ dōngxi shōushi hǎo**
Hurry up and make things tidy.

Other conventional face-to-face expressions are likewise succinct, without subjects or objects being mentioned:

对不起。	**duìbuqǐ**	Sorry. (lit. Face-not-rise.)
谢谢。	**xièxie**	Thanks./Thank you. (lit. Thank-thank.)
没关系。	**méi guānxi**	It doesn't matter. (lit. Has not concern.)

25.3 ABBREVIATIONS IN COMPARISONS

In Chinese syntax, it is the norm for the second element in a comparison not to be expressed in full. For example in the following sentences the words in square brackets would usually be omitted:

那件衣服比这件[衣服]漂亮。 **nèi jiàn yīfu bǐ zhèi jiàn [yīfu] piàoliang**
(lit that mw clothes cv:compared with this mw [clothes] attractive)
That suit/piece of clothing is prettier/more attractive than this one.

你打羽毛球打得比我[打羽毛球打得]好。
nǐ dǎ yǔmáoqiú dǎ de bǐ wǒ [dǎ yǔmáoqiú dǎ de] hǎo
(lit. you play badminton play *de* cv:compared with me [play badminton play *de*] well)
You play badminton better than I do.

---

[1] Note that the subject 你 **nǐ** 'you' is omitted in this follow-up question but the verb is retained.
[2] See §25.5 below.

这儿的天气比北京[的天气]热。 **zhèr de tiānqì bǐ běijīng [de tiānqì] rè**
(lit. here *de* weather cv:compared with beijing [*de* weather] hot)
The weather here is hotter than in Beijing.

25.4 THE HIDDEN PRESENCE OF THE NARRATOR IN A NARRATIVE

The narrator in a piece of narration is omnipresent but not always visible. In Chinese there is a range of set expressions which establish a narrative presentation, introducing the description of a situation or creating an atmosphere. They usually take the form of an impersonalised verbal phrase and are placed at the beginning of the sentence:

只见远远走来两个人。 **zhǐ jiàn yuǎnyuǎn zǒu lái liǎng ge rén**
(lit. only see far-far walk-come two mw people)
One could see that in the distance two people approached.

据说他已出国去了。 **jùshuō tā yǐ chūguó qù le**
(lit. according to talk he already exit country go *le*)
They say he's already gone abroad.

不知不觉已经过了一年。 **bùzhī bùjué yǐjīng guò le yī nián**
(lit. not know not feel already pass *le* one year)
Imperceptibly, a year had already passed.

谁知道那年冬天没有下雪。
shuí/shéi zhīdao nèi nián dōngtiān méiyǒu xià xuě
(lit. who know that year winter not have fall snow)
Nobody expected it not to snow that winter./Unexpectedly it did not snow that winter.

怪不得她生气了。 **guàibude tā shēngqì le**
(lit. wonder not possible she angry *le*)
No wonder she got angry.

25.5 OMISSIONS IN A DISCOURSE

The omission of sentence elements we observed in §25.1 is most apparent in longer sentences in Chinese. They usually take the form of chain constructions[3] that bring together, in a linear sequence of time and action, a series of basic 'subject + predicate' or 'topic + comment' sentences. They also establish, by definition, a broader contextual and co-textual base which allows for extensive omissions of elements like subjects and objects from the constituent basic sentences, because these elements have already been identified in the text.

---

[3] See Chapter 14.

Take a sentence like the following (arranged vertically to identify the constituent sentences):

那天我去找一个老朋友， **nèi tiān wǒ qù zhǎo yī ge lǎo péngyou**
敲了两下门， **qiāo le liǎng xià mén**
没人回答， **méi rén huídá**
想他准是出去了， **xiǎng tā zhǔn shì chū qù le**
便留了个字条， **biàn liú le ge zìtiáo**
从门上的信箱口里塞了进去，
cóng mén shàng de xìnxiāngkǒu li sāi le jìnqu
约好改日再去拜访， **yuē hǎo gǎirì zài qù bàifǎng**
并说回来后， **bìng shuō huí lái hòu**
最好给我一个答复， **zuìhǎo gěi wǒ yǐ ge dáfù**
没想到过了几天， **méi xiǎng dào guò le jǐ tiān**
收到一封没署名的信， **shōudào yī fēng méi shùmíng de xìn**
说他已经搬走了， **shuō tā yǐjīng bān zǒu le**
不知去了什么地方。 **bùzhī qù le shénme dìfang**

To highlight the omissions, we will first provide a literal translation and then a full translation, which introduces in brackets the pronominal and other elements required by English but 'omitted' by Chinese:

literal translation:

那天我去找一个老朋友，	that day I go find one mw old friend
敲了两下门，	knock *le* two mw:times door
没人回答，	no people reply
想他准是出去了，	think he definitely exit-go *le*
便留了个字条，	then leave *le* mw note
从门上的信箱口里塞了进去，	cv:from door-on *de* letter box opening inside push *le* enter-go
约好改日再去拜访，	fix another day again go visit
并说回来后，	and say return-come after
最好给我一个答复，	best give me one mw reply
没想到过了几天，	not expect pass *le* few days
收到一封没署名的信，	receive one mw not sign *de* letter
说他已经搬走了，	say he already move out *le*
不知去了什么地方。	not know go *le* what place

full translation:

那天我去找一个老朋友，	That day I went to see an old friend.
敲了两下门，	(I) knocked on the door,
没人回答，	(but) nobody answered.
想他准是出去了，	(I) thought that he must have gone out,
便留了个字条，	(and) so (I) left a note

从门上的信箱口里塞了进去，	(and) pushed (it) through the letter box in the door,
约好改日再去拜访，	indicating that (I) would come back another day.
并说回来后，	(I) also said that as soon as (he) comes back,
最好给我一个答复，	it would be nice if (he) could drop me a note.
没想到过了几天，	(I) never expected that a few days later
收到一封没署名的信，	(I) would receive an anonymous letter
说他已经搬走了，	saying that he had already moved out
不知去了什么地方。	(and) (it) was not known where (he) had moved to.

This sentence, centred around the single theme of a fruitless visit, consists of thirteen constituent sentences, simply strung together following an inherent time sequence. There are few linking words and the sentence is a mini-discourse, which holds its shape through the rhythm of the sequentially juxtaposed constituent sentences. Pronouns are generally redundant and are not present since the noun subjects or objects they would represent are clearly identifiable from the context.

Below are a few more examples for illustration.

我养了一只猫，可是不会抓老鼠，妹妹说，算了，不要养了，送给别人吧。
wǒ yǎng le yī zhī māo | kěshì bùhuì zhuā lǎoshu | mèimei shuō | suàn le | bùyào yǎng le | sòng gěi biérén ba
(lit. I rear *le* one mw cat, but not can catch mice, younger sister said, that's enough, don't keep *le*, send-give others *ba*)
I had a cat, but (it) could not catch mice. Younger sister said, 'That's enough. Don't keep (it) any more. Give (it) to someone else'.

体育锻炼可以增强体质，早上起来跑跑步，使你整天精神饱满，有什么不好呢?
tǐyù duànliàn kěyǐ zēngqiáng tǐzhì | zǎoshàng qǐlái pǎopǎo bù | shǐ nǐ zhěngtiān jīngshén bǎomǎn | yǒu shénme bù hǎo ne
(lit. physical training can strengthen constitution, morning get up jog steps, makes you whole day spirit full, has what not good *ne*)
Physical education can strengthen (the) constitution. Getting up in the morning for a run, can make you full of vigour all day, (and) what is wrong (with that)?

时间很宽裕，可以从从容容地做。
shíjiān hěn kuānyù | kěyǐ cóngcóngróngróng de zuò
(lit. time very ample, can leisurely *de* do)
There's plenty of time (you) can do (it) without any rush.

听他的口音，好象是浙江人。 **tīng tāde kǒuyīn | hǎoxiàng shì zhèjiāng rén**
(lit. listen to his accent, seems to be Zhejiang person)
From his accent, (he) sounds like someone from Zhejiang.

我常常到那儿去买龙虾，有时有，有时没有。
wǒ chángcháng dào nàr qù mǎi lóngxiā | yǒu shí yǒu | yǒu shí méiyǒu
(lit. I often get there go buy lobster, sometimes have, sometimes not have)
I often go there to buy lobsters, sometimes (they) have (some) and
sometimes (they) don't.

26 PROSODIC FEATURES

Prosodic features, and particularly those relating to rhythm, are essential elements in Chinese syntax. Sentences that do not observe prosodic principles are often regarded not only as stylistically implausible but also as syntactically unacceptable. Consider the following:

*他很喜欢浏览书。 ***tā hěn xǐhuan liúlǎn shū**
He very much likes browsing through books.

The sentence does not infringe any lexical, collocational or grammatical rules, but it is not acceptable because it is out of line with prosodic needs. It can be improved with the following small amendment:

他很喜欢浏览书籍。 **tā hěn xǐhuan liúlǎn shūjí**
He very much likes browsing through books.

Here the addition of a syllable to the noun object, changing the monosyllabic 书 **shū** into the disyllabic 书籍 **shūjí** 'books', ensures rhythmic balance and makes the sentence easy on the Chinese ear. Clearly rhythm, like grammar and collocation, plays a vital role in Chinese syntax.

In the following sections, we will first analyse the basic rhythmic structure of the Chinese language and then look more closely at the interplay between this basic rhythm and syntactic sequences.

26.1 THE OVERALL RHYTHM OF CHINESE SPEECH

Owing to the disyllabic dominance of the lexical items in the language's vocabulary, Chinese has gradually developed a preference for disyllabic rhythms. In fact, the Tang poetry of medieval China was based on **disyllabic trochaic rhythms**:

Xx Xx X[1]

王之涣 登鹳雀楼 **Wáng Zhīhuàn Dēng Guànquè Lóu**
Climbing Crane Pagoda

---

[1] Upper-case X is used to indicate stress whereas lower-case x is used to indicate non-stress.

白日 | 依山 | 尽， **bái rì | yī shān | jìn**	white sun | lean on mountain | ends
黄河 | 入海 | 流。 **huáng hé | rù hǎi | liú**	yellow river | enter sea | flows
欲穷 | 千里 | 目， **yù qióng | qiān lǐ | mù**	desire exhaust | thousand *li* | eyes
更上 | 一层 | 楼。 **gèng shàng | yī céng | lóu**	further mount | one level | building

The white sun sinks behind the mountains,
The Yellow River flows into the sea.
Desiring to extend my gaze over a thousand *li*
I climb another floor of the pagoda.

or

Xx Xx Xx X

张继 枫桥夜泊 **Zhāng Jì Fēng Qiáo Yè Bó**
Mooring at Night by Maple Bridge

月落 \| 乌啼 \| 霜满 \| 天， **yuè luò \| wū tí \| shuāng mǎn \| tiān**
江枫 \| 渔火 \| 对愁 \| 眠。 **jiāng fēng \| yú huǒ \| duì chóu \| mián**
姑苏 \| 城外 \| 寒山 \| 寺， **gū sū \| chéng wài \| hán shān \| sì**
夜半 \| 钟声 \| 到客 \| 船。 **yè bàn \| zhōng shēng \| dào kè \| chuán**

moon fall \| crows call \| frost fill \| sky
river maples \| fishing light \| cv:facing sadly \| sleep
Suzhou \| walls outside \| Hanshan \| monastery
night middle \| bell sound \| arrive traveller \| boat

The moon sinks, the crows call and frost fills the sky,
By the river maples, the fishing boat lights confront my troubled sleep.
Beyond the walls of Suzhou, the Hanshan monastery
In the middle of the night the sound of its bell reaches the traveller's boat.

This basic rhythm carries over into modern speech and prose. The length of a sentence or that piece of language between plausible pauses may of course vary, and the number of unstressed syllables between stressed ones may be one or two. However, the first syllable stress remains the basic feature, with a speaker or writer using a range of rhythmic patterns based on this, e.g.:

Xx Xxx Xx X
Xxx Xx Xx Xx

Xxx Xx Xxx
etc.

An unstressed or introductory syllable is often used at the beginning of a pattern:

xXx Xx Xx X^2

The rhythm of Chinese speech hinges on the insistent front stressing of disyllabic items. Under no circumstances does one find the first syllable of a disyllable losing its tone, whereas this can sometimes be the case with the second syllable. These structures are underpinned by the fact that disyllabic words across all grammatical categories are naturally of a trochaic rhythm:

	Xx	Xx
disyllabic noun	杯子 **bēizi** cup/glass	酒杯 **jiǔbēi**
disyllabic verb	打架 **dǎjià** to fight	研究 **yánjiū** to study
disyllabic adjective	美丽 **měilì** beautiful	残酷 **cánkù** cruel
disyllabic modal verb	可以 **kěyǐ** may	愿意 **yuànyi** willing
disyllabic adverb	已经 **yǐjīng** already	常常 **chángcháng** often
disyllabic conjunction	如果 **rúguǒ** if	虽然 **suīrán** although
numeral	二十 **èrshí** twenty	三百 **sān bǎi** three hundred
negator	没有 **méiyǒu** (did/have) not	

In relation to the last two categories, it must be noted that monosyllabic numerals or negators like 一 **yī** 'one' or 不 **bù** 'not' are invariably stressed.

On the other hand, the following monosyllabic grammatical categories are always unstressed and remain so whatever the context:

	X	X	X
adjectival particle	的 **de**		
adverbial particle	地 **de**		
complemental particle	得 **de**		
sentence particle	了 **le**		
functional particle	把 **bǎ**	被 **bèi**	
aspect or style indicator	了 **le**	过 **guò**	在 **zài**
measure word	个 **ge**	杯 **bēi**	本 **běn**

Finally, some parts of speech can be either stressed or unstressed, depending on emphasis required and on their position in predominantly trochaic sentence patterns:

---

^{2} Allowing an extra unstressed syllable at the beginning (xXx) is similar to introducing an extra unstressed syllable (i.e. Xxx Xx) between two stressed syllables. The overall rhythm remains trochaic.

monosyllabic pronoun	我 **wǒ** I	你 **nǐ** you	他 **tā** he
monosyllabic verb	去 **qù** to go	是 **shì** to be	有 **yǒu** to have
monosyllabic adjective	新 **xīn** new	旧 **jiù** old	
monosyllabic adverb	再 **zài** again	又 **yòu** again	很 **hěn** very
monosyllabic modal verb	能 **néng** can	要 **yào** want	
monosyllabic conjunction	如 **rú** if	和 **hé** and	跟 **gēn** with/and
reference adverb	都 **dōu** all/both	也 **yě** also	就 **jiù** then

In summary, we may say that disyllabic items of the vocabulary are always first-syllable stressed and monosyllabic items of a grammatical rather than lexical nature are always unstressed. Only monosyllabic items of the lexical vocabulary may adjust their stressed or unstressed status depending on the stress of adjacent items. In other words, when two monosyllabic lexical items come together, either may become stressed or unstressed in relation to the other so long as the overall trochaic rhythm is maintained.

Let us look at the following example:

Xx   Xx   Xx   X
我想 | 再买 | 一杯 | 酒。
wǒ xiǎng | **zài mǎi** | **yī bēi** | **jiǔ**
I'd like to buy another glass of wine.

In the first beat, a monosyllabic pronoun and a monosyllabic modal verb come together, and the pronoun is stressed to start a trochaic rhythm; the same applies in the second beat where a monosyllabic adverb because of emphasis is stressed before an unstressed monosyllabic verb; similarly in the third beat, a numeral takes precedence in stress before the measure word that follows it; and the final mono-syllabic noun is stressed because it stands in isolation unaffected by other syllables.

The above is therefore a well-formed sentence on all counts. However, if the monosyllabic verb 去 **qù** 'to go' is introduced:

我想再去买一杯酒。
wǒ xiǎng zài qù mǎi yī bēi jiǔ

the sentence remains grammatical, but it is rhythmically unbalanced because of the clash of two consecutive stressed syllables in the middle:

Xx   Xx   X   Xx   X
+我想 | 再去 | 买 | 一杯 | 酒。
wǒ xiǎng | **zài qù** | **mǎi** | **yī bēi** | **jiǔ**

If the stress is adjusted to make the two monsyllabic verbs following the adverb unstressed, the necessary emphasis on 'buying' is lost:

Xx   Xxx   Xx   X
+我想 | 再去买 | 一杯 | 酒。
wǒ xiǎng | zài qù mǎi | yī bēi | jiǔ

If the first syllable is made introductory, the required emphasis on 'another' will be lost:

xXx   Xx   Xx   X
+我想再 | 去买 | 一杯 | 酒。
wǒ xiǎng zài | qù mǎi | yī bēi | jiǔ

This will leave unstressed the concept of 'again', which is central to the intended meaning of the sentence.

The mechanical imposition of a trochaic rhythm to the sentence will of course make it sound gibberish altogether:

Xx   Xx   Xx   Xx
+我想 | 再去 | 买一 | 杯酒。
wǒ xiǎng | zài qù | mǎi yī | bēi jiǔ

From this we can see that an acceptable rhythmic structure must also be imposed on a Chinese sentence, which may otherwise have proper collocation and good grammar, if full understanding of the meaning is not to be jeopardised.

The obvious solution for the sentence above with 去 **qù** 'to go' included is in fact to delete a syllable[3] to retrieve the trochaic rhythm:

Xx   Xx   Xx   X
我想 | 再去 | 买杯 | 酒。
wǒ xiǎng | zài qù | mǎi bēi | jiǔ

This would be a natural way of formulating the sentence and native speakers would express it in these terms instinctively following trochaic cadence.

Let's now look at another example:

Xx   Xx   Xx   Xx
谁都 | 吃了 | 两个 | 鸡蛋。
shuí dōu | chī le | liǎng ge | jīdàn
Everybody has eaten two eggs.

---

[3] The numeral 一 **yī** 'one' in a 'numeral + measure word' collocation can often be deleted to leave the measure word on its own.

Here in the first beat a monosyllabic pronoun and a reference adverb come together, and the pronoun is stressed to start a trochaic rhythm; in the second beat, the verb is stressed leaving the particle naturally unstressed; in the third beat the numeral is as usual stressed while the measure word is not; in the last beat, the first syllable of a disyllabic noun is stressed and the second unstressed. The utterance is therefore acceptable in every way.

However, the sentence could be rephrased without changing the meaning by substituting the disyllabic 大家 **dàjiā** 'everybody' for 谁 **shuí** 'everybody':

Xxx   Xx   Xx   Xx
大家都 | 吃了 | 两个 | 鸡蛋。
dàjiā dōu | chī le | liǎng ge | jīdàn
Everybody has eaten two eggs.

In this case there is no problem with rhythm since the verb remains primarily accented, and an additional unstressed syllable is simply introduced into the first beat.

Similarly there is no difficulty in converting the sentence into an imperative by introducing an extra verb 来 **lái** 'to come' before 吃 **chī** 'to eat':

Xx   Xx   Xx   X
大家 | 都来 | 吃鸡 | 蛋！
dàjiā | dōu lái | chī jī- | dàn
Everybody, come and eat eggs.

Here the verb in the penultimate beat (吃 **chī**) reaches across the lexical boundary and builds the first syllable of its disyllabic object (鸡 **jī**) into an unaccented second syllable of its own in order to keep to the rhythmic pattern. This is possible because disyllabic nouns can in fact have its first syllable unstressed following a monosyllabic verb on condition that its second syllable stands free and stressed.

However, if the imperative becomes a question with the addition of the particle 吗 **ma** at the end, the rhythmic pattern starts to interfere with understanding by having 蛋吗 **dàn ma** thrown together as a meaningless unit in the last beat.

Xx   Xx   Xx   Xx
+大家 | 都来 | 吃鸡 | 蛋吗？
dàjiā | dōu lái | chī jī- | dàn ma
Will everybody come and eat eggs?

As a remedy, the stress pattern can be easily adjusted as follows:

Xxx   Xx   Xxx
大家都 | 来吃 | 鸡蛋吗?
dàjiā dōu | lái chī | jīdàn ma
Will everybody come and eat eggs?

From this it can be seen how unstressed syllables can be accommodated to keep the trochaic rhythm alive so long as the meaning remains clear.

We will now move on to the further question of the link between grammatical sequences and rhythmic structures.

26.2 SYNTACTIC SEQUENCES AND THEIR UNDERLYING RHYTHM

Meaning is usually realised by the strictly ordered sequence of grammatical patterns or lexical idioms. The more strictly ordered the sequence is, the more rule-governed the rhythmic structure becomes.

26.2.1 'VERB + OBJECT' PATTERNS

First, in the case of 'verb + object' patterns, three rhythmic structures are possible:

(a) monosyllabic verb + monosyllabic object: Xx
e.g. 看书 **kànshū**
(b) disyllabic verb + disyllabic object: Xx + Xx
e.g. 浏览书籍 **liúlǎn shūjí**
(c) monosyllabic verb + disyllabic object: Xx + X[4]
e.g. 看电影 **kàn diànyǐng**

If we go back to the first sentence quoted at the beginning of this chapter, we can see that the verb–object sequence at the end of the sentence, 浏览书 **liúlǎn shū**, has a disyllabic verb + monosyllabic object pattern. Because of this, it does not conform to any of the three structures above and it is not an acceptable sentence

monosyllabic verb and monosyllabic object:

This pattern Xx embraces a large number of words in the lexicon, e.g.

开会 **kāihuì**	看戏 **kànxì**	打拳 **dǎquán**	跳舞 **tiàowǔ**	唱歌 **chànggē**
hold a meeting	see a play	(shadow) box (lit. hit fist)	dance (lit. leap dance)	sing (lit. sing song)

---

[4] Please note that the rhythmic cluster does not have to coincide with the lexical boundary, as we have already seen above.

These 'verb + object' words are all established lexical items and to make the object disyllabic, e.g. 开会议 **kāi huìyì**, 看戏剧 **kàn xìjù**, 打拳术 **dǎ quánshù**, 跳舞蹈 **tiào wǔdǎo**, 唱歌曲 **chàng gēqǔ**, while grammatically and apparently rhythmically correct, would in fact be unacceptable as it conflicts with established lexical convention.

However, to extend these words into phrases presents no problem if the following pattern is used:

   Xx   Xx   X
   看了 | 一场 | 戏
   kàn le | yī chǎng | xì
   (lit. see *le* | one mw | play) saw a play

   唱了 | 一首 | 歌
   chàng le | yī shǒu | gē
   (lit. sing *le* | one mw | song) sang a song

or:

   Xx   X
   看场 | 戏
   kàn chǎng | xì
   (lit. see (one) mw | play) see a play

   唱首 | 歌
   chàng shǒu | gē
   (lit. sing (one) mw | song) sing a song

These all conform to the established rhythm. However, they are less admissible in the following form:

   X   Xx   X
   +看 | 一场 | 戏
   kàn | yī chǎng | xì
   +唱 | 一首 | 歌
   chàng | yī shǒu | gē

or:

   Xx   xX
   *看了 | 场戏
   kàn le | chǎng xì

*唱了 | 首歌
chàng le | shǒu gē

and as we have seen in §26.1, their rhythmic pattern would have to be adjusted
to:

Xxx　　X
看一场 | 戏
kàn yī chǎng | xì

唱一首 | 歌
chàng yī shǒu | gē

or:

看了场 | 戏
kàn le chǎng | xì

唱了首 | 歌
chàng le shǒu | gē

This rhythmic requirement with verbal patterns explains why verbal reduplications follow similar principles:

Xx	看看 **kànkàn**
Xx | X	看一看 **kàn yī kàn**
Xx | X	看了看 **kàn le kàn**
Xx | Xx	讨论讨论 **tǎolùn tǎolùn**
*Xx | Xx | X	*讨论一讨论[5] **tǎolùn yī tǎolùn**

26.2.2 THE 'ATTRIBUTIVE + HEADWORD' PATTERN

This follows two basic rhythmic rules:

(**a**) if the attributive is monosyllabic, the headword does not normally exceed
two syllables. For example:

新书	Xx **xīn shū**	new books
新房子	xXx **xīn fángzi**	new house
*新运动场	xXx | X **xīn yùndòngchǎng**	(new sportsground)

---

[5] 一讨 **yī tǎo** can, of course, make no sense, and that explains why this pattern is impermissible.

(b) if the attributive is disyllabic or polysyllabic, the headword can be of any length.[6] For example:

新买的书	Xxx | X	**xīn mǎi de | shū**
		newly bought book(s)
新买的房子	Xxx | Xx	**xīn mǎi de | fángzi**
		newly bought house
新买的洗衣机	Xxx | Xx | X	**xīn mǎi de | xǐyī | jī**
		newly bought washing
		machine
新买的电子游戏	Xxx | Xx | Xx	**xīn mǎi de | diànzǐ | yóuxì**
		newly bought electronic
		game(s)
新买的电子游戏机	Xxx | Xx | Xx | X	**xīn mǎi de | diànzǐ |**
		yóuxì | jī
		newly bought electronic
		game machine

In some cases where a disyllabic attributive is followed by a monosyllabic headword (which can be a suffix-like noun), the combination becomes an established item in the language's lexicon. For example:

XxX	运动 | 员	**yùndòng | yuán**	athlete
XxX	计算 | 机	**jìsuàn | jī**	computer
XxX	电话 | 亭	**diànhuà | tíng**	telephone kiosk
XxX	时刻 | 表	**shíkè | biǎo**	timetable
XxX	压岁 | 钱	**yāsuì | qián**	New Year (gift) money

and also:

| XxX | 两点 \| 钟 | **liǎng diǎn \| zhōng** | two o'clock |
| XxX | 三块 \| 钱 | **sān kuài \| qián** | three yuan |

This trisyllabic rhythm for established words may supersede a word's underlying semantic structure. For example:

XxX	手风 | 琴 **shǒufēng | qín**	手 | 风琴 **shǒu | fēngqín**
	whereas the semantic structure is	
	accordian (lit. hand organ)	
XxX	电风 | 扇 **diànfēng | shàn**	电 | 风扇 **diàn | fēngshàn**
	electric fan	
XxX	高速 | 度 **gāosù | dù**	高 | 速度 **gāo | sùdù**
	high speed	

---

[6] As we have seen in Chapters 4 and 18, the particle 的 **de** usually marks longer attributives.

There is much evidence of newly coined words following this trisyllabic pattern:

XxX	系列 | 舞	**xìliè | wǔ**	sequence dancing
XxX	肥皂 | 剧	**féizào | jù**	soap opera
XxX	小人 | 书	**xiǎorén | shū**	picture (story) book
XxX	电饭 | 锅	**diànfàn | guō**	electric cooker

26.3 ECHOING PATTERNS OF RHYTHM

Language conventions are of course regularly ignored if a specific effect or style is required and the rules of rhythmic patterning are no exception. However, if non-standard cadence is introduced, it is usually echoed by a similarly non-standard pattern to ease the deviation for the listener's ear. For instance, take the following sentence:

Xx | X | xXx | Xx | (X | Xx | X) | Xx | Xx | Xx
临睡 | 前 | 我弟弟 | 总是 | (翻 | 故事 | 书) | 折腾 | 一番 | 才睡。
lín shuì | qián | wǒ dìdi | zǒngshì | (fān | gùshi | shū) | zhéténg | yī fān | cái shuì
(lit. on the point of sleep | before | my younger brother | always | finger through | story | book | dilly-dally | one mw:occasion | only then sleep)
When he goes to bed, my younger brother never goes to sleep until he has glanced through a storybook and dilly-dallied for a while.

Obviously, the rhythmic pattern X | Xx | X (i.e. **fān | gùshi | shū**) in the middle of the utterance disregards the trochaic principle, and as a result, the sentence sounds not only awkward but also incomplete. However, if an echoing phrase with a similar rhythm is introduced, the sentence becomes acceptable:

Xx | X | xXx | Xx | (X | Xx | X) | (X | Xx | X) | Xx | Xx | Xx
临睡 | 前 | 我弟弟 | 总是 | (翻 | 故事 | 书) | (玩 | 玩具 | 熊) | 折腾 | 一番 | 才睡。
lín shuì | qián | wǒ dìdi | zǒngshì | (fān | gùshi | shū) | (wán | wánjù | xióng) | zhéténg | yī fān | cái shuì
(lit. on the point of sleep | before | my younger brother | always | finger through | story | book | play with | toy | bear | dilly-dally | one mw:occasion | only then sleep)
When he goes to bed, my younger brother never goes to sleep until he has glanced through a storybook, played with his toy bear, and dilly-dallied for a while.

This manipulation of unfamiliar rhythms, in fact, provides a refreshing variety to trochaic regularity, and can breathe life into the flow of the prose rhythm.

If a particular rhythmic pattern is used in a sequence, it is unusual for it to be followed by another sequence with a different rhythm, especially when there is also a semantic affinity between the two sequences. For example, take the following:

xXx | Xx | Xx | Xx | xXx
*我一路走去，心情舒畅，很振奋。
wǒ yī lù | zǒu qù | xīnqíng | shūchàng | hěn zhènfèn
(lit. I whole way walk-go, mood carefree, very enthused)
All along the way, I was in a carefree mood and very enthused.

Here the cadence of the final sequence xXx, which is closely related semantically to the previous sequence XxXx, undermines the rhythmic consistency and makes the sentence jar on the ear.

However, the problem disappears if the sentence is reworded with an echoing pattern:

xXx | Xx | Xx | xXx | xXx
我一路走去，心情很舒畅，很振奋。
wǒ yī lù | zǒu qù | xīnqíng | hěn shūchàng | hěn zhènfèn
All along the way my mood was carefree and enthused.

or:

xXx | Xx | Xx | Xx | Xx | Xx
我一路走去，心情舒畅，精神振奋。
wǒ yī lù zǒu qù | xīnqíng shūchàng | jīngshén zhènfèn
All along the way my mood was carefree and my spirits enthused.

26.4 EXPANDING, CONDENSING AND PADDING TO GET INTO THE APPROPRIATE RHYTHM

It is plain that the Chinese speaker is concerned with rhythm as well as grammar and collocation. To achieve rhythmic balance he or she will expand or condense the individual items in an utterance. Compare the following two sentences:

(a) Xx | Xx | Xx | Xx | X | Xx | Xxx
如果 | 能够 | 见到 | 您的 | 话， | 那就 | 太好了。
rúguǒ | nénggòu | jiàn dào | nín de | huà | nà jiù | tài hǎo le
If (I/we) can meet you, that will be splendid.
(b) Xx | Xx | xXx | Xx
如能 | 见您， | 将十分 | 荣幸。
rú néng | jiàn nín | jiāng shífēn | róngxìng
If (I/we) can meet you, (we) will be extremely honoured.

In (a) (expanded) the initial disyllabic 能够 **nénggòu** 'can', especially after 如果 **rúguǒ** 'if', inevitably leads on to the two syllable verb 见到 **jiàndào** 'meet', with the object 您 **nín** 'you' (polite) linking in convenient rhythm with the end-clause conditional marker 的话 **de huà**. In (b) (condensed), on the other hand, the trochaic stress pattern has to be reformulated to take account of the use of the monosyllabic words 如 **rú** 'if', 能 **néng** 'can', 见 **jiàn** 'to see', 您 **nín** 'you' (polite). In both of them, whether disyllabic or monosyllabic, the underlying pattern of stress is maintained.

In addition to generating expansion and condensation of utterances, rhythmic requirements can also lead to the introduction of padding words. Consider the following pair of sentences, which both mean 'Let's go and have a drink tonight':

(a) Xx | Xxx | Xx | Xx
    咱们 | 今晚去 | 喝杯 | 酒吧。
    zánmen | **jīnwǎn qù** | **hē bēi** | **jiǔ ba**
    (lit. we | this evening go | drink (one) mw:glass | beer ***ba***)

(b) Xx | Xxx | Xx | Xx
    咱们 | 今晚去 | 喝它 | 一杯。
    zánmen | **jīnwǎn qù** | **hē tā** | **yī bēi**
    (lit. we | this evening go | drink it | one mw:glass)

In the first sentence, the numeral 一 **yī** 'one' is omitted before 杯 **bēi** 'glass' in the standard way to achieve a trochaic rhythm. In the second, the numeral 一 **yī** 'one' is retained, and to avoid the clash of two consecutive accented syllables, the meaningless padding word 它 **tā** is introduced to complete the trochaic rhythm with the verb 喝 **hē** 'to drink'.

27 STYLISTIC CONSIDERATIONS IN SYNTACTIC CONSTRUCTIONS

Chinese syntactic constructions, as we have seen, are not merely governed by syntactic rules, but are subject to lexical and prosodic requirements as well. Only when all the conventions of syntax, collocation and prosody are taken into account can one decide if a particular construction is grammatical or not. These grammatical structures then provide the basis on which stylistically varying constructions may be built.

Communication, as we know, does not involve syntax alone; it also needs to exploit ranges of style to be completely effective. Stylistic considerations are, therefore, an important flourish added to the melody of syntax, and without these considerations, syntax is unlikely to break out of its prosaic limits and turn language into literature or poetry.

If we analyse the main stylistic features in Chinese syntactic construction, it is possible to identify two determining factors: one presentational and the other rhetorical, which separate or combine to provide qualities of tone and rhythm. They are both, of course, particularly characteristic of literary writing.

In order to give clear illustrations of these stylistic features, we have selected below examples of writing from the works of modern Chinese authors who make conscious use of the poetic dimensions of prose. In each case the quotation is set out vertically on a section-by-section basis.

27.1 THE PRESENTATIONAL FACTOR

Presentational needs, which are predominantly found in the realm of description, lead to the configuration of syntactic structures in order to exploit features like repetition, to register different focuses and emphases, and simply to display variety of expression.

The following are commonly used stylistic configurations:

27.1.1 LAYERED OR SEQUENTIAL IMAGES

(a) S S S . . . P (multi-subject structure)

S   她那毛茸茸的头发， **tā nà máoróngróng de tóufa**
Her downy hair,

S   她那被雨水和眼泪冲没了的脂粉，
tā nà bèi yǔshuǐ hé yǎnlèi chōngmò le de zhīfěn
her make-up washed away by rain and tears,

S   有着一只尖削的鼻子和一张微瘪的嘴的黄脸，
yǒu zhe yī zhī jiānxuē de bízi hé yī zhāng wēi biě de zuǐ de huáng liǎn
her pale face with its pointed nose and wizened mouth,

S   她那蜷缩着的单薄的身体， **tā nà quánsuō zhe de dānbó de shēntǐ**
her thin, bent frame/body

S   以及她的假笑， **yǐjí tā de jiǎ xiào**
and her false smile

S   她的不大耐烦的声口， **tā de bù dà nàifán de shēng kǒu**
her somewhat impatient tone

P   都在引起他的不满。 **dōu zài yǐnqǐ tā de bùmǎn**
All made him resentful.

> **Sha Ding** 沙汀, **yī ge qiūtiān de wǎnshàng**
> 一个秋天的晚上, One Autumn Night

Here the cumulative impact of the sequence of subjects is enhanced by the variety of attributes – adjective, phrase, clause – that the language allows.

(b) S P, P, P . . . (multi-predicate structure)

S   他 **tā**
He

P   拿着一把点燃的香 **ná zhe yī bǎ diǎnrán de xiāng**
holding a bunch of lighted incense(-sticks)

P   从长阶的左端走过来， **cóng chángjiē de zuǒduān zǒu guòlai**
walked over from the left side of the staircase,

P 跨过那两尺高的专和小孩的腿为难的门坎 **kuà guò nèi liǎng chǐ gāo de zhuān hé xiǎohái de tuǐ wéinán de ménkǎn**
stepped over the two-foot-high threshold, which purposely caused problems for children,

P 走进堂屋去， **zǒu jìn tángwū qù**
walked into the hall,

P 在所有的神龛的香炉中插上一炷香， **zài suǒyǒu de shénkān qián de xiānglú zhōng chā shàng yī zhù xiāng**
and stuck an incense-stick into each of the incense burners in front of the ancestral shrines,

P 然后虔诚地敲响了那圆圆的碗形的铜罄。 **ránhòu qiánchéng de qiāo xiǎng le nà yuányuán de wǎnxíng de tóngqìng**
and afterwards piously struck/sounded the round, bowl-like brass bell.

He Qifang 何其芳, **lǎoren** 老人, An Old Man

This description is built on a series of verbal phrases in the predicate. Their syntactic structures differ from one to the next, and these distinctions add to the sense of precision in the actions of the man involved.

27.1.2 REITERATION FOR CUMULATIVE EFFECT

In these two quotations, the writers again seek to build up a picture through repeating the elements that are linked syntactically and semantically.

(a) **AX, BX, CX . . .**

S AX 茉莉的香， **mòli de xiāng**
The fragrance of jasmine,

BX 白兰花的香， **báilánhuā de xiāng**
(the fragrance) of white orchid,

CX 脂粉的香， **zhīfěn de xiāng**
(the fragrance) of cosmetics,

DX 沙衣裳的香 . . . **shā yīshang de xiāng**
(the fragrance) of silk robes,

EX 微波泛溢出甜的暗香， **wēibō fànyì chū tián de ànxiāng**
and a hint of sweet fragrance issuing from the ripples

P AY 随着她们那些船儿荡， **suízhe tāmen nèixiē chuánr dàng**
followed the motion of their boat,

BY 随着我们这船儿荡， **suízhe wǒmen zhèi chuánr dàng**
followed the motion of our boat,

CY 随着大大小小一切的船儿荡。
suízhe dàdà xiǎoxiǎo yīqiè de chuánr dàng
and followed the motion of all the boats, large and small.

> **Yu Pingbo** 俞平伯, **jiǎngshēng dēngyǐng li de qínhuáihé**
> 桨声灯影里的秦淮河, Qinhuai River with its Lights and Oars

In the above quotation, for example, by repeating the two key words 香 **xiāng** 'fragrance' and 荡 **dàng** 'to bob up and down or move from side to side' in similar constructions, the author recreates the atmosphere and sensation of a personal experience.

(b) AX, AY, AZ . . .

S 他 **tā**
He

P 深信 **shēnxìn**
firmly believed

S 理想的人生 **lǐxiǎng de rénshēng**
an ideal life

P AX 必须有爱， **bìxū yǒu ài**
must have love,

AY 必须有美， **bìxū yǒu měi**
must have beauty,

AZ 必须有自由， **bìxū yǒu zìyóu**
must have freedom.

S 他 **tā**
He

P 深信 **shēnxìn**
firmly believed

S 这三位一体的人生 **zhè sān wèi yītǐ de rénshēng**
this three-in-one life

P BX 是可以追求的，**shì kěyǐ zhuīqiú de**
could be pursued,

BY 至少是可以用纯洁的心血培养出来的。
zhìshǎo shì kěyǐ yòng chúnjié de xīnxuè péiyǎng chūlai de
and at least could be fostered with honest effort.

Hu Shi 胡适, **dào xúzhìmō** 悼徐志摩, In Memory of Xu Zhimo[1]

Here the insistent repetition of 必须 **bìxū** 'must' and 深信 **shēnxìn** 'firmly believe', reinforces the description of the conviction and determination of the person being remembered.

27.1.3 FACTORISATION

In factorisation, the author tries to get across his message in small similarly constructed segments of language, one after another, in order to achieve maximum impact.

(a) A (X, Y, Z)

S 我 **wǒ**
I

P A 和 **hé**
with

X 那些谦卑的菜蔬，**nèixiē qiānbēi de càishū**
those humble vegetables,

Y 那些高大的果树，**nèixiē gāodà de guǒshù**
those lofty fruit trees,

Z 那些开着美丽的花的草木 **nèixiē kāi zhe měilì de huā de cǎomù**
those plants with beautiful blossoms,

一块儿生活着。**yī kuàir shēnghuó zhe**
was living together.

He Qifang 何其芳, **lǎoren** 老人, An Old Man

---

[1] China's leading poet of the 1920s and 1930s who was killed in a plane crash.

(b) A (X, Y, Z)

P   X 在睡眠减少的长长的夜里，
zài shuìmián jiǎnshǎo de chángcháng de yè li
In long nights of reduced sleep,

     X' 在荧荧的油灯下， **zài yíngyíng de yóudēng xià**
under a glimmering oil lamp,

S   我 **wǒ**
I

P   Y 迟缓地、 **chíhuǎn de**
slowly

     Y' 详细地 **xiángxì de**
minutely

     Z 回忆着 **huíyì zhe**
recollected

     Z' 而且写着 **érqiě xiě zhe**
and wrote

O   我自己的一生的故事 . . . **wǒ zìjǐ de yīshēng de gùshi**
the story of my life.

                     He Qifang 何其芳, **lǎoren** 老人, An Old Man

27.1.4 PARALLEL MATCHING

In parallel matching, what the author seeks to achieve is to present closely connected ideas in consecutive and similar structures, so that they come across more forcibly.

(a) AX, BY, CZ . . .

这榆树在园子的西北角上， **zhè yúshù zài yuánzi de xīběi jiǎo shàng**
This elm tree was in the northwest corner of the garden,

A   来了风， **lái le fēng**
when the wind blew,

X   这榆树先啸； **zhè yúshù xiān xiào**
This elm tree whistled;

B 来了雨， **lái le yǔ**
when it rained,

Y 这榆树先就冒烟了。 **zhè yúshù xiān jiù mào yān le**
This elm tree gave off steam;

C 太阳一出来， **tàiyáng yī chūlái**
as soon as the sun came out,

Z 大榆树的叶子就发光了， **dà yúshù de yèzi jiù fāguāng le**
This elm tree's leaves shone

它们闪烁得和沙滩上的蚌壳一样了。
tāmen shǎnshuò de hé shātān shàng de bàngké yīyàng le
(and) they glittered like clam shells on the sand.

> **Xiao Hong** 肖红, **hūlánhé zhuàn**
> 呼兰河传, Story of the Hulan River

(b) (A, B, C) (X, Y, Z)

A 虽同是灯船， **suī tóng shì dēngchuán**
Though it was also a light vessel,

B 虽同是秦淮， **suī tóng shì qínhuái**
though it was the same Qinhuai (River),

C 虽同是我们； **suī tóng shì wǒmen**
though it was still us,

X 却是灯影淡了， **què shì dīngyǐng dàn le**
yet the shadow from the light grew weaker,

Y 河水静了， **héshuǐ jìng le**
the river water went quiet,

Z 我们倦了， **wǒmen juàn le**
(and) we grew tired.

－ 况且月儿将上了。 **kuàngqiě yuèr jiāng shàng le**
Moreover the moon was about to rise.

> Yu Pingbo 俞平伯, **jiǎngshēng dēngyǐng li de qínhuáihé**
> 桨声灯影里的秦淮河, Qinhuai River with its Lights and Oars

27.1.5 INVERSION: ATTRIBUTIVES OR ADVERBIALS AFTER THEIR HEADWORDS

Authors use inversion, which undermines linguistic expectations, as a means to attract the attention of their readers.

> 荷塘四面，**hétáng sìmiàn**
> All round the lotus pond
>
> 长着许多树，**zhǎng zhe xǔduō shù**
> were growing numerous trees,

attributive: 蓊蓊郁郁的。**wěngwěngyùyù de**
lush and luxuriant.

> **Zhu Ziqing** 朱自清, **lǜ** 绿 Green

> 我用手拍着你，**wǒ yòng shǒu pāi zhe nǐ**
> I patted you with my hand
>
> 抚摩着你，**fǔmó zhe nǐ**
> stroked you

adverbial: 如同一个十二三岁的小姑娘。
rútóng yī ge shí'èr sān suì de xiǎo gūniang
like a 12- or 13-year-old girl.

> **Zhu Ziqing** 朱自清, **hétáng yuèsè** 荷塘月色,
> Moonlight Over the Lotus Pond

27.2 THE RHETORICAL FACTOR

When elegance merges with forcefulness, the resulting structures display features such as balance, symmetry, crescendo and regularity and variety of rhythm and cadence.

27.2.1 COUPLING: XY, XY

X 我爱热闹，**wǒ ài rènao**
I like bustle

Y 也爱冷静；**yě ài lěngjìng**
and (I) like calm too;

X 爱群居， **ài qúnjū**
(I) like living in crowds

Y 也爱独处。 **yě ài dúchǔ**
and (I) like being alone.

> **Zhu Ziqing** 朱自清, **hétáng yuèsè** 荷塘月色,
> Moonlight Over the Lotus Pond

X 我若能裁你以为带， **wǒ ruò néng cái nǐ yǐ wéi dài**
If I could cut you and make you into a girdle,

Y 我将赠给那轻盈的舞女； **wǒ jiāng zèng gěi nà qīngyíng de wǔnǚ**
I would give (it) to that slim and graceful dancing girl,

Z 她必能临风飘举了。 **tā bì néng línfēng piāojǔ le**
(and) she would surely rise in the breeze;

X 我若能挹你以为眼，**wǒ ruò néng yì nǐ yǐ wéi yǎn**
If I could ladle you out and make you into an eye

Y 我将赠给那善歌的盲妹； **wǒ jiāng zèng gěi nà shàngē de mángmèi**
I would give (it) to that blind girl with the beautiful voice,

Z 她必明眸善睐了。 **tā bì míngmóu shàn lài le**
(and) she would certainly have bright eyes and a good gaze.

> **Zhu Ziqing** 朱自清, **lǜ** 绿, Green

Aphorisms, of course, have their obvious rhythms and parallels:

X 玉不琢， **yù bù zhuó**
If jade is not carved,

Y 不成器。 **bù chéng qì**
(it) does not make a piece.

X 明枪易躲， **míngqiāng yì duǒ**
Guns in the open are easy to avoid;

Y 暗箭难防。 **àn jiàn nán fáng**
hidden arrows are hard to defend against.

X 只要功夫深， **zhǐyào gōngfu shēn**
If (you) work hard,

Y 铁杵磨成针。 **tiěchǔ móchéng zhēn**
(you) can grind an iron rod into a needle.

X 世上无难事， **shìshàng wú nánshì**
There is nothing difficult in the world

Y 只怕有心人。 **zhǐpà yǒuxīnrén**
provided there are people with will.

(Aphorisms)

27.2.2 PROGRESSION: XY, XY, XY . . .

我问他为什么带芭蕉扇， **wǒ wèn tā wèishénme dài bājiāoshàn**
I asked him why he had brought a palm-leaf fan.

他回答说， **tā huídá shuō**
He replied saying

这东西妙用无穷： **zhè dōngxi miàoyòng wúqióng**
this thing has endless magical uses:

X 热的时候 **rè de shíhou**
when (it's) hot,

Y 扇风， **shān fēng**
it fans (up) a breeze;

X 太阳大的时候 **tàiyáng dà de shíhou**
when the sun is beating down,

Y 遮荫， **zhē yīn**
(it) gives shade;

X 下雨的时候 **xià yǔ de shíhou**
when it rains,

Y 代伞， **dài sǎn**
(it) acts as an umbrella;

X 休息的时候 **xiūxi de shíhou**
when it's time to rest,

Y 当坐垫， **dàng zuòdiàn**
(it) serves as a cushion (to sit on).

这好比济公活佛的芭蕉扇。 **zhè hǎobǐ jìgōng huófó de bājiāoshàn**
It is exactly like the Living Buddha's palm-leaf fan.

> **Feng Zikai** 丰子恺, **lúshān miànmù** 庐山面目,
> The True Face of (Mount) Lushan

27.2.3 ECHOING

Echoing may often be achieved through word-for-word repetition:

远处， **yuǎnchù**
In the distance

有一条小瀑布， **yǒu yī tiáo xiǎo pùbù**
there's a small waterfall

哗哗哗， **huāhuāhuā**
gurgling, gurgling

日夜不停地往下流， **rìyè bùtíng de wǎng xià liú**
night and day without cease it flows down,

E 往下流。 **wǎng xià liú**
flows down.

> **Liu Zhen** 刘真, **chángcháng de liúshuǐ**
> 长长的流水, A Long Stream

他见过许多少男少女， **tā jiàn guò xǔduō shàonán shàonǚ**
He had seen very many young men and women,

有的是在笑， **yǒude shì zài xiào**
some smiling,

E 笑得那样痴呆， **xiào de nèiyàng chīdāi**
smiling in that stupid manner;

有的哭， **yǒude kū**
others weeping,

E 哭得又那样失态。 **kū de yòu nèiyàng shītài**
weeping too in that unmannerly way.

    Feng Zhi 冯至, **sàinàhé pàn de wúmíng shàonǚ** 塞纳河畔的无名少女,
Unknown Girls by the Seine

It can also, as the following aphorisms demonstrate, bring together for contrast expressions of similar construction:

远亲 **yuǎnqīn**
A distant relative

不如 **bùrú**
is not as good as

E 近邻。 **jìnlín**
a close neighbour.

言有尽 **yán yǒu jìn**
Words are limited,

而 **ér**
but

E 意无穷。 **yì wúqióng**
the meaning is infinite.

(Aphorisms)

27.2.4 ALTERNATION: LONG AND SHORT SENTENCES

short 没有风。 **méiyǒu fēng**
There was no wind.

long 门前池中的残荷梗 **mén qián chí zhōng de cánhégěng**
The remaining lotus stems in the pool in front of the gate

时时忽然急剧地动摇起来， **shí shí hūrán jíjù de dòngyáo qǐlai**
would from time to time suddenly begin to shake rapidly

接着便有如鲤鱼的活泼地跳跃 **jiēzhe biàn yǒurú lǐyú de huópo de tiàoyuè**
and then flapping vigorously like live carps

划破了死一样平静的水面。 **huà pò le sǐ yīyàng píngjìng de shuǐmiàn**
and break the death-like calm of the water's surface.

Mao Dun 茅盾, **wù** 雾, Mist

short 志摩走了。 **zhìmō zǒu le**
(Xu) Zhimo has gone.

long 我们这个世界里 **wǒmen zhèi ge shìjiè li**
In this world of ours,

被带走了不少云彩。 **bèi dài zǒu le bùshǎo yúncai**
many colourful clouds have been carried off.

long 他在我们这些朋友之中， **tā zài wǒmen zhèixiē péngyou zhīzhōng**
He amongst these friends of ours

真是一片可爱的云彩， **zhēnshi yī piàn kě'ài de yúncai**
was truly a lovable cloud,

永远是温暖的颜色， **yǒngyuǎn shì wēnnuǎn de yánsè**
always a warm colour,

永远是美的花样， **yǒngyuǎn shì měi de huāyàng**
always a beautiful pattern,

永远是可爱。 **yǒngyuǎn shì kě'ài**
always lovable.

Hu Shi 胡适, **dào xúzhìmō** 悼徐志摩, In Memory of Xu Zhimo

27.3 CONCLUDING REMARKS

Syntax establishes general rules regarding the relationships between component elements in sentential construction, and any stereotypical sentence will therefore conform to these rules. However, as we have seen throughout this book, the actual realisations of these stereotypical patterns take diverse forms. Such diversity stems not only from varied communicative objectives, but also from different linguistic foci, emphases, contexts and intentions. These differences in turn entail differing organising principles: contextual, functional, focal, presentational and rhetorical.

In this book, variations that are contextual (e.g. abbreviations and omissions), functional (e.g. statements vs questions, narrative vs expository), and focal (e.g. emphatic sentences with 是 **shì**) have been covered in all our discussions of syntax proper. Presentational and rhetorical variations, being more of a stylistic nature, were therefore dealt with here in this last chapter with the hope that it may give some additional insight into how Chinese writers exploit and manipulate their language.

BIBLIOGRAPHY

Chao, Yuen-ren (1968). *A Grammar of Spoken Chinese*. Berkeley and Los Angeles: University of California Press.

Chen, Jianmin (陈建民) (1984). 《北京口语》。北京出版社。

Chu, Chauncey C. (1998). *A Discourse Grammar of Mandarin Chinese*. New York: Peter Lang Publishing, Inc.

Fang, Yuqing (房玉清) (1992). 《实用汉语语法》。北京语言学院出版社。

Gao, Gengsheng and Wang, Hongqi (高更生 王红旗) (1996). 《汉语教学语法研究》。语文出版社。

Gao, Gengsheng *et al.* (高更生等) (1984). 《现代汉语》。济南：山东教育出版社。

Hong, Xinheng (洪心衡) (1980). 《汉语词法句法阐要》。吉林人民出版社。

Hu, Fu and Wen, Lian (胡附 文炼) (1990). 《现代汉语语法探索》。北京：商务印书馆。

Hu, Mingyang (胡明扬) (ed.) (1996). 《词类问题考察》。北京语言学院出版社。

Hu, Shuxian (胡树鲜) (1990). 《现代汉语语法理论初探》。北京：中国人民大学出版社。

Hu, Yushu (胡裕树) (ed.) (1962). 《现代汉语》。上海教育出版社。

Hu, Yushu and Fan, Xiao (胡裕树 范晓) (eds) (1996). 《动词研究综述》。太原：山西高校联合出版社。

Hu, Zhuanglin *et al.* (胡壮麟等)(1989). 《系统功能语法概论》。湖南教育出版社。

Huang, Borong and Liao, Xudong (黄伯荣 廖序东) (1983). 《现代汉语》。兰州：甘肃人民出版社。

Huang, Hansheng *et al.* (黄汉生等) (1982). 《现代汉语》。北京：书目文献出版社。

Jin, Zhaozi (金兆梓) (1983). 《国文法之研究》 (new edition). 北京：商务印书馆。

Li, Charles N. and Thompson, Sandra A. (1981). *Mandarin Chinese – A Functional Reference Grammar*. Berkeley: University of California Press.

Li, Dejin and Cheng, Meizhen (李德津 程美珍) (1988). *A Practical Chinese Grammar for Foreigners*. Beijing: Sinolingua.

Li, Jinxi (黎锦熙) (1992). 《新著国语文法》 (new edition). 北京：商务印书馆。

Li, Linding (李临定) (1988). 《汉语比较变换语法》。北京：中国社会科学出版社。

Li, Ying-che *et al.* (李英哲等) (eds), Xiong, Wenhua (熊文华) (trans.) (1990). 《实用汉语参考语法》。北京语言学院出版社。

Lin, Xiangmei (林祥楣) (ed.) (1991). 《现代汉语》。北京：语文出版社。

Liu, Yuehua *et al.* (刘月华等) (1983). 《实用现代汉语语法》。北京：外语教学与研究出版社。

Lu, Fubo (卢福波) (1997). 《对外汉语教学实用语法》。北京语言文化大学出版社。

Lu, Jianming (陆俭明) (1993). 《现代汉语句法论》。北京：商务印书馆。

Luo, Huayan (罗华炎) (1998). 《现代汉语语法》。Taman Ipoh Timur: Penerbitan Seni Hijau SDN. BHD. (艺青出版社有限公司).

Lü, Shuxiang (吕叔湘) (1979). 《汉语语法分析问题》。北京: 商务印书馆。

Lü, Shuxiang (吕叔湘) (ed.) (1980). 《现代汉语八百词》。北京: 商务印书馆。

Lü, Shuxiang (吕叔湘) (1982). 《中国文法要略》。北京: 商务印书馆。

Lü, Wenhua (吕文华) (1999). 《对外汉语教学语法体系研究》。北京语言学院出版社。

Ma, Qingzhu (马庆株) (ed.) (2000). 《语法研究入门》。北京: 商务印书馆。

Ma, Zhen (马真) (1981). 《简明实用汉语语法》。北京大学出版社。

Seybolt, Peter J. and Chiang, Gregory Kuei-Ke (ed.) (1979). *Language Reform in China – Documents and Commentary*. New York: M. E. Sharpe, Inc.

Shao, Jingmin (邵敬敏) (1996). 《现代汉语疑问句研究》。上海: 华东师范大学出版社。

Shao, Jingmin (邵敬敏) (2000). 《汉语语法的立体研究》。北京: 商务印书馆。

Shen, Xiaolong (申小龙) (1995). 《当代中国语法学》。广州: 广东教育出版社。

Shen, Xiaolong (申小龙) (1988). 《中国句型文化》。长春: 东北师范大学出版社。

Shen, Yang and Zheng, Ding'ou (沈阳 郑定欧) (eds) (1995). 《现代汉语配价语法研究》。北京大学出版社。

Shi, Cunzhi (史存直) (1980). 《语法三论》。上海教育出版社。

Shi, Yuzhi (石毓智) (1997). 《语法的认知语义基础》。江西教育出版社。

Teng, Shou-hsin (邓守信) (1991). 'The semantics of causatives in Chinese' in Tai, James H-Y, Hsueh, F. S. (eds). *Functionalism and Chinese Grammar*. Chinese Language Teachers' Association Monograph Series No. 1.

Wang, Huan (王还) (ed.) (1995). 《对外汉语教学语法大纲》。北京语言学院出版社。

Wang, Li (王力) (1985). 《中国现代语法》。北京: 商务印书馆。

Wu, Weizhang (吴为章) (1982). '单向动词及其句型' in 中国语文 1982 No. 5.

Xiao, Guozheng (萧国政) (1994). 《现代汉语语法问题研究》。华中师范大学出版社。

Xing, Fuyi (刑福义) (1997). 《汉语语法学》。长春: 东北师范大学出版社。

Xing, Fuyi (刑福义) (ed.) (1999). 《汉语语法特点面面观》。北京语言文化大学出版社。

Yang, Shuda (杨树达) (1984). 《高等国文法 》 (new edition). 北京: 商务印书馆。

Yip Po-Ching and Don Rimmington (1997). *Chinese – An Essential Grammar*. London and New York: Routledge.

Yip Po-Ching and Don Rimmington (1998). *Basic Chinese – A Grammar and Workbook*. London and New York: Routledge.

Yip Po-Ching and Don Rimmington (1998). *Intermediate Chinese – A Grammar and Workbook*. London and New York: Routledge.

Yuan, Yulin and Guo Rui (袁毓林 郭锐) (eds) (1998). 《现代汉语配价语法研究 (二)》。北京大学出版社。

Zhang, Bin and Hu, Yushu (张斌 胡裕树) (1989). 《汉语语法研究》。北京: 商务印书馆。

Zhang, Jin and Chen, Yunqing (张今 陈云清) (eds) (1981). 《英汉比较语法纲要》。北京: 商务印书馆。

Zhao, Jinming (赵金铭) (1997). 《汉语研究与对外汉语教学》。北京: 语文出版社。

Zhao, Jinming *et al.* (赵金铭) (eds) (1997). 《新视角汉语语法研究》。北京语言文化大学出版社。

Zhao, Shikai (赵世开) (ed.) (2000). 《汉英对比语法论集》。上海外语教育出版社。

Zhu, Dexi (朱德熙) (1982). 《语法讲义》。北京: 商务印书馆。

Zhu, Dexi (朱德熙) (1990). 《语法丛稿》。上海: 上海教育出版社。

Zhu, Xing (朱星) (1979). 《汉语语法学的若干问题》。石家庄: 河北人民出版社。

INDEX